Economy.
Where I lived, and what I lived for.
Reading.
Sounds.
Solitude.
        Preface. Note.
    Visitors.

Nearly all of this volume was written
eight or nine years ago on the
scenery & under the circumstances
which it describes, and a considerable part was read at that time
as lectures before the Concord Lyceum. In what is now added the
object has been chiefly to make it
a completer & truer account of
that portion of the author's life.

The Bean-Field   Spring.
    The Village   Conclusion.
    The Ponds.
    Baker Farm
    Animal Food. Higher Laws
    Animals Brute Neighbors
    House-warming.
    Winter Animals.
    Former Inhabitants; & Winter Visitors
    The Pond in Winter

Walden

An Annotated Edition

I DO NOT PROPOSE TO WRITE AN
ODE TO DEJECTION, BUT TO BRAG
AS LUSTILY AS CHANTICLEER IN THE
MORNING, STANDING ON HIS ROOST,
IF ONLY TO WAKE MY NEIGHBORS UP.

Walden

HENRY D. THOREAU

AN ANNOTATED EDITION

Foreword and Notes by
WALTER HARDING

HOUGHTON MIFFLIN COMPANY

Boston   New York

For information about permission to reproduce selections from
this book, write to Permissions, Houghton Mifflin Company,
215 Park Avenue South, New York, New York 10003.

LIBRARY OF CONGRESS CATALOGING-IN-PUBLICATION DATA

Thoreau, Henry David, 1817–1862
Walden: an annotated edition / Henry D. Thoreau;
foreword and notes by Walter Harding.
p.   cm.
Includes bibliographical references (p.) and index.
ISBN 0-395-72042-7
1. Thoreau, Henry David, 1817–1862 — Homes and haunts — Massachusetts —
Walden Woods.   2. Walden Woods (Mass.) — Social life and customs.
3. Wilderness areas — Massachusetts — Walden Woods.   4. Natural history —
Massachusetts — Walden Woods.   5. Authors, American — 19th century —
Biography.   6. Solitude.   I. Harding, Walter Roy. 1917-   .   II. Title
PS3048.A1   1995B
818'.309 — dc20   94-45347
CIP

Book design by Anne Chalmers
Notes type: Bulmer (Monotype)
Text type: Electra (Linotype-Hell)
Map on page vi by Jacques Chazaud

Printed in the United States of America
QUM   10   9   8

Endpapers: Manuscript pages from *Walden*
(title page, v. 7; pp. 83-84, v. 3; HM 924), reproduced
by permission of The Huntington Library,
San Marino, California.

Contents

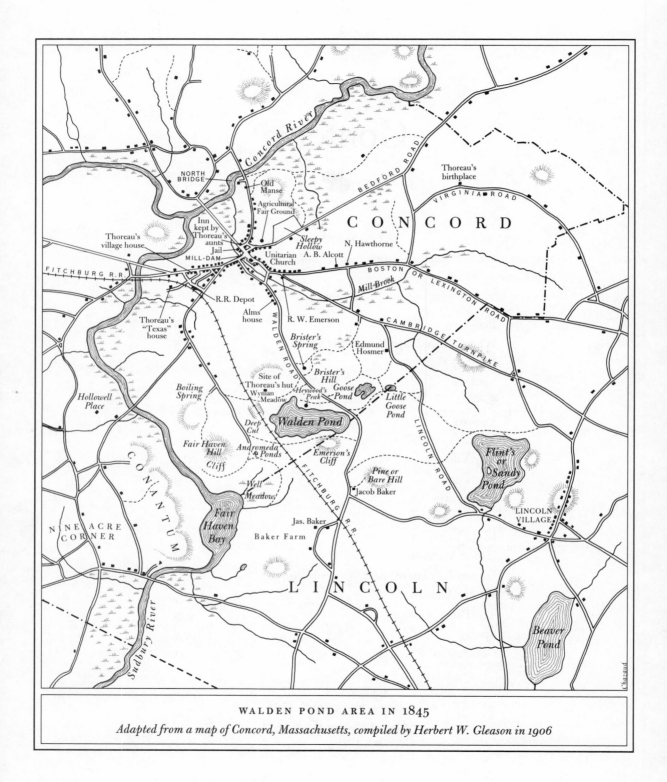

WALDEN POND AREA IN 1845

Adapted from a map of Concord, Massachusetts, compiled by Herbert W. Gleason in 1906

Foreword

Henry David Thoreau was a few days short of his twenty-eighth birthday when he moved into his cabin on Walden Pond in Concord, Massachusetts, on July 4, 1845, and began what was to become one of the most famous experiments in living in American history.

Thoreau was born in Concord on July 12, 1817. After graduating from Harvard College in 1837, he turned to teaching, first for a few weeks in the Concord public schools, where he found himself in disagreement with his school committee who wanted stricter discipline than he thought necessary, and then in a highly successful private school that he and his brother John maintained for three years and in which they anticipated many of the techniques of twentieth-century education. But his brother's illness in 1841 forced abandonment of the school, and Thoreau's interest, at his friend Emerson's urging, turned to writing. With John's death in 1842, Thoreau decided to write a memorial tribute, an account of an excursion the two brothers had taken on the Concord and Merrimack Rivers in 1839. But the necessity of earning a living kept him from his task until he moved out to Walden, where he had built a cabin on some of Emerson's property, with the avowed purpose of writing his book there.

Thoreau had long been attracted by the idea of building a cabin in the woods and living by himself. At the age of five when he had first visited Walden Pond, he had told others that he wanted to live on its shores. While he was a student at Harvard, his friend and roommate Charles Stearns Wheeler spent a vacation living in a cabin on Flint's Pond, only a few miles from Walden, and Thoreau lived with him there for several weeks in the summer of 1837. Another close friend, Ellery Channing, had for a time lived in a cabin alone on the Illinois prairie. So there was ample precedent for Thoreau's experiment.

In 1841 Thoreau's interest in such a project intensified. On April 5 he wrote in his journal, "I will build my lodge on the southern slope of some hill, and take there the life the gods send me. Will it not be employment enough to accept gratefully all that is yielded me between sun and sun?" On October 18 Margaret Fuller wrote him, "Let me know whether you go to the lonely hut." And on December 24 he wrote again in his journal, "I want to go soon and live away by the pond, where I shall hear only the wind whispering among the reeds. It will be success if I shall have left myself behind. But my friends ask what I will do when I get there. Will it not be employment enough to watch the progress of the seasons?"

In the fall of 1844 Ralph Waldo Emerson purchased several woodlots on the shores of Walden

Pond to preserve them from the ax. On March 5, 1845, Ellery Channing wrote to Thoreau, "I see nothing for you in this earth but that field [at Walden] which I once christened 'Briars'; go out upon that, build yourself a hut, & there begin the grand process of devouring yourself alive." By the end of the month Thoreau had worked out an agreement with Emerson for the use of his land and started construction of his cabin.

The writing of *Walden* was apparently not among Thoreau's original plans when he went to live at the pond. *A Week on the Concord and Merrimack Rivers* was the book he proposed to write, and did write, there. But from the beginning of his stay at the pond he was noting his impressions in his journal, and most of these notes he eventually incorporated into the text of *Walden*. By February 1847 he was delivering lectures to his fellow townsmen at their request on his experiences at Walden, and these lectures, too, eventually became part of the text. And by 1849 he had sufficiently worked out the first draft of the book, so he was able to announce its publication "soon" in the back pages of the first edition of *A Week*. The announcement proved to be premature, for the commercial failure of *A Week* — only slightly more than two hundred copies were sold in the first four years — frightened publishers away from *Walden*. It was finally published in August 1854, although by a new and different publisher, the rising firm of Ticknor & Fields, which later became Houghton Mifflin Company.

What happened in those intervening years, how the manuscript was reworked, revamped, revised, reworded, and polished through at least seven distinct versions, has been told so well by J. Lyndon Shanley in his *Making of Walden* that I shall not attempt to retell it here. The important fact is that out of all Thoreau's labor, the masterpiece that is *Walden* emerged.

Walden too was not a notable success when it first appeared. True, it did much better than *A Week*. It achieved much wider notice and did receive some excellent reviews. But it took five years, until 1859, to sell out the first printing of two thousand copies. And it was 1862, the year of Thoreau's death, before *Walden* was brought back into print. The book has never been out of print since then. It has been reissued in hundreds of editions, from inexpensive paperbacks to leather-bound limited editions. It has been translated into virtually every major modern language. It is one of the best-selling American nonfiction classics.

To most people, Thoreau is primarily a naturalist, and a large percentage of the readers of *Walden,* particularly in the years shortly after its publication, read the book as they did Gilbert White's *Selbourne,* primarily for its natural history. Nineteenth-century readers were often advised by critics to ignore the more philosophical chapters such as "Economy" and "Higher Laws," which were considered transcendentalist nonsense, and to concentrate on the nature writing in "Sounds," "Brute Neighbors," and "The Pond in Winter." As a nature writer, Thoreau has few if any peers. He is a master of the art of descriptive writing. The loons, the frogs, the ants, and the mice of *Walden* not only come alive, they become almost human. As long as man continues his interest in the world of nature, *Walden* seems assured of readers.

To another large group of readers, *Walden,* like *Robinson Crusoe,* is escape literature. Thoreau, like Crusoe, was able to get away from it all, to shed the cares and tribulations of modern civilization. No more alarm clocks, time schedules, dinner jackets, or headache powders. The reader can vicariously enjoy the pleasures of the simple life, and at the same time just as vicariously meet the challenge of pitting himself against his environment, finding food, clothing, shelter, and fuel, living as his pioneer ancestors did a century or more ago — and never move from his comfortable armchair in front of his thermopane picture window and his gas-log fireplace.

Walden can be read in an armchair, but it is not likely that the reader will remain there. He may start it as escape literature, but almost inevitably he becomes involved. He begins to think not in terms of escape but in terms of reform, and particularly of reform of himself. *Walden* is a book that impels its reader to action.

For some reason, it is not obvious to all of Thoreau's readers that *Walden,* like *Gulliver's Travels,* is a subtle — and often not so subtle — satire on contemporary civilization. Even so eminent a critic as James Russell Lowell missed that side of *Walden,* and so was able to come to the astounding conclusion that Thoreau lacked a sense of humor. It is true that often Thoreau's humor, for the so-called man in the street, is of a topsy-turvy kind. Thoreau laughs at what many take seriously, and takes seriously what many laugh at. But there is barely a page of *Walden* without its satirical humor, and anyone who cannot see humor in the book may be assured that he is missing the whole point of it. Thoreau announced on his title page that he is bragging like chanticleer, if only to wake his neighbors up. And most of that

bragging is satire. Once the reader begins to view the world through Thoreau's eyes, it becomes a very different world.

But *Walden* reaches its highest levels as a spiritual autobiography, a *Pilgrim's Progress* to the good life. I would not denigrate the other levels of appeal. It is one of the book's claims to greatness that it can be appreciated on many different levels. But to Thoreau and to the perceptive reader, *Walden* is as much a religious document as any scripture. It is not concerned with theological disputation; he does not count angels on pinheads. "Metaphysics was his aversion," said his good friend Ellery Channing. But Thoreau is concerned with spiritual values throughout *Walden,* and particularly in those very chapters — "Economy," "Higher Laws," and "Conclusion" — that some of his early readers tended to ignore.

Thoreau assures us:

> If one advances confidently in the direction of his dreams, and endeavors to live the life which he has imagined, he will meet with a success unexpected in common hours. He will put some things behind, will pass an invisible boundary; new, universal, and more liberal laws will begin to establish themselves around and within him; or the old laws be expanded, and interpreted in his favor in a more liberal sense, and he will live with the license of a higher order of beings.

It is true our success may be only momentary, but it is worth the effort, for in those moments we achieve a higher plane of life. On the *Robinson Crusoe* level it may at times appear to be escapist, on the *Gulliver's Travels* level, carping and negative, but on its highest level it is dynamic, positive, and optimistic. To see that this was the final impression Thoreau wished to leave with his reader, we need only turn to the final paragraph of *Walden:*

> I do not say that John or Jonathan will realize all this; but such is the character of that morrow which mere lapse of time can never make to dawn. The light which puts out our eyes is darkness to us. Only that day dawns to which we are awake. There is more day to dawn. The sun is but a morning star.

Nor is this theme relegated to the final paragraph alone. The predominant images throughout, starting with the epigraph on the title page, are those of rebirth, of morning, of spring, of the new life that is ahead. The whole book is shaped around the cycle of the seasons, beginning with spring, passing through summer, autumn, winter, and ending with the rebirth of spring. The chapter "Sounds" follows the same pattern in miniature for a day, beginning with the morning, progressing through afternoon, evening, night, and concluding with the sounds of a reawakening world at dawn. We read of the purification ceremonies of the Indians and the Mexicans. We learn of the rebirth of a marvelous insect buried for sixty years in the wood of an apple-tree table. We see even Thoreau's beloved Walden Pond become torpid with the ice of winter, only to revive once more with the coming of spring. *Walden* is fundamentally an optimistic book. Thoreau feels no need of waiting to attain heaven in another world. He has high hopes of attaining his heaven right here on earth, and he does his level best to do so.

In his third chapter of *Walden* Thoreau says, "How many a man has dated a new era in his life from the reading of a book." *Walden* has become just such a book for more and more of its readers. Written a century and a half ago, it grows more meaningful with each new day.

I would like to alert readers of the existence of the Thoreau Society, an informal gathering of fifteen hundred students and followers of Thoreau spread around the world who publish a quarterly bulletin and an annual devoted to Thoreau. The society meets each year in Concord on the Saturday closest to Thoreau's birthday, July 12. If you want more details, write to the Thoreau Society, 44 Baker Farm, Lincoln, Massachusetts 01773.

WALTER HARDING

A Note on the Annotations and Illustrations

After nearly a century and a half in print, the text of *Walden* retains its obscurities. These I have tried to clear up in the marginal notes. I have tried to give the sources for all the quotations in the text, although a few have escaped me. I have also tried to give the source of all allusions in the text that might puzzle the reader. When words have changed their meanings or spellings over the hundred and fifty years, I have tried to point that fact out. I have added Thoreau's own comments written in his personal copy of *Walden,* now in the Abernethy Library of Middlebury College, and some of Ellery Channing's notes in his own copy, now in the Berg Collection of the New York Public Library. And I have added many pertinent comments from the vast body of Thoreau literature.

I have used the current Modern Language Association system for indicating my sources, appending to this volume a list of works cited. To save space, I have reduced "Thoreau" and "*Walden*" to T and W. In the Works Cited section, where my references are to the editorial apparatus rather than to the main text, I have listed the work under the editor's name rather than the author's. (Shanley's edition of *Walden,* for example, is listed under Shanley rather

than under Thoreau.) To help readers who are not familiar with Concord and the Walden Pond area, I have included a modified version of Herbert Gleason's map of Concord, made for the 1906 edition of Thoreau's *Journal,* and refer to it in the notes. The drawings and captions are taken from Thoreau's *Journal* and are not from the period when he was living at Walden.

I am greatly indebted to many, many friends for information used in this volume. I have already thanked most of them in my *Variorum Walden* (Twayne, 1962), a predecessor of this volume, but I would also like to acknowledge the help of Judith Bushnell, Barbara Chadburn, James Dawson, Bradley Dean, Kenneth Eble, Daniel Fink, Ronald Gottesman, Kenneth Harber, Allen Harding, Norvin Hein, John Finely Kiser, Jane Langton, Tom Mansbridge, Elizabeth Marshall, Austin Meredith, Rodney Owen, Ronald Pesha, Paul Ransohoff, Susan Rawleigh, Russell Ready, Gordon Rohman, Robert Sattelmeyer, Mark Shanks, William Bysshe Stein, Philip Van Doren Stern, James Stronks, and Thomas Woodson, and particularly Richard O'Connor, who generously shared with me his knowledge of the Walden Pond area and of its early residents.

WALDEN;

OR,

LIFE IN THE WOODS.

By HENRY D. THOREAU,

AUTHOR OF "A WEEK ON THE CONCORD AND MERRIMACK RIVERS."

I do not propose to write an ode to dejection, but to brag as lustily as chanticleer in the morning, standing on his roost, if only to wake my neighbors up. — Page 92.

BOSTON:
TICKNOR AND FIELDS.
M DCCC LIV.

Title page of the 1854 edition

1 Although the first edition gives the title *Walden; or, Life in the Woods,* on March 4, 1862, two months before he died, T wrote to his publishers, Ticknor & Fields, asking them to omit the subtitle in a new edition. They complied with this request, although it has rarely been followed since. Paul (75) suggests that T may have dropped the subtitle because he feared his audience was taking it too literally and thus missing the more important philosophy permeating the book. T could have derived the subtitle from his friend Charles Lane's essay "Life in the Woods" in the *Dial* (IV, 1844, 415) or from John S. Williams, "Our Cabin; or, Life in the Woods" in the October 1843 *American Pioneer* (DeMott), but not from the then popular *The Adirondack: or Life in the Woods,* by J. T. Headley (New York, 1849), which did not appear until after T had used the subtitle in an advertisement for W in the back pages of the first edition of *A Week.* For a comprehensive study of the types of books on which T based the structure of W, see Linck Johnson. For a discussion of the organic structure of W, see Lane (1960). Kurtz is one of the most straightforward analyses of W's style.

2 The drawing of T's cabin was made by his sister Sophia, an amateur artist. T himself complained of it, "Thoreau would suggest a little alteration, chiefly in the door, in the wide projection of the roof at the front; and that the bank more immediately about the house be brought out more distinctly" (Sanborn, 1917, 338). Sanborn adds, "He must have noticed that her trees were firs and not pines, with a few deciduous trees that did not then grow there." Ellery Channing thought it "a feeble caricature." Other contemporary drawings of the cabin may be found in Meltzer and Harding (144–5).

3 The epigraph is quoted from the second chapter of W. It is omitted from many modern editions, and unfortunately so, for it sets the mood for the whole book. Broderick (1954) points out how this awakening and morning theme is a basic image carried throughout W. A possible source for T's idea is Orestes Brownson's statement in his *Boston Quarterly Review* in 1839 that he "aimed to startle, and made it a point to be as paradoxical and extravagant as he could."

1   Saunders suggests that T's surprising use of economic terms to convey the joys of a natural and spiritual life is intended to demonstrate how overwhelmingly our vision of life is dominated by commercial values. For further discussion of T's use of the word "economy," see Werge and see Heinzelman. Blasing's "The Economics of W" is a thoughtful and much broader study than its title implies. It includes a good discussion of W as autobiography. Neufeldt (1966, 156) points out that T in his earliest version of the W manuscript used one series of page numberings for "Economy" and a second for the rest of the book, as though "Economy" were an extended preface to W. The most extensive analysis of T's economic theories is Neufeldt (1989). Birch and Metting give an interesting contrast of T's economic theory with that of his contemporaries, saying, "T wanted to make it clear that the real quarrel between himself and his neighbors did not involve the necessity of work and industry but centered on the Calvinist doctrine that earthly duties, such as work, were necessarily a hardship to be endured and that accumulation of material wealth was a symbol of spiritual success."

2   Morse (150), choosing these opening lines as a notable example, says, "In truth W is a self-dramatizing, self-advertising and deeply duplicitous book that seeks to mask its excessive ambitions behind a facade of commonsense and practicality."

W is filled with wordplay of all sorts. Lane (1970) analyzes at length the puns in the first three paragraphs of the book. Donald Ross (1971) provides a checklist of the wordplay T uses.

3   T wrote no more than half the text while at the pond. The rest was worked on in the later versions before publication (Shanley, 1957, 25). "The bulk of them" is an aside quite typical of T, as Broderick (1982) wittily demonstrates — a sort of precursor of the modern footnote — and T uses it deftly.

4   Actually there was a whole hamlet of huts and shanties occupied by Irish railroad laborers less than half a mile from T's cabin, but

(Notes to page 1 continued on next page)

Standing on the middle of Walden I see with perfect distinctness the form and outlines of the low hills which surround it, though they are wooded, because they are quite white, being covered with snow, while the woods are for the most part bare or very thin-leaved. I see thus the outline of the hills eight or ten rods back through the trees. This I can never do in the summer, when the leaves are thick and the ground is nearly the same color with them. (January 6, 1859)

Economy

WHEN I WROTE the following pages, or rather the bulk of them, I lived alone, in the woods, a mile from any **2, 3** neighbor, in a house which I had built myself, on the **4** shore of Walden Pond, in Concord, Massachusetts, and **5, 6** earned my living by the labor of my hands only. I lived there two years and two months. At present I am a so- **7** journer in civilized life again.

I should not obtrude my affairs so much on the notice of my readers if very particular inquiries had not been **8, 9** made by my townsmen concerning my mode of life, which some would call impertinent, though they do not appear **10** to me at all impertinent, but, considering the circumstances, very natural and pertinent. Some have asked what I **11** got to eat; if I did not feel lonesome; if I was not afraid; and the like. Others have been curious to learn what portion of my income I devoted to charitable purposes; and some, who have large families, how many poor children I maintained. I will therefore ask those of my readers who feel no particular interest in me to pardon me if I undertake to answer some of these questions in this book. In most books, the *I*, or first person, is omitted; in this it will be retained; that, in respect to egotism, is the main difference. We commonly do not remember that it is, after all, always the first person that is speaking. I should not talk so much about myself if there were anybody else whom I knew as well. Unfortunately, I am confined to this theme by the narrowness of my experience. Moreover, I, on my side, require of every writer, first or last, a simple and sincere account of his own life, and not **12** merely what he has heard of other men's lives; some such

(Notes to page 1 continued)

T chose to ignore them. Hawthorne (395) gives a vivid description of this colony.

While there is a general impression that T lived in a hut or shanty at Walden, he himself, in W, refers to it more than eighty times as a "house," only twice as a "hut," and never as a shanty. It was undoubtedly much better built than many other houses in Concord (Robbins).

5 Lyon discusses Walden Pond as a symbol. "Walden remains Thoreau's ultimate image of God upon Earth and the central symbol of the work to which it gives its name" (299).

6 Concord, then a village of about 2,000 people, is 18 miles northwest of Boston. It is now a prosperous suburb with a population of 15,000.

7 Exactly two years, two months, and two days — that is, from July 4, 1845, to September 6, 1847.

8 For a particularly thoughtful study of the relationship between T and his intended audience, see Railton.

9 Although T is undoubtedly referring to many direct inquiries, some of which he describes later in the book, he is also probably referring to the fact that he was asked by his fellow townsmen to give three lectures before the Concord Lyceum on his experiences at Walden. The texts of these lectures were later incorporated into the book itself. Much of the material on this page, for example, was taken from his lecture of February 10, 1847. Rossi (251) suggests that T started his account of his life at Walden earlier and used the inquiries as a rhetorical pretext for explaining his purpose in writing.

10 Note that "impertinent" can refer to "inquiries," "townsmen," or "life" (Cavell, 45).

11 "In all, the first-person pronoun occurs almost three thousand times in W: 'I' 1816 times, 'my' 723 times, 'me' 306 times, and 'myself' 65 times" (Neufeldt, 1989, 181). In fact, T used "I" so frequently that the printer ran out of the letter occasionally in setting type (Stern, 145).

12 There are those who question just how "simple and sincere" T's own account is — and not without reason.

1 "Poor" in the sense of needy, rather than inferior. Note the particular audience to whom T is addressing the book. He later suggests W is primarily for those who are dissatisfied with their present life.

2 The common nineteenth-century name for Hawaiians.

3 Upper-caste Hindus who frequently subjected themselves to various penances as acts of devotion. For an extensive analysis of Hindu influences on this chapter, see Stein (1969).

4 The sun acts as a key symbol in W; see Hyman.

5 T is quoting from *The Library of Entertaining Knowledge: The Hindoos* (London, 1834, II, 57–8), which in turn quotes from James Mill, *The History of India* (1817; London, 1848, I, 410). Hoch (1971 and 1975) gives good brief surveys of Hindu influences on T, as does McShane.

6 Hercules, the most celebrated of all heroes of antiquity, was commanded to perform twelve feats before he could obtain his release from servitude to Eurystheus. They included such tasks as fetching the golden apples of the Hesperides and cleaning the stables of Augeas.

account as he would send to his kindred from a distant land; for if he has lived sincerely, it must have been in a distant land to me. Perhaps these pages are more particu-
1 larly addressed to poor students. As for the rest of my readers, they will accept such portions as apply to them. I trust that none will stretch the seams in putting on the coat, for it may do good service to him whom it fits.

I would fain say something, not so much concerning
2 the Chinese and Sandwich Islanders as you who read these pages, who are said to live in New England; something about your condition, especially your outward condition or circumstances in this world, in this town, what it is, whether it is necessary that it be as bad as it is, whether it cannot be improved as well as not. I have travelled a good deal in Concord; and everywhere, in shops, and offices, and fields, the inhabitants have appeared to me to be doing penance in a thousand remarkable ways. What I
3 have heard of Bramins sitting exposed to four fires and
4 looking in the face of the sun; or hanging suspended, with their heads downward, over flames; or looking at the heavens over their shoulders 'until it becomes impossible for them to resume their natural position, while from the twist of the neck nothing but liquids can pass into the
5 stomach;' or dwelling, chained for life, at the foot of a tree; or measuring with their bodies, like caterpillars, the breadth of vast empires; or standing on one leg on the tops of pillars — even these forms of conscious penance are hardly more incredible and astonishing than the scenes
6 which I daily witness. The twelve labors of Hercules were trifling in comparison with those which my neighbors have undertaken; for they were only twelve, and had an end; but I could never see that these men slew or captured any monster or finished any labor. They have no

friend Iolaus to burn with a hot iron the root of the hydra's **1** head, but as soon as one head is crushed, two spring up.

I see young men, my townsmen, whose misfortune it is to have inherited farms, houses, barns, cattle, and farming tools; for these are more easily acquired than got rid of. Better if they had been born in the open pasture and suckled by a wolf, that they might have seen with clearer **2** eyes what field they were called to labor in. Who made them serfs of the soil? Why should they eat their sixty acres, when man is condemned to eat only his peck of **3** dirt? Why should they begin digging their graves as soon **4** as they are born? They have got to live a man's life, pushing all these things before them, and get on as well as they can. How many a poor immortal soul have I met wellnigh crushed and smothered under its load, creeping down the road of life, pushing before it a barn seventy-five feet by forty, its Augean stables never cleansed, and one hun- **5** dred acres of land, tillage, mowing, pasture, and woodlot! The portionless, who struggle with no such unnecessary inherited encumbrances, find it labor enough to subdue and cultivate a few cubic feet of flesh.

But men labor under a mistake. The better part of the man is soon plowed into the soil for compost. By a seeming fate, commonly called necessity, they are employed, as it **6** says in an old book, laying up treasures which moth and **7** rust will corrupt and thieves break through and steal. It is a fool's life, as they will find when they get to the end of it, if not before. It is said that Deucalion and Pyrrha created **8** men by throwing stones over their heads behind them:

> Inde genus durum sumus, experiensque laborum,
> Et documenta damus quâ simus origine nati. **9**

Or, as Raleigh rhymes it in his sonorous way, **10**

1 One of the labors of Hercules was to fight the Lernean Hydra, a serpent with nine heads. As fast as Hercules cut off one head, two grew in its place. But finally with the aid of his servant Iolas he burned away the heads and buried the ninth, immortal one beneath a rock. T took this sentence almost word for word from Lemprière's *Classical Dictionary,* including the spelling of Iolas. The more common spelling is Iolaus (Eddleman, 63).

2 Romulus, the founder of Rome, and his brother Remus are fabled to have been stranded as babies at the foot of the Palatine hill and adopted and suckled by a she-wolf.

3 The then typical size of a farm in the Concord area.

4 "We must eat a peck of dirt before we die" is a proverb that can be traced at least as far back as Oswald Dyke's *English Proverbs* of 1709.

5 Augeas had 3,000 oxen, and his stables had not been cleaned for thirty years.

6 Called: T, by the use of this word, stresses how frequently we are misled by the names of things (Cavell, 65).

7 "Lay not up for yourselves treasures upon earth, where moth and rust doth corrupt, and where thieves break through and steal" (Matthew 6:19). T's referring to the Bible as "an old book" did not ingratiate him among his religiously conservative contemporaries. For a checklist of biblical allusions in W, see Long.

8 Deucalion, the son of Prometheus, and his wife Pyrrha were the only mortals saved when Zeus decided to annihilate the degenerate race of man. Upon the advice of Themis, they covered their heads and cast stones over their shoulders which turned into men, thereby repopulating the earth.

9 Ovid, *Metamorphoses,* I, 414–5.

10 Sir Walter Raleigh, *History of the World,* book 1, part 1, chap. 2, sec. 5.

1 On the limits: to the point of overdrawing a bank account.

'From thence our kind hard-hearted is, enduring
        pain and care,
Approving that our bodies of a stony nature are.'

So much for a blind obedience to a blundering oracle, throwing the stones over their heads behind them, and not seeing where they fell.

Most men, even in this comparatively free country, through mere ignorance and mistake, are so occupied with the factitious cares and superfluously coarse labors of life that its finer fruits cannot be plucked by them. Their fingers, from excessive toil, are too clumsy and tremble too much for that. Actually, the laboring man has not leisure for a true integrity day by day; he cannot afford to sustain the manliest relations to men; his labor would be depreciated in the market. He has no time to be anything but a machine. How can he remember well his ignorance — which his growth requires — who has so often to use his knowledge? We should feed and clothe him gratuitously sometimes, and recruit him with our cordials, before we judge of him. The finest qualities of our nature, like the bloom on fruits, can be preserved only by the most delicate handling. Yet we do not treat ourselves nor one another thus tenderly.

Some of you, we all know, are poor, find it hard to live, are sometimes, as it were, gasping for breath. I have no doubt that some of you who read this book are unable to pay for all the dinners which you have actually eaten, or for the coats and shoes which are fast wearing or are already worn out, and have come to this page to spend borrowed or stolen time, robbing your creditors of an hour. It is very evident what mean and sneaking lives many of you live, for my sight has been whetted by experi-
1 ence; always on the limits, trying to get into business and

trying to get out of debt, a very ancient slough, called by **1**
the Latins *aes alienum*, another's brass, for some of their
coins were made of brass; still living, and dying, and buried by this other's brass; always promising to pay, promising to pay, tomorrow, and dying today, insolvent; seeking
to curry favor, to get custom, by how many modes, only
not state-prison offences; lying, flattering, voting, con- **2**
tracting yourselves into a nutshell of civility or dilating **3**
into an atmosphere of thin and vaporous generosity, that
you may persuade your neighbor to let you make his
shoes, or his hat, or his coat, or his carriage, or import his
groceries for him; making yourselves sick, that you may
lay up something against a sick day, something to be
tucked away in an old chest, or in a stocking behind the
plastering, or, more safely, in the brick bank; no matter **4**
where, no matter how much or how little.

I sometimes wonder that we can be so frivolous, I may
almost say, as to attend to the gross but somewhat foreign **5**
form of servitude called Negro Slavery, there are so many
keen and subtle masters that enslave both North and
South. It is hard to have a Southern overseer; it is worse to **6**
have a Northern one; but worst of all when you are the **7**
slave-driver of yourself. Talk of a divinity in man! Look at **8**
the teamster on the highway, wending to market by day or
night; does any divinity stir within him? His highest duty **9**
to fodder and water his horses! What is his destiny to him
compared with the shipping interests? Does not he drive
for Squire Make-a-stir? How godlike, how immortal, is **10**
he? See how he cowers and sneaks, how vaguely all the
day he fears, not being immortal nor divine, but the slave
and prisoner of his own opinion of himself, a fame won by
his own deeds. Public opinion is a weak tyrant compared
with our own private opinion. What a man thinks of himself, that it is which determines, or rather indicates, his

1   T is undoubtedly referring to the
"Slough of Despond" in Bunyan's *Pilgrim's
Progress* where insolvent debtors were mired.

2   Misdemeanors are punished by imprison-
ment in county jail; felonies, in state prison.

3   "I could be bounded in a nutshell" (*Hamlet,* II, ii, 260).

4   Traditional places to hide one's savings.

5   "Foreign" because it was limited to the
southern states.

6   Overseer: supervisor of slaves. T was an
active abolitionist all his adult life.

7   Despite the popular understanding that
T fled the problems of modern civilization, he
was one of the earliest Americans to protest the
northern factory system. He favored beginning
one's reforms at home, rather than in a distant
land.

8   Although the Puritans concerned themselves with man as a sinner, the transcendentalists of T's day talked more of the divinity of
man. See, for example, Emerson's "Divinity
School Address."

9   "Tis the Divinity that stirs within us"
(Joseph Addison, *Cato,* V, 1).

10   This name does not occur in *Pilgrim's
Progress,* but it is certainly in that tradition.

1 The transcendentalists regularly contrasted two types of creative power, fancy and imagination, with the former thought of as more superficial and decorative, and the latter deeper and more serious.

2 William Wilberforce (1759–1833), an English antislavery crusader who led the parliamentary battle for the abolition of slavery in the British West Indies.

3 Embroidered cushions popular in ladies' dressing rooms in T's day.

4 T uses the words "desperation" and "desperate" six times in this one brief paragraph (Cavell, 55).

5 Minks and muskrats, when caught in steel traps, will even chew their own feet off to free themselves (Dean).

6 "What is the chief end of man? Man's chief end is to glorify God and to enjoy Him forever" (the Shorter Catechism, from *The New England Primer*). While T quotes twice from this major document of orthodox Protestantism, he was anything but orthodox in his own religious beliefs (Bush).

7 Dry wood under a pot: a reference to railroads, which in the 1840s were beginning to spread throughout the country.

8 I have been unable to find this phrase in any collection of sayings or proverbs.

fate. Self-emancipation even in the West Indian prov-
1 inces of the fancy and imagination — what Wilberforce
2 is there to bring that about? Think, also, of the ladies of
3 the land weaving toilet cushions against the last day, not to betray too green an interest in their fates! As if you could kill time without injuring eternity.

4 The mass of men lead lives of quiet desperation. What is called resignation is confirmed desperation. From the desperate city you go into the desperate country, and have to console yourself with the bravery of minks and musk-
5 rats. A stereotyped but unconscious despair is concealed even under what are called the games and amusements of mankind. There is no play in them, for this comes after work. But it is a characteristic of wisdom not to do desperate things.

When we consider what, to use the words of the cate-
6 chism, is the chief end of man, and what are the true necessaries and means of life, it appears as if men had deliberately chosen the common mode of living because they preferred it to any other. Yet they honestly think there is no choice left. But alert and healthy natures remember that the sun rose clear. It is never too late to give up our prejudices. No way of thinking or doing, however ancient, can be trusted without proof. What everybody echoes or in silence passes by as true today may turn out to be falsehood tomorrow, mere smoke of opinion, which some had trusted for a cloud that would sprinkle fertilizing rain on their fields. What old people say you cannot do, you try and find that you can. Old deeds for old people, and new deeds for new. Old people did not know enough once, perchance, to fetch fresh fuel to keep the
7 fire a-going; new people put a little dry wood under a pot, and are whirled round the globe with the speed of birds,
8 in a way to kill old people, as the phrase is. Age is no

better, hardly so well, qualified for an instructor as youth, for it has not profited so much as it has lost. One may almost doubt if the wisest man has learned anything of absolute value by living. Practically, the old have no very important advice to give the young, their own experience has been so partial, and their lives have been such miserable failures, for private reasons, as they must believe; and it may be that they have some faith left which belies that experience, and they are only less young than they were. I have lived some thirty years on this planet, and I have yet **1** to hear the first syllable of valuable or even earnest advice from my seniors. They have told me nothing, and prob- **2** ably cannot tell me anything to the purpose. Here is life, an experiment to a great extent untried by me; but it does not avail me that they have tried it. If I have any experience which I think valuable, I am sure to reflect that this my Mentors said nothing about. **3**

One farmer says to me, 'You cannot live on vegetable food solely, for it furnishes nothing to make bones with;' **4** and so he religiously devotes a part of his day to supplying his system with the raw material of bones; walking all the while he talks behind his oxen, which, with vegetable-made bones, jerk him and his lumbering plow along in spite of every obstacle. Some things are really necessaries of life in some circles, the most helpless and diseased, **5** which in others are luxuries merely, and in others still are entirely unknown.

The whole ground of human life seems to some to have been gone over by their predecessors, both the heights and the valleys, and all things to have been cared for. According to Evelyn, 'the wise Solomon prescribed ordi- **6** nances for the very distances of trees; and the Roman praetors have decided how often you may go into your neighbor's land to gather the acorns which fall on it with-

1 Although T was eight days short of twenty-eight years of age when he went to Walden Pond to live, he wrote a large portion of the book in later years, not completing it until 1854, when he was thirty-six. In the campus rebellions of the 1960s and '70s, a common cry of college students was "Don't trust anyone over thirty." T, appropriately, was one of the few heroes of those rebelling students.

2 Yet T quotes continually from his "seniors" — Confucius, Darwin, Chapman, and so on — throughout the book (Bickman, 35).

3 Mentor was the friend and counselor of Telemachus, the son of Odysseus in Homer's *Odyssey*. The term has come to mean a wise counselor.

4 Although T was not an absolute vegetarian, as were some of his transcendentalist friends, he did follow a modified vegetarian diet for many years. See the chapter "Higher Laws." See also Joseph Jones.

5 For an elaborate discussion of the circle images in W, see Tuerk.

6 John Evelyn, *Sylva; or, A Discourse of Forest Trees* (London, 1679, 227).

1 "The nails neither to exceed nor come short of the finger tips" (Hippocrates, "In the Surgery," *Works* [Loeb, 1928, III, 63]).

2 "Be not afflicted, my child, for who shall efface what thou hast formerly done, or shall assign to thee what thou hast left undone?" (H. H. Wilson, trans., *The Vishnu Purana* [London, 1840, p. 871]).

3 "The days of our years are three-score and ten" (Psalms 90:10).

out trespass, and what share belongs to that neighbor.' Hippocrates has even left directions how we should cut our nails; that is, even with the ends of the fingers, neither shorter nor longer. Undoubtedly the very tedium and ennui which presume to have exhausted the variety and the joys of life are as old as Adam. But man's capacities have never been measured; nor are we to judge of what he can do by any precedents, so little has been tried. Whatever have been thy failures hitherto, 'be not afflicted, my child, for who shall assign to thee what thou hast left undone?'

We might try our lives by a thousand simple tests; as, for instance, that the same sun which ripens my beans illumines at once a system of earths like ours. If I had remembered this it would have prevented some mistakes. This was not the light in which I hoed them. The stars are the apexes of what wonderful triangles! What distant and different beings in the various mansions of the universe are contemplating the same one at the same moment! Nature and human life are as various as our several constitutions. Who shall say what prospect life offers to another? Could a greater miracle take place than for us to look through each other's eyes for an instant? We should live in all the ages of the world in an hour; ay, in all the worlds of the ages. History, Poetry, Mythology! — I know of no reading of another's experience so startling and informing as this would be.

The greater part of what my neighbors call good I believe in my soul to be bad, and if I repent of anything, it is very likely to be my good behavior. What demon possessed me that I behaved so well? You may say the wisest thing you can, old man — you who have lived seventy years, not without honor of a kind — I hear an irresistible voice which invites me away from all that. One genera-

tion abandons the enterprises of another like stranded
vessels.   **1**

I think that we may safely trust a good deal more than
we do. We may waive just so much care of ourselves as we
honestly bestow elsewhere. Nature is as well adapted to
our weakness as to our strength. The incessant anxiety
and strain of some is a well-nigh incurable form of disease. We are made to exaggerate the importance of what
work we do; and yet how much is not done by us! or, what
if we had been taken sick? How vigilant we are! determined not to live by faith if we can avoid it; all the day
long on the alert, at night we unwillingly say our prayers
and commit ourselves to uncertainties. So thoroughly
and sincerely are we compelled to live, reverencing our
life, and denying the possibility of change. This is the
only way, we say; but there are as many ways as there can
be drawn radii from one centre. All change is a miracle to
contemplate; but it is a miracle which is taking place
every instant. Confucius said, 'To know that we know **2**
what we know, and that we do not know what we do not
know, that is true knowledge.' When one man has reduced a fact of the imagination to be a fact to his understanding, I foresee that all men will at length establish
their lives on that basis.

Let us consider for a moment what most of the trouble
and anxiety which I have referred to is about, and how
much it is necessary that we be troubled, or at least careful. It would be some advantage to live a primitive and
frontier life, though in the midst of an outward civilization, if only to learn what are the gross necessaries of life
and what methods have been taken to obtain them; or
even to look over the old day-books of the merchants, to **3**
see what it was that men most commonly bought at the
stores, what they stored, that is, what are the grossest gro-

1 Both Bonner (1985) and Springer discuss the surprisingly large number of nautical images throughout W.

2 *Confucian Analects,* II, xvii. For analysis of this and other quotations from Confucius, see Cady.

3 In several places in his *Journal* (I, 474; VI, 69) T records his delight in going over old account books of Concord merchants. See the chapter "Winter Animals."

1   Except for the fact that so many have called T "without humor," it would seem almost pointless to note that he particularly delighted in puns. For a catalog of puns in W, see Skwire.

2   Interestingly enough, when five years after the publication of W Charles Darwin published his *Origin of Species,* refuting this statement, T became one of the earlier admirers of Darwin's thesis.

3   "We were well clothed, and though sitting close to the fire, were far from too warm; yet these naked savages, though further off, were observed, to our great surprise, to be streaming with perspiration at undergoing such a roasting" (Charles Darwin, *Voyage of a Naturalist Round the World* [New York, 1846, I, 284]).

4   New Holland was an early name for Australia. T's reference is to Darwin, *Voyage of a Naturalist,* 220–1.

1   ceries. For the improvements of ages have had but little influence on the essential laws of man's existence: as our skeletons, probably, are not to be distinguished from those of 2 our ancestors.

By the words, *necessary of life,* I mean whatever, of all that man obtains by his own exertions, has been from the first, or from long use has become, so important to human life that few, if any, whether from savageness, or poverty, or philosophy, ever attempt to do without it. To many creatures there is in this sense but one necessary of life, Food. To the bison of the prairie it is a few inches of palatable grass, with water to drink; unless he seeks the Shelter of the forest or the mountain's shadow. None of the brute creation requires more than Food and Shelter. The necessaries of life for man in this climate may, accurately enough, be distributed under the several heads of Food, Shelter, Clothing, and Fuel; for not till we have secured these are we prepared to entertain the true problems of life with freedom and a prospect of success. Man has invented, not only houses, but clothes and cooked food; and possibly from the accidental discovery of the warmth of fire, and the consequent use of it, at first a luxury, arose the present necessity to sit by it. We observe cats and dogs acquiring the same second nature. By proper Shelter and Clothing we legitimately retain our own internal heat; but with an excess of these, or of Fuel, that is, with an external heat greater than our own internal, may 3 not cookery properly be said to begin? Darwin, the naturalist, says of the inhabitants of Tierra del Fuego, that while his own party, who were well clothed and sitting close to a fire, were far from too warm, these naked savages, who were farther off, were observed, to his great surprise, 'to be streaming with perspiration at undergoing 4 such a roasting.' So, we are told, the New Hollander goes naked with impunity, while the European shivers in his clothes. Is it impossible to combine the hardiness of these savages with the intellectualness of the civilized man? According to Liebig, man's body is a stove, and food the **1** fuel which keeps up the internal combustion in the lungs. In cold weather we eat more, in warm less. The animal heat is the result of a slow combustion, and disease and death take place when this is too rapid; or for want of fuel, or from some defect in the draught, the fire goes out. Of course the vital heat is not to be confounded with fire; but so much for analogy. It appears, therefore, from the above list, that the expression, *animal life,* is nearly synonymous with the expression, *animal heat;* for while Food may be regarded as the Fuel which keeps up the fire within us — and Fuel serves only to prepare that Food or to increase the warmth of our bodies by addition from without — Shelter and Clothing also serve only to retain the *heat* thus generated and absorbed.

The grand necessity, then, for our bodies, is to keep warm, to keep the vital heat in us. What pains we accordingly take, not only with our Food, and Clothing, and Shelter, but with our beds, which are our night-clothes, robbing the nests and breasts of birds to prepare this shelter within a shelter, as the mole has its bed of grass and leaves at the end of its burrow! The poor man is wont to complain that this is a cold world; and to cold, no less physical than social, we refer directly a great part of our ails. The summer, in some climates, makes possible to man a sort of Elysian life. Fuel, except to cook his Food, is **2** then unnecessary; the sun is his fire, and many of the fruits are sufficiently cooked by its rays; while Food generally is more various, and more easily obtained, and Clothing and Shelter are wholly or half unnecessary. At the present day, and in this country, as I find by my own

1   Justus Liebig (1803–1873), a professor of chemistry at the University of Giessen, wrote many volumes using this metaphor, among them *Animal Chemistry* (Philadelphia, 1842).
2   In Greek mythology, Elysium was the home of the virtuous in the afterlife.

1   When T wrote his book, the clipper trade with the Orient was at its height.
2   In the current fashion.

experience, a few implements, a knife, an axe, a spade, a wheelbarrow, etc., and for the studious, lamplight, stationery, and access to a few books, rank next to necessaries, and can all be obtained at a trifling cost. Yet some, not 1 wise, go to the other side of the globe, to barbarous and unhealthy regions, and devote themselves to trade for ten or twenty years, in order that they may live — that is, keep comfortably warm — and die in New England at last. The luxuriously rich are not simply kept comfortably warm, but unnaturally hot; as I implied before, they are cooked, 2 of course *à la mode*.

Most of the luxuries, and many of the so-called comforts of life, are not only not indispensable, but positive hindrances to the elevation of mankind. With respect to luxuries and comforts, the wisest have ever lived a more simple and meagre life than the poor. The ancient philosophers, Chinese, Hindoo, Persian, and Greek, were a class than which none has been poorer in outward riches, none so rich in inward. We know not much about them. It is remarkable that *we* know so much of them as we do. The same is true of the more modern reformers and benefactors of their race. None can be an impartial or wise observer of human life but from the vantage ground of what *we* should call voluntary poverty. Of a life of luxury the fruit is luxury, whether in agriculture, or commerce, or literature, or art. There are nowadays professors of philosophy, but not philosophers. Yet it is admirable to profess because it was once admirable to live. To be a philosopher is not merely to have subtle thoughts, nor even to found a school, but so to love wisdom as to live according to its dictates, a life of simplicity, independence, magnanimity, and trust. It is to solve some of the problems of life, not only theoretically, but practically. The success of great scholars and thinkers is commonly a courtier-like success, not kingly, not manly. They make shift to live merely by conformity, practically as their fathers did, and are in no sense the progenitors of a noble race of men. But why do men degenerate ever? What makes families run out? What is the nature of the luxury which enervates and destroys nations? Are we sure that there is none of it in our own lives? The philosopher is in advance of his age even in the outward form of his life. He is not fed, sheltered, clothed, warmed, like his contemporaries. How can a man be a philosopher and not maintain his vital heat by better methods than other men?

When a man is warmed by the several modes which I have described, what does he want next? Surely not more warmth of the same kind, as more and richer food, larger and more splendid houses, finer and more abundant clothing, more numerous, incessant, and hotter fires, and the like. When he has obtained those things which are necessary to life, there is another alternative than to obtain the superfluities; and that is, to adventure on life now, his vacation from humbler toil having commenced. The soil, it appears, is suited to the seed, for it has sent its radicle downward, and it may now send its shoot upward also with confidence. Why has man rooted himself thus firmly in the earth, but that he may rise in the same proportion into the heavens above? — for the nobler plants are val- **1** ued for the fruit they bear at last in the air and light, far from the ground, and are not treated like the humbler esculents, which, though they may be biennials, are culti- **2** vated only till they have perfected their root, and often cut down at top for this purpose, so that most would not know them in their flowering season.

I do not mean to prescribe rules to strong and valiant natures, who will mind their own affairs whether in heaven or hell, and perchance build more magnificently and

1 It was a pet theory of T's friend and neighbor Bronson Alcott that man's diet should not be confined to vegetables merely, but to those species of plants that showed their higher nature by growing up toward the sun and not down into the earth. Thus one should eat corn, but not carrots, which were considered "humbler" (Sears, 39).

2 The carrot, for instance.

1 T once again calls the reader's attention to the fact that he is addressing his book not to the general public but to a special audience — those who are dissatisfied with their present life.

2 "A fool I to him firmly hold, that loves his fetters though they were of gold" (Spenser, *The Faerie Queene,* III, vii).

3 T was probably thinking of Robinson Crusoe's method of keeping his calendar.

4 "One life, a little gleam of Time between two Eternities" (Thomas Carlyle, *On Heroes and Hero-Worship,* lecture V). Tripp (1969) suggests another source in Marcus Aurelius.

spend more lavishly than the richest, without ever impoverishing themselves, not knowing how they live — if, indeed, there are any such, as has been dreamed; nor to those who find their encouragement and inspiration in precisely the present condition of things, and cherish it with the fondness and enthusiasm of lovers — and, to some extent, I reckon myself in this number; I do not speak to those who are well employed, in whatever circumstances, and they know whether they are well employed or not; — but mainly to the mass of men who are discontented, and idly complaining of the hardness of their lot or of the times, when they might improve them. There are some who complain most energetically and inconsolably of any, because they are, as they say, doing their duty. I also have in my mind that seemingly wealthy, but most terribly impoverished class of all, who have accumulated dross, but know not how to use it, or get rid of it, and thus have forged their own golden or silver fetters.

If I should attempt to tell how I have desired to spend my life in years past, it would probably surprise those of my readers who are somewhat acquainted with its actual history; it would certainly astonish those who know nothing about it. I will only hint at some of the enterprises which I have cherished.

In any weather, at any hour of the day or night, I have been anxious to improve the nick of time, and notch it on my stick too; to stand on the meeting of two eternities, the past and future, which is precisely the present moment; to toe that line. You will pardon some obscurities, for there are more secrets in my trade than in most men's, and yet not voluntarily kept, but inseparable from its very nature.

I would gladly tell all that I know about it, and never paint 'No Admittance' on my gate.

I long ago lost a hound, a bay horse, and a turtle-dove, **1** and am still on their trail. Many are the travellers I have spoken concerning them, describing their tracks and what calls they answered to. I have met one or two who had heard the hound, and the tramp of the horse, and even seen the dove disappear behind a cloud, and they seemed as anxious to recover them as if they had lost them themselves.

To anticipate, not the sunrise and the dawn merely, but, if possible, Nature herself! How many mornings, summer and winter, before yet any neighbor was stirring about his business, have I been about mine! No doubt, many of my townsmen have met me returning from this enterprise, farmers starting for Boston in the twilight, or **2** woodchoppers going to their work. It is true, I never assisted the sun materially in his rising, but, doubt not, it was of the last importance only to be present at it.

So many autumn, ay, and winter days, spent outside the town, trying to hear what was in the wind, to hear and **3** carry it express! I well-nigh sunk all my capital in it, and lost my own breath into the bargain, running in the face of it. If it had concerned either of the political parties, depend upon it, it would have appeared in the Gazette **4** with the earliest intelligence. At other times watching from the observatory of some cliff or tree, to telegraph any **5** new arrival; or waiting at evening on the hill-tops for the **6** sky to fall, that I might catch something, though I never caught much, and that, manna-wise, would dissolve again **7** in the sun.

For a long time I was reporter to a journal, of no very **8** wide circulation, whose editor has never yet seen fit to print the bulk of my contributions, and, as is too common

1   See the Appendix.

2   Many Concord farmers raised crops especially for the Boston market.

3   Pribeck discusses the many wind images in W, saying, "T consistently uses the wind to symbolize the spirit at the heart of man and nature, both the 'sublime' and the 'mean.'"

4   T was probably thinking of Concord's own *Yeoman's Gazette* (1826–1841).

5   Bonner (1969) points out that T is referring to the then prevalent custom of using semaphore to announce the progress of ships along the coast.

6   When T lived on Staten Island in 1843, he loved to climb a hilltop and watch the ships coming and going in New York harbor (T, 1958, 99).

7   Manna: the food God provided the children of Israel in the Sinai desert which rained from the heavens (Exodus 16).

8   T may be referring facetiously either to his own journal, which was not published until forty-four years after his death, or to the *Dial*, whose editors, Emerson and Margaret Fuller, rejected a number of his contributions, and whose circulation never exceeded several hundred.

1 T felt the day was wasted if he did not spend at least four or five hours walking in the woods and fields of Concord, taking note of the world of nature. In his later years he became more and more concerned with keeping a precise record of the progress of the seasons and, with the urging of Bronson Alcott, hoped to publish an "Atlas of Concord" with a complete record of its natural phenomena. He died before he was able to do this.

2 For the last ten or fifteen years of his life, T earned a large portion of his income by surveying (Chase).

3 All of these species were rarities in Concord and so especially cherished.

4 American Indians were always of great interest to T. He gathered more than 2,800 pages of notes from his readings on them and mentions them nearly fifty times in W (Sayre).

5 In his *Journal* (II, 84) T identifies the well-known lawyer as Samuel Hoar, the town's leading citizen and father of T's friends Elizabeth and Edward Hoar.

with writers, I got only my labor for my pains. However, in this case my pains were their own reward.

1   For many years I was self-appointed inspector of snow-storms and rain-storms, and did my duty faithfully; sur-
2 veyor, if not of highways, then of forest paths and all across-lot routes, keeping them open, and ravines bridged and passable at all seasons, where the public heel had testified to their utility.

I have looked after the wild stock of the town, which give a faithful herdsman a good deal of trouble by leaping fences; and I have had an eye to the unfrequented nooks and corners of the farm; though I did not always know whether Jonas or Solomon worked in a particular field today; that was none of my business. I have watered the red huckleberry, the sand cherry and the nettle-tree, the red pine and the black ash, the white grape and the yel-
3 low violet, which might have withered else in dry seasons.

In short, I went on thus for a long time (I may say it without boasting), faithfully minding my business, till it became more and more evident that my townsmen would not after all admit me into the list of town officers, nor make my place a sinecure with a moderate allowance. My accounts, which I can swear to have kept faithfully, I have, indeed, never got audited, still less accepted, still less paid and settled. However, I have not set my heart on that.

4   Not long since, a strolling Indian went to sell baskets at
5 the house of a well-known lawyer in my neighborhood. 'Do you wish to buy any baskets?' he asked. 'No, we do not want any,' was the reply. 'What!' exclaimed the Indian as he went out the gate, 'do you mean to starve us?' Having seen his industrious white neighbors so well off — that the lawyer had only to weave arguments, and, by some magic, wealth and standing followed — he had said to himself: I will go into business; I will weave baskets; it is

In the sluiceway of Pole Brook, by the road just beyond, I found another kind of Indian pot. It was an eel-pot (?) or creel, a wattled basket or wicker-work, made of willow osiers with the bark on, very artfully. It was about four feet long and shaped thus. (March 20, 1858)

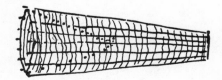

a thing which I can do. Thinking that when he had made the baskets he would have done his part, and then it would be the white man's to buy them. He had not discovered that it was necessary for him to make it worth the other's while to buy them, or at least make him think that it was so, or to make something else which it would be worth his while to buy. I too had woven a kind of basket of a delicate texture, but I had not made it worth any one's while to buy them. Yet not the less, in my case, did I think **1** it worth my while to weave them, and instead of studying how to make it worth men's while to buy my baskets, I studied rather how to avoid the necessity of selling them. The life which men praise and regard as successful is but one kind. Why should we exaggerate any one kind at the expense of the others?

Finding that my fellow-citizens were not likely to offer me any room in the court house, or any curacy or living anywhere else, but I must shift for myself, I turned my face more exclusively than ever to the woods, where I was better known. I determined to go into business at once, and not wait to acquire the usual capital, using such slender means as I had already got. My purpose in going to Walden Pond was not to live cheaply nor to live dearly there, but to transact some private business with the few- **2** est obstacles; to be hindered from accomplishing which for want of a little common sense, a little enterprise and business talent, appeared not so sad as foolish.

I have always endeavored to acquire strict business habits; they are indispensable to every man. If your trade is with the Celestial Empire, then some small counting house on the coast, in some Salem harbor, will be fixture enough. **3** You will export such articles as the country affords, purely native products, much ice and pine timber and a little granite, always in native bottoms. These will be good

1   Tripp (1988) suggests that T may be echoing both Chaucer's *Canterbury Tales* (VI, 444–6) and Virgil's *Eclogues* (X, 70–2).

Paul (1958, 322) suggests that T is here giving a thinly veiled account of the publishing failure of his *Week*.

2   At least one piece of "private business" that T wished to transact at Walden Pond was the writing of *A Week*, his memorial tribute to his brother John, who had died in 1842. For three years he had been kept from the task by worldly affairs. By retiring to the pond, he was able to find time to complete the book.

3   Salem, Massachusetts, was the center of trade with China, the Celestial Empire. The products listed were all prominent in that trade (Morison).

1   The coast of New Jersey was long noted as the site of many shipwrecks.

2   Jean-François de Galaup, Comte de La Pérouse (1741–1788), a French explorer who disappeared in 1788 while exploring the Pacific. His fate was not learned until 1826, when his shipwreck was discovered on Vanikoro Island, north of the New Hebrides.

3   Hanno was a Carthaginian navigator of the sixth and fifth centuries B.C.

4   The two ordinary deductions in calculating the net weight of goods to be sold by retail, "tare" making allowance for the weight of the container, "tret" for that of waste matter.

5   Both the railroad and the ice trade were new to Walden Pond when T lived there. See the chapter "The Pond in Winter."

6   In T's own copy of W, he corrected "post" to "port," and it is clearly "port" in the manuscript. Either word makes sense, and critics have argued for both.

7   St. Petersburg is built in the lowlands of the Neva River.

ventures. To oversee all the details yourself in person; to be at once pilot and captain, and owner and underwriter; to buy and sell and keep the accounts; to read every letter received, and write or read every letter sent; to superintend the discharge of imports night and day; to be upon many parts of the coast almost at the same time — often **1** the richest freight will be discharged upon a Jersey shore; — to be your own telegraph, unweariedly sweeping the horizon, speaking all passing vessels bound coastwise; to keep up a steady despatch of commodities, for the supply of such a distant and exorbitant market; to keep yourself informed of the state of the markets, prospects of war and peace everywhere, and anticipate the tendencies of trade and civilization — taking advantage of the results of all exploring expeditions, using new passages and all improvements in navigation; — charts to be studied, the position of reefs and new lights and buoys to be ascertained, and ever, and ever, the logarithmic tables to be corrected, for by the error of some calculator the vessel often splits upon a rock that should have reached a friendly pier — **2** there is the untold fate of La Pérouse; — universal science to be kept pace with, studying the lives of all great discoverers and navigators, great adventurers and mer- **3** chants, from Hanno and the Phoenicians down to our day; in fine, account of stock to be taken from time to time, to know how you stand. It is a labor to task the faculties of a man — such problems of profit and loss, of **4** interest, of tare and tret, and gauging of all kinds in it, as demand a universal knowledge.

I have thought that Walden Pond would be a good place for business, not solely on account of the railroad **5** and the ice trade; it offers advantages which it may not be **6** good policy to divulge; it is a good port and a good foun- **7** dation. No Neva marshes to be filled; though you must everywhere build on piles of your own driving. It is said that a flood-tide, with a westerly wind, and ice in the Neva, would sweep St. Petersburg from the face of the earth.

As this business was to be entered into without the usual capital, it may not be easy to conjecture where those means, that will still be indispensable to every such undertaking, were to be obtained. As for Clothing, to **1** come at once to the practical part of the question, perhaps we are led oftener by the love of novelty and a regard for the opinions of men, in procuring it, than by a true utility. Let him who has work to do recollect that the object of clothing is, first, to retain the vital heat, and secondly, in this state of society, to cover nakedness, and **2** he may judge how much of any necessary or important work may be accomplished without adding to his wardrobe. Kings and queens who wear a suit but once, though made by some tailor or dressmaker to their majesties, cannot know the comfort of wearing a suit that fits. They are no better than wooden horses to hang the clean clothes **3** on. Every day our garments become more assimilated to ourselves, receiving the impress of the wearer's character, until we hesitate to lay them aside without such delay and medical appliances and some such solemnity even as our bodies. No man ever stood the lower in my estimation for having a patch in his clothes; yet I am sure that there is greater anxiety, commonly, to have fashionable, or at least clean and unpatched clothes, than to have a sound conscience. But even if the rent is not mended, perhaps the worst vice betrayed is improvidence. I sometimes try my acquaintances by such tests as this — Who could wear a patch, or two extra seams only, over the knee? Most behave as if they believed that their prospects for life would be ruined if they should do it. It would be easier for them to hobble to town with a broken leg than with a broken

1   The relationship of the following material on clothing to the "clothes philosophy" of Carlyle's *Sartor Resartus* will quickly be seen by any student familiar with that work.

2   T did not have the usual mid-Victorian objections to nudity, but delighted in swimming and wading naked in rivers. Modern nudists often claim him as one of their precursors (MacDonald).

3   Clothes horses: wooden frames used to air out clothes, and also persons who think clothes are all-important.

1   The *New York Times* for May 16, 1969, reported that thieves in Trujillo, Peru, used this technique to rob houses. I doubt they got the idea from W.

2   Ida Pfeiffer, *A Lady's Voyage Round the World* (New York, 1852, 265).

3   "Man may work from sun to sun, / But woman's work is never done" (Bartlett, 920).

pantaloon. Often if an accident happens to a gentleman's legs, they can be mended; but if a similar accident happens to the legs of his pantaloons, there is no help for it; for he considers, not what is truly respectable, but what is respected. We know but few men, a great many coats and breeches. Dress a scarecrow in your last shift, you standing shiftless by, who would not soonest salute the scarecrow? Passing a cornfield the other day, close by a hat and coat on a stake I recognized the owner of the farm. He was only a little more weather-beaten than when I saw him last. I have heard of a dog that barked at every stranger who approached his master's premises with clothes on, but was easily quieted by a naked thief. It is an interesting question how far men would retain their relative rank if they were divested of their clothes. Could you, in such a case, tell surely of any company of civilized men which belonged to the most respected class? When Madam Pfeiffer, in her adventurous travels round the world, from east to west, had got so near home as Asiatic Russia, she says that she felt the necessity of wearing other than a travelling dress, when she went to meet the authorities, for she 'was now in a civilized country, where. . . people are judged of by their clothes.' Even in our democratic New England towns the accidental possession of wealth, and its manifestation in dress and equipage alone, obtain for the possessor almost universal respect. But they who yield such respect, numerous as they are, are so far heathen, and need to have a missionary sent to them. Beside, clothes introduced sewing, a kind of work which you may call endless; a woman's dress, at least, is never done.

A man who has at length found something to do will not need to get a new suit to do it in; for him the old will do, that has lain dusty in the garret for an indeterminate period. Old shoes will serve a hero longer than they have

served his valet — if a hero ever has a valet — bare feet **1**
are older than shoes, and he can make them do. Only
they who go to soirées and legislative halls must have new
coats, coats to change as often as the man changes in
them. But if my jacket and trousers, my hat and shoes, are
fit to worship God in, they will do; will they not? Who
ever saw his old clothes — his old coat, actually worn out,
resolved into its primitive elements, so that it was not a
deed of charity to bestow it on some poor boy, by him
perchance to be bestowed on some poorer still, or shall
we say richer, who could do with less? I say, beware of all
enterprises that require new clothes, and not rather a new
wearer of clothes. If there is not a new man, how can the
new clothes be made to fit? If you have any enterprise
before you, try it in your old clothes. All men want, not
something to *do with*, but something to *do*, or rather
something to *be*. Perhaps we should never procure a new
suit, however ragged or dirty the old, until we have so
conducted, so enterprised or sailed in some way, that we
feel like new men in the old, and that to retain it would
be like keeping new wine in old bottles. Our moulting **2**
season, like that of the fowls, must be a crisis in our lives.
The loon retires to solitary ponds to spend it. Thus also
the snake casts ·its slough, and the caterpillar its wormy
coat, by an internal industry and expansion; for clothes
are but our outmost cuticle and mortal coil. Otherwise **3**
we shall be found sailing under false colors, and be inevi- **4**
tably cashiered at last by our own opinion, as well as that
of mankind.

We don garment after garment, as if we grew like ex-
ogenous plants by addition without. Our outside and often **5**
thin and fanciful clothes are our epidermis, or false skin,
which partakes not of our life, and may be stripped off
here and there without fatal injury; our thicker garments,

1 "No man is a hero to his valet" (Madame Cornuel, 1605–1694).

2 "Neither do men put new wine into old bottles else the bottles break" (Matthew 9:17).

3 "When we have shuffled off this mortal coil" (*Hamlet*, III, i, 67).

4 Pirates and other unscrupulous merchant-men often sailed flying the flag of another nation to disguise their activities.

5 Plants that grow by adding an annual layer just beneath the bark.

1   T was thinking of Bias (c. sixth century
B.C.), as he indicates in his *Journal* (1906, I,
169–70).

2   She has been identified by Sanborn
(1909, I, 79) as Mary Minot of Concord.

constantly worn, are our cellular integument, or cortex;
but our shirts are our liber, or true bark, which cannot be
removed without girdling and so destroying the man. I
believe that all races at some seasons wear something
equivalent to the shirt. It is desirable that a man be clad
so simply that he can lay his hands on himself in the
dark, and that he live in all respects so compactly and
preparedly that, if an enemy take the town, he can, like
1 the old philosopher, walk out the gate empty-handed without anxiety. While one thick garment is, for most purposes, as good as three thin ones, and cheap clothing can
be obtained at prices really to suit customers; while a
thick coat can be bought for five dollars, which will last as
many years, thick pantaloons for two dollars, cowhide
boots for a dollar and a half a pair, a summer hat for a
quarter of a dollar, and a winter cap for sixty-two and a
half cents, or a better be made at home at a nominal cost,
where is he so poor that, clad in such a suit, *of his own
earning*, there will not be found wise men to do him
reverence?

When I ask for a garment of a particular form, my
2 tailoress tells me gravely, 'They do not make them so
now,' not emphasizing the 'They' at all, as if she quoted
an authority as impersonal as the Fates, and I find it
difficult to get made what I want, simply because she
cannot believe that I mean what I say, that I am so rash.
When I hear this oracular sentence, I am for a moment
absorbed in thought, emphasizing to myself each word
separately that I may come at the meaning of it, that I may
find out by what degree of consanguinity *They* are related
to *me*, and what authority they may have in an affair
which affects me so nearly; and, finally, I am inclined to
answer her with equal mystery, and without any more
emphasis of the 'they' — 'It is true, they did not make

them so recently, but they do now.' Of what use this measuring of me if she does not measure my character, but only the breadth of my shoulders, as it were a peg to hang the coat on? We worship not the Graces, nor the **1** Parcae, but Fashion. She spins and weaves and cuts with **2** full authority. The head monkey at Paris puts on a traveller's cap, and all the monkeys in America do the same. I sometimes despair of getting anything quite simple and honest done in this world by the help of men. They would have to be passed through a powerful press first, to squeeze their old notions out of them, so that they would not soon get upon their legs again; and then there would be some one in the company with a maggot in his head, hatched from an egg deposited there nobody knows when, for not even fire kills these things, and you would have lost your labor. Nevertheless, we will not forget that some Egyptian wheat was handed down to us by a mummy.   **3**

On the whole, I think that it cannot be maintained that dressing has in this or any country risen to the dignity of an art. At present men make shift to wear what they can get. Like shipwrecked sailors, they put on what they can find on the beach, and at a little distance, whether of space or time, laugh at each other's masquerade. Every generation laughs at the old fashions, but follows religiously the new. We are amused at beholding the costume **4** of Henry VIII, or Queen Elizabeth, as much as if it was that of the King and Queen of the Cannibal Islands. All **5** costume off a man is pitiful or grotesque. It is only the serious eye peering from and the sincere life passed within it which restrain laughter and consecrate the costume of any people. Let Harlequin be taken with a fit of the colic **6** and his trappings will have to serve that mood too. When the soldier is hit by a cannon-ball, rags are as becoming as purple.   **7**

1 Graces: the Roman goddesses of charm and beauty.

2 Parcae: the Fates in Roman mythology.

3 The *Concord Freeman* for Nov. 12, 1841, gives such an account, and T probably saw it there. Such stories have appeared in many places, and although they have often been dismissed as myth, present-day scientists acknowledge that dormant seeds can germinate even after thousands of years. See, for example, the *New York Times* for March 7, 1951.

4 T originally made these statements on costume about a group of Tyrolian singers who visited Concord in 1841 (Journal, 1906, I, 196).

5 T is here using the common generic term for islands inhabited by uncivilized natives.

6 A droll character in comedy and pantomime usually dressed in parti-colored clothes.

7 The color of royal garments.

1   Ellery Channing, in his notes on W, points out that T had visited the Bigelow mills in Clinton, Massachusetts. T reports at length on this visit in his *Journal* (1906, II, 134–6).

2   Here again, it is significant that T was an early protester against the evils of the factory system, which was already producing slums and paupers in New England cities.

3   Samuel Laing, *Journal of a Residence in Norway* (London, 1837, 295).

The childish and savage taste of men and women for new patterns keeps how many shaking and squinting through kaleidoscopes that they may discover the particular figure which this generation requires today. The manufacturers have learned that this taste is merely whimsical. Of two patterns which differ only by a few threads more or less of a particular color, the one will be sold readily, the other lie on the shelf, though it frequently happens that after the lapse of a season the latter becomes the most fashionable. Comparatively, tattooing is not the hideous custom which it is called. It is not barbarous merely because the printing is skin-deep and unalterable.

I cannot believe that our factory system is the best mode by which men may get clothing. The condition of the operatives is becoming every day more like that of the English; and it cannot be wondered at, since, as far as I have heard or observed, the principal object is, not that mankind may be well and honestly clad, but, unquestionably, that the corporations may be enriched. In the long run men hit only what they aim at. Therefore, though they should fail immediately, they had better aim at something high.

As for a Shelter, I will not deny that this is now a necessary of life, though there are instances of men having done without it for long periods in colder countries than this. Samuel Laing says that 'the Laplander in his skin dress, and in a skin bag which he puts over his head and shoulders, will sleep night after night on the snow . . . in a degree of cold which would extinguish the life of one exposed to it in any woollen clothing.' He had seen them asleep thus. Yet he adds, 'They are not hardier than other people.' But, probably, man did not live long on the earth without discovering the convenience which there is in a house, the domestic comforts, which phrase may have originally signified the satisfactions of the house more than of the family; though these must be extremely partial and occasional in those climates where the house is associated in our thoughts with winter or the rainy season chiefly, and two thirds of the year, except for a parasol, is unnecessary. In our climate, in the summer, it was formerly almost solely a covering at night. In the Indian gazettes a wigwam was the symbol of a day's march, and a row of them cut or painted on the bark of a tree signified that so many times they had camped. Man was not made so large limbed and robust but that he must seek to narrow his world, and wall in a space such as fitted him. He was at first bare and out of doors; but though this was pleasant enough in serene and warm weather, by daylight, the rainy season and the winter, to say nothing of the torrid sun, would perhaps have nipped his race in the bud if he had not made haste to clothe himself with the shelter of a house. Adam and Eve, according to the fable, wore the bower before other clothes. Man wanted a **1** home, a place of warmth, or comfort, first of physical warmth, then the warmth of the affections.

We may imagine a time when, in the infancy of the human race, some enterprising mortal crept into a hollow in a rock for shelter. Every child begins the world again, to some extent, and loves to stay outdoors, even in wet and cold. It plays house, as well as horse, having an instinct for it. Who does not remember the interest with which, when young, he looked at shelving rocks, or any approach to a cave? It was the natural yearning of that portion of our most primitive ancestor which still survived in us. From the cave we have advanced to roofs of palm leaves, of bark and boughs, of linen woven and stretched, of grass and straw, of boards and shingles, of stones and tiles. At last, we know not what it is to live in the open air,

1 Genesis 3:7. Calling the Bible a fable alienated some of T's more devout contemporaries, but he was not one to mince words to soothe his neighbors' feelings.

I took refuge from the thunder-shower this afternoon by running for a high pile of wood near Second Division, and while it was raining, I stuck three stout cat-sticks into the pile, higher than my head, each a little lower than the other, and piled large flattish wood on them and tossed on dead pine tops, making a little shed, under which I stood dry. (May 29, 1860)

1   Labyrinth: any complicated structure, but specifically a building in Crete built by Daedalus where the Minotaur was housed. Theseus was able to penetrate it, slay the Minotaur, and escape with the aid of Ariadne, who gave him the clue — a thread to follow.

2   The Penobscots of northern Maine frequently visited Concord and camped outside the town.

3   Although T suggests a man might well live in a large box, only seven pages later he condemns the "degraded poor" for living in "sties," which Bridgman (79) says are surely more livable than boxes.

4   "If I have freedom in my love, / And in my soul am free" (Richard Lovelace, "To Althea from Prison").

and our lives are domestic in more senses than we think. From the hearth the field is a great distance. It would be well, perhaps, if we were to spend more of our days and nights without any obstruction between us and the celestial bodies, if the poet did not speak so much from under a roof, or the saint dwell there so long. Birds do not sing in caves, nor do doves cherish their innocence in dovecots.

However, if one designs to construct a dwelling-house, it behooves him to exercise a little Yankee shrewdness, 1 lest after all he find himself in a workhouse, a labyrinth without a clue, a museum, an almshouse, a prison, or a splendid mausoleum instead. Consider first how slight a shelter is absolutely necessary. I have seen Penobscot In- 2 dians, in this town, living in tents of thin cotton cloth, while the snow was nearly a foot deep around them, and I thought that they would be glad to have it deeper to keep out the wind. Formerly, when how to get my living honestly, with freedom left for my proper pursuits, was a question which vexed me even more than it does now, for unfortunately I am become somewhat callous, I used to 3 see a large box by the railroad, six feet long by three wide, in which the laborers locked up their tools at night; and it suggested to me that every man who was hard pushed might get such a one for a dollar, and, having bored a few auger holes in it, to admit the air at least, get into it when it rained and at night, and hook down the lid, and so have 4 freedom in his love, and in his soul be free. This did not appear the worst, nor by any means a despicable alternative. You could sit up as late as you pleased, and, whenever you got up, go abroad without any landlord or houselord dogging you for rent. Many a man is harassed to death to pay the rent of a larger and more luxurious box who would not have frozen to death in such a box as this. I am far from jesting. Economy is a subject which admits

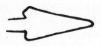

The Red Man, his mark (March 28, 1859)

of being treated with levity, but it cannot so be disposed of. A comfortable house for a rude and hardy race, that lived mostly out of doors, was once made here almost entirely of such materials as Nature furnished ready to their hands. Gookin, who was superintendent of the Indi- [1] ans subject to the Massachusetts Colony, writing in 1674, says, 'The best of their houses are covered very neatly, tight and warm, with barks of trees, slipped from their bodies at those seasons when the sap is up, and made into great flakes, with pressure of weighty timber, when they are green. . . . The meaner sort are covered with mats which they make of a kind of bulrush and are also indifferently tight and warm, but not so good as the former. . . . Some I have seen, sixty or a hundred feet long and thirty feet broad. . . . I have often lodged in their wigwams, and found them as warm as the best English houses.' He adds that they were commonly carpeted and lined within with well-wrought embroidered mats, and were furnished with various utensils. The Indians had advanced so far as to regulate the effect of the wind by a mat suspended over the hole in the roof and moved by a string. Such a lodge was in the first instance constructed in a day or two at most, and taken down and put up in a few hours; and every family owned one, or its apartment in one.

In the savage state every family owns a shelter as good as the best, and sufficient for its coarser and simpler wants; but I think that I speak within bounds when I say that, though the birds of the air have their nests, and the foxes [2] their holes, and the savages their wigwams, in modern civilized society not more than one half the families own a shelter. In the large towns and cities, where civilization especially prevails, the number of those who own a shelter is a very small fraction of the whole. The rest pay an annual tax for this outside garment of all, become indis-

1   Daniel Gookin, *Historical Collections of the Indians in New England* (Boston, 1792, chap. III, 9).

2   "The foxes have holes, and the birds of the air have nests; but the Son of Man hath not where to lay his head" (Matthew 8:20).

1 A nonsmoking fireplace invented by Benjamin Thompson, Count Rumford (1753–1814).

2 Formerly builders plastered between the studding; now thick paper takes the place of this back plaster.

Returning along the shore, we saw a man and woman putting off in a small boat. . . . Their boat was of peculiar construction, and T. said it was called a sharper. . . . R. told the squaw that we were interested in those of the old stock, now they were so few. "Yes," said she, "and you'd be glad if they were all gone." (October 2, 1855)

pensable summer and winter, which would buy a village of Indian wigwams, but now helps to keep them poor as long as they live. I do not mean to insist here on the disadvantage of hiring compared with owning, but it is evident that the savage owns his shelter because it costs so little, while the civilized man hires his commonly because he cannot afford to own it; nor can he, in the long run, any better afford to hire. But, answers one, by merely paying this tax the poor civilized man secures an abode which is a palace compared with the savage's. An annual rent of from twenty-five to a hundred dollars (these are the country rates) entitles him to the benefit of the improvements of centuries, spacious apartments, clean paint and paper, Rumford fireplace, back plastering, Venetian blinds, copper pump, spring lock, a commodious cellar, and many other things. But how happens it that he who is said to enjoy these things is so commonly a *poor* civilized man, while the savage, who has them not, is rich as a savage? If it is asserted that civilization is a real advance in the condition of man — and I think that it is, though only the wise improve their advantages — it must be shown that it has produced better dwellings without making them more costly; and the cost of a thing is the amount of what I will call life which is required to be exchanged for it, immediately or in the long run. An average house in this neighborhood costs perhaps eight hundred dollars, and to lay up this sum will take from ten to fifteen years of the laborer's life, even if he is not encumbered with a family — estimating the pecuniary value of every man's labor at one dollar a day, for if some receive more, others receive less; — so that he must have spent more than half his life commonly before *his* wigwam will be earned. If we suppose him to pay a rent instead, this is but a doubtful choice of evils. Would the savage have been wise to exchange his wigwam for a palace on these terms?

It may be guessed that I reduce almost the whole advantage of holding this superfluous property as a fund in store against the future, so far as the individual is concerned, mainly to the defraying of funeral expenses. But perhaps a man is not required to bury himself. Nevertheless this points to an important distinction between the civilized man and the savage; and, no doubt, they have designs on us for our benefit, in making the life of a civilized people an *institution*, in which the life of the individual is to a great extent absorbed, in order to preserve and perfect that of the race. But I wish to show at what a sacrifice this advantage is at present obtained, and to suggest that we may possibly so live as to secure all the advantage without suffering any of the disadvantage. What mean ye by saying that the poor ye have always with 1 you, or that the fathers have eaten sour grapes, and the 2 children's teeth are set on edge?

'As I live, saith the Lord God, ye shall not have occasion any more to use this proverb in Israel.

'Behold all souls are mine; as the soul of the father, so also the soul of the son is mine: the soul that sinneth, it shall die.'   3

When I consider my neighbors, the farmers of Concord, who are at least as well off as the other classes, I find that for the most part they have been toiling twenty, thirty, or forty years, that they may become the real owners of their farms, which commonly they have inherited with encumbrances, or else bought with hired money — and we may regard one third of that toil as the cost of their houses — but commonly they have not paid for them yet. It is true, the encumbrances sometimes outweigh the

1   "For ye have the poor always with you" (Matthew 26:11).

2   "The fathers have eaten sour grapes, and the children's teeth are set on edge" (Ezekiel 18:2). See Taylor.

3   Ezekiel 18:3–4.

This boat had a singular "wooden grapple," as Tom called it, made in form of a cross, thus: with a stone within. (October 2, 1855)

1 The Middlesex Cattle Show was held in Concord each September, and T usually joined the throng visiting it. In 1860 he was its principal speaker, delivering a paper on "The Succession of Forest Trees."

2 Ostentatious display.

3 A dialect word meaning "proceeding regularly," and more usually spelled "suant." T's usage is so unusual that it is often cited in dictionaries. He comments in some detail on this word in his *Journal* (III, 272).

4 The first edition of W reads "springe," but Shanley (1971, 396) has changed it to "spring," which is the spelling T uses in some of the early drafts.

value of the farm, so that the farm itself becomes one great encumbrance, and still a man is found to inherit it, being well acquainted with it, as he says. On applying to the assessors, I am surprised to learn that they cannot at once name a dozen in the town who own their farms free and clear. If you would know the history of these homesteads, inquire at the bank where they are mortgaged. The man who has actually paid for his farm with labor on it is so rare that every neighbor can point to him. I doubt if there are three such men in Concord. What has been said of the merchants, that a very large majority, even ninety-seven in a hundred, are sure to fail, is equally true of the farmers. With regard to the merchants, however, one of them says pertinently that a great part of their failures are not genuine pecuniary failures, but merely failures to fulfil their engagements, because it is inconvenient; that is, it is the moral character that breaks down. But this puts an infinitely worse face on the matter, and suggests, beside, that probably not even the other three succeed in saving their souls, but are perchance bankrupt in a worse sense than they who fail honestly. Bankruptcy and repudiation are the spring-boards from which much of our civilization vaults and turns its somersets, but the savage stands on the unelastic plank of famine. Yet the **1, 2** Middlesex Cattle Show goes off here with *éclat* annually, **3** as if all the joints of the agricultural machine were suent.

The farmer is endeavoring to solve the problem of a livelihood by a formula more complicated than the problem itself. To get his shoestrings he speculates in herds of cattle. With consummate skill he has set his trap with **4** a hair spring to catch comfort and independence, and then, as he turned away, got his own leg into it. This is the reason he is poor; and for a similar reason we are all poor in respect to a thousand savage comforts, though surrounded by luxuries. As Chapman sings,   1

> 'The false society of men —
> — for earthly greatness
> All heavenly comforts rarefies to air.'

And when the farmer has got his house, he may not be the richer but the poorer for it, and it be the house that has got him. As I understand it, that was a valid objection urged by Momus against the house which Minerva made, **2, 3** that she 'had not made it movable, by which means a bad neighborhood might be avoided;' and it may still be urged, for our houses are such unwieldy property that we are often imprisoned rather than housed in them; and the bad neighborhood to be avoided is our own scurvy selves. I know one or two families, at least, in this town, who, for nearly a generation, have been wishing to sell their houses in the outskirts and move into the village, but have not been able to accomplish it, and only death will set them free.

Granted that the *majority* are able at last either to own or hire the modern house with all its improvements. While civilization has been improving our houses, it has not equally improved the men who are to inhabit them. It has created palaces, but it was not so easy to create noblemen and kings. And *if the civilized man's pursuits are no worthier than the savage's, if he is employed the greater part of his life in obtaining gross necessaries and comforts merely, why should he have a better dwelling than the former?*

But how do the poor *minority* fare? Perhaps it will be found that just in proportion as some have been placed in outward circumstances above the savage, others have been degraded below him. The luxury of one class is

1 George Chapman, *The Tragedy of Caesar and Pompey*, V, ii.

2 Among the ancients, a god of pleasure and the son of Nox, according to Hesiod. The following quotation is from the entry under Momus in Lemprière's *Bibliotheca Classica* (New York, 1842, 744).

3 The Roman goddess of wisdom.

1 "Silent poor" refers to a fund established in Concord in the eighteenth century for the care of those who hid their poverty to avoid going to the poorhouse.

2 "There are writings on the pyramids in Egyptian characters showing how much was spent on purges and onions and garlic for the workmen" (Herodotus 2.125).

3 Oddly enough, in his later chapter on "Former Inhabitants" of the area, T never mentions that there was a whole colony of such shanties, inhabited by Irish railroad workers, just a few hundred yards north of the pond, along the railroad tracks.

4 England was the first nation to take advantage of the Industrial Revolution.

5 It was still the custom in T's day to leave all unexplored areas white on the maps.

6 T, in W, often speaks disparagingly of the Irish, who were at that time swarming into New England as a result of the potato famine. Finding only menial jobs open to them, they were forced to live in poverty and were openly despised by the resident Yankees. However, as T got to know them personally, he changed his mind about them and became their defender. Why he did not then excise his disparaging remarks is not known.

7 Throughout his adult life T was actively engaged both in protesting slavery and in anti-slavery activities.

counterbalanced by the indigence of another. On the one side is the palace, on the other are the almshouse and 1 'silent poor.' The myriads who built the pyramids to be 2 the tombs of the Pharaohs were fed on garlic, and it may be were not decently buried themselves. The mason who finishes the cornice of the palace returns at night perchance to a hut not so good as a wigwam. It is a mistake to suppose that, in a country where the usual evidences of civilization exist, the condition of a very large body of the inhabitants may not be as degraded as that of savages. I refer to the degraded poor, not now to the degraded rich. To know this I should not need to look farther than to the 3 shanties which everywhere border our railroads, that last improvement in civilization; where I see in my daily walks human beings living in sties, and all winter with an open door, for the sake of light, without any visible, often imaginable, wood-pile, and the forms of both old and young are permanently contracted by the long habit of shrinking from cold and misery, and the development of all their limbs and faculties is checked. It certainly is fair to look at that class by whose labor the works which distinguish this generation are accomplished. Such too, to a greater or less extent, is the condition of the operatives of every 4 denomination in England, which is the great workhouse of the world. Or I could refer you to Ireland, which is 5 marked as one of the white or enlightened spots on the 6 map. Contrast the physical condition of the Irish with that of the North American Indian, or the South Sea Islander, or any other savage race before it was degraded by contact with the civilized man. Yet I have no doubt that that people's rulers are as wise as the average of civilized rulers. Their condition only proves what squalidness may consist with civilization. I hardly need refer now to 7 the laborers in our Southern States who produce the staple exports of this country, and are themselves a staple [1] production of the South. But to confine myself to those who are said to be in *moderate* circumstances. [2]

Most men appear never to have considered what a house is, and are actually though needlessly poor all their lives because they think that they must have such a one as their neighbors have. As if one were to wear any sort of coat which the tailor might cut out for him, or, gradually leaving off palm-leaf hat or cap of woodchuck skin, com- [3, 4] plain of hard times because he could not afford to buy him a crown! It is possible to invent a house still more convenient and luxurious than we have, which yet all would admit that man could not afford to pay for. Shall we always study to obtain more of these things, and not sometimes to be content with less? Shall the respectable citizen thus gravely teach, by precept and example, the necessity of the young man's providing a certain number of superfluous glow-shoes, and umbrellas, and empty guest [5] chambers for empty guests, before he dies? Why should not our furniture be as simple as the Arab's or the Indian's? When I think of the benefactors of the race, whom we have apotheosized as messengers from heaven, bearers of divine gifts to man, I do not see in my mind any retinue at their heels, any carload of fashionable furniture. Or what if I were to allow — would it not be a singular allowance? — that our furniture should be more complex than the Arab's, in proportion as we are morally and intellectually his superiors! At present our houses are cluttered and defiled with it, and a good housewife would sweep out the greater part into the dust hole, and not [6] leave her morning's work undone. Morning work! By the blushes of Aurora and the music of Memnon, what [7, 8] should be man's *morning work* in this world? I had three pieces of limestone on my desk, but I was terrified to find

1   Slave breeding was one of the "industries" of the South at this time.
2   In his own copy of W, T questioned the italicizing of this word by the printer.
3   Hats made of palm leaves were then fashionable in the summer.
4   Hunters often made winter hats out of woodchuck fur.
5   A variant spelling of "galoshes," overshoes for wet weather.
6   A hole cut in the floor enabling one to sweep dust and debris directly into the basement.
7   Aurora: the Roman goddess of dawn.
8   Memnon: a king of Egypt. His subjects erected a statue of him that uttered a melodious sound every morning when the first rays of the sun fell upon it.

1   The printer of the first edition of W misread "best" as "lust," with rather amusing results. Fortunately T caught the error in the proof sheets and corrected it.

2   The last king of Assyria, whose effeminacy irritated his military officers and led them to revolt. See Byron's tragedy of this name. Thoreau may have read of Sardanapalus in Diodorus 2.23.

3   There was a vogue for Oriental decoration in the mid-nineteenth century, inspired by the China trade.

4   The name for a typical American, as "John Bull" was for an Englishman.

5   A reference to his friend Nathaniel Hawthorne's satire on liberal religions, "The Celestial Railroad." "Malaria" literally means "bad air."

that they required to be dusted daily, when the furniture of my mind was all undusted still, and I threw them out the window in disgust. How, then, could I have a furnished house? I would rather sit in the open air, for no dust gathers on the grass, unless where man has broken ground.

It is the luxurious and dissipated who set the fashions which the herd so diligently follow. The traveller who stops at the best houses, so called, soon discovers this, for the publicans presume him to be a Sardanapalus, and if he resigned himself to their tender mercies he would soon be completely emasculated. I think that in the railroad car we are inclined to spend more on luxury than on safety and convenience, and it threatens without attaining these to become no better than a modern drawing-room, with its divans, and ottomans, and sunshades, and a hundred other oriental things, which we are taking west with us, invented for the ladies of the harem and the effeminate natives of the Celestial Empire, which Jonathan should be ashamed to know the names of. I would rather sit on a pumpkin and have it all to myself than be crowded on a velvet cushion. I would rather ride on earth in an ox cart, with a free circulation, than go to heaven in the fancy car of an excursion train and breathe a *malaria* all the way.

The very simplicity and nakedness of man's life in the primitive ages imply this advantage, at least, that they left him still but a sojourner in nature. When he was refreshed with food and sleep, he contemplated his journey again. He dwelt, as it were, in a tent in this world, and was either threading the valleys, or crossing the plains, or climbing the mountain-tops. But lo! men have become the tools of their tools. The man who independently plucked the fruits when he was hungry is become a farmer; and he who stood under a tree for shelter, a housekeeper. We now no longer camp as for a night, but have settled down on earth and forgotten heaven. We have adopted Christianity merely as an improved method of *agri*-culture. We [1] have built for this world a family mansion, and for the next a family tomb. The best works of art are the expression of man's struggle to free himself from this condition, but the effect of our art is merely to make this low state comfortable and that higher state to be forgotten. There is actually no place in this village for a work of *fine* art, if any had come down to us, to stand, for our lives, our houses and streets, furnish no proper pedestal for it. There is not a nail to hang a picture on, nor a shelf to receive the bust of a hero or a saint. When I consider how our houses are built and paid for, or not paid for, and their internal economy managed and sustained, I wonder that the floor does not give way under the visitor while he is admiring the gewgaws upon the mantelpiece, and let him through [2] into the cellar, to some solid and honest though earthy foundation. I cannot but perceive that this so-called rich and refined life is a thing jumped at, and I do not get on in the enjoyment of the *fine* arts which adorn it, my attention being wholly occupied with the jump; for I remember that the greatest genuine leap, due to human muscles alone, on record, is that of certain wandering Arabs, who are said to have cleared twenty-five feet on [3] level ground. Without factitious support, man is sure to come to earth again beyond that distance. The first question which I am tempted to put to the proprietor of such great impropriety is, Who bolsters you? Are you one of the ninety-seven who fail, or the three who succeed? Answer me these questions, and then perhaps I may look at your bawbles and find them ornamental. The cart before [4] the horse is neither beautiful nor useful. Before we can

[1] The hyphenation and italic type call attention to the derivation of the word from the Latin *agri cultura,* the cultivation or tilling of a field.

[2] Gaudy trifles.

[3] I have been unable to uncover T's source for this tale.

[4] "Set the cart before the horse" (John Heywood, *Proverbs,* 1546).

1   Edward Johnson, "Wonder-Working Providence of Sions Saviour," *A History of New England* (London, 1654, chap. 36, p. 83). T has modernized the English slightly.

2   E. B. O'Callaghan, *The Documentary History of the State of New York* (Albany, 1851, IV, 31–2).

adorn our houses with beautiful objects the walls must be stripped, and our lives must be stripped, and beautiful housekeeping and beautiful living be laid for a foundation: now, a taste for the beautiful is most cultivated out of doors, where there is no house and no housekeeper.

1   Old Johnson, in his 'Wonder-Working Providence,' speaking of the first settlers of this town, with whom he was contemporary, tells us that 'they burrow themselves in the earth for their first shelter under some hillside, and, casting the soil aloft upon timber, they make a smoky fire against the earth, at the highest side.' They did not 'provide them houses,' says he, 'till the earth, by the Lord's blessing, brought forth bread to feed them,' and the first year's crop was so light that 'they were forced to cut their bread very thin for a long season.' The secretary of the

2   Province of New Netherland, writing in Dutch, in 1650, for the information of those who wished to take up land there, states more particularly that 'those in New Netherland, and especially in New England, who have no means to build farmhouses at first according to their wishes, dig a square pit in the ground, cellar fashion, six or seven feet deep, as long and as broad as they think proper, case the earth inside with wood all round the wall, and line the wood with the bark of trees or something else to prevent the caving in of the earth; floor this cellar with plank, and wainscot it overhead for a ceiling, raise a roof of spars clear up, and cover the spars with bark or green sods, so that they can live dry and warm in these houses with their entire families for two, three, and four years, it being understood that partitions are run through those cellars which are adapted to the size of the family. The wealthy and principal men in New England, in the beginning of the colonies, commenced their first dwelling-houses in

this fashion for two reasons: firstly, in order not to waste time in building, and not to want food the next season; secondly, in order not to discourage poor laboring people whom they brought over in numbers from Fatherland. In the course of three or four years, when the country became adapted to agriculture, they built themselves handsome houses, spending on them several thousands.'

In this course which our ancestors took there was a show of prudence at least, as if their principle were to satisfy the more pressing wants first. But are the more pressing wants satisfied now? When I think of acquiring for myself one of our luxurious dwellings, I am deterred, for, so to speak, the country is not yet adapted to *human* 1 culture, and we are still forced to cut our *spiritual* bread far thinner than our forefathers did their wheaten. Not that all architectural ornament is to be neglected even in the rudest periods; but let our houses first be lined with beauty, where they come in contact with our lives, like the tenement of the shellfish, and not overlaid with it. But, alas! I have been inside one or two of them, and know what they are lined with.

Though we are not so degenerate but that we might possibly live in a cave or a wigwam or wear skins today, it certainly is better to accept the advantages, though so dearly bought, which the invention and industry of mankind offer. In such a neighborhood as this, boards and shingles, lime and bricks, are cheaper and more easily obtained than suitable caves, or whole logs, or bark in sufficient quantities, or even well-tempered clay or flat stones. I speak understandingly on this subject, for I have made myself acquainted with it both theoretically and practically. With a little more wit we might use these materials so as to become richer than the richest now are,

1   T was probably thinking of his friend Bronson Alcott's book *The Doctrine and Discipline of Human Culture* (Boston, 1836).

1 According to tradition, T borrowed the ax from Bronson Alcott, and Alcott states, "When he [T] projected the Walden cabin he came to me and said, 'Mr. Alcott, lend me an ax,' and with this he built the temple of a grand primeval man." But George Willis Cooke (81) says Emerson was the lender, and Ellery Channing, in his personal copy of W, has a note claiming the ax to be his. The real question is, Why did T have to borrow an ax in the first place? The year before he went to Walden to build his cabin, he and his father together built a house for the family, the one usually referred to as the Texas House. Surely he must have had tools to build that. And how do we explain the ax or axes that he refers to numerous times later in W? Did he finally acquire one of his own?

Kappeler discusses the tools T probably used at Walden, thirty-one of them, and includes drawings of some of them.

2 Matson (68) wonders how T could be so naive as to use unseasoned pine for his studs, and what the resulting warping and shrinking of the wood must have done to his cabin. Yet the cabin remained sturdy for a number of years. For its later history, see Harding, *Days* (1993, 222–4).

3 "He kept him as the apple of his eye" (Deuteronomy 32:10).

4 T refers to the meadowlark and the phoebe. Both begin singing in the Concord area in late March. He is not referring to the wood pewee, which does not arrive in Concord until late May.

5 "Now is the winter of our discontent" (*Richard III*, I, i).

and make our civilization a blessing. The civilized man is a more experienced and wiser savage. But to make haste to my own experiment.

1 Near the end of March, 1845, I borrowed an axe and went down to the woods by Walden Pond, nearest to where I intended to build my house, and began to cut **2** down some tall, arrowy white pines, still in their youth, for timber. It is difficult to begin without borrowing, but perhaps it is the most generous course thus to permit your fellow-men to have an interest in your enterprise. The owner of the axe, as he released his hold on it, said that it **3** was the apple of his eye; but I returned it sharper than I received it. It was a pleasant hillside where I worked, covered with pine woods, through which I looked out on the pond, and a small open field in the woods where pines and hickories were springing up. The ice in the pond was not yet dissolved, though there were some open spaces, and it was all dark-colored and saturated with water. There were some slight flurries of snow during the days that I worked there; but for the most part when I came out on to the railroad, on my way home, its yellow sand-heap stretched away gleaming in the hazy atmosphere, and the rails shone in the spring sun, and I heard **4** the lark and pewee and other birds already come to commence another year with us. They were pleasant spring **5** days, in which the winter of man's discontent was thawing as well as the earth, and the life that had lain torpid began to stretch itself. One day, when my axe had come off and I had cut a green hickory for a wedge, driving it with a stone, and had placed the whole to soak in a pond-hole in order to swell the wood, I saw a striped snake run into the water, and he lay on the bottom, apparently without inconvenience, as long as I stayed there, or more than a quarter of an hour; perhaps because he had not yet fairly come out of the torpid state. It appeared to me that for a like reason men remain in their present low and primitive condition; but if they should feel the influence of the spring of springs arousing them, they would of necessity rise to a higher and more ethereal life. I had previously seen the snakes in frosty mornings in my path with portions of their bodies still numb and inflexible, waiting for the sun to thaw them. On the 1st of April it rained and melted the ice, and in the early part of the day, which was very foggy, I heard a stray goose groping about over the pond and cackling as if lost, or like the spirit of the fog.

So I went on for some days cutting and hewing timber, **1** and also studs and rafters, all with my narrow axe, not having many communicable or scholar-like thoughts, singing to myself,

> Men say they know many things;
> But lo! they have taken wings —
> The arts and sciences,
> And a thousand appliances;
> The wind that blows
> Is all that anybody knows. **2**

I hewed the main timbers six inches square, most of the studs on two sides only, and the rafters and floor timbers on one side, leaving the rest of the bark on, so that they were just as straight and much stronger than sawed ones. Each stick was carefully mortised or tenoned by its stump, for I had borrowed other tools by this time. My days in the woods were not very long ones; yet I usually carried my dinner of bread and butter, and read the newspaper in which it was wrapped, at noon, sitting amid the green pine boughs which I had cut off, and to my bread was imparted some of their fragrance, for my hands were covered with a thick coat of pitch. Before I had done I was

1 Yannella (18) expresses his astonishment that T did not adopt the much simpler "balloon frame" construction, which was already popular around the country, but actually balloon framing is used only for houses of more than one story.

2 T's own poem. Although he quotes other authors frequently, he is always careful to put all but his own poetry within quotation marks.

1   There is no James Collins listed in Concord town records in T's time, but some years ago I met a James Collins, then a resident of Lowell, Massachusetts, who claimed to be a descendant of this Collins. He was undoubtedly one of the many Irish who left their native country because of the potato famine and came to this country to work on the railroad as day laborers.

2   The railroad, running from Boston to Fitchburg, had reached Concord only the year before, in 1844. The tracks are still in use today.

3   The site of Collins's shanty is not known, but it was probably one of the little community of shanties constructed by the Irish laborers. The cellar holes of these shanties can still be found adjacent to the railroad tracks just north of Walden Pond.

more the friend than the foe of the pine tree, though I had cut down some of them, having become better acquainted with it. Sometimes a rambler in the wood was attracted by the sound of my axe, and we chatted pleasantly over the chips which I had made.

By the middle of April, for I made no haste in my work, but rather made the most of it, my house was framed and ready for the raising. I had already bought the shanty of **1** James Collins, an Irishman who worked on the Fitchburg **2** Railroad, for boards. James Collins' shanty was consid- **3** ered an uncommonly fine one. When I called to see it he was not at home. I walked about the outside, at first unobserved from within, the window was so deep and high. It was of small dimensions, with a peaked cottage roof, and not much else to be seen, the dirt being raised five feet all around as if it were a compost heap. The roof was the soundest part, though a good deal warped and made brittle by the sun. Doorsill there was none, but a perennial passage for the hens under the door-board. Mrs. C. came to the door and asked me to view it from the inside. The hens were driven in by my approach. It was dark, and had a dirt floor for the most part, dank, clammy, and aguish, only here a board and there a board which would not bear removal. She lighted a lamp to show me the inside of the roof and the walls, and also that the board floor extended under the bed, warning me not to step into the cellar, a sort of dust hole two feet deep. In her own words, they were 'good boards overhead, good boards all around, and a good window' — of two whole squares originally, only the cat had passed out that way lately. There was a stove, a bed, and a place to sit, an infant in the house where it was born, a silk parasol, gilt-framed looking-glass, and a patent new coffee-mill nailed to an oak sapling, all told. The bargain was soon concluded, for James had in the meanwhile returned. I to pay four dollars and twenty-five cents tonight, he to vacate at five tomorrow morning, selling to nobody else meanwhile: I to take possession at six. It were well, he said, to be there early, and anticipate certain indistinct but wholly unjust claims on the score of ground rent and fuel. This he assured me was the only encumbrance. At six I passed him and his family on the road. One large bundle held their all — bed, coffee-mill, looking-glass, hens — all but the cat; she took to the woods and became a wild cat, and, as I learned afterward, trod in a trap set for woodchucks, and so became a dead cat at last.

I took down this dwelling the same morning, drawing the nails, and removed it to the pond-side by small cart-loads, spreading the boards on the grass there to bleach and warp back again in the sun. One early thrush gave me a note or two as I drove along the woodland path. I was informed treacherously by a young Patrick that neigh- **1** bor Seeley, an Irishman, in the intervals of the carting, **2** transferred the still tolerable, straight, and drivable nails, staples, and spikes to his pocket, and then stood when I came back to pass the time of day, and look freshly up, unconcerned, with spring thoughts, at the devastation; there being a dearth of work, as he said. He was there to represent spectatordom, and help make this seemingly insignificant event one with the removal of the gods of Troy. **3**

I dug my cellar in the side of a hill sloping to the south, **4** where a woodchuck had formerly dug his burrow, down through sumach and blackberry roots, and the lowest stain of vegetation, six feet square by seven deep, to a fine sand where potatoes would not freeze in any winter. The sides were left shelving, and not stoned; but the sun having never shone on them, the sand still keeps its place. It was but two hours' work. I took particular pleasure in this **5** breaking of ground, for in almost all latitudes men dig

1 The name Yankees used for a typical Irishman.

2 Concord town records list a William Se-ley at this time, but no Seeleys.

3 T is referring, in Virgil's *Aeneid,* either to the theft of the Palladium by Odysseus and Diomedes (II, 351) or to Aeneas's rescue of his household gods (I, 6). In either case, he is poking fun by contrasting the ne'er-do-well Collins with the heroic Greeks (Miller; Woodson, 1975).

4 Ellery Channing wrote in his copy of W, "There is nothing like a hill here and never was. . . . H. means the small rise in the ground, but it is no hill, no 20 foot rise" (Sanborn, 1909).

5 Paul Williams (1971) asserts that in digging his cellar, T moved 194.25 cubic feet of dirt, weighing 9.7 tons, lifting it an average of six feet. Translating that into horsepower, one comes up with .03. An average person can work at a rate of from .033 to .05 horsepower, so T should not have had much difficulty in completing his task, as he says, in two hours, since he was digging mostly in sand.

1 There is still a noticeable dent in the earth nearly a century and a half after the cabin was moved away.

2 Cooke (81) says these acquaintances were Alcott, Emerson, Ellery Channing, Burrill and George William Curtis, Edmund Hosmer and his sons John, Edmund, and Andrew. The Curtis brothers had been residents of Brook Farm before moving to Concord. George later became a well-known editor and critic. Hosmer was T's favorite farmer, and his farm was a short distance from Walden.

3 T was declaring his own independence. He was too astute not to take advantage of the symbolism of the day.

4 On the boards to be nailed horizontally, the top and bottom edges were cut at forty-five-degree angles and overlapped so as to shed rain (Gottesman, 1559).

5 As we learn later, T brought his own copy of the *Iliad* out to the pond.

into the earth for an equable temperature. Under the most splendid house in the city is still to be found the cellar where they store their roots as of old, and long after the superstructure has disappeared posterity remark its 1 dent in the earth. The house is still but a sort of porch at the entrance of a burrow.

At length, in the beginning of May, with the help of 2 some of my acquaintances, rather to improve so good an occasion for neighborliness than from any necessity, I set up the frame of my house. No man was ever more honored in the character of his raisers than I. They are destined, I trust, to assist at the raising of loftier structures one 3 day. I began to occupy my house on the 4th of July, as soon as it was boarded and roofed, for the boards were 4 carefully feather-edged and lapped, so that it was perfectly impervious to rain, but before boarding I laid the foundation of a chimney at one end, bringing two cartloads of stones up the hill from the pond in my arms. I built the chimney after my hoeing in the fall, before a fire became necessary for warmth, doing my cooking in the meanwhile out of doors on the ground, early in the morning which mode I still think is in some respects more convenient and agreeable than the usual one. When it stormed before my bread was baked, I fixed a few boards over the fire, and sat under them to watch my loaf, and passed some pleasant hours in that way. In those days, when my hands were much employed, I read but little, but the least scraps of paper which lay on the ground, my holder, or tablecloth, afforded me as much entertain-5 ment, in fact answered the same purpose as the Iliad.

It would be worth the while to build still more deliberately than I did, considering, for instance, what foundation a door, a window, a cellar, a garret, have in the nature of man, and perchance never raising any superstructure until we found a better reason for it than our temporal necessities even. There is some of the same fitness in a man's building his own house that there is in a bird's building its own nest. Who knows but if men constructed their dwellings with their own hands, and provided food for themselves and families simply and honestly enough, the poetic faculty would be universally developed, as birds universally sing when they are so engaged? But alas! we do like cowbirds and cuckoos, which lay their eggs in **1** nests which other birds have built, and cheer no traveller with their chattering and unmusical notes. Shall we forever resign the pleasure of construction to the carpenter? What does architecture amount to in the experience of the mass of men? I never in all my walks came across a man engaged in so simple and natural an occupation as building his house. We belong to the community. It is not the tailor alone who is the ninth part of a man; it is as **2** much the preacher, and the merchant, and the farmer. Where is this division of labor to end? and what object **3** does it finally serve? No doubt another *may* also think for me; but it is not therefore desirable that he should do so to the exclusion of my thinking for myself.

True, there are architects so called in this country, and I have heard of one at least possessed with the idea of **4** making architectural ornaments have a core of truth, a **5** necessity, and hence a beauty, as if it were a revelation to him. All very well perhaps from his point of view, but only a little better than the common dilettantism. A sentimental reformer in architecture, he began at the cornice, not at the foundation. It was only how to put a core of truth within the ornaments, that every sugarplum, in fact, might have an almond or caraway seed in it — though I hold

1   The American cowbird and the English cuckoo lay their eggs in other birds' nests, avoiding the task of providing for their offspring.

2   "Nine tailors make but one man" is an old proverb that can be traced at least as far back as John Ray's *English Proverbs* of 1678.

3   Masteller suggests that T is here parodying the house pattern books so popular in his day.

4   As T points out in his *Journal* (III, 182-3), this was Horatio Greenough, the sculptor. Matthiessen (153–7) and Metzger (79) both point out that this paragraph seems to reflect a gross misunderstanding of Greenough's ideas. But Griffin demonstrates that T's opinions were based on a letter Greenough had written Emerson, and not on his published theories.

5   This is the fundamental theory of modern functional architecture. Significantly, Frank Lloyd Wright, our greatest modern architect, has said in a letter to me, "The history of American architecture would be incomplete without T's wise observations on the subject."

that almonds are most wholesome without the sugar — and not how the inhabitant, the indweller, might build truly within and without, and let the ornaments take care of themselves. What reasonable man ever supposed that ornaments were something outward and in the skin merely — that the tortoise got his spotted shell, or the shell-fish its mother-o'-pearl tints, by such a contract as the inhabitants of Broadway their Trinity Church? But a man has no more to do with the style of architecture of his house than a tortoise with that of its shell: nor need the soldier be so idle as to try to paint the precise *color* of his virtue on his standard. The enemy will find it out. He may turn pale when the trial comes. This man seemed to me to lean over the cornice, and timidly whisper his half truth to the rude occupants who really knew it better than he. What of architectural beauty I now see, I know has gradually grown from within outward, out of the necessities and character of the indweller, who is the only builder — out of some unconscious truthfulness, and nobleness, without ever a thought for the appearance and whatever additional beauty of this kind is destined to be produced will be preceded by a like unconscious beauty of life. The most interesting dwellings in this country, as the painter knows, are the most unpretending, humble log huts and cottages of the poor commonly; it is the life of the inhabitants whose shells they are, and not any peculiarity in their surfaces merely, which makes them *picturesque*; and equally interesting will be the citizen's suburban box, when his life shall be as simple and as agreeable to the imagination, and there is as little straining after effect in the style of his dwelling. A great proportion of architectural ornaments are literally hollow, and a September gale would strip them off, like borrowed plumes, without

1 The famed church in downtown New York had been burned and rebuilt while T was at Walden.

2 T's precise meaning here eludes me, but he is apparently alluding to ancient soldiers who painted on their shields the symbols of their supposed capabilities.

3 The vogue of the "picturesque" in the early nineteenth century was considerable, and T read avidly all the works of the Reverend William Gilpin on the subject (Templeman).

4 The strongest winds of the year in the Concord area typically come in September.

injury to the substantials. They can do without *architecture* who have no olives nor wines in the cellar. What if an 1 equal ado were made about the ornaments of style in literature, and the architects of our bibles spent as much time about their cornices as the architects of our churches do? So are made the *belles-lettres* and the *beaux-arts* and their professors. Much it concerns a man, forsooth, how a few sticks are slanted over him or under him, and what colors are daubed upon his box. It would signify somewhat, if, in any earnest sense, *he* slanted them and daubed it; but the spirit having departed out of the tenant, it is of a piece with constructing his own coffin — the architecture of the grave — and 'carpenter' is but another name for 'coffin-maker.' One man says, in his despair or indif- 2 ference to life, take up a handful of the earth at your feet, and paint your house that color. Is he thinking of his last and narrow house? Toss up a copper for it as well. What 3 an abundance of leisure he must have! Why do you take up a handful of dirt? Better paint your house your own complexion; let it turn pale or blush for you. An enterprise to improve the style of cottage architecture! When 4 you have got my ornaments ready, I will wear them.

Before winter I built a chimney, and shingled the sides 5 of my house, which were already impervious to rain, with imperfect and sappy shingles made of the first slice of the log, whose edges I was obliged to straighten with a plane.

I have thus a tight shingled and plastered house, ten 6, 7 feet wide by fifteen long, and eight-feet posts, with a garret and a closet, a large window on each side, two trap-doors, one door at the end, and a brick fireplace opposite. The exact cost of my house, paying the usual price for such materials as I used, but not counting the work, all of which was done by myself, was as follows; and I give the

1 That is, those who do not have rare and expensive foods in their homes.

2 In T's time, one would order a coffin to be made by the local carpenter. In the first edition of W, T placed a comma after "carpenter."

3 The grave.

4 For Wordsworth's influence on this section and other portions of W, see Moldenhauer (1990).

5 The details of building his chimney can be found in the "House-Warming" chapter.

6 He did not plaster the house until late fall (Robbins). See "House-Warming."

7 This was no hut or shanty. It was sturdily built and survived being moved twice (Zimmer).

1 Half-cent coins were still in circulation then (Paul Williams, 1987).

2 Lime and hair were used to make plaster. The hair was added as a binder (Proulx).

3 A metal strip above a fireplace opening, supporting the masonry above.

4 Nails at this time typically sold for three cents a pound. Did he really use 130 pounds of nails (Kenner, 210)? That would have been more than enough to build an entire house. When the site was excavated in 1945, many bent nails were found, but not enough to account for all those nails (Robbins).

5 The modern replacement value of these materials would probably be four or five thousand dollars.

6 Although T liked to pretend that he was no more than a squatter on Emerson's land, Canby (215) asserts that he had made an arrangement with Emerson to clear the land in return for its use.

7 Main Street in Concord still displays a notable line of grand and luxurious mansions, some of the loveliest in any New England town. Ironically, shortly after T left the pond and before he published W, his parents purchased one of these mansions, spent money to make it even grander, and T lived there with them for the remainder of his life. The house was sold in 1988 for well over a million dollars.

8 One of many biblical allusions (as Jeremiah 23:28) to the difficulty of separating the wheat from the chaff.

details because very few are able to tell exactly what their houses cost, and fewer still, if any, the separate cost of the various materials which compose them:

1 Boards	$8 03 ½,	mostly shanty boards.
Refuse shingles for roof and sides	4 00	
Laths	1 25	
Two second-hand windows with glass	2 43	
One thousand old brick	4 00	
Two casks of lime	2 40	That was high.
2 Hair	0 31	More than I needed.
3 Mantle-tree iron	0 15	
4 Nails	3 90	
Hinges and screws	0 14	
Latch	0 10	
Chalk	0 01	
Transportation	1 40	{ I carried a good part on my back.
5 In all	$28 12 ½	

6 These are all the materials, excepting the timber, stones, and sand, which I claimed by squatter's right. I have also a small woodshed adjoining, made chiefly of the stuff which was left after building the house.

7 I intend to build me a house which will surpass any on the main street in Concord in grandeur and luxury, as soon as it pleases me as much and will cost me no more than my present one.

I thus found that the student who wishes for a shelter can obtain one for a lifetime at an expense not greater than the rent which he now pays annually. If I seem to boast more than is becoming, my excuse is that I brag for humanity rather than for myself; and my shortcomings and inconsistencies do not affect the truth of my state-**8** ment. Notwithstanding much cant and hypocrisy — chaff which I find it difficult to separate from my wheat, but for which I am as sorry as any man — I will breathe freely and stretch myself in this respect, it is such a relief to both the moral and physical system; and I am resolved that I will not through humility become the devil's attorney. I [1] will endeavor to speak a good word for the truth. At Cam- [2] bridge College the mere rent of a student's room, which is only a little larger than my own, is thirty dollars each year, though the corporation had the advantage of building thirty-two side by side and under one roof, and the occupant suffers the inconvenience of many and noisy neighbors, and perhaps a residence in the fourth story. I [3] cannot but think that if we had more true wisdom in these respects, not only less education would be needed, because, forsooth, more would already have been acquired, but the pecuniary expense of getting an education would in a great measure vanish. Those conveniences which the student requires at Cambridge or elsewhere cost him or somebody else ten times as great a sacrifice of life as they would with proper management on both sides. Those things for which the most money is demanded are never the things which the student most wants. Tuition, for instance, is an important item in the term bill, while for the far more valuable education which he gets by associating with the most cultivated of his contemporaries no charge is made. The mode of founding a college is, commonly, to get up a subscription of dollars and cents, and then, following blindly the principles of a division of labor to its extreme — a principle which should never be followed but with circumspection — to call in a contractor who makes this a subject of speculation, and he employs [4] Irishmen or other operatives actually to lay the foundations, while the students that are to be are said to be fitting themselves for it; and for these oversights successive gen-

1 In the Roman Catholic Church it is customary to appoint a cardinal as devil's advocate to bring up every conceivable argument against the raising of a candidate to sainthood.

2 Harvard College, from which T graduated in 1837.

3 T had his own problems with a fourth-floor dormitory room, for he occupied one in Hollis Hall when he was at Harvard (Salt, 9).

4 Another reference to the fact that recent Irish immigrants were hired chiefly to do menial labor.

1 One of Thoreau's acquaintances, Horace Mann, then the president of Antioch College in Ohio, was developing a curriculum that involved studying and working outside the classroom.

2 In 1846 William Lassell discovered a satellite of Neptune, a few months after the planet itself was first observed.

3 "And why beholdest thou the mote that is in thy brother's eye, but perceivest not the beam that is in thine own?" (Luke 6:41).

4 In the 1840s technological institutes, such as the Rochester Institute of Technology, were being established in many American cities to help further the education of workingmen.

erations have to pay. I think that it would be *better than this,* for the students, or those who desire to be benefited by it, even to lay the foundation themselves. The student who secures his coveted leisure and retirement by systematically shirking any labor necessary to man obtains but an ignoble and unprofitable leisure, defrauding himself of the experience which alone can make leisure fruitful. 'But,' says one, 'you do not mean that the students should go to work with their hands instead of their heads?' I do not mean that exactly, but I mean something which he might think a good deal like that; I mean that they should not *play* life, *or study* it merely, while the community supports them at this expensive game, but earnestly *live* it from beginning to end. How could youths better learn to live than by at once trying the experiment of living? Methinks this would exercise their minds as much as mathematics. If I wished a boy to know something about the arts and sciences, for instance, I would not pursue the common course, which is merely to send him into the neighborhood of some professor, where anything is professed and practised but the art of life; — to survey the world through a telescope or a microscope, and never with his natural eye; to study chemistry, and not learn how his bread is made, or mechanics, and not learn how it is earned; to discover new satellites to Neptune, and not detect the motes in his eyes, or to what vagabond he is a satellite himself; or to be devoured by the monsters that swarm all around him, while contemplating the monsters in a drop of vinegar. Which would have advanced the most at the end of a month — the boy who had made his own jackknife from the ore which he had dug and smelted, reading as much as would be necessary for this — or the boy who had attended the lectures on metallurgy at the Institute in the meanwhile, and had received a Rodgers penknife from his father? Which would be [1] most likely to cut his fingers?. . . To my astonishment I was informed on leaving college that I had studied navi- [2] gation! — why, if I had taken one turn down the harbor I should have known more about it. Even the *poor* student studies and is taught only *political* economy, while that economy of living which is synonymous with philosophy is not even sincerely professed in our colleges. The consequence is, that while he is reading Adam Smith, Ricardo, [3] and Say, he runs his father in debt irretrievably.

As with our colleges, so with a hundred 'modern improvements;' there is an illusion about them; there is not always a positive advance. The devil goes on exacting compound interest to the last for his early share and numerous succeeding investments in them. Our inventions are wont to be pretty toys, which distract our attention from serious things. They are but improved means to an unimproved end, an end which it was already but too easy to arrive at; as railroads lead to Boston or New York. We are in great haste to construct a magnetic telegraph from [4] Maine to Texas; but Maine and Texas, it may be, have nothing important to communicate. Either is in such a predicament as the man who was earnest to be introduced to a distinguished deaf woman, but when he was [5] presented, and one end of her ear trumpet was put into his hand, had nothing to say. As if the main object were to talk fast and not to talk sensibly. We are eager to tunnel [6] under the Atlantic and bring the Old World some weeks nearer to the New; but perchance the first news that will leak through into the broad, flapping American ear will be that the Princess Adelaide has the whooping cough. [7] After all, the man whose horse trots a mile in a minute does not carry the most important messages; he is not an evangelist, nor does he come round eating locusts and

[1] Manufactured by Joseph Rodgers & Sons of Sheffield, England, long one of the most noted cutlers. Although T had written "Rogers'," Shanley (1971, 397) corrected the spelling.

[2] The Harvard College catalogs of the 1830s list "nautical astronomy" as one part of sophomore mathematics.

[3] Adam Smith (1723–1790), Scottish economist, author of *The Wealth of Nations;* David Ricardo (1772–1823), English economist; and Jean-Baptiste Say (1767–1832), French economist (Yanella).

[4] Samuel F. B. Morse had invented the magnetic telegraph in 1835. It first reached Concord in 1851 after T had left Walden Pond.

[5] Harriet Martineau, who made a famous tour of America in 1834 and 1835.

[6] They were not thinking seriously of tunneling the Atlantic, but they were attempting to lay an Atlantic cable.

[7] Possibly the Princess Adelaide (1792–1849) who in 1818 married the Duke of Clarence, who became William IV in 1830. Although I have not succeeded in finding it, I would not be surprised if T was thinking of a specific item he had seen in a newspaper.

1 Wild honey: the food of John the Baptist in the desert (Matthew 3:4).

2 A famous racehorse in eighteenth-century England, owned by a Mr. Childers of Carr House.

3 The terminus of the Boston and Fitchburg Railroad, which passed by Walden Pond.

4 It is an indication of T's preciseness that in the manuscript this reads one dollar, then is corrected to seventy cents, only to be changed in the page proof to ninety cents, with the marginal comment to the printer, "They have changed the fare within the last week" (Shanley, 1957, 36).

5 This expression can be traced back at least to John Ray, *English Proverbs* (1678).

6 A typical newspaper headline of T's time.

1, 2 wild honey. I doubt if Flying Childers ever carried a peck of corn to mill.

One says to me, 'I wonder that you do not lay up money; you love to travel; you might take the cars and go **3** to Fitchburg today and see the country.' But I am wiser than that. I have learned that the swiftest traveller is he that goes afoot. I say to my friend, Suppose we try who will get there first. The distance is thirty miles; the fare **4** ninety cents. That is almost a day's wages. I remember when wages were sixty cents a day for laborers on this very road. Well, I start now on foot, and get there before night; I have travelled at that rate by the week together. You will in the meanwhile have earned your fare, and arrive there some time tomorrow, or possibly this evening, if you are lucky enough to get a job in season. Instead of going to Fitchburg, you will be working here the greater part of the day. And so, if the railroad reached round the world, I think that I should keep ahead of you; and as for seeing the country and getting experience of that kind, I should have to cut your acquaintance altogether.

Such is the universal law, which no man can ever outwit, and with regard to the railroad even we may say it **5** is as broad as it is long. To make a railroad round the world available to all mankind is equivalent to grading the whole surface of the planet. Men have an indistinct notion that if they keep up this activity of joint stocks and spades long enough all will at length ride somewhere, in next to no time, and for nothing; but though a crowd rushes to the depot, and the conductor shouts 'All aboard!' when the smoke is blown away and the vapor condensed, it will be perceived that a few are riding, but the rest are run over — and it will be called, and will be, 'A melan- **6** choly accident.' No doubt they can ride at last who shall have earned their fare, that is, if they survive so long, but they will probably have lost their elasticity and desire to travel by that time. This spending of the best part of one's life earning money in order to enjoy a questionable liberty during the least valuable part of it reminds me of the Englishman who went to India to make a fortune first, in **1** order that he might return to England and live the life of a poet. He should have gone up garret at once. 'What!' exclaim a million Irishmen starting up from all the shanties in the land, 'is not this railroad which we have built a good thing?' Yes, I answer, *comparatively* good, that is, you might have done worse; but I wish, as you are brothers of mine, that you could have spent your time better than digging in this dirt.

Before I finished my house, wishing to earn ten or twelve dollars by some honest and agreeable method, in order to meet my unusual expenses, I planted about two acres and **2** a half of light and sandy soil near it chiefly with beans, but also a small part with potatoes, corn, peas, and turnips. The whole lot contains eleven acres, mostly growing up **3** to pines and hickories, and was sold the preceding season for eight dollars and eight cents an acre. One farmer said that it was 'good for nothing but to raise cheeping squirrels on.' I put no manure whatever on this land, not being **4** the owner, but merely a squatter, and not expecting to cultivate so much again, and I did not quite hoe it all once. I got out several cords of stumps in plowing, which supplied me with fuel for a long time, and left small circles of virgin mould, easily distinguishable through the summer by the greater luxuriance of the beans there. The dead and for the most part unmerchantable wood behind my house, and the driftwood from the pond, have supplied the remainder of my fuel. I was obliged to hire a

1   T may be thinking of Robert Clive (Baron Clive of Passey), who served the British government in India and also wrote poetry.

2   In 1859 T replanted his old garden to trees, chiefly pines, for Emerson. Although the last of these trees has long since died, most of them having burned or blown down, their stumps can still easily be discerned a hundred feet or so north of his cabin site.

3   Emerson records the purchase of this first of his Walden Pond woodlots in a letter to his brother William on October 4, 1844 (Rusk, III, 262). The lot was pie-shaped, with only the point touching the shore on what is now known as Thoreau's Cove. Over the years, Emerson purchased other parcels, until he had bought most of the land around the pond. In 1922 his heirs deeded the property to the Commonwealth of Massachusetts, and it eventually became a state park.

4   The printer ignored T's deletion of the word "whatever" in the page proof.

1 Richardson (175) suggests that T had a smaller crop the second year because a severe frost on June 12, 1846, destroyed many of his vegetables. But his decision to spade up less ground that year would normally have been made weeks earlier than that.

2 Arthur Young wrote many books on agriculture, including Rural Oeconomy (London, 1773).

team and a man for the plowing, though I held the plow myself. My farm outgoes for the first season were, for implements, seed, work, etc., $14.72 ½. The seed corn was given me. This never costs anything to speak of, unless you plant more than enough. I got twelve bushels of beans, and eighteen bushels of potatoes, beside some peas and sweet corn. The yellow corn and turnips were too late to come to anything. My whole income from the farm was

$$\begin{array}{lr} & \$23\ 44 \\ \text{Deducting the outgoes}\dots\dots\dots & \$14\ 72\,½ \\ \text{There are left}\dots\dots\dots\dots\dots & \$\ 8\ 71\,½ \end{array}$$

beside produce consumed and on hand at the time this estimate was made of the value of $4.50 — the amount on hand much more than balancing a little grass which I did not raise. All things considered, that is, considering the importance of a man's soul and of today, notwithstanding the short time occupied by my experiment, nay, partly even because of its transient character, I believe that that was doing better than any farmer in Concord did that year.

The next year I did better still, for I spaded up all the land which I required, about a third of an acre, and I learned from the experience of both years, not being in the least awed by many celebrated works on husbandry, Arthur Young among the rest, that if one would live simply and eat only the crop which he raised, and raise no more than he ate, and not exchange it for an insufficient quantity of more luxurious and expensive things, he would need to cultivate only a few rods of ground, and that it would be cheaper to spade up that than to use oxen to plow it, and to select a fresh spot from time to time than to manure the old, and he could do all his necessary farm work as it were with his left hand at odd hours in the summer; and thus he would not be tied to an ox, or horse, or cow, or pig, as at present. I desire to speak impartially on this point, and as one not interested in the success or failure of the present economical and social arrangements. I was more independent than any farmer in Concord, for I was not anchored to a house or farm, but could follow the bent of my genius, which is a very crooked one, every moment. Beside being better off than they already, if my house had been burned or my crops had failed, I should have been nearly as well off as before.

I am wont to think that men are not so much the keepers of herds as herds are the keepers of men, the **1** former are so much the freer. Men and oxen exchange work; but if we consider necessary work only, the oxen will be seen to have greatly the advantage, their farm is so much the larger. Man does some of his part of the exchange work in his six weeks of haying, and it is no boy's play. Certainly no nation that lived simply in all respects, that is, no nation of philosophers, would commit so great **2** a blunder as to use the labor of animals. True, there never was and is not likely soon to be a nation of philosophers, nor am I certain it is desirable that there should be. However, *I* should never have broken a horse or bull and taken him to board for any work he might do for me, for fear I should become a horseman or a herds-man merely; and if society seems to be the gainer by so doing, are we certain that what is one man's gain is not another's loss, **3** and that the stable-boy has equal cause with his master to be satisfied? Granted that some public works would not have been constructed without this aid, and let man share the glory of such with the ox and horse; does it follow that he could not have accomplished works yet more worthy of himself in that case? When men begin to do, not

1 "I understand you well, said my master, it is now very plain, from all you have spoken, that whatever share of reason the *Yahoos* pretend to, the *Howyhnhnms* are your masters" (Jonathan Swift, *Gulliver's Travels*, IV, iv).

2 T may have been thinking of his friend Bronson Alcott, whose transcendentalist community at nearby Harvard, Massachusetts, did not use work animals.

3 "Gain cannot be made without some other person's loss" (Publilius Syrus).

1 T was speaking from bitter experience. In 1844 when Emerson wished to address a gathering of abolitionists on the anniversary of the liberation of the West Indian slaves, no Concord church would open its doors to the convention, and T finally obtained the use of the courthouse and rang the bell to announce the meeting (Cabot, 430).

2 This classic of Hindu religious literature was T's favorite Oriental work. Stein, in his three articles on W, discusses at length the impact of the book on T.

3 A pastoral region in ancient Greece, now used figuratively as the name of an ideal land. Rees expounds at some length on the hammering stone. See also Reginald Cook.

4 Not the famous Greek city, but an ancient city in Egypt, also called Hecatompylos for its hundred gates. Thoreau may have read about it in Diodorus 1.15.

5 Since New England is a heavily glaciated area, the farmers gathered the many boulders on their land and formed stone walls to mark boundaries and fence in their farm animals.

merely unnecessary or artistic, but luxurious and idle work, with their assistance, it is inevitable that a few do all the exchange work with the oxen, or, in other words, become the slaves of the strongest. Man thus not only works for the animal within him, but, for a symbol of this, he works for the animal without him. Though we have many substantial houses of brick or stone, the prosperity of the farmer is still measured by the degree to which the barn overshadows the house. This town is said to have the largest houses for oxen, cows, and horses hereabouts, and it is not behindhand in its public buildings; but there **1** are very few halls for free worship or free speech in this county. It should not be by their architecture, but why not even by their power of abstract thought, that nations should seek to commemorate themselves? How much **2** more admirable the Bhagvat-Geeta than all the ruins of the East! Towers and temples are the luxury of princes. A simple and independent mind does not toil at the bidding of any prince. Genius is not a retainer to any emperor, nor is its material silver, or gold, or marble, except to a trifling extent. To what end, pray, is so much stone ham- **3** mered? In Arcadia, when I was there, I did not see any hammering stone. Nations are possessed with an insane ambition to perpetuate the memory of themselves by the amount of hammered stone they leave. What if equal pains were taken to smooth and polish their manners? One piece of good sense would be more memorable than a monument as high as the moon. I love better to see **4** stones in place. The grandeur of Thebes was a vulgar **5** grandeur. More sensible is a rod of stone wall that bounds an honest man's field than a hundred-gated Thebes that has wandered farther from the true end of life. The religion and civilization which are barbaric and heathenish build splendid temples; but what you might call Christianity does not. Most of the stone a nation hammers goes toward its tomb only. It buries itself alive. As for the Pyra- **1** mids, there is nothing to wonder at in them so much as the fact that so many men could be found degraded enough to spend their lives constructing a tomb for some ambitious booby, whom it would have been wiser and manlier to have drowned in the Nile, and then given his body to the dogs. I might possibly invent some excuse for them and him, but I have no time for it. As for the relig- ion and love of art of the builders, it is much the same all the world over, whether the building be an Egyptian tem- **2** ple or the United States Bank. It costs more than it comes to. The mainspring is vanity, assisted by the love of garlic and bread and butter. Mr. Balcom, a promising young **3** architect, designs it on the back of his Vitruvius, with **4** hard pencil and ruler, and the job is let out to Dobson & **5** Sons, stonecutters. When the thirty centuries begin to **6** look down on it, mankind begin to look up at it. As for your high towers and monuments, there was a crazy fel- low once in this town who undertook to dig through to **7** China, and he got so far that, as he said, he heard the Chinese pots and kettles rattle; but I think that I shall not go out of my way to admire the hole which he made. Many are concerned about the monuments of the West and the East — to know who built them. For my part, I should like to know who in those days did not build them — who were above such trifling. But to proceed with my statistics.

By surveying, carpentry, and day-labor of various other kinds in the village in the meanwhile, for I have as many trades as fingers, I had earned $13.34. The expense of food for eight months, namely, from July 4th to March 1st, the time when these estimates were made, though I lived there more than two years — not counting potatoes, a

1   Emerson, in his *Journal* for August 18, 1852 (VIII, 320), attributes a very similar opin- ion of the worth of the pyramids to Horatio Greenough. But Greenough apparently made his statement that month, whereas T's is re- corded in his own *Journal* for April 21, 1852 (III, 454).

2   A vogue for Egyptian-style architecture flourished in Philadelphia in the mid-nineteenth century, and the Second Bank of the United States there is a notable example of that style.

3   While there is a Balcomb family listed in the Concord records of T's time, I can find no one of that name in the list of Massachusetts ar- chitects of that period. I suspect T was playing a little joke on one of his neighbors.

4   A celebrated architect in the age of Augustus. His is the only classical work on ar- chitecture that is still extant.

5   I can find no trace of any Dobsons in Concord records or in the directories of Massa- chusetts stonecutters of T's time.

6   T probably meant to say forty centuries. Napoleon, in a short address to his soldiers in Egypt, said of the pyramids, "From the summit of those monuments forty centuries look down upon you."

7   There is in the Easterbrook Woods, north of Concord center, a slight excavation that is still pointed out as "the hole to China."

1 Cavell (30) suggests that T, in his use of fractions of cents, is parodying American methods of bookkeeping, but half-cent coins were still in circulation in the United States until the 1850s (Paul Williams, 1987).

2 In the first edition, the bracket covering "experiments which failed" did not include salt, but through a printer's error, the bracket was extended in many later editions. This detail offers a simple check as to whether a particular edition has been edited with care.

3 Charles Anderson (27) points out that this is almost exactly the sum recommended by William Alcott, in *The Young Housekeeper* (Boston, 1838), for a healthy diet for that period of time. Since William Alcott was Bronson Alcott's cousin, Anderson suggests T might have been familiar with the book. But as Yanella (24) says, such family budgets were common at the time, and T's friend Horace Greeley printed them regularly in his *New York Tribune*. Wesolowski (141) evaluates T's diet against modern nutritional standards and states that it does not imply "nutritional frugality."

4 There is a little legend, probably apocryphal, that T caught alive in a box trap one of the woodchucks that had been ravaging his beans. But not having the heart to kill it, he carted it off two miles and freed it, letting it become someone else's worry (Canby, 219).

5 A resident of central Asia. Most Oriental religions include the doctrine of transmigration of the soul after death, even for animals. Sattelmeyer (63) suggests T is referring to Évariste Régis Huc's *Recollections of a Journey Through Tartary, Thibet and China*.

little green corn, and some peas, which I had raised, nor considering the value of what was on hand at the last date — was

1	Rice	$1 73 ½	
	Molasses	1 73	Cheapest form of the saccharine.
	Rye meal	1 04 ¾	
	Indian meal	0 99 ¾	Cheaper than rye.
	Pork	0 22	
2	Flour	0 88	{ Costs more than Indian meal, both money and trouble
	Sugar	0 80	
	Lard	0 65	
	Apples	0 25	
	Dried apple	0 22	
	Sweet potatoes. .	0 10	
	One pumpkin . .	0 6	
	One watermelon	0 2	
	Salt.	0 3	

Experiment which failed.

3 Yes, I did eat $8.74, all told; but I should not thus unblushingly publish my guilt, if I did not know that most of my readers were equally guilty with myself, and that their deeds would look no better in print. The next year I sometimes caught a mess of fish for my dinner, and once **4** I went so far as to slaughter a woodchuck which ravaged **5** my bean-field — effect his transmigration, as a Tartar would say — and devour him, partly for experiment's sake; but though it afforded me a momentary enjoyment, notwithstanding a musky flavor, I saw that the longest use would not make that a good practice, however it might seem to have your woodchucks ready dressed by the village butcher.

Clothing and some incidental expenses within the same dates, though little can be inferred from this item, amounted to

<table>
<tr><td>Oil and some household utensils . . . .</td><td>$8 40 ¾</td></tr>
<tr><td></td><td>2 00</td></tr>
</table>

So that all the pecuniary outgoes, excepting for washing and mending, which for the most part were done out of the house, and their bills have not yet been received — **1** and these are all and more than all the ways by which money necessarily goes out in this part of the world — were

House.	$28 12 ½	**2**
Farm one year	14 72 ½	
Food eight months.	8 74	
Clothing, etc., eight months	8 40 ¾	
Oil, etc., eight months.	2 00	
In all.	$61 99 ¾	

I address myself now to those of my readers who have a living to get. And to meet this I have for farm produce sold

	$23 44
Earned by day-labor.	13 34
In all.	$36 78

which subtracted from the sum of the outgoes leaves a balance of $25.21 ¾ on the one side — this being very nearly the means with which I started, and the measure of expenses to be incurred — and on the other, beside the leisure and independence and health thus secured, a comfortable house for me as long as I choose to occupy it.

These statistics, however accidental and therefore un-instructive they may appear, as they have a certain completeness, have a certain value also. Nothing was given

1   Their bills: his mother and sisters did most such work for him as a friendly service.

2   Although Crawford asserts that the fractions did not appear in the original manuscript, that they were "whimsical additions" by T, Shanley has informed me that they are indeed there.

1   Although those cavillers still try to assert that T hastened to heed the sound of Mrs. Emerson's dinner bell, since his cabin was a mile and a quarter from her kitchen door, he would have had to have remarkable hearing in order to hear it. Cooke (81) tells us, "It was T's custom while at Walden to dine on Sundays with Emerson, and to stop at [Edmund] Hosmer's on his way back to the pond, often remaining to supper."

2   Much comment has been made about T's diet. Many have thought it accounted for his poor health, but in general it was no worse, according to present-day standards, than that of most of his contemporaries. For a comprehensive analysis of his diet, see Stephen and Barbara Adams. See also Wesolowski.

3   A native of India, purslane is widely used around the world as a potherb. (Paul Williams, 1965).

4   He is using the word in the biological sense of a specific, as opposed to a generic, name. T is exceedingly careful in his choice of words, and one will often find his use of them enlightening.

5   The word "water" occurs 177 times in W (Ogden and Keller, 246), and T makes much symbolic use of it, as Gupta demonstrates.

me of which I have not rendered some account. It appears from the above estimate, that my food alone cost me in money about twenty-seven cents a week. It was, for nearly two years after this, rye and Indian meal without yeast, potatoes, rice, a very little salt pork, molasses, and salt; and my drink, water. It was fit that I should live on rice, mainly, who love so well the philosophy of India. To

1 meet the objections of some inveterate cavillers, I may as well state, that if I dined out occasionally, as I always had done, and I trust shall have opportunities to do again, it was frequently to the detriment of my domestic arrangements. But the dining out, being, as I have stated, a constant element, does not in the least affect a comparative statement like this.

I learned from my two years' experience that it would cost incredibly little trouble to obtain one's necessary food,

2 even in this latitude; that a man may use as simple a diet as the animals, and yet retain health and strength. I have made a satisfactory dinner, satisfactory on several accounts,

3 simply off a dish of purslane (*Portulaca oleracea*) which I gathered in my cornfield, boiled and salted. I give the

4 Latin on account of the savoriness of the trivial name. And pray what more can a reasonable man desire, in peaceful times, in ordinary noons, than a sufficient number of ears of green sweet corn boiled, with the addition of salt? Even the little variety which I used was a yielding to the demands of appetite, and not of health. Yet men have come to such a pass that they frequently starve, not for want of necessaries, but for want of luxuries; and I know a good woman who thinks that her son lost his life because

5 he took to drinking water only.

The reader will perceive that I am treating the subject rather from an economic than a dietetic point of view, and he will not venture to put my abstemiousness to the test unless he has a well-stocked larder.

Bread I at first made of pure Indian meal and salt, genuine hoe-cakes, which I baked before my fire out of [1] doors on a shingle or the end of a stick of timber sawed off in building my house; but it was wont to get smoked and to have a piny flavor. I tried flour also; but have at last found a mixture of rye and Indian meal most convenient and agreeable. In cold weather it was no little amusement to bake several small loaves of this in succession, tending and turning them as carefully as an Egyptian his hatching [2] eggs. They were a real cereal fruit which I ripened, and they had to my senses a fragrance like that of other noble fruits, which I kept in as long as possible by wrapping them in cloths. I made a study of the ancient and indispensable art of bread-making, consulting such authorities as offered, going back to the primitive days and first invention of the unleavened kind, when from the wildness of nuts and meats men first reached the mildness and refinement of this diet, and travelling gradually down in my studies through that accidental souring of the dough which, it is supposed, taught the leavening process, and through the various fermentations thereafter, till I came to 'good, sweet, wholesome bread,' the staff of life. Leaven, which [3] some deem the soul of bread, the *spiritus* which fills its cellular tissue, which is religiously preserved like the ves- [4] tal fire — some precious bottleful, I suppose, first brought over in the Mayflower, did the business for America, and its influence is still rising, swelling, spreading, in cere- [5] alian billows over the land — this seed I regularly and faithfully procured from the village, till at length one morning I forgot the rules, and scalded my yeast; by which accident I discovered that even this was not indispensable

1 A bread made of cornmeal, so called because it was originally baked on the blade of a hoe.

2 "For the Egyptians do not use the birds for hatching the eggs, in effecting this themselves artificially by their own wit and skill in an astounding manner, they are not surpassed by the operations of nature" (Diodorus 1.74.4).

3 "Bread . . . called the staff of life" (Matthew Henry, *Commentaries*, 1708).

4 In ancient Rome, a fire in the temple of Vesta was kept constantly burning. If the flame went out, it boded calamity.

5 Apparently T's own coinage, but clear in its meaning and a pun on "cerulean."

1   Crystalized sodium carbonate, used as a leavening agent.

2   Marcus Porcius Cato, *De Agri Cultura*, chap. 74. Seybold (55) points out that T apparently did not have access to this volume until 1851, so it was a late addition to W. Note that T almost invariably follows any Latin or Greek quotation with an English translation, often his own, for the convenience of the reader (Pritchard).

— for my discoveries were not by the synthetic but analytic process — and I have gladly omitted it since, though most housewives earnestly assured me that safe and wholesome bread without yeast might not be, and elderly people prophesied a speedy decay of the vital forces. Yet I find it not to be an essential ingredient, and after going without it for a year am still in the land of the living; and I am glad to escape the trivialness of carrying a bottleful in my pocket, which would sometimes pop and discharge its contents to my discomfiture. It is simpler and more respectable to omit it. Man is an animal who more than any other can adapt himself to all climates and circumstances. Neither did I put any sal-soda, or other acid or alkali, into my bread. It would seem that I made it according to the recipe which Marcus Porcius Cato gave about two centuries before Christ. 'Panem depsticium sic facito. Manus mortariumque bene lavato. Farinam in mortarium indito, aquae paulatim addito, subigitoque pulchre. Ubi bene subegeris, defingito, coquitoque sub testu.' Which I take to mean, 'Make kneaded bread thus. Wash your hands and trough well. Put the meal into the trough, add water gradually, and knead it thoroughly. When you have kneaded it well, mould it, and bake it under a cover,' that is, in a baking-kettle. Not a word about leaven. But I did not always use this staff of life. At one time, owing to the emptiness of my purse, I saw none of it for more than a month.

Every New Englander might easily raise all his own breadstuffs in this land of rye and Indian corn, and not depend on distant and fluctuating markets for them. Yet so far are we from simplicity and independence that, in Concord, fresh and sweet meal is rarely sold in the shops, and hominy and corn in a still coarser form are hardly used by any. For the most part the farmer gives to his cattle and hogs the grain of his own producing, and buys flour, which is at least no more wholesome, at a greater cost, at the store. I saw that I could easily raise my bushel or two of rye and Indian corn, for the former will grow on the poorest land, and the latter does not require the best, and grind them in a hand-mill, and so do without rice and pork; and if I must have some concentrated sweet, I found by experiment that I could make a very good molasses either of pumpkins or beets, and I knew that I needed only to set out a few maples to obtain it more easily still, and while these were growing I could use various substitutes beside those which I have named. 'For,' as the Forefathers sang,

> 'we can make liquor to sweeten our lips
> Of pumpkins and parsnips and walnut-tree
>   chips.' **1**

Finally, as for salt, that grossest of groceries, to obtain this might be a fit occasion for a visit to the seashore, or, if I did without it altogether, I should probably drink the less water. I do not learn that the Indians ever troubled themselves to go after it.

Thus I could avoid all trade and barter, so far as my food was concerned, and having a shelter already, it would only remain to get clothing and fuel. The pantaloons which I now wear were woven in a farmer's family — thank Heaven there is so much virtue still in man; for I think the fall from the farmer to the operative as great and memorable as that from the man to the farmer; — and in **2** a new country, fuel is an encumbrance. As for a habitat, if I were not permitted still to squat, I might purchase one acre at the same price for which the land I cultivated was

1   T undoubtedly used John Warner Barber, *Historical Collections . . . of . . . Massachusetts* (Worcester, 1839, 195), where the whole, an untitled poem, is quoted.

2   When Adam was driven out of Eden, he was forced to become a farmer (Genesis 3:23).

1   Raymond Adams (1948) gives an amusing account of Emerson's purchase of the Walden land, telling how Emerson was outwitted by the farmer.

2   Swift (103) identifies this young man as Isaac Hecker.

3   A widow's share, according to the laws of inheritance, was a third.

4   Most of the furniture that T used at Walden is now on display in a room at the Concord Museum. In his *Journal* (III, 200) T says he carted all his furniture out to Walden in a hay-rigging.

5   Skillet and frying-pan: Although these two terms are now used interchangeably, both referring to round, shallow pans used for frying, then a skillet was sometimes thought of as being deeper and raised on legs.

6   Japanned lamp: made of lacquer ware.

7   There seems to be no record of a Concord Spaulding, but it was a common name in some of the neighboring towns.

1 sold — namely, eight dollars and eight cents. But as it was, I considered that I enhanced the value of the land by squatting on it.

There is a certain class of unbelievers who sometimes ask me such questions as, if I think that I can live on vegetable food alone; and to strike at the root of the matter at once — for the root is faith — I am accustomed to answer such, that I can live on board nails. If they cannot understand that, they cannot understand much that I have to say. For my part, I am glad to hear of experiments **2** of this kind being tried; as that a young man tried for a fortnight to live on hard, raw corn on the ear, using his teeth for all mortar. The squirrel tribe tried the same and succeeded. The human race is interested in these experiments, though a few old women who are incapacitated **3** for them, or who own their thirds in mills, may be alarmed.

❦

4 My furniture, part of which I made myself — and the rest cost me nothing of which I have not rendered an account — consisted of a bed, a table, a desk, three chairs, a looking-glass three inches in diameter, a pair of tongs and **5** andirons, a kettle, a skillet, and a frying-pan, a dipper, a wash-bowl, two knives and forks, three plates, one cup, one spoon, a jug for oil, a jug for molasses, and a ja- **6** panned lamp. None is so poor that he need sit on a pumpkin. That is shiftlessness. There is a plenty of such chairs as I like best in the village garrets to be had for taking them away. Furniture! Thank God, I can sit and I can stand without the aid of a furniture warehouse. What man but a philosopher would not be ashamed to see his furniture packed in a cart and going up country exposed to the light of heaven and the eyes of men, a beggarly **7** account of empty boxes? That is Spaulding's furniture. I could never tell from inspecting such a load whether it belonged to a so-called rich man or a poor one; the owner always seemed poverty-stricken. Indeed, the more you have of such things the poorer you are. Each load looks as if it contained the contents of a dozen shanties; and if one shanty is poor, this is a dozen times as poor. Pray, for what do we *move* ever but to get rid of our furniture, our *exu-* [1] *viae*; at last to go from this world to another newly furnished, and leave this to be burned? It is the same as if all these traps were buckled to a man's belt, and he could not move over the rough country where our lines are cast without dragging them — dragging his trap. He was a lucky fox that left his tail in the trap. The muskrat will [2] gnaw his third leg off to be free. No wonder man has lost his elasticity. How often he is at a dead set! 'Sir, if I may be so bold, what do you mean by a dead set?' If you are a [3] seer, whenever you meet a man you will see all that he owns, ay, and much that he pretends to disown, behind him, even to his kitchen furniture and all the trumpery which he saves and will not burn, and he will appear to be harnessed to it and making what headway he can. I think that the man is at a dead set who has got through a knot-hole or gate-way where his sledge load of furniture cannot follow him. I cannot but feel compassion when I hear some trig, compact-looking man, seemingly free, all [4] girded and ready, speak of his 'furniture,' as whether it is insured or not. 'But what shall I do with my furniture?' My gay butterfly is entangled in a spider's web then. Even those who seem for a long while not to have any, if you inquire more narrowly you will find have some stored in somebody's barn. I look upon England today as an old gentleman who is travelling with a great deal of baggage, trumpery which has accumulated from long housekeeping, which he has not the courage to burn; great trunk,

1 Latin for "castoff."
2 A reference to Aesop's fable "The Fox Without a Tail."
3 A collegiate term meaning a complete failure in recitation.
4 Neat, trim-looking.

Log trap to catch many kinds of animals. Some for bears let the log fall six or seven feet. First there is a frame, then the little stick which the animal moves, presses down, as he goes through under the log; then the crooked stick is hung over the top of the frame, and holds up the log by a string; the weight of the log on this keeps the little stick up. (November 26, 1850)

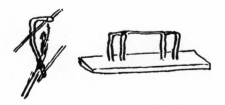

1 "Take up thy bed and walk" (John 5:8).

2 Sour milk: an old superstition.

3 Economical New England housewives kept the curtains drawn in their parlors to keep the sun from fading the carpet.

4 Ellery Channing comments in his copy of W, "Deacon Brown, a penurious old curmudgeon, who lived next house to me in the middle of town, — a human rat." T gives further details of this auction in his *Journal* (VI, 80).

5 *Julius Caesar,* III, ii.

6 The word was formerly applied to fires for the burning of heretics, proscribed books, etc.

little trunk, bandbox, and bundle. Throw away the first three at least. It would surpass the powers of a well man 1 nowadays to take up his bed and walk, and I should certainly advise a sick one to lay down his bed and run. When I have met an immigrant tottering under a bundle which contained his all — looking like an enormous wen which had grown out of the nape of his neck — I have pitied him, not because that was his all, but because he had all *that* to carry. If I have got to drag my trap, I will take care that it be a light one and do not nip me in a vital part. But perchance it would be wisest never to put one's paw into it.

I would observe, by the way, that it costs me nothing for curtains, for I have no gazers to shut out but the sun and moon, and I am willing that they should look in. The 2 moon will not sour milk nor taint meat of mine, nor will 3 the sun injure my furniture or fade my carpet; and if he is sometimes too warm a friend, I find it still better economy to retreat behind some curtain which nature has provided, than to add a single item to the details of housekeeping. A lady once offered me a mat, but as I had no room to spare within the house, nor time to spare within or without to shake it, I decline it, preferring to wipe my feet on the sod before my door. It is best to avoid the beginnings of evil.

Not long since I was present at the auction of a dea- 4 con's effects, for his life had not been ineffectual:

'The evil that men do lives after them.'
5

As usual, a great proportion was trumpery which had begun to accumulate in his father's day. Among the rest was a dried tapeworm. And now, after lying half a century in his garret and other dust holes, these things were not 6 burned; instead of a *bonfire*, or purifying destruction of

them, there was an *auction*, or increasing of them. The **1**
neighbors eagerly collected to view them, bought them
all, and carefully transported them to their garrets and
dust holes, to lie there till their estates are settled, when **2**
they will start again. When a man dies he kicks the dust. **3**

The customs of some savage nations might, perchance,
be profitably imitated by us, for they at least go through
the semblance of casting their slough annually; they have **4**
the idea of the thing, whether they have the reality or not.
Would it not be well if we were to celebrate such a 'busk,' **5**
or 'feast of first fruits,' as Bartram describes to have been **6**
the custom of the Mucclasse Indians? 'When a town cele-
brates the busk,' says he, 'having previously provided themselves with new clothes, new pots, pans, and other household utensils and furniture, they collect all their worn out
clothes and other despicable things, sweep and cleanse
their houses, squares, and the whole town, of their filth,
which with all the remaining grain and other old provi-
sions they cast together into one common heap, and con-
sume it with fire. After having taken medicine, and fasted
for three days, all the fire in the town is extinguished.
During this fast they abstain from the gratification of
every appetite and passion whatever. A general amnesty is
proclaimed; all malefactors may return to their town.'

'On the fourth morning, the high priest, by rubbing dry
wood together, produces new fire in the public square,
from whence every habitation in the town is supplied
with the new and pure flame.'

They then feast on the new corn and fruits, and dance
and sing for three days, 'and the four following days they
receive visits and rejoice with their friends from neighboring towns who have in like manner purified and prepared
themselves.'

The Mexicans also practised a similar purification at **7**

1 The emphasis is on the derivation of the
word from the Latin *auctio,* meaning an increase, that is, in the price by bidding.

2 A cranny used for storage of seldom-used
materials.

3 T is probably thinking of the *Iliad*
(22.330), wherein the death of Hector is usually
described as his "kicking the dust."

4 A snake sheds its skin.

5 Davidson (1947) points out the similarity
between the description of the busk and Hawthorne's short story "Earth's Holocaust," and
suggests that T may have inspired Hawthorne
to write the story.

6 William Bartram, *Travels Through North
and South Carolina . . . (Philadelphia, 1791,
507).*

7 William H. Prescott, History of the Con-
quest of Mexico (New York, 1843, book 1,
chap. V).

1 Noah Webster, *An American Dictionary of the English Language* (Springfield, Mass., 1848, 974).

2 In his commencement speech at his graduation from Harvard, T suggested we should reverse the biblical order, working one day and resting six. He thus was practicing roughly what he had preached.

3 T had three experiences as a school-teacher. In order to earn some money, he left Harvard for a few months and taught in Canton. After graduation, he taught for a few weeks in the public schools in Concord. But when the authorities insisted that he use the rod, he whipped six children at random and then resigned. Shortly thereafter he started a private school with his brother John. The school pioneered many of the principles of modern education and was so successful that there was a waiting list of students. But it was later abandoned when John became too ill to teach. T also spent a number of months as a private tutor for Emerson's nephews on Staten Island.

4 Fink (262) suggests T may here be referring to Emerson's urging him to publish *A Week* at his own expense.

the end of every fifty-two years, in the belief that it was time for the world to come to an end.

1 I have scarcely heard of a truer sacrament, that is, as the dictionary defines it, 'outward and visible sign of an inward and spiritual grace,' than this, and I have no doubt that they were originally inspired directly from Heaven to do thus, though they have no Biblical record of the revelation.

❦

For more than five years I maintained myself thus solely by the labor of my hands, and I found that, by working 2 about six weeks in a year, I could meet all the expenses of living. The whole of my winters, as well as most of my summers, I had free and clear for study. I have thoroughly 3 tried school-keeping, and found that my expenses were in proportion, or rather out of proportion, to my income, for I was obliged to dress and train, not to say think and believe, accordingly, and I lost my time into the bargain. As I did not teach for the good of my fellow-men, but simply for a livelihood, this was a failure. I have tried trade; but I found that it would take ten years to get under way in that, and that then I should probably be on my way to the devil. I was actually afraid that I might by that time be doing what is called a good business. When formerly I was looking about to see what I could do for a living, some 4 sad experience in conforming to the wishes of friends being fresh in my mind to tax my ingenuity, I thought often and seriously of picking huckleberries; that surely I could do, and its small profits might suffice — for my greatest skill has been to want but little — so little capital it required, so little distraction from my wonted moods, I foolishly thought. While my acquaintances went unhesitatingly into trade or the professions, I contemplated this occupation as most like theirs; ranging the hills all summer to pick the berries which came in my way, and thereafter carelessly dispose of them; so, to keep the flocks of Admetus. I also dreamed that I might gather the wild [1] herbs, or carry evergreens to such villagers as loved to be reminded of the woods, even to the city, by hay-cart loads. But I have since learned that trade curses everything it handles; and though you trade in messages from heaven, the whole curse of trade attaches to the business.

As I preferred some things to others, and especially valued my freedom, as I could fare hard and yet succeed well, I did not wish to spend my time in earning rich carpets or other fine furniture, or delicate cookery, or a house in the Grecian or the Gothic style just yet. If there [2] are any to whom it is no interruption to acquire these things, and who know how to use them when acquired, I relinquish to them the pursuit. Some are 'industrious,' and appear to love labor for its own sake, or perhaps because it keeps them out of worse mischief; to such I have at present nothing to say. Those who would not know what to do with more leisure than they now enjoy, I might advise to work twice as hard as they do — work till they pay for themselves, and get their free papers. For [3] myself I found that the occupation of a day-laborer was the most independent of any, especially as it required only thirty or forty days in a year to support one. The laborer's day ends with the going down of the sun, and he is then free to devote himself to his chosen pursuit, independent of his labor; but his employer, who speculates from month to month, has no respite from one end of the year to the other.

In short, I am convinced, both by faith and experience, that to maintain one's self on this earth is not a hardship but a pastime, if we will live simply and wisely; as the

1 Apollo, when banished from heaven, was forced to tend the flocks of Admetus, son of the king of Pherae, for nine years. This is a favorite allusion of T's, and is found again and again in his writings. Seybold (59) thinks that T derived this legend from his reading of *Alcestis,* but the legend appears so frequently that it might have come from a number of other places.

2 The Greek Revival in American architecture was nearing its end by the time T went to Walden, and was being replaced by the more ornate pseudo-Gothic style.

3 In colonial America, immigrants often indentured themselves to pay for their passage across the Atlantic. They were granted "free papers" when they had paid off their debt.

1 This paragraph, taken almost word for word from a letter T wrote Horace Greeley on May 19, 1848, provides an insight into his methods of composition.

2 An interesting parallel to the story of the rich young man told in Luke 18.

3 It is important to call attention to this line, for so many ask, "What if everyone lived like T?" An anonymous reviewer of W in the *National Anti-Slavery Standard* for December 16, 1854, aptly commented, "No man could pursue his course who was a mere superficial imitator, any more than it would be a real imitation of Christ if all men were to make it their main business to go about preaching the gospel to each other."

4 Fugitive slaves trying to make their way to Canada used the North Star as their guide.

5 T was probably thinking in particular of J. A. Etzler's proposals, in his *The Paradise Within the Reach of All Men,* that the construction of huge apartment houses would save much time, money, and energy. T wrote a devastating review of the book for the *Democratic Review* (XIII, 1843, 427).

pursuits of the simpler nations are still the sports of the
1 more artificial. It is not necessary that a man should earn his living by the sweat of his brow, unless he sweats easier than I do.

2 One young man of my acquaintance, who has inherited some acres, told me that he thought he should live as I did, *if he had the means.* I would not have any one adopt
3 *my* mode of living on any account; for, beside that before he has fairly learned it I may have found out another for myself, I desire that there may be as many different persons in the world as possible; but I would have each one be very careful to find out and pursue *his own* way, and not his father's or his mother's or his neighbor's instead. The youth may build or plant or sail, only let him not be hindered from doing that which he tells me he would like to do. It is by a mathematical point only that we are wise, as the sailor or the fugitive slave keeps the polestar in his
4 eye; but that is sufficient guidance for all our life. We may not arrive at our port within a calculable period, but we would preserve the true course.

Undoubtedly, in this case, what is true for one is truer
5 still for a thousand, as a large house is not proportionally more expensive than a small one, since one roof may cover, one cellar underlie, and one wall separate several apartments. But for my part, I preferred the solitary dwelling. Moreover, it will commonly be cheaper to build the whole yourself than to convince another of the advantage of the common wall; and when you have done this, the common partition, to be much cheaper, must be a thin one, and that other may prove a bad neighbor, and also not keep his side in repair. The only coöperation which is commonly possible is exceedingly partial and superficial; and what little true coöperation there is, is as if it were not, being a harmony inaudible to men. If a man has

faith, he will cooperate with equal faith everywhere; if he
has not faith, he will continue to live like the rest of the
world, whatever company he is joined to. To coöperate in
the highest as well as the lowest sense, means *to get our
living together.* I heard it proposed lately that two young
men should travel together over the world, the one without money, earning his means as he went, before the mast **1**
and behind the plow, the other carrying a bill of exchange **2**
in his pocket. It was easy to see that they could not long be
companions or coöperate, since one would not *operate* at
all. They would part at the first interesting crisis in their
adventures. Above all, as I have implied, the man who
goes alone can start today; but he who travels with another must wait till that other is ready, and it may be a
long time before they get off.

❧

But all this is very selfish, I have heard some of my townsmen say. I confess that I have hitherto indulged very little
in philanthropic enterprises. I have made some sacrifices **3**
to a sense of duty, and among others have sacrificed this
pleasure also. There are those who have used all their arts
to persuade me to undertake the support of some poor
family in the town; and if I had nothing to do — for the
devil finds employment for the idle — I might try my **4**
hand at some such pastime as that. However, when I have
thought to indulge myself in this respect, and lay their
Heaven under an obligation by maintaining certain poor
persons in all respects as comfortably as I maintain myself, and have even ventured so far as to make them the
offer, they have one and all unhesitatingly preferred to
remain poor. While my townsmen and women are devoted in so many ways to the good of their fellows, I trust
that one at least may be spared to other and less humane

1 That is, as a sailor. On sailing vessels the
crew traditionally slept in the front portion of
the ship, ahead of the mast.

2 Bill of exchange: a kind of check direct-
ing a person to pay a second person a certain
sum of money and charging it to the account of
a third person.

3 Despite T's protests to the contrary, he
did perhaps more than any other Concordian to
better the conditions of the Irish laborers of the
town (Buckley; Ryan).

4 "The devil finds work for idle hands" is
an old proverb that can be traced at least as far
back as John Ray's *Compleat Collection of English Proverbs,* 1670.

1 Possibly a reference to Cotton Mather's *Essays to Do Good* (1710), to Benjamin Franklin's *Dogood Papers,* or, as Doudna suggests, to James Freeman Clarke's writings.

2 A merry domestic fairy known also as Puck (*Midsummer Night's Dream,* II, i).

3 "No light, but rather darkness visible" (*Paradise Lost,* I, 63).

pursuits. You must have a genius for charity as well as for anything else. As for Doing-good, that is one of the professions which are full. Moreover, I have tried it fairly, and, strange as it may seem, am satisfied that it does not agree with my constitution. Probably I should not consciously and deliberately forsake my particular calling to do the good which society demands of me, to save the universe from annihilation; and I believe that a like but infinitely greater steadfastness elsewhere is all that now preserves it. But I would not stand between any man and his genius; and to him who does this work, which I decline, with his whole heart and soul and life, I would say, Persevere, even if the world call it doing evil, as it is most likely they will.

I am far from supposing that my case is a peculiar one; no doubt many of my readers would make a similar defence. At doing something — I will not engage that my neighbors shall pronounce it good — I do not hesitate to say that I should be a capital fellow to hire; but what that is, it is for my employer to find out. What *good* I do, in the common sense of that word, must be aside from my main path, and for the most part wholly unintended. Men say, practically, Begin where you are and such as you are, without aiming mainly to become of more worth, and with kindness aforethought go about doing good. If I were to preach at all in this strain, I should say rather, Set about being good. As if the sun should stop when he had kindled his fires up to the splendor of a moon or a star of the sixth magnitude, and go about like a Robin Goodfellow, peeping in at every cottage window, inspiring lunatics, and tainting meats, and making darkness visible, instead of steadily increasing his genial heat and beneficence till he is of such brightness that no mortal can look him in the face, and then, and in the meanwhile too, going about the world in his own orbit, doing it good, or rather, as a truer philosophy has discovered, the world going about him getting good. When Phaëton, wishing to prove his [1] heavenly birth by his beneficence, had the sun's chariot but one day, and drove out of the beaten track, he burned several blocks of houses in the lower streets of heaven, and scorched the surface of the earth, and dried up every spring, and made the great desert of Sahara, till at length Jupiter hurled him headlong to the earth with a thunderbolt, and the sun, through grief at his death, did not shine for a year.

There is no odor so bad as that which arises from goodness tainted. It is human, it is divine, carrion. If I knew for a certainty that a man was coming to my house with the conscious design of doing me good, I should run for my life, as from that dry and parching wind of the African deserts called the simoom, which fills the mouth and nose and ears and eyes with dust till you are suffocated, for fear that I should get some of his good done to me — some of its virus mingled with my blood. No — in this case I would rather suffer evil the natural way. A man is not a good *man* to me because he will feed me if I should be starving, or warm me if I should be freezing, or pull me out of a ditch if I should ever fall into one. I can find you a Newfoundland dog that will do as much. Philan- [2] thropy is not love for one's fellow-man in the broadest sense. Howard was no doubt an exceedingly kind and [3] worthy man in his way, and has his reward; but, comparatively speaking, what are a hundred Howards to *us*, if their philanthropy do not help *us* in our best estate, when we are most worthy to be helped? I never heard of a philanthropic meeting in which it was sincerely proposed to do any good to me, or the like of me.

The Jesuits were quite balked by those Indians who, [4] being burned at the stake, suggested new modes of tor-

1   The son of the sun in Greek mythology. The tale is told in *Metamorphoses* and many other classical sources. As Eddleman (64) shows, T here quotes almost word for word from Lemprière's *Classical Dictionary*.

2   "Why a water spaniel would have done as much" (Richard B. Sheridan, *The Rivals,* I, i) (Stronks). T's walking companion Ellery Channing owned a Newfoundland that often accompanied them on their walks.

3   John Howard (1726?–1790), English philanthropist and prison reformer.

4   There are many such incidents recorded in *The Jesuit Relations and Allied Documents,* which were favorite reading for T. See, for example, XVII, 109 (Cleveland, 1898).

1 "And as ye would that men should do to you, do ye also to them likewise" (Luke 6:31).

2 "Love your enemies" (Matthew 5:44).

3 "Then said Jesus, Father forgive them, for they know not what they do" (Luke 23:34).

4 For further details of the ice cutting, see "The Pond in Winter" chapter.

5 Latin for "outside" and "inside."

6 A store where cheap clothes were sold.

ture to their tormentors. Being superior to physical suffering, it sometimes chanced that they were superior to any consolation which the missionaries could offer; and the 1 law to do as you would be done by fell with less persuasiveness on the ears of those who, for their part, did not 2 care how they were done by, who loved their enemies 3 after a new fashion, and came very near freely forgiving them all they did.

Be sure that you give the poor the aid they most need, though it be your example which leaves them far behind. If you give money, spend yourself with it, and do not merely abandon it to them. We make curious mistakes sometimes. Often the poor man is not so cold and hungry as he is dirty and ragged and gross. It is partly his taste, and not merely his misfortune. If you give him money, he will perhaps buy more rags with it. I was wont to pity the 4 clumsy Irish laborers who cut ice on the pond, in such mean and ragged clothes, while I shivered in my more tidy and somewhat more fashionable garments, till, one bitter cold day, one who had slipped into the water came to my house to warm him, and I saw him strip off three pairs of pants and two pairs of stockings ere he got down to the skin, though they were dirty and ragged enough, it 5 is true, and that he could afford to refuse the *extra* garments which I offered him, he had so many *intra* ones. This ducking was the very thing he needed. Then I began to pity myself, and I saw that it would be a greater charity 6 to bestow on me a flannel shirt than a whole slop-shop on him. There are a thousand hacking at the branches of evil to one who is striking at the root, and it may be that he who bestows the largest amount of time and money on the needy is doing the most by his mode of life to produce that misery which he strives in vain to relieve. It is the pious slave-breeder devoting the proceeds of every tenth slave to buy a Sunday's liberty for the rest. Some show their kindness to the poor by employing them in their kitchens. Would they not be kinder if they employed themselves there? You boast of spending a tenth part of [1] your income in charity; maybe you should spend the nine tenths so, and done with it. Society recovers only a tenth part of the property then. Is this owing to the generosity of him in whose possession it is found, or to the remissness of the officers of justice?

Philanthropy is almost the only virtue which is sufficiently appreciated by mankind. Nay, it is greatly overrated; and it is our selfishness which overrates it. A robust poor man, one sunny day here in Concord, praised a fellow-townsman to me, because, as he said, he was kind to the poor; meaning himself. The kind uncles and aunts of the race are more esteemed than its true spiritual fathers and mothers. I once heard a reverend lecturer on [2] England, a man of learning and intelligence, after enumerating her scientific, literary, and political worthies, Shakespeare, Bacon, Cromwell, Milton, Newton, and others, speak next of her Christian heroes, whom, as if his profession required it of him, he elevated to a place far above all the rest, as the greatest of the great. They were Penn, Howard, and Mrs. Fry. Every one must feel the false- [3] hood and cant of this. The last were not England's best men and women; only, perhaps, her best philanthropists.

I would not subtract anything from the praise that is due to philanthropy, but merely demand justice for all who by their lives and works are a blessing to mankind. I do not value chiefly a man's uprightness and benevolence, which are, as it were, his stem and leaves. Those plants of whose greenness withered we make herb tea for the sick serve but a humble use, and are most employed by quacks. I want the flower and fruit of a man; that some

1 The biblical injunction to tithe one's income for the Lord. T, of course, sees the full irony of the situation.

2 In all probability, this was the Reverend Frederick Henry Hedge, the Unitarian clergyman and transcendentalist from Bangor, Maine, who spoke on "The English Nation" before the Concord Lyceum on January 16, 1850 (Cameron, 1959, 164).

3 William Penn (1644–1718), Quaker reformer and founder of Pennsylvania; John Howard (1726?–1790), English prison reformer; and Elizabeth Fry (1780–1845), Quaker prison reformer.

1   "Charity shall cover the multitude of sins" (I Peter 4:8).

2   T was always skeptical of Christian missionary efforts.

3   An ancient belief, as in Song of Solomon 5:4: "My bowels were moved for him."

4   A traditional source of stomach upsets.

fragrance be wafted over from him to me, and some ripeness flavor our intercourse. His goodness must not be a partial and transitory act, but a constant superfluity, which costs him nothing and of which he is unconscious. This is **1** a charity that hides a multitude of sins. The philanthropist too often surrounds mankind with the remembrance of his own castoff griefs as an atmosphere, and calls it sympathy. We should impart our courage, and not our despair, our health and ease, and not our disease, and take care that this does not spread by contagion. From what southern plains comes up the voice of wailing? Under what latitudes reside the heathen to whom we would **2** send light? Who is that intemperate and brutal man whom we would redeem? If anything ail a man, so that he does **3** not perform his functions, if he have a pain in his bowels even — for that is the seat of sympathy — he forthwith sets about reforming — the world. Being a microcosm himself, he discovers — and it is a true discovery, and he is the man to make it — that the world has been eating **4** green apples; to his eyes, in fact, the globe itself is a great green apple, which there is danger awful to think of that the children of men will nibble before it is ripe; and straightway his drastic philanthropy seeks out the Esquimau and the Patagonian, and embraces the populous Indian and Chinese villages; and thus, by a few years of philanthropic activity, the powers in the meanwhile using him for their own ends, no doubt, he cures himself of his dyspepsia, the globe acquires a faint blush on one or both of its cheeks, as if it were beginning to be ripe, and life loses its crudity and is once more sweet and wholesome to live. I never dreamed of any enormity greater than I have committed. I never knew, and never shall know, a worse man than myself.

I believe that what so saddens the reformer is not his

sympathy with his fellows in distress, but, though he be the holiest son of God, is his private ail. Let this be righted, let the spring come to him, the morning rise over his couch, and he will forsake his generous companions without apology. My excuse for not lecturing against the use of tobacco is, that I never chewed it, that is a penalty which reformed tobacco-chewers have to pay; though there are things enough I have chewed which I could lecture against. If you should ever be betrayed into any of these philanthropies, do not let your left hand know what your **1** right hand does, for it is not worth knowing. Rescue the drowning and tie your shoestrings. Take your time, and set about some free labor.

Our manners have been corrupted by communication **2** with the saints. Our hymn-books resound with a melodious cursing of God and enduring Him forever. One would **3** say that even the prophets and redeemers had rather consoled the fears than confirmed the hopes of man. There is nowhere recorded a simple and irrepressible satisfaction with the gift of life, any memorable praise of God. All health and success does me good, however far off and withdrawn it may appear; all disease and failure helps to make me sad and does me evil, however much sympathy it may have with me or I with it. If, then, we would indeed restore mankind by truly Indian, botanic, magnetic, or **4** natural means, let us first be as simple and well as Nature ourselves, dispel the clouds which hang over our own brows, and take up a little life into our pores. Do not stay to be an overseer of the poor, but endeavor to become **5** one of the worthies of the world.

I read in the Gulistan, or Flower Garden, of Sheik Sadi **6** of Shiraz, that 'they asked a wise man, saying: Of the many celebrated trees which the Most High God has created lofty and umbrageous, they call none azad, or **7**

1 "But when thou doest alms, let not thy left hand know what thy right hand doeth" (Matthew 6:3).

2 "Evil communications corrupt good manners" (I Corinthians 15:33).

3 The opening lines of the Shorter Catechism in *The New England Primer* are "Man's chief End is to Glorify God, and to Enjoy Him for ever."

4 One of the popular healing fads of T's day was mesmerism, or animal magnetism.

5 Most New England towns of T's day had an officer designated "overseer of the poor" who looked after their welfare.

6 Musee-Huddeen Sheik Saadi, *The Gulistan, or Rose Garden*. Saadi, a Persian poet of the thirteenth century, was popular among the transcendentalists. Emerson wrote a preface to an English translation of *The Gulistan*. T's quotation comes from chap. VIII, "Rules for Conduct in Life."

7 For a discussion of T as an azad, or free man, see Douglas Anderson.

1 Another name for the Tigris River. Also spelled Dijla or Dojail.

free, excepting the cypress, which bears no fruit; what mystery is there in this? He replied: Each has its appropriate produce, and appointed season, during the continuance of which it is fresh and blooming, and during their absence dry and withered; to neither of which states is the cypress exposed, being always flourishing; and of this nature are the azads, or religious independents. — Fix not thy heart on that which is transitory; for the Dijlah, or Tigris, will continue to flow through Bagdad after the race of caliphs is extinct: if thy hand has plenty, be liberal as the date tree; but if it affords nothing to give away, be an azad, or free man, like the cypress.'

COMPLEMENTAL VERSES
THE PRETENSIONS OF POVERTY

Thou dost presume too much, poor needy
    wretch,
To claim a station in the firmament
Because thy humble cottage, or thy tub,
Nurses some lazy or pedantic virtue
In the cheap sunshine or by shady springs,
With roots and pot-herbs; where thy right hand,
Tearing those humane passions from the mind,
Upon whose stocks fair blooming virtues flourish,
Degradeth nature, and benumbeth sense,
And, Gorgon-like, turns active men to stone.
We not require the dull society
Of your necessitated temperance,
Or that unnatural stupidity
That knows nor joy nor sorrow; nor your forc'd
Falsely exalted passive fortitude
Above the active. This low abject brood,
That fix their seats in mediocrity,
Become your servile minds; but we advance
Such virtues only as admit excess,
Brave, bounteous acts, regal magnificence,
All-seeing prudence, magnanimity
That knows no bound, and that heroic virtue
For which antiquity hath left no name,
But patterns only, such as Hercules,
Achilles, Theseus. Back to thy loath'd cell;
And when thou seest the new enlightened
    sphere,
Study to know but what those worthies were.

T. CAREW

1 This poem was taken from the Cavalier poet Thomas Carew's masque *Coelum Britannicum.* They are the words of Mercury after "the fifth anti-masque of Gipsies." They are "complemental," rounding out a one-sided view of things. Bickman (51) says this poem has "been inserted not to support or amplify a text but, rather to disagree with or qualify it. It provides literally another voice from that of the author, asking the reader to consider also the obverse of everything just said." Gozzi (1964) argues that T is presenting the argument that one needs spirituality as well as poverty for the ideal life.

2 This title is T's own.

3 Any of three snake-haired sisters in Greek mythology whose glance changed the beholder to stone.

4 In Homer's *Iliad,* the Greek hero of the Trojan War.

5 In Greek legend, Theseus is famed for killing the Minotaur.

1 In his copy of W, Ellery Channing lists Weird Dell, the orchard side of Fairhaven Hill, the Cliff Hill, and Baker Farm as other sites that T considered.

2 Poirier (86), in a discussion of T's use of puns, points out that "premises" here can appropriately mean both property and a proposition from which a conclusion is drawn.

3 The "picturesque" school of landscape architecture, popular in T's day, reveled in displaying deformed trees.

The farmer accustomed to look at his crops from a mercenary point of view is not aware how beautiful they are. (July 22, 1860)

Where I Lived, and What I Lived For

AT A CERTAIN season of our life we are accustomed to
1 consider every spot as the possible site of a house. I have thus surveyed the country on every side within a dozen miles of where I live. In imagination I have bought all the farms in succession, for all were to be bought, and I knew
2 their price. I walked over each farmer's premises, tasted his wild apples, discoursed on husbandry with him, took his farm at his price, at any price, mortgaging it to him in my mind; even put a higher price on it — took everything but a deed of it — took his word for his deed, for I dearly love to talk — cultivated it, and him too to some extent, I trust, and withdrew when I had enjoyed it long enough, leaving him to carry it on. This experience entitled me to be regarded as a sort of real-estate broker by my friends. Wherever I sat, there I might live, and the landscape radiated from me accordingly. What is a house but a *sedes*, a seat? — better if a country seat. I discovered many a site for a house not likely to be soon improved, which some might have thought too far from the village, but to my eyes the village was too far from it. Well, there I might live, I said; and there I did live, for an hour, a summer and a winter life; saw how I could let the years run off, buffet the winter through, and see the spring come in. The future inhabitants of this region, wherever they may place their houses, may be sure that they have been anticipated. An afternoon sufficed to lay out the land into orchard, wood-lot, and pasture, and to decide what fine oaks or pines should be left to stand before the door, and whence
3 each blasted tree could be seen to the best advantage; and then I let it lie, fallow perchance, for a man is rich in

proportion to the number of things which he can afford to let alone. **1**

My imagination carried me so far that I even had the refusal of several farms — the refusal was all I wanted — but I never got my fingers burned by actual possession. The nearest that I came to actual possession was when I bought the Hollowell place, and had begun to sort my **2** seeds, and collected materials with which to make a wheelbarrow to carry it on or off with; but before the owner gave me a deed of it, his wife — every man has such a wife — changed her mind and wished to keep it, and he offered me ten dollars to release him. Now, to speak the truth, I had but ten cents in the world, and it surpassed my arithmetic to tell, if I was that man who had ten cents, or who had a farm, or ten dollars, or all together. However, I let him keep the ten dollars and the farm too, for I had carried it far enough; or rather, to be generous, I sold him the farm for just what I gave for it, and, as he was not a rich man, made him a present of ten dollars, and still had my ten cents, and seeds, and materials for a wheelbarrow left. I found thus that I had been a rich man without any damage to my poverty. But I retained the landscape, and I have since annually carried off what it yielded without a wheelbarrow. With respect to landscapes,

> 'I am monarch of all I *survey*, **3**
> My right there is none to dispute.' **4**

I have frequently seen a poet withdraw, having enjoyed **5** the most valuable part of a farm, while the crusty farmer supposed that he had got a few wild apples only. Why, the owner does not know it for many years when a poet has put his farm in rhyme, the most admirable kind of invisible fence, has fairly impounded it, milked it, skimmed

1 The first, second, third, and fifth paragraphs of this chapter were first published in *Sartain's Union Magazine* (XI, 1852, 127), with slight variations in wording and punctuation. A short segment from "Sounds" was published in the same volume. Since they were the last issues of *Sartain's* published, it raises the question of whether T intended to serialize more of W, only to have the magazine fail on him.

2 An old farm on the Sudbury River just below Hubbard's Bridge.

3 The word is italicized to call attention to the pun on T's own means of earning a living.

4 From "Verses supposed to be written by Alexander Selkirk" by William Cowper.

5 Undoubtedly Ellery Channing, who often accompanied T on his walks and who often described Concord landscapes in his poetry.

1 According to Greek mythology, Atlas carried the world on his shoulders.

2 T was famous in Concord for his gardens. He delighted particularly in raising many varieties of melons and each fall gave a melon party, which was one of Concord's social events of the year (Harding, 1993, 89).

Paddling through the wild Sudbury meadows, I am struck with the regularity with which the phalanxes of bulrushes *(Scirpus lacustris)* occur. They do not grow in a continuous line, like pipes or pontederia, but in small isolated patches. (July 9, 1859)

it, and got all the cream, and left the farmer only the skimmed milk.

The real attractions of the Hollowell farm, to me, were: its complete retirement, being about two miles from the village, half a mile from the nearest neighbor, and separated from the highway by a broad field; its bounding on the river, which the owner said protected it by its fogs from frosts in the spring, though that was nothing to me; the gray color and ruinous state of the house and barn, and the dilapidated fences, which put such an interval between me and the last occupant; the hollow and lichen-covered apple trees, gnawed by rabbits, showing what kind of neighbors I should have; but above all, the recollection I had of it from my earliest voyages up the river, when the house was concealed behind a dense grove of red maples, through which I heard the house-dog bark. I was in haste to buy it, before the proprietor finished getting out some rocks, cutting down the hollow apple trees, and grubbing up some young birches which had sprung up in the pasture, or, in short, had made any more of his improvements. To enjoy these advantages I was ready to

1 carry it on; like Atlas, to take the world on my shoulders — I never heard what compensation he received for that — and do all those things which had no other motive or excuse but that I might pay for it and be unmolested in my possession of it; for I knew all the while that it would yield the most abundant crop of the kind I wanted, if I could only afford to let it alone. But it turned out as I have said.

All that I could say, then, with respect to farming on a

2 large scale — I have always cultivated a garden — was, that I had had my seeds ready. Many think that seeds improve with age. I have no doubt that time discriminates between the good and the bad; and when at last I shall plant, I shall be less likely to be disappointed. But I would

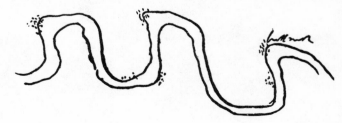

say to my fellows, once for all, As long as possible live free and uncommitted. It makes but little difference whether you are committed to a farm or the county jail.

Old Cato, whose 'De Re Rusticâ' is my 'Cultivator,' **1** says — and the only translation I have seen makes sheer nonsense of the passage — 'When you think of getting a farm turn it thus in your mind, not to buy greedily; nor spare your pains to look at it, and do not think it enough to go round it once. The oftener you go there the more it will please you, if it is good.' I think I shall not buy greed- **2** ily, but go round and round it as long as I live, and be buried in it first, that it may please me the more at last.

The present was my next experiment of this kind, which I purpose to describe more at length, for convenience put- ting the experience of two years into one. As I have said, I **3, 4** do not propose to write an ode to dejection, but to brag as lustily as chanticleer in the morning, standing on his **5** roost, if only to wake my neighbors up.

When first I took up my abode in the woods, that is, began to spend my nights as well as days there, which, by accident, was on Independence Day, or the Fourth of July, 1845, my house was not finished for winter, but was merely a defence against the rain, without plastering or chimney, the walls being of rough, weather-stained boards, with wide chinks, which made it cool at night. The up- right white hewn studs and freshly planed door and win- dow casings gave it a clean and airy look, especially in the morning, when its timbers were saturated with dew, so that I fancied that by noon some sweet gum would exude from them. To my imagination it retained throughout the day more or less of this auroral character, reminding me of a certain house on a mountain which I had visited a **6** year before. This was an airy and unplastered cabin, fit to entertain a travelling god, and where a goddess might trail

1 T is probably referring to either the *Boston Cultivator* or the *New England Cultivator,* both of which were published in Boston in his lifetime.

2 Cato, *De Agri Cultura* 1.1. T would have little complaint about the current Ash-Hooper translation. "When you are thinking of acquir- ing a farm, keep in mind these points: that you be not over eager in buying nor spare your pains in examining, and that you consider it not sufficient to go over it once. However often you go, a good piece of land will please you more at each visit."

3 Note the structure of the book. To give it unity, he combined the experience of two years (and, indeed, some of the experiences of the period from 1847 to 1854, when W was finally published) into one. This was a favorite device of T's. He had used the unit of a week for his first book, *A Week,* and in *Cape Cod* combined several excursions into one. Lane (1969) sug- gests that combining the two years into one added to the mythic qualities of the book, but in turn lessened the realism.

4 He said this before on the title page, where these lines are set forth as the theme of the book. The "ode to dejection" refers to Coleridge's poem of that name.

5 The rooster, a standard symbol of dawn.

6 A house he had seen in the Catskill Mountains in 1844, as he tells us in his *Journal* (V, 361).

1   The *Iliad* (Maxwell).

2   The residence of the gods in Greek mythology. Cavell (56) suggests, "The abode of the gods is to be entered not merely at the outermost point of the earth or at the top of the highest mountain, and maybe not at all; but anywhere, only at the point of the present."

3   T built the boat himself and used it on his excursion on the Concord and Merrimack Rivers. He sold it to Nathaniel Hawthorne, who was then living in the Old Manse, who in turn passed it on to Ellery Channing. It eventually rotted away and was disposed of. Hawthorne tells at some length the story of his acquiring the boat in his *American Notebooks,* in the entries for September 1 and 2, 1842.

4   "Et un séjour sans oiseaux est comme un mets sans assaisonnement" (M. A. Langlois, trans., *Harivansa, ou Histoire de la Famille de Hari* [Paris, 1834, I, 282]). The English translation is undoubtedly T's.

5   Cavell (53–4) notes how frequently T speaks of "finding himself" and suggests its transcendentalist implications.

6   T is mistaken here about the field sparrow, for as the name implies, it is a bird of the open fields rather than of the woods.

7   T did not retire far from civilization. He was within easy walking distance of Concord village and only twenty miles from Boston.

8   Site of the battle of April 19, 1775, the opening skirmish of the American Revolution.

---

1   her garments. The winds which passed over my dwelling were such as sweep over the ridges of mountains, bearing the broken strains, or celestial parts only, of terrestrial music. The morning wind forever blows, the poem of creation is uninterrupted; but few are the ears that hear it.

2   Olympus is but the outside of the earth everywhere.

3   The only house I had been the owner of before, if I except a boat, was a tent, which I used occasionally when making excursions in the summer, and this is still rolled up in my garret; but the boat, after passing from hand to hand, has gone down the stream of time. With this more substantial shelter about me, I had made some progress toward settling in the world. This frame, so slightly clad, was a sort of crystallization around me, and reacted on the builder. It was suggestive somewhat as a picture in outlines. I did not need to go outdoors to take the air, for the atmosphere within had lost none of its freshness. It was not so much within-doors as behind a door where I

4   sat, even in the rainiest weather. The Harivansa says, 'An abode without birds is like a meat without seasoning.'

5   Such was not my abode, for I found myself suddenly neighbor to the birds; not by having imprisoned one, but having caged myself near them. I was not only nearer to some of those which commonly frequent the garden and the orchard, but to those wilder and more thrilling songsters of the forest which never, or rarely, serenade a villager — the wood thrush, the veery, the scarlet tanager,

6   the field sparrow, the whip-poor-will, and many others.

7   I was seated by the shore of a small pond, about a mile and a half south of the village of Concord and somewhat higher than it, in the midst of an extensive wood between that town and Lincoln, and about two miles south of that

8   our only field known to fame, Concord Battle Ground; but I was so low in the woods that the opposite shore, half

a mile off, like the rest, covered with wood, was my most distant horizon. For the first week, whenever I looked out on the pond it impressed me like a tarn high up on the side of a mountain, its bottom far above the surface of other lakes, and, as the sun arose, I saw it throwing off its nightly clothing of mist, and here and there, by degrees, its soft ripples or its smooth reflecting surface was revealed, while the mists, like ghosts, were stealthily withdrawing in every direction into the woods, as at the breaking up of some nocturnal conventicle. The very dew seemed to **1** hang upon the trees later into the day than usual, as on the sides of mountains.

This small lake was of most value as a neighbor in the **2** intervals of a gentle rain-storm in August, when, both air and water being perfectly still, but the sky overcast, mid-afternoon had all the serenity of evening, and the wood thrush sang around, and was heard from shore to shore. A lake like this is never smoother than at such a time; and the clear portion of the air above it being shallow and darkened by clouds, the water, full of light and reflections, becomes a lower heaven itself so much the more important. From a hill-top near by, where the wood had **3** been recently cut off, there was a pleasing vista southward across the pond, through a wide indentation in the hills which form the shore there, where their opposite sides sloping toward each other suggested a stream flowing out in that direction through a wooded valley, but stream there was none. That way I looked between and over the near green hills to some distant and higher ones in the horizon, tinged with blue. Indeed, by standing on tiptoe I could catch a glimpse of some of the peaks of the still bluer and more distant mountain ranges in the north- **4** west, those true-blue coins from heaven's own mint, and also of some portion of the village. But in other directions,

1 A secret or illegal religious meeting.

2 As he tells us later, in "The Ponds," the lake is ½ mile long, 1¾ miles in circumference, and covers about 61½ acres.

3 Channing identifies this as Heywood's Peak, which is directly south of Walden Pond.

4 The Peterborough range in southern New Hampshire.

1 In the days before refrigeration, butter was submerged in the well on summer days to keep it from melting and becoming rancid.

2 The rivers of Concord (including the Sudbury) still overflow their banks each spring.

3 More commonly known as the scrub oak.

4 The grasslands of Asiatic Russia.

5 "Il n'y a d'heureux dans le monde que les êtres qui jouissent librement d'un vaste horizon." (M. A. Langlois, trans., *Harivansa, ou Histoire de la Famille de Hari* [Paris, 1834, I, 283]). Again, the English translation is most likely T's. Damodara is another name for Krishna.

6 The names of various stars and constellations.

even from this point, I could not see over or beyond the woods which surrounded me. It is well to have some water in your neighborhood, to give buoyancy to and float the earth. One value even of the smallest well is, that when you look into it you see that earth is not continent **1** but insular. This is as important as that it keeps butter cool. When I looked across the pond from this peak to- **2** ward the Sudbury meadows, which in time of flood I distinguished elevated perhaps by a mirage in their seething valley, like a coin in a basin, all the earth beyond the pond appeared like a thin crust insulated and floated even by this small sheet of intervening water, and I was reminded that this on which I dwelt was but *dry land.*

Though the view from my door was still more contracted, I did not feel crowded or confined in the least. There was **3** pasture enough for my imagination. The low shrub oak plateau to which the opposite shore arose stretched away **4** toward the prairies of the West and the steppes of Tartary, affording ample room for all the roving families of men. 'There are none happy in the world but beings who enjoy **5** freely a vast horizon' — said Damodara, when his herds required new and larger pastures.

Both place and time were changed, and I dwelt nearer to those parts of the universe and to those eras in history which had most attracted me. Where I lived was as far off as many a region viewed nightly by astronomers. We are wont to imagine rare and delectable places in some remote and more celestial corner of the system, behind the constellation of Cassiopeia's Chair, far from noise and disturbance. I discovered that my house actually had its site in such a withdrawn, but forever new and unprofaned, part of the universe. If it were worth the while to settle in those parts near to the Pleiades or the Hyades, to **6** Aldebaran or Altair, then I was really there, or at an equal

In one or two places on this side of the mountain, which . . . terminated in an abrupt precipice, I saw bogs or meadows four or six rods wide or more. (June 3, 1858)

remoteness from the life which I had left behind, dwindled and twinkling with as fine a ray to my nearest neighbor, and to be seen only in moonless nights by him. Such was that part of creation where I had squatted;

> 'There was a shepherd that did live,
>   And held his thoughts as high
> As were the mounts whereon his flocks
>   Did hourly feed him by.'

[1]

What should we think of the shepherd's life if his flocks always wandered to higher pastures than his thoughts?

Every morning was a cheerful invitation to make my life of equal simplicity, and I may say innocence, with Nature herself. I have been as sincere a worshipper of Aurora as the Greeks. I got up early and bathed in the [2] pond; that was a religious exercise, and one of the best things which I did. They say that characters were engraven on the bathing tub of King Tching-thang to this effect: 'Renew thyself completely each day; do it again, and again, and forever again.' I can understand that. Morning [3] brings back the heroic ages. I was as much affected by the faint hum of a mosquito making its invisible and unimaginable tour through my apartment at earliest dawn, when I was sitting with door and windows open, as I could be by any trumpet that ever sang of fame. It was Homer's re- [4, 5] quiem; itself an Iliad and Odyssey in the air, singing its own wrath and wanderings. There was something cosmi- [6] cal about it; a standing advertisement, till forbidden, of [7] the everlasting vigor and fertility of the world. The morning, which is the most memorable season of the day, is the awakening hour. Then there is least somnolence in us; and for an hour, at least, some part of us awakes which slumbers all the rest of the day and night. Little is to be expected of that day, if it can be called a day, to which we

1 The author of these lines is unknown, but they were set to music in 1611 by Robert Jones as the ninth song in *The Muses Gardin of Delights, or The Fift Booke of Ayres* (Leach; Schultz).

2 The Roman goddess of dawn.

3 Confucius, *The Great Learning*, "Commentary of the Philosopher Tsang," chap. I, p. 1.

4 "And the trumpet that sings of fame" (Felicia Hemans, "The Landing of the Pilgrims").

5 T was probably thinking of Homer's tribute to the mosquito in the *Iliad* (17.567–73) (Weissman).

6 The *Iliad* opens with a reference to Achilles' wrath, and the *Odyssey* to the wanderings of Odysseus.

7 "Till forbidden," abbreviated to "tf," was a printer's term for a standing advertisement.

1 The *Sanchya Karika,* translated by Henry Thomas Colebrooke and H. V. Wilson (Oxford, 1837, LXXII, Comment) (Stein, 1970, 304).

are not awakened by our Genius, but by the mechanical nudgings of some servitor, are not awakened by our own newly acquired force and aspirations from within, accompanied by the undulations of celestial music, instead of factory bells, and a fragrance filling the air — to a higher life than we fell asleep from; and thus the darkness bear its fruit, and prove itself to be good, no less than the light. That man who does not believe that each day contains an earlier, more sacred, and auroral hour than he has yet profaned, has despaired of life, and is pursuing a descending and darkening way. After a partial cessation of his sensuous life, the soul of man, or its organs rather, are reinvigorated each day, and his Genius tries again what noble life it can make. All memorable events, I should say, transpire in morning time and in a morning atmos-
1 phere. The Vedas say, 'All intelligences awake with the morning.' Poetry and art, and the fairest and most memorable of the actions of men, date from such an hour. All poets and heroes, like Memnon, are the children of Aurora, and emit their music at sunrise. To him whose elastic and vigorous thought keeps pace with the sun, the day is a perpetual morning. It matters not what the clocks say or the attitudes and labors of men. Morning is when I am awake and there is a dawn in me. Moral reform is the effort to throw off sleep. Why is it that men give so poor an account of their day if they have not been slumbering? They are not such poor calculators. If they had not been overcome with drowsiness, they would have performed something. The millions are awake enough for physical labor; but only one in a million is awake enough for effective intellectual exertion, only one in a hundred millions to a poetic or divine life. To be awake is to be alive. I have never yet met a man who was quite awake. How could I have looked him in the face?

We must learn to reawaken and keep ourselves awake, not by mechanical aids, but by an infinite expectation of the dawn, which does not forsake us in our soundest sleep. I know of no more encouraging fact than the unquestionable ability of man to elevate his life by a conscious endeavor. It is something to be able to paint a particular picture, or to carve a statue, and so to make a few objects beautiful; but it is far more glorious to carve and paint the very atmosphere and medium through which we look, which morally we can do. To affect the quality of the day, that is the highest of arts. Every man is tasked to make his life, even in its details, worthy of the contemplation of his most elevated and critical hour. If we refused, or rather used up, such paltry information as we get, the oracles would distinctly inform us how this might be done.

I went to the woods because I wished to live deliber- **1** ately, to front only the essential facts of life, and see if I could not learn what it had to teach, and not, when I came to die, discover that I had not lived. I did not wish to live what was not life, living is so dear; nor did I wish to practise resignation, unless it was quite necessary. I wanted to live deep and suck out all the marrow of life, to live so sturdily and Spartan-like as to put to rout all that was not life, to cut a broad swath and shave close, to drive life into a corner, and reduce it to its lowest terms, and, if it proved to be mean, why then to get the whole and genuine meanness of it, and publish its meanness to the world; or if it were sublime, to know it by experience, and be able to give a true account of it in my next excursion. **2** For most men, it appears to me, are in a strange uncertainty about it, whether it is of the devil or of God, and have *somewhat hastily* concluded that it is the chief end of man here to 'glorify God and enjoy him forever.'

Still we live meanly, like ants; though the fable tells us **3**

1 "He went to the woods . . . with no intention of abandoning society or of going primitive. Instead, by beginning from scratch, he would relive all human life and history and test the achievement of civilization by what he found, hoping, of course to demonstrate that choice was still possible and to reorient society by showing what had been lost on the way" (Paul, 306). For an exceptionally interesting stylistic analysis of T's paragraph, see Shwartz, 67–8.

2 T usually referred to his travel essays as "excursions."

3 Aeacus, son of Jupiter in Greek mythology, was king of Oenopia. When a pestilence destroyed his subjects, he entreated Jupiter to repopulate his kingdom by changing all the ants in an old oak tree into men.

1　The opening lines of *Iliad* III compare the Trojans to cranes fighting with pygmies.

2　"If we can get a garment to cover without / Our other garments are clout upon clout." From "New England Annoyances," with which T was familiar, in John Warner Barber's *Historical Collections . . . of . . . Massachusetts* (Worcester, 1841, 195).

3　If T really meant simplicity seriously, why did he repeat it twice? A number of critics have asked — I trust facetiously.

4　A method of determining the location of a ship by its last known position and its course and direction. Dead reckoning was used especially in bad weather or when stars could not be seen.

5　The German Confederation was constantly changing its borders, until national unification in 1871.

6　As we shall see in "The Pond in Winter," the practice of shipping ice from New England to warmer regions for refrigeration was just beginning.

7　The Morse telegraph had been invented in 1835, and by the 1840s was rapidly spreading through the nation.

8　Railroad trains, the first vehicles to reach such speeds, were just coming into the area, and in fact had reached Concord just the year before T moved out to Walden. While T admired the vigor of the railroads, he despaired of its devotion to material ends (Cronkhite).

that we were long ago changed into men; like pygmies we **1** fight with cranes; it is error upon error, and clout upon **2** clout, and our best virtue has for its occasion a superfluous and evitable wretchedness. Our life is frittered away by detail. An honest man has hardly need to count more than his ten fingers, or in extreme cases he may add his ten toes, and lump the rest. Simplicity, simplicity, sim-**3** plicity! I say, let your affairs be as two or three, and not a hundred or a thousand; instead of a million count half a dozen, and keep your accounts on your thumb-nail. In the midst of this chopping sea of civilized life, such are the clouds and storms and quicksands and thousand-and-one items to be allowed for, that a man has to live, if he would not founder and go to the bottom and not make his **4** port at all, by dead reckoning, and he must be a great calculator indeed who succeeds. Simplify, simplify. Instead of three meals a day, if it be necessary eat but one; instead of a hundred dishes, five; and reduce other things **5** in proportion. Our life is like a German Confederacy, made up of petty states, with its boundary forever fluctuating, so that even a German cannot tell you how it is bounded at any moment. The nation itself, with all its so-called internal improvements, which, by the way are all external and superficial, is just such an unwieldy and overgrown establishment, cluttered with furniture and tripped up by its own traps, ruined by luxury and heedless expense, by want of calculation and a worthy aim, as the million households in the land; and the only cure for it, as for them, is in a rigid economy, a stern and more than Spartan simplicity of life and elevation of purpose. It lives too fast. Men think that it is essential that the *Nation* have **6, 7** commerce, and export ice, and talk through a telegraph, **8** and ride thirty miles an hour, without a doubt, whether *they* do or not; but whether we should live like baboons or

like men, is a little uncertain. If we do not get out sleep- **1**
ers, and forge rails, and devote days and nights to the
work, but go to tinkering upon our *lives* to improve *them*,
who will build railroads? And if railroads are not built,
how shall we get to heaven in season? But if we stay at
home and mind our business, who will want railroads?
We do not ride on the railroad; it rides upon us. Did you
ever think what those sleepers are that underlie the rail- **2**
road? Each one is a man, an Irishman, or a Yankee man.
The rails are laid on them, and they are covered with
sand, and the cars run smoothly over them. They are **3**
sound sleepers, I assure you. And every few years a new
lot is laid down and run over; so that, if some have the
pleasure of riding on a rail, others have the misfortune to **4**
be ridden upon. And when they run over a man that
is walking in his sleep, a supernumerary sleeper in the
wrong position, and wake him up, they suddenly stop the
cars, and make a hue and cry about it, as if this were an
exception. I am glad to know that it takes a gang of men
for every five miles to keep the sleepers down and level in
their beds as it is, for this is a sign that they may sometime
get up again.

Why should we live with such hurry and waste of life?
We are determined to be starved before we are hungry.
Men say that a stitch in time saves nine, and so they take
a thousand stitches today to save nine tomorrow. As for **5**
work, we haven't any of any consequence. We have the
Saint Vitus' dance, and cannot possibly keep our heads **6**
still. If I should only give a few pulls at the parish bell-
rope, as for a fire, that is, without setting the bell, there is **7**
hardly a man on his farm in the outskirts of Concord,
notwithstanding that press of engagements which was his
excuse so many times this morning, nor a boy, nor a
woman, I might almost say, but would forsake all and

1 Ties upon which the railroad tracks were laid. Note the pun, which T makes much of later.

2 Another reference to Hawthorne's satire "The Celestial Railroad."

3 Moldenhauer (1964) discusses at length T's use of paradox here and throughout W.

4 Note the punning allusion to running a person out of town.

5 A proverb that can be traced at least as far back as Thomas Fuller's *Gnomologia* (1732).

6 A nervous disease characterized by involuntary motions of the limbs.

7 The parish bell was rung in one way (known as "setting the bell") to call people to church, and in another to call them to a fire.

1 In May 1844 T and his friend Edward Hoar accidentally set the woods on fire at Fairhaven Bay, destroying a number of acres of trees. T felt guilty about it for years. For his own account of the fire, see his *Journal* (II, 21–5). For a contemporary newspaper account, see *Thoreau Society Bulletin* 32 (1950).

2 The Washito (or Ouachita, as it is now called) flows from Arkansas into the Red River in Louisiana. According to Allen, when the residents of that area got into a fight, they would try to gouge out their opponents' eyes with a turn of the thumb.

3 "Dark unfathomed caves of ocean" (Thomas Gray, "Elegy in a Country Churchyard"). T is referring to Mammoth Cave in Kentucky, noted for its blind fish.

4 Actually T was a fairly regular letter writer; the new edition of his correspondence, being prepared for the Princeton edition of his writings, will fill three volumes.

5 England had established the so-called penny post in 1839. At the time of the publication of W, letter postage in the United States was three cents.

6 "A penny for your thought" can be traced at least as far back as John Heywood's *Proverbs* (1546).

7 A railroad formerly connecting Worcester and Albany, now a part of the Boston and Albany Railroad.

follow that sound, not mainly to save property from the flames, but, if we will confess the truth, much more to see it burn, since burn it must, and we, be it known, did not **1** set it on fire — or to see it put out, and have a hand in it, if that is done as handsomely; yes, even if it were the parish church itself. Hardly a man takes a half-hour's nap after dinner, but when he wakes he holds up his head and asks, 'What's the news?' as if the rest of mankind had stood his sentinels. Some give directions to be waked every half-hour, doubtless for no other purpose; and then, to pay for it, they tell what they have dreamed. After a night's sleep the news is as indispensable as the breakfast. 'Pray tell me anything new that has happened to a man anywhere on this globe' — and he reads it over his coffee and rolls, that a man has had his eyes gouged out this **2** morning on the Wachito River; never dreaming the while **3** that he lives in the dark unfathomed mammoth cave of this world, and has but the rudiment of an eye himself.

For my part, I could easily do without the post-office. I think that there are very few important communications made through it. To speak critically, I never received **4** more than one or two letters in my life — I wrote this some years ago — that were worth the postage. The penny-**5** post is, commonly, an institution through which you seri-**6** ously offer a man that penny for his thoughts which is so often safely offered in jest. And I am sure that I never read any memorable news in a newspaper. If we read of one man robbed, or murdered, or killed by accident, or one house burned, or one vessel wrecked, or one steamboat **7** blown up, or one cow run over on the Western Railroad, or one mad dog killed, or one lot of grasshoppers in the winter — we never need read of another. One is enough. If you are acquainted with the principle, what do you care for a myriad instances and applications? To a philosopher all *news*, as it is called, is gossip, and they who edit and read it are old women over their tea. Yet not a few are greedy after this gossip. There was such a rush, as I hear, the other day at one of the offices to learn the foreign news by the last arrival, that several large squares of plate glass belonging to the establishment were broken by the pressure — news which I seriously think a ready wit might write a twelvemonth, or twelve years, beforehand with sufficient accuracy. As for Spain, for instance, if you know 1 how to throw in Don Carlos and the Infanta, and Don Pedro and Seville and Granada, from time to time in the right proportions — they may have changed the names a little since I saw the papers — and serve up a bull-fight when other entertainments fail, it will be true to the letter, and give us as good an idea of the exact state or ruin of things in Spain as the most succinct and lucid reports under this head in the newspapers: and as for England, almost the last significant scrap of news from that quarter was the revolution of 1649; and if you have learned the 2 history of her crops for an average year, you never need attend to that thing again, unless your speculations are of a merely pecuniary character. If one may judge who rarely looks into the newspapers, nothing new does ever happen in foreign parts, a French revolution not excepted.

What news! how much more important to know what that is which was never old! 'Kieou-pe-u (great dignitary 3 of the state of Wei) sent a man to Khoung-tseu to know his news. Khoung-tseu caused the messenger to be seated near him, and questioned him in these terms: What is your master doing? The messenger answered with respect: My master desires to diminish the number of his faults, but he cannot accomplish it. The messenger being gone, 4 the philosopher remarked: What a worthy messenger! What a worthy messenger!' The preacher, instead of vex- 5

1 "The persons here named appear prominently in the annals of Spain during the 'thirties and early 'forties. During the first part of the period, King Ferdinand and his brother Don Carlos were struggling for power. With the death of the king in 1839, Maria Christina succeeded to the throne as regent. In 1841 she was temporarily replaced by General Espartero, also as regent; but in 1843 the thirteen-year-old Infanta was crowned Queen Isabella" (Crawford, 367).

2 When the Commonwealth, under Cromwell, abolished the British monarchy.

3 Shanley (1971, 397) has corrected the typographical error of the first edition of W, which read "Kieou-Pe-you."

4 Cannot accomplish it: In the first edition of W, this reads "cannot come to the end of them," but in his personal copy of W, T changed it to the present reading, which Shanley accepts.

5 *Confucian Analects,* XIV, xxvi, 2.

1 According to Genesis, the Sabbath is the last day of the week, rather than the first, as in the modern calendar. The Seventh-Day Adventists were particularly active in calling attention to this in T's day.

2 Possibly an allusion to Father Taylor of the Boston Seamen's Bethel, who was famous for the nautical allusions in his sermons. He was the model for the character of Father Mapple in Melville's *Moby-Dick*.

3 For a complex analysis of the remaining paragraphs of this chapter, see Balthazor.

4 The idea, which was common to the English romanticists and the American transcendentalists and most notably expressed in Wordsworth's "Intimations of Immortality," is that the child has a superior understanding of the universe which he loses as he grows older.

5 *The Sanchya Karika*, translated by Henry Thomas Colebrooke and H. V. Wilson (Oxford, 1837, 72) (Stein, 1970; Hoch, 1970).

ing the ears of drowsy farmers on their day of rest at the **1** end of the week — for Sunday is the fit conclusion of an ill-spent week, and not the fresh and brave beginning of a new one — with this one other draggle-tail of a sermon, should shout with thundering voice, 'Pause! Avast! Why **2** so seeming fast, but deadly slow?'

3 Shams and delusions are esteemed for soundest truths, while reality is fabulous. If men would steadily observe realities only, and not allow themselves to be deluded, life, to compare it with such things as we know, would be like a fairy tale and the Arabian Nights' Entertainments. If we respected only what is inevitable and has a right to be, music and poetry would resound along the streets. When we are unhurried and wise, we perceive that only great and worthy things have any permanent and absolute existence, that petty fears and petty pleasures are but the shadow of the reality. This is always exhilarating and sublime. By closing the eyes and slumbering, and consenting to be deceived by shows, men establish and confirm their daily life of routine and habit everywhere, which still is **4** built on purely illusory foundations. Children, who play life, discern its true law and relations more clearly than men, who fail to live it worthily, but who think that they are wiser by experience, that is, by failure. I have read in a **5** Hindoo book, that 'there was a king's son, who, being expelled in infancy from his native city, was brought up by a forester, and, growing up to maturity in that state, imagined himself to belong to the barbarous race with which he lived. One of his father's ministers having discovered him, revealed to him what he was, and the misconception of his character was removed, and he knew himself to be a prince. So soul,' continues the Hindoo philosopher, 'from the circumstances in which it is placed, mistakes its own character, until the truth is revealed to it by some holy teacher, and then it knows itself to be *Brahme*.' I perceive that we inhabitants of New England live this mean life that we do because our vision does not penetrate the surface of things. We think that that *is* which *appears* to be. If a man should walk through this town and see only the reality, where, think you, would the 'Mill-dam' go to? If he should give us an account of the realities he beheld there, we should not recognize the place in his description. Look at a meeting-house, or a court-house, or a jail, or a shop, or a dwelling-house, and say what that thing really is before a true gaze, and they would all go to pieces in your account of them. Men esteem truth remote, in the outskirts of the system, behind the farthest star, before Adam and after the last man. In eternity there is indeed something true and sublime. But all these times and places and occasions are now and here. God himself culminates in the present moment, and will never be more divine in the lapse of all the ages. And we are enabled to apprehend at all what is sublime and noble only by the perpetual instilling and drenching of the reality that surrounds us. The universe constantly and obediently answers to our conceptions; whether we travel fast or slow, the track is laid for us. Let us spend our lives in conceiving then. The poet or the artist never yet had so fair and noble a design but some of his posterity at least could accomplish it.

Let us spend one day as deliberately as Nature, and not be thrown off the track by every nutshell and mosquito's **2** wing that falls on the rails. Let us rise early and fast, or break fast, gently and without perturbation; let company come and let company go, let the bells ring and the children cry — determined to make a day of it. Why should we knock under and go with the stream? Let us not be upset and overwhelmed in that terrible rapid and whirl- **3**

1 Still the name of the business center of Concord, so called because it was originally built on the dam of a mill pond, long since filled in.

2 The trains then spreading their tracks over New England were easily derailed.

3 An allusion to the Scylla and Charybdis of Ulysses' journey, recorded in the *Odyssey*.

1 Meridian: noontime.

2 So that he might hear the song of the Sirens yet not succumb to the fatal desire to go to them, Ulysses had himself tied to the mast of his ship and had his sailors' ears filled with wax.

3 A point of support.

4 "Because of the anxiety occasioned by the rise of the river the kings have constructed a Nilometer at Memphis, where those who are charged with the administration of it accurately measure the rise and despatch messages to the cities" (Diodorus 1.36.10).

5 A scimitar, a sword with a curved blade.

1 pool called a dinner, situated in the meridian shallows. Weather this danger and you are safe, for the rest of the way is down hill. With unrelaxed nerves, with morning

2 vigor, sail by it, looking another way, tied to the mast like Ulysses. If the engine whistles, let it whistle till it is hoarse for its pains. If the bell rings, why should we run? We will consider what kind of music they are like. Let us settle ourselves, and work and wedge our feet downward through the mud and slush of opinion, and prejudice, and tradition, and delusion, and appearance, that alluvion which covers the globe, through Paris and London, through New York and Boston and Concord, through Church and State, through poetry and philosophy and religion, till we come to a hard bottom and rocks in place, which we can call *reality*, and say, This is, and no mistake;

3 and then begin, having a *point d'appui*, below freshet and frost and fire, a place where you might found a wall or a state, or set a lamp-post safely, or perhaps a gauge, not a

4 Nilometer, but a Realometer, that future ages might know how deep a freshet of shams and appearances had gathered from time to time. If you stand right fronting and face to face to a fact, you will see the sun glimmer on both

5 its surfaces, as if it were a cimeter, and feel its sweet edge dividing you through the heart and marrow, and so you will happily conclude your mortal career. Be it life or death, we crave only reality. If we are really dying, let us hear the rattle in our throats and feel cold in the extremities; if we are alive, let us go about our business.

Time is but the stream I go a-fishing in. I drink at it; but while I drink I see the sandy bottom and detect how shallow it is. Its thin current slides away, but eternity remains. I would drink deeper; fish in the sky, whose bottom is pebbly with stars. I cannot count one. I know not the first letter of the alphabet. I have always been

regretting that I was not as wise as the day I was born. The **1**
intellect is a cleaver; it discerns and rifts its way into the
secret of things. I do not wish to be any more busy with
my hands than is necessary. My head is hands and feet. I
feel all my best faculties concentrated in it. My instinct
tells me that my head is an organ for burrowing, as some
creatures use their snout and fore paws, and with it I
would mine and burrow my way through these hills. I
think that the richest vein is somewhere hereabouts; so by
the divining-rod and thin rising vapors I judge; and here I **2**
will begin to mine.

1 Another allusion to the romantic belief in
the superior wisdom of the child.

2 According to folklore, a stick, usually of
willow, that when held in a certain way would,
of its own volition, point to the nearest underground source of water (Noverr).

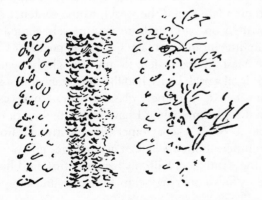

Looking north from Hubbard's Bridge about 4 P.M., the wind
being southeasterly, I am struck by the varied lights of the river. The
wind, which is a considerable breeze, strikes the water by a very
irregular serrated edge about mid-channel, and then abruptly leaves
it on a distinct and regular meandering line, about eight feet from
the outer edge of the pads on the west side. The rippled portion of
the river is blue, the rest smooth, silvery. Thus to my eye the river is
divided into five portions. (August 8, 1858)

READING

1 For an extensive analysis of this chapter, see Knott.

2 To lift the veil of Isis, the principal goddess of ancient Egypt, is to pierce the heart of a great mystery. In the Hindu religion, the successful unveiling of Maya, the cosmic illusion, results in a direct knowledge of God and the secret of creation.

3 T is exaggerating here, for Albert Stacy ran a bookstore with a circulating library (that is, book rental) in Concord for many years.

4 "Etant assis, parcourir la région du monde spirituel: j'ai eu cet avantage dans les livres. Être enivré par une seule coupe de vin: j'ai éprouvé ce plaisir lorsque j'ai bu la liqueur des doctrines ésotériques" (M. Garcin de Tassy, *Histoire de la Littérature Hindoui*, Paris, 1839, I, 331). The translation from the French is undoubtedly T's own. Mast was a Hindu poet of the eighteenth century.

5 For the influence of Homer upon T, particularly in the writing of W, see Seybold.

WITH A LITTLE more deliberation in the choice of their pursuits, all men would perhaps become essentially students and observers, for certainly their nature and destiny are interesting to all alike. In accumulating property for ourselves or our posterity, in founding a family or a state, or acquiring fame even, we are mortal; but in dealing with truth we are immortal, and need fear no change nor accident. The oldest Egyptian or Hindoo philosopher raised a corner of the veil from the statue of the divinity; and still the trembling robe remains raised, and I gaze upon as fresh a glory as he did, since it was I in him that was then so bold, and it is he in me that now reviews the vision. No dust has settled on that robe; no time has elapsed since that divinity was revealed. That time which we really improve, or which is improvable, is neither past, present, nor future.

My residence was more favorable, not only to thought, but to serious reading, than a university; and though I was beyond the range of the ordinary circulating library, I had more than ever come within the influence of those books which circulate round the world, whose sentences were first written on bark, and are now merely copied from time to time on to linen paper. Says the poet Mîr Camar Uddin Mast, 'Being seated, to run through the region of the spiritual world; I have had this advantage in books. To be intoxicated by a single glass of wine; I have experienced this pleasure when I have drunk the liquor of the esoteric doctrines.' I kept Homer's Iliad on my table through the summer, though I looked at his page only now and then. Incessant labor with my hands, at first, for I had my house to finish and my beans to hoe at the same time, made more study impossible. Yet I sustained myself by the prospect of such reading in future. I read one or two shallow books of travel in the intervals of my work, till that **1** employment made me ashamed of myself, and I asked where it was then that *I* lived.

The student may read Homer or Aeschylus in the Greek **2, 3** without danger of dissipation or luxuriousness, for it implies that he in some measure emulate their heroes, and consecrate morning hours to their pages. The heroic books, even if printed in the character of our mother tongue, will always be in a language dead to degenerate times; and we must laboriously seek the meaning of each word and line, conjecturing a larger sense than common use permits out of what wisdom and valor and generosity we have. The modern cheap and fertile press, with all its translations, has done little to bring us nearer to the heroic writers of antiquity. They seem as solitary, and the letter in which they are printed as rare and curious, as ever. It is worth the expense of youthful days and costly hours, if you learn only some words of an ancient language, which are raised out of the trivialness of the street, to be perpetual suggestions and provocations. It is not in vain that the farmer remembers and repeats the few Latin words which he has heard. Men sometimes speak as if the study of the classics would at length make way for more modern and practical studies; but the adventurous student will always study classics, in whatever language they may be written and however ancient they may be. For what are the classics but the noblest recorded thoughts of man? They are the only oracles which are not decayed, and there are such answers to the most modern inquiry in them as Delphi and Dodona never gave. We might as **4** well omit to study Nature because she is old. To read well, that is, to read true books in a true spirit, is a noble

1 T was actually an inveterate reader of travel books, averaging about one a month (Christie).

2 Greek dramatist (525–456 B.C.) whose *Prometheus Bound* and *Seven Against Thebes* T had translated (Rossi).

3 T had perhaps a better knowledge of Greek and Latin than any other transcendentalist, and translated a number of classical works into modern English.

4 The two most famous oracles of ancient Greece.

1 "Except a man be born again, he cannot see the kingdom of God" (John 3:3).

2 Some of the ancient classics have survived only because churchmen of the Middle Ages, not appreciating their value, used the manuscripts as scrap paper for their own notes.

exercise, and one that will task the reader more than any exercise which the customs of the day esteem. It requires a training such as the athletes underwent, the steady intention almost of the whole life to this object. Books must be read as deliberately and reservedly as they were written. It is not enough even to be able to speak the language of that nation by which they are written, for there is a memorable interval between the spoken and the written language, the language heard and the language read. The one is commonly transitory, a sound, a tongue, a dialect merely, almost brutish, and we learn it unconsciously, like the brutes, of our mothers. The other is the maturity and experience of that; if that is our mother tongue, this is our father tongue, a reserved and select expression, too significant to be heard by the ear, which we must be born again in order to speak. The crowds of men who merely *spoke* the Greek and Latin tongues in the Middle Ages were not entitled by the accident of birth to *read* the works of genius written in those languages; for these were not written in that Greek or Latin which they knew, but in the select language of literature. They had not learned the nobler dialects of Greece and Rome, but the very materials on which they were written were waste paper to them, and they prized instead a cheap contemporary literature. But when the several nations of Europe had acquired distinct though rude written languages of their own, sufficient for the purposes of their rising literatures, then first learning revived, and scholars were enabled to discern from that remoteness the treasures of antiquity. What the Roman and Grecian multitude could not *hear*, after the lapse of ages a few scholars *read*, and a few scholars only are still reading it.

However much we may admire the orator's occasional bursts of eloquence, the noblest written words are com-

Why, then, make so great ado about the Roman and the Greek, and neglect the Indian? (October 22, 1857)

monly as far behind or above the fleeting spoken language as the firmament with its stars is behind the clouds. *There* are the stars, and they who can may read them. The astronomers forever comment on and observe them. They are not exhalations like our daily colloquies and vaporous breath. What is called eloquence in the forum is commonly found to be rhetoric in the study. The orator yields **1** to the inspiration of a transient occasion, and speaks to the mob before him, to those who can *hear* him; but the writer, whose more equable life is his occasion, and who would be distracted by the event and the crowd which inspire the orator, speaks to the intellect and heart of mankind, to all in any age who can *understand* him.

No wonder that Alexander carried the Iliad with him **2** on his expeditions in a precious casket. A written word is the choicest of relics. It is something at once more intimate with us and more universal than any other work of art. It is the work of art nearest to life itself. It may be translated into every language, and not only be read but actually breathed from all human lips; — not be represented on canvas or in marble only, but be carved out of the breath of life itself. The symbol of an ancient man's thought becomes a modern man's speech. Two thousand summers have imparted to the monuments of Grecian literature, as to her marbles, only a maturer golden and autumnal tint, for they have carried their own serene and celestial atmosphere into all lands to protect them against the corrosion of time. Books are the treasured wealth of the world and the fit inheritance of generations and nations. Books, the oldest and the best, stand naturally and rightfully on the shelves of every cottage. They have no cause of their own to plead, but while they enlighten and sustain the reader his common sense will not refuse them. Their authors are a natural and irresistible aristocracy in

1 T was not always a successful lecturer, and after a failure was wont to deride the value of the lecture platform.

2 This fact is recorded in Plutarch's life of Alexander.

1   It need hardly be said that T did not intend us to take this statement literally. He means simply that no translation has ever succeeded in carrying over fully the spirit of the original.

2   The Vatican in Rome houses one of the greatest libraries of ancient classics in the world.

3   The Vedas are the entire sacred scriptures of the Hindus; the Zendavesta, the scripture of Zoroastrianism. T was always ready to point out that the bibles of other religions meant as much to him as did the Christian one.

every society, and, more than kings or emperors, exert an influence on mankind. When the illiterate and perhaps scornful trader has earned by enterprise and industry his coveted leisure and independence, and is admitted to the circles of wealth and fashion, he turns inevitably at last to those still higher but yet inaccessible circles of intellect and genius, and is sensible only of the imperfection of his culture and the vanity and insufficiency of all his riches, and further proves his good sense by the pains which he takes to secure for his children that intellectual culture whose want he so keenly feels; and thus it is that he becomes the founder of a family.

Those who have not learned to read the ancient classics in the language in which they were written must have a very imperfect knowledge of the history of the human race; for it is remarkable that no transcript of them has ever been made into any modern tongue, unless our civilization itself may be regarded as such a transcript. Homer has never yet been printed in English, nor Aeschylus, nor Virgil even — works as refined, as solidly done, and as beautiful almost as the morning itself; for later writers, say what we will of their genius, have rarely, if ever, equalled the elaborate beauty and finish and the lifelong and heroic literary labors of the ancients. They only talk of forgetting them who never knew them. It will be soon enough to forget them when we have the learning and the genius which will enable us to attend to and appreciate them. That age will be rich indeed when those relics which we call Classics, and the still older and more than classic but even less known Scriptures of the nations, shall have still further accumulated, when the Vaticans shall be filled with Vedas and Zendavestas and Bibles, with Homers and Dantes and Shakespeares, and all the centuries to come shall have successively deposited their trophies in the

forum of the world. By such a pile we may hope to scale **1**
heaven at last.

The works of the great poets have never yet been read
by mankind, for only great poets can read them. They
have only been read as the multitude read the stars, at
most astrologically, not astronomically. Most men have
learned to read to serve a paltry convenience, as they have
learned to cipher in order to keep accounts and not be
cheated in trade; but of reading as a noble intellectual
exercise they know little or nothing; yet this only is reading, in a high sense, not that which lulls us as a luxury and
suffers the nobler faculties to sleep the while, but what we
have to stand on tip-toe to read and devote our most alert
and wakeful hours to.

I think that having learned our letters we should read
the best that is in literature, and not be forever repeating
our a-b-abs, and words of one syllable, in the fourth or **2**
fifth classes, sitting on the lowest and foremost form all **3**
our lives. Most men are satisfied if they read or hear read,
and perchance have been convicted by the wisdom of
one good book, the Bible, and for the rest of their lives
vegetate and dissipate their faculties in what is called easy
reading. There is a work in several volumes in our Circulating Library entitled 'Little Reading,' which I thought **4**
referred to a town of that name which I had not been to. **5**
There are those who, like cormorants and ostriches, can **6**
digest all sorts of this, even after the fullest dinner of meats
and vegetables, for they suffer nothing to be wasted. If
others are the machines to provide this provender, they
are the machines to read it. They read the nine thou-
sandth tale about Zebulon and Sophronia, and how they **7**
loved as none had ever loved before, and neither did the
course of their true love run smooth — at any rate, how it **8**
did run and stumble, and get up again and go on! how

1 An allusion to the building of the Tower
of Babel.

2 This is the first part of a mnemonic
device once used in country schools to teach
children the alphabet.

3 In one-room country schools, the youngest children sat on the lowest benches in the
front row.

4 *Little Reading* (New York, 1827) (Gross,
1988).

5 Reading, Massachusetts, north of Boston.

6 An old bit of folklore that T may have become familiar with through Sir Thomas
Browne's discussion of "That the Ostrich Di-
gesteth Iron," in *Pseudodoxia Epidemica*, book
III, chap. 22.

7 Apparently an allusion to typical characters in the sentimental novels of T's day.

8 "The course of true love never did run
smooth" (*Midsummer Night's Dream*, I, i).

1 Perhaps a reference to a well-known Baron Munchausen tale in which, during a great snowstorm, he ties his horse to a post, only to discover when the snow melts that he has tied it to the top of a church steeple.

2 Perhaps a jibe at James Fenimore Cooper's *The Wept of the Wish-ton-Wish,* or possibly taken from the *Arabian Nights* (Leisy).

3 In his essay "Walking" (V, 236), T speaks of "the child's rigmarole, Iery wiery ichery van, tittle-tol-tan."

4 In the mid-nineteenth century long novels often first appeared in monthly installments. Dickens is the outstanding example.

5 Again, a reference to the fact that in country schools small children sat on low benches in the front of the room.

6 Just at the time T was at Walden, Dr. Sylvester Graham, the inventor of the graham cracker, was leading a campaign to change people's diets by substituting whole grain flours for the more highly milled products. Many of T's friends among the transcendentalists were followers of Graham.

1 some poor unfortunate got up on to a steeple, who had better never have gone up as far as the belfry; and then, having needlessly got him up there, the happy novelist rings the bell for all the world to come together and hear, O dear! how he did get down again! For my part, I think that they had better metamorphose all such aspiring heroes of universal noveldom into man weather-cocks, as they used to put heroes among the constellations, and let them swing round there till they are rusty, and not come down at all to bother honest men with their pranks. The next time the novelist rings the bell I will not stir though the meeting-house burn down. 'The Skip of the Tip-Toe-

2 Hop, a Romance of the Middle Ages, by the celebrated

3 author of "Tittle-Tol-Tan," to appear in monthly parts; a

4 great rush; don't all come together.' All this they read with saucer eyes, and erect and primitive curiosity, and with unwearied gizzard, whose corrugations even yet need no

5 sharpening, just as some little four-year-old bencher his two-cent gilt-covered edition of Cinderella — without any improvement, that I can see, in the pronunciation, or accent, or emphasis, or any more skill in extracting or inserting the moral. The result is dulness of sight, a stagnation of the vital circulations, and a general deliquium and sloughing off of all the intellectual faculties. This sort of gingerbread is baked daily and more sedulously than

6 pure wheat or rye-and-Indian in almost every oven, and finds a surer market.

The best books are not read even by those who are called good readers. What does our Concord culture amount to? There is in this town, with a very few exceptions, no taste for the best or for very good books even in English literature, whose words all can read and spell. Even the college-bred and so-called liberally educated men here and elsewhere have really little or no acquaintance with the English classics; and as for the recorded wisdom of mankind, the ancient classics and Bibles, which are accessible to all who will know of them, there are the feeblest efforts anywhere made to become acquainted with them. I know a woodchopper, of middle age, who takes a French **1** paper, not for news as he says, for he is above that, but to 'keep himself in practice,' he being a Canadian by birth; and when I ask him what he considers the best thing he can do in this world, he says, beside this, to keep up and add to his English. This is about as much as the college-bred generally do or aspire to do, and they take an English paper for the purpose. One who has just come from reading perhaps one of the best English books will find how many with whom he can converse about it? Or suppose he comes from reading a Greek or Latin classic in the original, whose praises are familiar even to the so-called illiterate; he will find nobody at all to speak to, but must keep silence about it. Indeed, there is hardly the professor in our colleges, who, if he has mastered the difficulties of the language, has proportionally mastered the difficulties of the wit and poetry of a Greek poet, and has any sympathy to impart to the alert and heroic reader; and as for the sacred Scriptures, or Bibles of mankind, who in this town can tell me even their titles? Most men do not know that any nation but the Hebrews have had a scripture. A man, any man, will go considerably out of his way to pick up a silver dollar; but here are golden words, which the wisest men of antiquity have uttered, and whose worth the wise of every succeeding age have assured us of; — and yet we learn to read only as far as Easy Reading, the primers and class-books, and when we **2, 3** leave school, the 'Little Reading,' and story-books, which

1 Allen (383) identifies this man as Alex Therien, who is described at greater length in the "Visitors" chapter. Therien is called middle-aged here, but T later describes him as being twenty-eight years old. His actual age was thirty-four.

2 T may have been thinking of *Easy Reading for Little Folks* (Boston, n.d.).

3 School textbooks for younger children were known as primers, and those for older children as classbooks.

1   "Tit" means "little," as in the bird name
"titlark."

2   And for many a man, W has been that
book!

are for boys and beginners; and our reading, our conversation and thinking, are all on a very low level, worthy only of pygmies and manikins.

I aspire to be acquainted with wiser men than this our Concord soil has produced, whose names are hardly known here. Or shall I hear the name of Plato and never read his book? As if Plato were my townsman and I never saw him — my next neighbor and I never heard him speak or attended to the wisdom of his words. But how actually is it? His Dialogues, which contain what was immortal in him, lie on the next shelf, and yet I never read them. We are underbred and low-lived and illiterate; and in this respect I confess I do not make any very broad distinction between the illiterateness of my townsman who cannot read at all and the illiterateness of him who has learned to read only what is for children and feeble intellects. We should be as good as the worthies of antiquity, but partly by first knowing how good they were. We are a race of tit-men, and soar but little higher in our intellectual flights than the columns of the daily paper.

It is not all books that are as dull as their readers. There are probably words addressed to our condition exactly, which, if we could really hear and understand, would be more salutary than the morning or the spring to our lives, and possibly put a new aspect on the face of things for us. How many a man has dated a new era in his life from the reading of a book! The book exists for us, perchance, which will explain our miracles and reveal new ones. The at present unutterable things we may find somewhere uttered. These same questions that disturb and puzzle and confound us have in their turn occurred to all the wise men; not one has been omitted; and each has answered them, according to his ability, by his words and his life. Moreover, with wisdom we shall learn liberality. The solitary hired man on a farm in the outskirts of Concord, who has had his second birth and peculiar religious expe- **1** rience, and is driven as he believes into silent gravity and exclusiveness by his faith, may think it is not true; but Zoroaster, thousands of years ago, travelled the same road **2** and had the same experience; but he, being wise, knew it to be universal, and treated his neighbors accordingly, and is even said to have invented and established worship among men. Let him humbly commune with Zoroaster then, and through the liberalizing influence of all the worthies, with Jesus Christ himself, and let 'our church' go by the board. **3**

We boast that we belong to the Nineteenth Century and are making the most rapid strides of any nation. But consider how little this village does for its own culture. I do not wish to flatter my townsmen, nor to be flattered by them, for that will not advance either of us. We need to be provoked — goaded like oxen, as we are, into a trot. We have a comparatively decent system of common schools, schools for infants only; but excepting the half-starved Lyceum in the winter, and latterly the puny beginning of **4** a library suggested by the State, no school for ourselves. **5** We spend more on almost any article of bodily aliment or ailment than on our mental aliment. It is time that we had uncommon schools, that we did not leave off our **6** education when we begin to be men and women. It is time that villages were universities, and their elder inhabitants the fellows of universities, with leisure — if they are, indeed, so well off — to pursue liberal studies the rest of their lives. Shall the world be confined to one Paris or one Oxford forever? Cannot students be boarded here and get a liberal education under the skies of Concord? Can we not hire some Abélard to lecture to us? Alas! what **7** with foddering the cattle and tending the store, we are

1 The religious conversion of a person is often spoken of as his second birth.

2 A Persian religious teacher of about the year 1000 B.C.

3 To fall overboard — that is, permit to be lost.

4 The lyceum was a common educational institution in the small towns of New England in the mid-nineteenth century. Its main purpose was to sponsor a series of lectures each winter. T was a frequent lecturer at such lyceums and was for a time one of the curators of the Concord Lyceum (Hoeltje; Harding, 1951).

5 On May 24, 1851, the Commonwealth of Massachusetts authorized and encouraged its towns to establish public libraries but did little else to assist them.

6 T may have derived some of these ideas from his friend Elizabeth Peabody, the Boston publisher (Joseph Jones, "Universities").

7 A French teacher and theologian (1079–1142).

kept from school too long, and our education is sadly neglected. In this country, the village should in some respects take the place of the nobleman of Europe. It should be the patron of the fine arts. It is rich enough. It wants only the magnanimity and refinement. It can spend money enough on such things as farmers and traders value, but it is thought Utopian to propose spending money for things which more intelligent men know to be of far more worth. This town has spent seventeen thousand 1 dollars on a town-house, thank fortune or politics, but probably it will not spend so much on living wit, the true meat to put into that shell, in a hundred years. The one 2 hundred and twenty-five dollars annually subscribed for a Lyceum in the winter is better spent than any other equal sum raised in the town. If we live in the Nineteenth Century, why should we not enjoy the advantages which the Nineteenth Century offers? Why should our life be in any respect provincial? If we will read newspapers, why not skip the gossip of Boston and take the best newspaper in the world at once? — not be sucking the pap of 'neu- 3 tral family' papers, or browsing 'Olive-Branches' here in 4 New England. Let the reports of all the learned societies come to us, and we will see if they know anything. Why 5 should we leave it to Harper & Brothers and Redding & 6 Co. to select our reading? As the nobleman of cultivated taste surrounds himself with whatever conduces to his culture — genius — learning — wit — books — paintings — statuary — music — philosophical instruments, and the like; so let the village do — not stop short at a pedagogue, 7 a parson, a sexton, a parish library, and three selectmen, 8 because our Pilgrim forefathers got through a cold winter once on a bleak rock with these. To act collectively is according to the spirit of our institutions; and I am confident that, as our circumstances are more flourishing, our

1   Concord built its present town offices on the square in 1851 (Wheeler, 171).

2   T was curator of the Concord Lyceum for the year 1842–43. With a budget of $109.20, he rented a lecture hall, paid for its lighting and heating, and invited twenty-three speakers, including such men as Emerson, Horace Greeley, Theodore Parker, and Wendell Phillips. Yet he was able to turn $9.20 back to the treasury at the end of the year (Sanborn, *Recollections,* 569–70).

3   Periodicals that did not take sides on political issues but provided a variety of reading matter for every member of the family.

4   The *Olive Branch* was published weekly in Boston, under the editorship of the Reverend Thomas F. Norris.

5   Harper & Brothers was a New York City book publisher. Redding & Co., booksellers and publishers, had offices at 8 State Street, Boston.

6   T is playing on the fact that Harper & Brothers published a series of books entitled "Select Library of Valuable Standard Literature." T preferred to do his own selecting.

7   The elected governing officials in most New England towns, including Concord, were a small group known as selectmen.

8   The founders of Plymouth, the earliest colony in Massachusetts.

means are greater than the nobleman's. New England can hire all the wise men in the world to come and teach her, and board them round the while, and not be provin- **1** cial at all. That is the *uncommon* school we want. Instead of noblemen, let us have noble villages of men. If it is necessary, omit one bridge over the river, go round a little there, and throw one arch at least over the darker gulf of ignorance which surrounds us.

1 In lieu of part of their salary, New England teachers were often given board and room by their students' parents.

As I stand on the sand-bank below the Assabet stone bridge and look up through the arch, the river makes a pretty picture. (May 25, 1857)

1 Lambden discusses the artistry of this chapter. Stein (1972) analyzes this chapter from the standpoint of yoga.

2 Notice how the opening paragraph carries over the idea from the preceding chapter. This was one of the many devices T used to unify the seemingly unrelated essays of the book. Note also that the sounds described in the chapter follow a chronological order starting with morning, going on through afternoon, evening, night, and ending up with morning once more. Just as the whole book epitomizes the year, so this chapter epitomizes the day, and both end on the theme of renewal — the book on the renewal of spring, and the chapter on the renewal of dawn.

3 Although some suggest this refers to a camera shutter, mechanical shutters did not come into use until after the first publication of W. T is more likely referring to window shutters, which were used in New England to keep the sun off parlor rugs.

4 Seer: a favorite term among transcendentalists for a person with extraordinary perceptions.

5 This paragraph is considered by many to be one of the outstanding expressions of the mystical experience in literature. For an analysis of T's use of sound and silence in achieving the mystical experience, see Paul (1949).

6 T took his daily bath in the cove nearest his cabin.

7 The road from Concord to Lincoln was then the closest highway to T's cabin. Route 2, the road just north of the pond, was not constructed until well into the twentieth century.

8 Corn is among the fastest growing of the common garden vegetables.

1

SOUNDS

2 BUT WHILE WE are confined to books, though the most select and classic, and read only particular written languages, which are themselves but dialects and provincial, we are in danger of forgetting the language which all things and events speak without metaphor, which alone is copious and standard. Much is published, but little **3** printed. The rays which stream through the shutter will be no longer remembered when the shutter is wholly removed. No method nor discipline can supersede the necessity of being forever on the alert. What is a course of history or philosophy, or poetry, no matter how well selected, or the best society, or the most admirable routine of life, compared with the discipline of looking always at what is to be seen? Will you be a reader, a student merely, **4** or a seer? Read your fate, see what is before you, and walk on into futurity.

5 I did not read books the first summer; I hoed beans. Nay, I often did better than this. There were times when I could not afford to sacrifice the bloom of the present moment to any work, whether of the head or hands. I love a broad margin to my life. Sometimes, in a summer morn-**6** ing, having taken my accustomed bath, I sat in my sunny doorway from sunrise till noon, rapt in a revery, amidst the pines and hickories and sumachs, in undisturbed solitude and stillness, while the birds sang around or flitted noiseless through the house, until by the sun falling in at my west window, or the noise of some traveller's wagon **7** on the distant highway, I was reminded of the lapse of **8** time. I grew in those seasons like corn in the night, and they were far better than any work of the hands would have been. They were not time subtracted from my life, but so much over and above my usual allowance. I realized what the Orientals mean by contemplation and the forsaking of works. For the most part, I minded not how the hours went. The day advanced as if to light some work of mine; it was morning, and lo, now it is evening, and nothing memorable is accomplished. Instead of singing like the birds, I silently smiled at my incessant good fortune. As the sparrow had its trill, sitting on the hickory before my door, so had I my chuckle or suppressed warble which he might hear out of my nest. My days were not days of the week, bearing the stamp of any heathen deity, 1 nor were they minced into hours and fretted by the ticking of a clock; for I lived like the Puri Indians, of whom it 2 is said that 'for yesterday, today, and tomorrow they have only one word, and they express the variety of meaning by pointing backward for yesterday, forward for tomorrow, and overhead for the passing day.' This was sheer idleness to my fellow-townsmen, no doubt; but if the birds and flowers had tried me by their standard, I should not have been found wanting. A man must find his occasions in 3 himself, it is true. The natural day is very calm, and will hardly reprove his indolence.

I had this advantage, at least, in my mode of life, over those who were obliged to look abroad for amusement, to society and the theatre, that my life itself was become my amusement and never ceased to be novel. It was a drama of many scenes and without an end. If we were always, indeed, getting our living, and regulating our lives according to the last and best mode we had learned, we should never be troubled with ennui. Follow your genius closely enough, and it will not fail to show you a fresh prospect every hour. Housework was a pleasant pastime. When my floor was dirty, I rose early, and, setting all my furniture out of doors on the grass, bed and bedstead

1 The days of our week are named after heathen deities — Thor, Woden, etc.

2 Ida Pfeiffer, *A Lady's Voyage Round the World* (New York, 1852, 36). The Puri Indians are natives of eastern Brazil.

3 "Thou art weighed in the balances, and art found wanting" (Daniel 5:27).

1 When T went to Staten Island in 1843 to tutor Emerson's nephews, he was given an inkstand by his friend and neighbor Elizabeth Hoar. He kept it throughout his life, and it is now on exhibit in the Concord Museum.

2 A common weed of the genus *Gnaphalium.*

3 A rod, a surveyor's measure, is 16½ feet. Surprisingly, since T was a professional surveyor, he greatly underestimated the distance, which was 204 feet, or more than twelve rods (Robbins, 9–10).

4 Compare this with T's description of the time he heard a tree fall at night in the Maine wilderness (*Maine Woods,* 103), which he thought one of the most impressive sounds he had ever heard. T emphasizes sounds and onomatopoeia throughout this chapter.

I find under one small pitch pine tree a heap of the cones which have been stripped of their scales, evidently by the red squirrels, the last winter and fall, they having sat upon some dead limbs above. (April 2, 1859)

making but one budget, dashed water on the floor, and sprinkled white sand from the pond on it, and then with a broom scrubbed it clean and white; and by the time the villagers had broken their fast the morning sun had dried my house sufficiently to allow me to move in again, and my meditations were almost uninterrupted. It was pleasant to see my whole household effects out on the grass, making a little pile like a gypsy's pack, and my three-legged table, from which I did not remove the books and **1** pen and ink, standing amid the pines and hickories. They seemed glad to get out themselves, and as if unwilling to be brought in. I was sometimes tempted to stretch an awning over them and take my seat there. It was worth the while to see the sun shine on these things, and hear the free wind blow on them; so much more interesting most familiar objects look out of doors than in the house. A **2** bird sits on the next bough, life-everlasting grows under the table, and blackberry vines run round its legs; pine cones, chestnut burs, and strawberry leaves are strewn about. It looked as if this was the way these forms came to be transferred to our furniture, to tables, chairs, and bedsteads — because they once stood in their midst.

My house was on the side of a hill, immediately on the edge of the larger wood, in the midst of a young forest of **3** pitch pines and hickories, and half a dozen rods from the pond, to which a narrow footpath led down the hill. In my front yard grew the strawberry, blackberry, and life-everlasting, johnswort and goldenrod, shrub oaks and sand cherry, blueberry and groundnut. Near the end of May, the sand cherry (*Cerasus pumila*)adorned the sides of the path with its delicate flowers arranged in umbels cylindrically about its short stems, which last, in the fall, weighed **4** down with goodsized and handsome cherries, fell over in wreaths like rays on every side. I tasted them out of com-

pliment to Nature, though they were scarcely palatable. The sumach (*Rhus glabra*) grew luxuriantly about the house, pushing up through the embankment which I had made, and growing five or six feet the first season. Its broad pinnate tropical leaf was pleasant though strange to look on. The large buds, suddenly pushing out late in the spring from dry sticks which had seemed to be dead, developed themselves as by magic into graceful green and tender boughs, an inch in diameter; and sometimes, as I sat at my window, so heedlessly did they grow and tax their weak joints, I heard a fresh and tender bough suddenly fall like a fan to the ground, when there was not a breath of air stirring, broken off by its own weight. In August, the large masses of berries, which, when in flower, had attracted many wild bees, gradually assumed their bright velvety crimson hue, and by their weight again bent down and broke the tender limbs.

As I sit at my window this summer afternoon, hawks are **1** circling about my clearing; the tantivy of wild pigeons, **2, 3** flying by twos and threes athwart my view, or perching restless on the white pine boughs behind my house, gives a voice to the air; a fish hawk dimples the glassy surface of the pond and brings up a fish; a mink steals out of the **4** marsh before my door and seizes a frog by the shore; the sedge is bending under the weight of the reed-birds flit- **5** ting hither and thither; and for the last half-hour I have heard the rattle of railroad cars, now dying away and then reviving like the beat of a partridge, conveying travellers **6** from Boston to the country. For I did not live so out of the world as that boy who, as I hear, was put out to a farmer in the east part of the town, but ere long ran away and came home again, quite down at the heel and homesick. He

1   The following nine paragraphs were first published as "The Iron Horse," in *Sartain's Union Magazine* (XI, 1852, 66–8), with numerous revisions of spelling, punctuation, and word choice.

2   Tantivy: at full gallop — or, in this case, fast flying.

3   Probably passenger pigeons, once so numerous, but in T's day becoming rarer, and now for nearly a century completely extinct.

4   The mink was not in T's original journal for August 6, 1845, but was added later after, he had left Walden and forgotten that he could not see the marsh from his doorstep (Robbins, 17).

5   Then a common name for bobolinks.

6   The partridge, or ruffed grouse, produces a loud noise during the mating season by beating its wings rapidly.

I see the fish hawk again. (April 28, 1858)

1 From Ellery Channing, "Walden Spring," *The Woodman and Other Poems* (Boston, 1849).

2 For discussions of T's literary use of the railroad, see Cronkhite and see Torsney.

3 "Come unto me, all ye that labour and are heavy laden, and I will give you rest" (Matthew 11:28).

had never seen such a dull and out-of-the-way place; the folks were all gone off; why, you couldn't even hear the whistle! I doubt if there is such a place in Massachusetts now:

> 'In truth, our village has become a butt
> For one of those fleet railroad shafts, and o'er
> Our peaceful plain its soothing sound is — Concord.'

1

2 The Fitchburg Railroad touches the pond about a hundred rods south of where I dwell. I usually go to the village along its causeway, and am, as it were, related to society by this link. The men on the freight trains, who go over the whole length of the road, bow to me as to an old acquaintance, they pass me so often, and apparently they take me for an employee; and so I am. I too would fain be a track-repairer somewhere in the orbit of the earth.

The whistle of the locomotive penetrates my woods summer and winter, sounding like the scream of a hawk sailing over some farmer's yard, informing me that many restless city merchants are arriving within the circle of the town, or adventurous country traders from the other side. As they come under one horizon, they shout their warning to get off the track to the other, heard sometimes through the circles of two towns. Here come your groceries, country; your rations, countrymen! Nor is there any man so independent on his farm that he can say them nay. And here's your pay for them! screams the countryman's whistle; timber like long battering-rams going twenty miles an hour against the city's walls, and chairs enough **3** to seat all the weary and heavy-laden that dwell within them. With such huge and lumbering civility the country hands a chair to the city. All the Indian huckleberry hills are stripped, all the cranberry meadows are raked into the city. Up comes the cotton, down goes the woven cloth; up comes the silk, down goes the woollen; up come the books, but down goes the wit that writes them.

When I meet the engine with its train of cars moving off with planetary motion — or, rather, like a comet, for the beholder knows not if with that velocity and with that direction it will ever revisit this system, since its orbit does not look like a returning curve — with its steam cloud like a banner streaming behind in golden and silver wreaths, like many a downy cloud which I have seen, high in the heavens, unfolding its masses to the light — as if this travelling demigod, this cloud-compeller, would ere long **1** take the sunset sky for the livery of his train; when I hear the iron horse make the hills echo with his snort like **2** thunder, shaking the earth with his feet, and breathing fire and smoke from his nostrils (what kind of winged horse or fiery dragon they will put into the new Mythology I don't know), it seems as if the earth had got a race now worthy to inhabit it. If all were as it seems, and men made the elements their servants for noble ends! If the cloud that hangs over the engine were the perspiration of heroic deeds, or as beneficent as that which floats over **3** the farmer's fields, then the elements and Nature herself would cheerfully accompany men on their errands and be their escort.

I watch the passage of the morning cars with the same feeling that I do the rising of the sun, which is hardly more regular. Their train of clouds stretching far behind and rising higher and higher, going to heaven while the **4** cars are going to Boston, conceals the sun for a minute and casts my distant field into the shade, a celestial train **5** beside which the petty train of cars which hugs the earth is but the barb of the spear. The stabler of the iron horse was up early this winter morning by the light of the stars amid the mountains, to fodder and harness his steed.

1 Zeus was sometimes referred to as "cloud-compeller."

2 This passage parallels in many respects Job 39:19–25.

3 Beneficient: Shanley (1971, 398) adds here the words "to men," which are not in the first edition. They are in the uncorrected page proof, and T did not indicate a deletion.

4 The antithesis here points out the triviality of the passengers' errands.

5 Still another reference to Hawthorne's satire "The Celestial Railroad."

1   Tate points out that the drill-barrow or seed-drill, a device that sows seeds evenly, was invented only four years before T went to Walden and would not have been widely known in Concord. This is another indication of how well T kept up with his times — remarkable for someone who supposedly fled from civilization.

2   An extensive swamp in southeastern Virginia and northeastern North Carolina.

Fire, too, was awakened thus early to put the vital heat in him and get him off. If the enterprise were as innocent as it is early! If the snow lies deep, they strap on his snow-shoes, and, with the giant plow, plow a furrow from the mountains to the seaboard, in which the cars, like a following drill-barrow, sprinkle all the restless men and floating merchandise in the country for seed. All day the fire-steed flies over the country, stopping only that his master may rest, and I am awakened by his tramp and defiant snort at midnight, when in some remote glen in the woods he fronts the elements incased in ice and snow; and he will reach his stall only with the morning star, to start once more on his travels without rest or slumber. Or perchance, at evening, I hear him in his stable blowing off the superfluous energy of the day, that he may calm his nerves and cool his liver and brain for a few hours of iron slumber. If the enterprise were as heroic and commanding as it is protracted and unwearied!

Far through unfrequented woods on the confines of towns, where once only the hunter penetrated by day, in the darkest night dart these bright saloons without the knowledge of their inhabitants; this moment stopping at some brilliant station-house in town or city, where a social crowd is gathered, the next in the Dismal Swamp, scaring the owl and fox. The startings and arrivals of the cars are now the epochs in the village day. They go and come with such regularity and precision, and their whistle can be heard so far, that the farmers set their clocks by them, and thus one well-conducted institution regulates a whole country. Have not men improved somewhat in punctuality since the railroad was invented? Do they not talk and think faster in the depot than they did in the stage-office? There is something electrifying in the atmosphere of the former place. I have been astonished at the miracles it has

The piers of the bridge by the railroad bridge are adorned with very handsome salver or waiter shaped ice three or four feet in diameter (bottom upward), the crenate edges all around being adorned with bell-shaped pendants. (March 2, 1859)

wrought; that some of my neighbors, who, I should have prophesied, once for all, would never get to Boston by so prompt a conveyance, were on hand when the bell rings. **1** To do things 'railroad fashion' is now the byword; and it is worth the while to be warned so often and so sincerely by any power to get off its track. There is no stopping to read the riot act, no firing over the heads of the mob, in this **2** case. We have constructed a fate, an *Atropos*, that never **3** turns aside. (Let that be the name of your engine.) Men are advertised that at a certain hour and minute these bolts will be shot toward particular points of the compass; yet it interferes with no man's business, and the children go to school on the other track. We live the steadier for it. We are all educated thus to be sons of Tell. The air is full **4** of invisible bolts. Every path but your own is the path of fate. Keep on your own track, then.

What recommends commerce to me is its enterprise and bravery. It does not clasp its hands and pray to Jupiter. I see these men every day go about their business with more or less courage and content, doing more even than they suspect, and perchance better employed than they could have consciously devised. I am less affected by their heroism who stood up for half an hour in the front line at Buena Vista, than by the steady and cheerful valor of the **5** men who inhabit the snowplow for their winter quarters; who have not merely the three-o'-clock-in-the-morning **6** courage, which Bonaparte thought was the rarest, but whose courage does not go to rest so early, who go to sleep only when the storm sleeps or the sinews of their iron steed are frozen. On this morning of the Great Snow, **7** perchance, which is still raging and chilling men's blood, I hear the muffled tone of their engine bell from out the fog bank of their chilled breath, which announces that the cars *are coming*, without long delay, notwithstanding

1   The first edition reads "are on hand," but T, in his personal copy of W, changed it to the present reading.

2   According to the Riot Act, which became law in England in 1715, if twelve or more individuals assemble and disturb the peace, they must disperse upon being read the law or face felony charges.

3   In Greek mythology Atropus, one of the three Fates who preside over mankind, cuts the thread of human destiny. "Atropus" means "never turn aside."

4   William Tell, the fourteenth-century Swiss folk hero, was required to shoot an apple from the head of his own son.

5   A battlefield in northern Mexico where American forces withstood a severe attack in 1847. T opposed the Mexican War, which might have resulted in extending slavery to new territory.

6   In *Mémorial de Sainte Hélène* (Dec. 4–5, 1815) Las Cases explains Napoleon's meaning, though the reference is to two o'clock: "As to moral courage, he had, he said, very rarely met with the two o'clock in the morning courage, unprepared courage." As Gottesman points out, "Courage not painstakingly worked up but coming forth spontaneously, as when a soldier is awakened suddenly in the dead of night."

7   T was probably thinking of the "Great Snow" of February 17, 1717, which Cotton Mather recorded in his *Magnalia Christi Americana*.

1 Plow blade.

2 T is referring to Robert Burns's poems "To a Mouse" and "To a Mountain Daisy."

3 Mountain range in Spain.

4 One of Boston's major wharves, the probable destination of much of the freight shipped down past Walden Pond from northern and western New England.

5 A large lake on the Vermont–New York border.

6 In the *Sartain's Union Magazine* version of these paragraphs, "parts" reads "ports," which makes more sense, but Shanley has assured me that it reads "parts" in the manuscript.

7 Again, the summer hats made from palm leaves that were popular at that time.

8 Cocoa-nut husks: used in making matting, particularly doormats.

9 Gunny is a coarse material made from jute and used for making sacks.

10 Old cloth was frequently pulverized and used in the making of good quality paper for books.

11 T frequently visited the Maine woods, where he saw the results of spring freshets on lumber being floated down to the mills: logs strewn high along the banks or washed out to sea.

12 Thomaston, Maine, one of the primary sources of lime in T's day.

13 More commonly spelled "slaked."

the veto of a New England northeast snow-storm, and I behold the plowmen covered with snow and rime, their

1 heads peering above the mould-board which is turning
2 down other than daisies and the nests of field mice, like
3 bowlders of the Sierra Nevada, that occupy an outside place in the universe.

Commerce is unexpectedly confident and serene, alert, adventurous, and unwearied. It is very natural in its methods withal, far more so than many fantastic enterprises and sentimental experiments, and hence its singular success. I am refreshed and expanded when the freight train rattles past me, and I smell the stores which go dispensing

4 their odors all the way from Long Wharf to Lake Cham-
5, 6 plain, reminding me of foreign parts, of coral reefs, and Indian oceans, and tropical climes, and the extent of the globe. I feel more like a citizen of the world at the sight of

7 the palm-leaf which will cover so many flaxen New England heads the next summer, the Manilla hemp and co-
8, 9 coanut husks, the old junk, gunny bags, scrap iron, and
10 rusty nails. This carload of torn sails is more legible and interesting now than if they should be wrought into paper and printed books. Who can write so graphically the history of the storms they have weathered as these rents have done? They are proof-sheets which need no correction.

11 Here goes lumber from the Maine woods, which did not go out to sea in the last freshet, risen four dollars on the thousand because of what did go out or was split up; pine, spruce, cedar — first, second, third, and fourth qualities, so lately all of one quality, to wave over the bear, and

12 moose, and caribou. Next rolls Thomaston lime, a prime
13 lot, which will get far among the hills before it gets slacked. These rags in bales, of all hues and qualities, the lowest condition to which cotton and linen descend, the final result of dress — of patterns which are now no longer

cried up, unless it be in Milwaukee, as those splendid [1] articles, English, French, or American prints, ginghams, muslins, etc., gathered from all quarters both of fashion and poverty, going to become paper of one color or a few shades only, on which, forsooth, will be written tales of real life, high and low, and founded on fact! This closed car smells of salt fish, the strong New England and commercial scent, reminding me of the Grand Banks and the [2] fisheries. Who has not seen a salt fish, thoroughly cured [3] for this world, so that nothing can spoil it, and putting the perseverance of the saints to the blush? with which you may sweep or pave the streets, and split your kindlings, and the teamster shelter himself and his lading against sun, wind, and rain behind it — and the trader, as a Concord trader once did, hang it up by his door for a sign [4] when he commences business, until at last his oldest customer cannot tell surely whether it be animal, vegeta- [5] ble, or mineral, and yet it shall be as pure as a snowflake, and if it be put into a pot and boiled, will come out an excellent dunfish for a Saturday's dinner. Next Spanish [6] hides, with the tails still preserving their twist and the angle of elevation they had when the oxen that wore them were careering over the pampas of the Spanish Main — a type of all obstinacy, and evincing how almost hopeless and incurable are all constitutional vices. I confess, that practically speaking, when I have learned a man's real disposition, I have no hopes of changing it for the better or worse in this state of existence. As the Orientals say, 'A cur's tail may be warmed, and pressed, and bound round with ligatures, and after a twelve years' labor bestowed upon it, still it will retain its natural form.' The [7] only effectual cure for such inveteracies as these tails exhibit is to make glue of them, which I believe is what is usually done with them, and then they will stay put and

1 Cried up: praised.

2 An extensive shoal southeast of Newfoundland, the Grand Banks is the major fishing ground of New England fishermen.

3 T, in *Cape Cod*, describes in detail the fish-curing process.

4 Emerson, in his *Journal* (V, 36–7), says that T told him this storekeeper was Deacon Parkman.

5 T was probably thinking of the old parlor game Twenty Questions, in which all substances are classified as animal, vegetable, or mineral.

6 A cod that has turned dun colored (dingy brown) in the curing process.

7 Charles Wilkins, trans., *Fables and Proverbs from the Sanskrit Being the Hitopadesa*, "The Lion and the Rabbit," chap. II, fable IX.

1   Another of T's numerous puns.
2   Although there is a Cuttingsville, Vermont, a village in the town of Shrewsbury, according to the town clerk there has never been a *Cuttingsville Times,* and while several John Smiths have lived there, none ever ran a store.
3   Milton, *Paradise Lost,* I, 293-4.
4   "The cattle upon a thousand hills" (Psalms 50:10).
5   "The mountains skipped like rams, and the little hills like lambs" (Psalms 114:4).

1   stick. Here is a hogshead of molasses or of brandy directed
2   to John Smith, Cuttingsville, Vermont, some trader among the Green Mountains, who imports for the farmers near his clearing, and now perchance stands over his bulkhead and thinks of the last arrivals on the coast, how they may affect the price for him, telling his customers this moment, as he has told them twenty times before this morning, that he expects some by the next train of prime quality. It is advertised in the Cuttingsville Times.

While these things go up other things come down. Warned by the whizzing sound, I look up from my book and see some tall pine, hewn on far northern hills, which has winged its way over the Green Mountains and the Connecticut, shot like an arrow through the township within ten minutes, and scarce another eye beholds it; going

> 'to be the mast
> Of some great ammiral.'

3

And hark! here comes the cattle-train bearing the cattle
4   of a thousand hills, sheepcots, stables, and cow-yards in the air, drovers with their sticks, and shepherd boys in the midst of their flocks, all but the mountain pastures, whirled along like leaves blown from the mountains by the September gales. The air is filled with the bleating of calves and sheep, and the hustling of oxen, as if a pastoral valley were going by, When the old bell-wether at the head rattles his bell, the mountains do indeed skip like
5   rams and the little hills like lambs. A carload of drovers, too, in the midst, on a level with their droves now, their vocation gone, but still clinging to their useless sticks as their badge of office. But their dogs, where are they? It is a stampede to them; they are quite thrown out; they have lost the scent. Methinks I hear them barking behind the

Peterboro' Hills, or panting up the western slope of the [1]
Green Mountains. They will not be in at the death. Their
vocation, too, is gone. Their fidelity and sagacity are below par now. They will slink back to their kennels in disgrace, or perchance run wild and strike a league with the
wolf and the fox. So is your pastoral life whirled past and
away. But the bell rings, and I must get off the track and
let the cars go by;

> What's the railroad to me?
> I never go to see
> Where it ends.
>
> It fills a few hollows,
> And makes banks for the swallows,
> It sets the sand a-blowing,
> And the blackberries a-growing,   [2]

but I cross it like a cart-path in the woods. I will not have
my eyes put out and my ears spoiled by its smoke and
steam and hissing.

Now that the cars are gone by and all the restless world
with them, and the fishes in the pond no longer feel their
rumbling, I am more alone than ever. For the rest of the
long afternoon, perhaps, my meditations are interrupted
only by the faint rattle of a carriage or team along the
distant highway.

Sometimes, on Sundays, I heard the bells, the Lincoln,
Acton, Bedford, or Concord bell, when the wind was
favorable, a faint, sweet, and, as it were, natural melody,
worth importing into the wilderness. At a sufficient distance over the woods this sound acquires a certain vibra-
tory hum, as if the pine needles in the horizon were the
strings of a harp which it swept. All sound heard at the
greatest possible distance produces one and the same

1   A range of hills in southwestern New
Hampshire, visible from Concord.
2   T's own poem.

effect, a vibration of the universal lyre, just as the intervening atmosphere makes a distant ridge of earth interesting to our eyes by the azure tint it imparts to it. There came to me in this case a melody which the air had strained, and which had conversed with every leaf and needle of the wood, that portion of the sound which the elements had taken up and modulated and echoed from vale to vale The echo is, to some extent, an original sound, and therein is the magic and charm of it. It is not merely a repetition of what was worth repeating in the bell, but partly the voice of the wood; the same trivial words and notes sung by a wood-nymph.

At evening, the distant lowing of some cow in the horizon beyond the woods sounded sweet and melodious, and at first I would mistake it for the voices of certain minstrels by whom I was sometimes serenaded, who might be straying over hill and dale; but soon I was not unpleasantly disappointed when it was prolonged into the cheap and natural music of the cow. I do not mean to be satirical, but to express my appreciation of those youths' singing, when I state that I perceived clearly that it was akin to the music of the cow, and they were at length one articulation of Nature.

Regularly at half-past seven, in one part of the summer, after the evening train had gone by, the whip-poor-wills chanted their vespers for half an hour, sitting on a stump by my door, or upon the ridge-pole of the house. They would begin to sing almost with as much precision as a clock, within five minutes of a particular time, referred to the setting of the sun, every evening. I had a rare opportunity to become acquainted with their habits. Sometimes I heard four or five at once in different parts of the wood, by accident one a bar behind another, and so near me that I distinguished not only the cluck after each note, but often

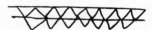

Silas Hosmer tells me how — and — sold the Heywood lot between the railroad and Fair Haven. They lotted it off in this wise: *i.e.* in triangles, and, carrying plenty of liquor, they first treated all round, and then proceeded to sell at auction, but the purchasers, excited with liquor, were not aware when the stakes were pointed out that the lots were not as broad in the rear as in the front, and the wood standing cost them as much as it should have done delivered at the door.
(November 17, 1860)

that singular buzzing sound like a fly in a spider's web, only proportionally louder. Sometimes one would circle round and round me in the woods a few feet distant as if tethered by a string, when probably I was near its eggs. They sang at intervals throughout the night, and were again as musical as ever just before and about dawn.

When other birds are still, the screech owls take up the strain, like mourning women their ancient u-lu-lu. Their [1] dismal scream is truly Ben Jonsonian. Wise midnight hags! [2,3] It is no honest and blunt tu-whit tu-who of the poets, but, [4] without jesting, a most solemn graveyard ditty, the mutual consolations of suicide lovers remembering the pangs and the delights of supernal love in the infernal groves. Yet I love to hear their wailing, their doleful responses, trilled along the woodside; reminding me sometimes of music and singing birds; as if it were the dark and tearful side of music, the regrets and sighs that would fain be sung. They are the spirits, the low spirits and melancholy forebodings, of fallen souls that once in human shape night-walked the earth and did the deeds of darkness, now expiating their sins with their wailing hymns or threnodies in the scenery of their transgressions. They give me a new sense of the variety and capacity of that nature which is our common dwelling. *(Oh-o-o-o-o that I never had been bor-r-r-n!* sighs one on this side of the pond, and circles [5] with the restlessness of despair to some new perch on the gray oaks. Then — *that I never had been bor-r-r-n!* echoes another on the farther side with tremulous sincerity, and — *bor-r-r-n!* comes faintly from far in the Lincoln woods.

I was also serenaded by a hooting owl. Near at hand you could fancy it the most melancholy sound in Nature, as if she meant by this to stereotype and make permanent in her choir the dying moans of a human being — some

[1]   The word seems to have been adapted by T from the Latin word *ulalo,* to howl.

[2]   T was probably thinking of "Wee give thee a shout: Hoo!" (Ben Jonson, *Masque of Queens,* II, 317–8).

[3]   "How now, you secret, black, and midnight hags?" (*Macbeth,* IV, i, 47).

[4]   "Then nightly sings the staring owl, 'Tu-whit, tu-who!'" (*Love's Labour's Lost,* V, ii, 911).

[5]   "Allas! that I was born!" (Chaucer, *The Book of the Duchess,* I, 686).

1 "Abandon hope, all ye who enter here" (Dante, *Inferno,* 3.1.9).

2 In his own copy of W, T corrected this from "single spruce." Double spruce is an old name for the black spruce, the common spruce of the New England swamps, found in the neighborhood of Concord. The single or white spruce is more northerly in its range. Adding irony to T's confusion of the species is the statement in his *Journal* (VI, 22) for December 22, 1853, before W was published. "It is remarkable how few inhabitants of Concord can tell a spruce from a fir, and probably not two a white from a black spruce, unless they are together."

3 In Greek mythology, the river Styx encircled Hades, so Stygian refers to the lower world.

The lower two-thirds of the white spruce has its branches retraced or turned downward, and then curving upward at the extremities, as much as the white pine commonly slants upwards. Above it is so thick that you cannot see through it. All the black spruce that I know hereabouts stand on higher land than this. (January 8, 1854)

1 poor weak relic of mortality who has left hope behind, and howls like an animal, yet with human sobs, on entering the dark valley, made more awful by a certain gurgling melodiousness — I find myself beginning with the letters *gl* when I try to imitate it — expressive of a mind which has reached the gelatinous, mildewy stage in the mortification of all healthy and courageous thought. It reminded me of ghouls and idiots and insane howlings. But now one answers from far woods in a strain made really melodious by distance — *Hoo hoo hoo, hoorer hoo;* and indeed for the most part it suggested only pleasing associations, whether heard by day or night, summer or winter.

I rejoice that there are owls. Let them do the idiotic and maniacal hooting for men. It is a sound admirably suited to swamps and twilight woods which no day illustrates, suggesting a vast and undeveloped nature which men have not recognized. They represent the stark twilight and unsatisfied thoughts which all have. All day the sun has shone on the surface of some savage swamp, **2** where the double spruce stands hung with usnea lichens, and small hawks circulate above, and the chickadee lisps amid the evergreens, and the partridge and rabbit skulk beneath; but now a more dismal and fitting day dawns, and a different race of creatures awakes to express the meaning of Nature there.

Late in the evening I heard the distant rumbling of wagons over bridges — a sound heard farther than almost any other at night — the baying of dogs, and sometimes again the lowing of some disconsolate cow in a distant barn-yard. In the meanwhile all the shore rang with the trump of bullfrogs, the sturdy spirits of ancient wine-bibbers and wassailers, still unrepentant, trying to sing a catch in **3** their Stygian lake — if the Walden nymphs will pardon the comparison, for though there are almost no weeds, there are frogs there — who would fain keep up the hilarious rules of their old festal tables, though their voices have waxed hoarse and solemnly grave, mocking at mirth, and the wine has lost its flavor, and become only liquor to distend their paunches, and sweet intoxication never comes to drown the memory of the past, but mere saturation and waterloggedness and distention. The most alder- **1** manic, with his chin upon a heart-leaf, which serves for a napkin to his drooling chaps, under this northern shore quaffs a deep draught of the once scorned water, and passes round the cup with the ejaculation *tr-r-r-oonk, tr-r-r-oonk, tr-r-r-oonk!* and straightway comes over the water from some distant cove the same password repeated, where the next in seniority and girth has gulped down to his mark; and when this observance has made the circuit of **2** the shores, then ejaculates the master of ceremonies, with satisfaction, *tr-r-r-oonk!* and each in his turn repeats the same down to the least distended, leakiest, and flabbiest paunched, that there be no mistake; and then the bowl goes round again and again, until the sun disperses the morning mist, and only the patriarch is not under the **3** pond, but vainly bellowing *troonk* from time to time, and pausing for a reply.

I am not sure that I ever heard the sound of cock-crowing from my clearing, and I thought that it might be worth the while to keep a cockerel for his music merely, as a singing bird. The note of this once wild Indian pheasant is certainly the most remarkable of any bird's, and if they could be naturalized without being domesticated, it would soon become the most famous sound in our woods, surpassing the clangor of the goose and the hooting of the owl; and then imagine the cackling of the hens to fill the pauses when their lords' clarions rested! No

1 Aldermen are often caricatured with vast bellies.

2 In drinking bouts it was customary to pass around a large cup with marks on the inside to indicate how much each man was expected to drink.

3 That is, under the table.

1 "Early to bed and early to rise / Makes a man healthy, wealthy, and wise" (Benjamin Franklin, *Poor Richard's Almanack,* 1757).

2 Cape Cod ship captains often took a coop of hens along on their whaling vessels to provide fresh meat and eggs.

3 A nocturnal bird (*Caprimulgus vociferus*), once common in the eastern United States, that often rested on house roofs at night to sing.

4 Now known as the great horned owl.

5 The meadowlark, a common resident of New England fields.

wonder that man added this bird to his tame stock — to say nothing of the eggs and drumsticks. To walk in a winter morning in a wood where these birds abounded, their native woods, and hear the wild cockerels crow on the trees, clear and shrill for miles over the resounding earth, drowning the feebler notes of other birds — think of it! It would put nations on the alert. Who would not be early to rise, and rise earlier and earlier every successive day of his life, till he became unspeakably healthy, wealthy, and wise? This foreign bird's note is celebrated by the poets of all countries along with the notes of their native songsters. All climates agree with brave Chanticleer. He is more indigenous even than the natives. His health is ever good, his lungs are sound, his spirits never flag. Even the sailor on the Atlantic and Pacific is awakened by his voice; but its shrill sound never roused me from my slumbers. I kept neither dog, cat, cow, pig, nor hens, so that you would have said there was a deficiency of domestic sounds; neither the churn, nor the spinning-wheel, nor even the singing of the kettle, nor the hissing of the urn, nor children crying, to comfort one. An old-fashioned man would have lost his senses or died of ennui before this. Not even rats in the wall, for they were starved out, or rather were never baited in — only squirrels on the roof and under the floor, a whip-poor-will on the ridge-pole, a blue jay screaming beneath the window, a hare or wood-chuck under the house, a screech owl or a cat owl behind it, a flock of wild geese or a laughing loon on the pond, and a fox to bark in the night. Not even a lark or an oriole, those mild plantation birds, ever visited my clearing. No cockerels to crow nor hens to cackle in the yard. No yard! but unfenced nature reaching up to your very sills. A young forest growing up under your windows, and wild sumachs and blackberry vines breaking through into your cellar; sturdy pitch pines rubbing and creaking against the shingles for want of room, their roots reaching quite under the house. Instead of a scuttle or a blind blown off **1** in the gale — a pine tree snapped off or torn up by the roots behind your house for fuel. Instead of no path to the front-yard gate in the Great Snow — no gate — no front- **2** yard — and no path to the civilized world.

1 Scuttle: a kind of bucket for carrying coal and other objects.

2 Another reference to Cotton Mather's Great Snow.

At 5 P.M. I saw, flying southwest high overhead, a flock of geese, and heard the faint honking of one or two. They were in the usual harrow form, twelve in the shorter line and twenty-four in the longer, the latter abutting on the former at the fourth bird from the front. I judged *hastily* that the interval between the geese was about double their alar extent, and, as the last is, according to Wilson, five feet and two inches, the former may safely be called eight feet. (November 23, 1853)

For an analysis of the structure of this chapter, see Ross (1970).

SOLITUDE

THIS IS A delicious evening, when the whole body is one sense, and imbibes delight through every pore. I go and come with a strange liberty in Nature, a part of herself. As I walk along the stony shore of the pond in my shirt-sleeves, though it is cool as well as cloudy and windy, and I see nothing special to attract me, all the elements are unusually congenial to me. The bullfrogs trump to usher in the night, and the note of the whip-poor-will is borne on the rippling wind from over the water. Sympathy with the fluttering alder and poplar leaves almost takes away my breath; yet, like the lake, my serenity is rippled but not ruffled. These small waves raised by the evening wind are as remote from storm as the smooth reflecting surface. Though it is now dark, the wind still blows and roars in the wood, the waves still dash, and some creatures lull the rest with their notes. The repose is never complete. The wildest animals do not repose, but seek their prey now; the fox, and skunk, and rabbit, now roam the fields and woods without fear. They are Nature's watchmen — links which connect the days of animated life.

When I return to my house I find that visitors have been there and left their cards, either a bunch of flowers, or a wreath of evergreen, or a name in pencil on a yellow walnut leaf or a chip. They who come rarely to the woods take some little piece of the forest into their hands to play with by the way, which they leave, either intentionally or accidentally. One has peeled a willow wand, woven it into a ring, and dropped it on my table. I could always tell if visitors had called in my absence, either by the bended twigs or grass, or the print of their shoes, and generally of what sex or age or quality they were by some slight trace

Saw a skunk in the Corner road, which I followed sixty rods or more. Out now about 4 P.M.,—partly because it is a dark, foul day. It is a slender black (and white) animal, with its back remarkably arched, standing high behind and carrying its head low; runs, even when undisturbed, with a singular teeter or undulation, like the walking of a Chinese lady. (March 10, 1854)

left, as a flower dropped, or a bunch of grass plucked and thrown away, even as far off as the railroad, half a mile distant, or by the lingering odor of a cigar or pipe. Nay, I was frequently notified of the passage of a traveller along the highway sixty rods off by the scent of his pipe.

There is commonly sufficient space about us. Our horizon is never quite at our elbows. The thick wood is not just at our door, nor the pond, but somewhat is always clearing, familiar and worn by us, appropriated and fenced in some way, and reclaimed from Nature. For what reason have I this vast range and circuit, some square miles of unfrequented forest, for my privacy, abandoned to me by men? My nearest neighbor is a mile distant, and no **1** house is visible from any place but the hill-tops within half a mile of my own. I have my horizon bounded by woods all to myself; a distant view of the railroad where it touches the pond on the one hand, and of the fence which skirts the woodland road on the other. But for the most part it is as solitary where I live as on the prairies. It is as much Asia or Africa as New England. I have, as it were, my own sun and moon and stars, and a little world **2** all to myself. At night there was never a traveller passed my house, or knocked at my door, more than if I were the first or last man; unless it were in the spring, when at long intervals some came from the village to fish for pouts — **3** they plainly fished much more in the Walden Pond of their own natures, and baited their hooks with darkness — but they soon retreated, usually with light baskets, and left 'the world to darkness and to me,' and the black ker- **4** nel of the night was never profaned by any human neighborhood. I believe that men are generally still a little afraid of the dark, though the witches are all hung, and **5** Christianity and candles have been introduced.

Yet I experienced sometimes that the most sweet and

1   As has been pointed out, there was a much nearer community of Irish shanties along the railroad track, but T preferred to ignore these in W.

2   Tuerk suggests this is an echo of "They know their own sun and their own stars" (*Aeneid,* VI, 640–1).

3   A common New England freshwater fish.

4   "And leaves the world to darkness and to me" (Thomas Gray, "Elegy in a Country Churchyard").

5   Salem had been the site of witch trials in the late seventeenth century.

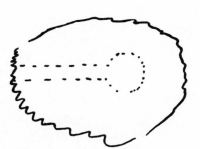

A pout's nest (at Pout's Nest) with a straight entrance some twenty inches long and a simple round nest at end. The young just hatched, all head, light-colored, under a mass of weedy hummock which is all under water. (June 13, 1859)

1 According to the physiological theory of the humors, the predominance of black bile caused melancholy.

2 Aeolus was the Greek god of the winds. One of T's favorite musical instruments was the Aeolian harp, whose strings made a sound when struck by wind. T's own self-made instrument is now in the Concord Museum.

tender, the most innocent and encouraging society may be found in any natural object, even for the poor misanthrope and most melancholy man. There can be no very **1** black melancholy to him who lives in the midst of nature and has his senses still. There was never yet such a storm **2** but it was Aeolian music to a healthy and innocent ear. Nothing can rightly compel a simple and brave man to a vulgar sadness. While I enjoy the friendship of the seasons I trust that nothing can make life a burden to me. The gentle rain which waters my beans and keeps me in the house today is not drear and melancholy, but good for me too. Though it prevents my hoeing them, it is of far more worth than my hoeing. If it should continue so long as to cause the seeds to rot in the ground and destroy the potatoes in the low lands, it would still be good for the grass on the uplands, and, being good for the grass, it would be good for me. Sometimes, when I compare myself with other men, it seems as if I were more favored by the gods than they, beyond any deserts that I am conscious of; as if I had a warrant and surety at their hands which my fellows have not, and were especially guided and guarded. I do not flatter myself, but if it be possible they flatter me. I have never felt lonesome, or in the least oppressed by a sense of solitude, but once, and that was a few weeks after I came to the woods, when, for an hour, I doubted if the near neighborhood of man was not essential to a serene and healthy life. To be alone was something unpleasant. But I was at the same time conscious of a slight insanity in my mood, and seemed to foresee my recovery. In the midst of a gentle rain while these thoughts prevailed, I was suddenly sensible of such sweet and beneficent society in Nature, in the very pattering of the drops, and in every sound and sight around my house, an infinite and unaccountable friendliness all at once like an atmosphere sustaining me, as made the fancied advantages of human neighborhood insignificant, and I have never thought of them since. Every little pine needle expanded and swelled with sympathy and befriended me. I was so distinctly made aware of the presence of something kindred to me, even in scenes which we are accustomed to call wild and dreary, and also that the nearest of blood of me and humanest was not a person nor a villager, that I thought no place could ever be strange to me again.

> 'Mourning untimely consumes the sad;
> Few are their days in the land of the living,
> Beautiful daughter of Toscar.' [1]

Some of my pleasantest hours were during the long rain-storms in the spring or fall, which confined me to the house for the afternoon as well as the forenoon, soothed by their ceaseless roar and pelting; when an early twilight ushered in a long evening in which many thoughts had time to take root and unfold themselves. In those driving northeast rains which tried the village houses so, when the maids stood ready with mop and pail in front entries to keep the deluge out, I sat behind my door in my little house, which was all entry, and thoroughly enjoyed its protection. In one heavy thunder-shower the lightning struck a large pitch pine across the pond, making a very conspicuous and perfectly regular spiral groove from top to bottom, an inch or more deep, and four or five inches wide, as you would groove a walking-stick. I passed it again the other day, and was struck with awe on looking up and beholding that mark, now more distinct than ever, where a terrific and resistless bolt came down out of the harmless sky eight years ago. Men frequently say to me, 'I should think you would feel lonesome down there, and

1   From Patrick MacGregor's "translation" of Ossian, *The Genuine Remains of Ossian,* "Croma" (London, 1841, 193).

I perceive that the low stratum of dark clouds under the red sky all dips one way, and to a remarkable degree presents the appearance of the butt ends of cannons slanted toward the sky, thus. (July 10, 1851)

1 Beacon Hill is the eminence on which the state house stands in Boston. Five Points was a section of lower Manhattan notorious for its squalor and crime.

2 Brighton, now part of Boston, was then the site of numerous slaughterhouses and farmers' markets. "Bright" was a common farm name for a favored ox.

want to be nearer to folks, rainy and snowy days and nights especially.' I am tempted to reply to such — This whole earth which we inhabit is but a point in space. How far apart, think you, dwell the two most distant inhabitants of yonder star, the breadth of whose disk cannot be appreciated by our instruments? Why should I feel lonely? is not our planet in the Milky Way? This which you put seems to me not to be the most important question. What sort of space is that which separates a man from his fellows and makes him solitary? I have found that no exertion of the legs can bring two minds much nearer to one another. What do we want most to dwell near to? Not to many men surely, the depot, the post-office, the barroom, the meeting-house, the school-house, the grocery,

1 Beacon Hill, or the Five Points, where men most congregate, but to the perennial source of our life, whence in all our experience we have found that to issue, as the willow stands near the water and sends out its roots in that direction. This will vary with different natures, but this is the place where a wise man will dig his cellar. . . . I one evening overtook one of my townsmen, who has accumulated what is called 'a handsome property' — though I never got a *fair* view of it — on the Walden road, driving a pair of cattle to market, who inquired of me how I could bring my mind to give up so many of the comforts of life. I answered that I was very sure I liked it passably well; I was not joking. And so I went home to my bed, and left him to pick his way through the darkness and the mud

2 to Brighton — or Bright-town — which place he would reach some time in the morning.

Any prospect of awakening or coming to life to a dead man makes indifferent all times and places. The place where that may occur is always the same, and indescribably pleasant to all our senses. For the most part we allow

The aspect of the sky varies every hour. About noon I observed it in the south, composed of short clouds horizontal and parallel to one another, each straight and dark below with a slight cumulus resting on it. (April 10, 1852)

only outlying and transient circumstances to make our occasions. They are, in fact, the cause of our distraction. Nearest to all things is that power which fashions their being. *Next* to us the grandest laws are continually being executed. *Next* to us is not the workman whom we have hired, with whom we love so well to talk, but the workman whose work we are.

'How vast and profound is the influence of the subtile powers of Heaven and of Earth!'

'We seek to perceive them, and we do not see them; we seek to hear them, and we do not hear them; identified with the substance of things, they cannot be separated from them.'

'They cause that in all the universe men purify and sanctify their hearts, and clothe themselves in their holiday garments to offer sacrifices and oblations to their ancestors. It is an ocean of subtile intelligences. They are everywhere, above us, on our left, on our right; they environ us on all sides.'   1

We are the subjects of an experiment which is not a little interesting to me. Can we not do without the society of our gossips a little while under these circumstances — have our own thoughts to cheer us? Confucius says truly, 2 'Virtue does not remain as an abandoned orphan; it must of necessity have neighbors.'

With thinking we may be beside ourselves in a sane sense. By a conscious effort of the mind we can stand aloof from actions and their consequences; and all things, good and bad, go by us like a torrent. We are not wholly involved in Nature. I may be either the driftwood in the stream, or Indra in the sky looking down on it. I *may be* 3 affected by a theatrical exhibition; on the other hand, I *may not* be affected by an actual event which appears to concern me much more. I only know myself as a human

1   Confucius, *The Doctrine of the Mean,* XVI, 1–3.

2   *Confucian Analects,* IV, xxv.

3   In Hindu mythology, the Vedic god who presides over the deities in the middle realm (the air).

The clouds are handsome this afternoon: on the north, some dark, windy clouds, with rain falling thus beneath. (April 23, 1857)

entity; the scene, so to speak, of thoughts and affections; and am sensible of a certain doubleness by which I can stand as remote from myself as from another. However intense my experience, I am conscious of the presence and criticism of a part of me, which, as it were, is not a part of me, but spectator, sharing no experience, but taking note of it, and that is no more I than it is you. When the play, it may be the tragedy, of life is over, the spectator goes his way. It was a kind of fiction, a work of the imagination only, so far as he was concerned. This doubleness may easily make us poor neighbors and friends sometimes.

I find it wholesome to be alone the greater part of the time. To be in company, even with the best, is soon wearisome and dissipating. I love to be alone. I never found the companion that was so companionable as solitude. We are for the most part more lonely when we go abroad among men than when we stay in our chambers. A man thinking or working is always alone, let him be where he will. Solitude is not measured by the miles of space that intervene between a man and his fellows. The really diligent student in one of the crowded hives of Cambridge College is as solitary as a dervis in the desert. The farmer can work alone in the field or the woods all day, hoeing or chopping, and not feel lonesome, because he is employed; but when he comes home at night he cannot sit down in a room alone, at the mercy of his thoughts, but must be where he can 'see the folks,' and recreate, and, as he thinks, remunerate himself for his day's solitude; and hence he wonders how the student can sit alone in the house all night and most of the day without ennui and 'the blues;' but he does not realize that the student, though in the house, is still at work in *his* field, and chopping in *his* woods, as the farmer in his, and in turn seeks the same recreation and society that the latter does, though it may be a more condensed form of it.

Society is commonly too cheap. We meet at very short intervals, not having had time to acquire any new value for each other. We meet at meals three times a day, and give each other a new taste of that old musty cheese that we are. We have had to agree on a certain set of rules, called etiquette and politeness, to make this frequent meeting tolerable and that we need not come to open war. We meet at the post-office, and at the sociable, and about the fireside every night; we live thick and are in each other's way, and stumble over one another, and I think that we thus lose some respect for one another. Certainly less frequency would suffice for all important and hearty communications. Consider the girls in a factory — never alone, **1** hardly in their dreams. It would be better if there were but one inhabitant to a square mile, as where I live. The value of a man is not in his skin, that we should touch him.

I have heard of a man lost in the woods and dying of **2** famine and exhaustion at the foot of a tree, whose loneliness was relieved by the grotesque visions with which, owing to bodily weakness, his diseased imagination surrounded him, and which he believed to be real. So also, owing to bodily and mental health and strength, we may be continually cheered by a like but more normal and natural society, and come to know that we are never alone.

I have a great deal of company in my house; especially in the morning, when nobody calls. Let me suggest a few comparisons, that some one may convey an idea of my situation. I am no more lonely than the loon in the pond that laughs so loud, or than Walden Pond itself. What company has that lonely lake, I pray? And yet it has not the blue devils, but the blue angels in it, in the azure tint **3** of its waters. The sun is alone, except in thick weather,

1 A famous social experiment of the time was conducted in Lowell, Massachusetts, where girls were hired to work in the textile mills and lived in factory dormitories nearby. Reformers roundly praised the artistic products of their leisure time, but T questioned the effect on their individual spirits.

2 I have been unable to discover the source of this story.

3 Blue devils: a popular name for hypochondriac melancholy.

1 A common natural phenomenon known as a parhelion or sundog.

2 When Jesus cast the evil spirit out of an unclean man, "He asked him, 'What is thy name?' and he answered, saying, 'My name is Legion: for we are many'" (Mark 5:9).

3 The Mill Brook still flows through the center of Concord, although now partly underground.

4 Since a few lines later T refers to the old settler as someone thought to be dead, it is likely that he is referring to Pan, the Greek god of all the inhabitants of the country. "The great God Pan is dead" is from Plutarch's "Why the Oracles Cease to Give Answers." Charles Anderson (77–8) questions the usual interpretation of this as Pan. Cameron (1991) suggests T is referring to Hawthorne's "Gray Champion."

5 Two of the regicides under indictment for killing King Charles I in 1649. They fled to America and hid in various places in the Connecticut River Valley.

6 Mother Nature.

7 Medicinal herbs.

when there sometimes appear to be two, but one is a mock sun. God is alone — but the devil, he is far from being alone; he sees a great deal of company; he is legion. I am no more lonely than a single mullein or dandelion in a pasture, or a bean leaf, or sorrel, or a horse-fly, or a humblebee. I am no more lonely than the Mill Brook, or a weathercock, or the north star, or the south wind, or an April shower, or a January thaw, or the first spider in a new house.

I have occasional visits in the long winter evenings, when the snow falls fast and the wind howls in the wood, from an old settler and original proprietor, who is reported to have dug Walden Pond, and stoned it, and fringed it with pine woods; who tells me stories of old time and of new eternity; and between us we manage to pass a cheerful evening with social mirth and pleasant views of things, even without apples or cider — a most wise and humorous friend, whom I love much, who keeps himself more secret than ever did Goffe or Whalley; and though he is thought to be dead, none can show where he is buried. An elderly dame, too, dwells in my neighborhood, invisible to most persons, in whose odorous herb garden I love to stroll sometimes, gathering simples and listening to her fables; for she has a genius of unequalled fertility, and her memory runs back farther than mythology, and she can tell me the original of every fable, and on what fact every one is founded, for the incidents occurred when she was young. A ruddy and lusty old dame, who delights in all weathers and seasons, and is likely to outlive all her children yet.

The indescribable innocence and beneficence of Nature — of sun and wind and rain, of summer and winter — such health, such cheer, they afford forever! and such sympathy have they ever with our race, that all Nature would be affected, and the sun's brightness fade, and the winds would sigh humanely, and the clouds rain tears, and the woods shed their leaves and put on mourning in midsummer, if any man should ever for a just cause grieve. Shall I not have intelligence with the earth? Am I not partly leaves and vegetable mould myself?

What is the pill which will keep us well, serene, contented? Not my or thy great-grandfather's, but our great-grandmother Nature's universal, vegetable, botanic medicines, by which she has kept herself young always, outlived so many old Parrs in her day, and fed her health with their decaying fatness. For my panacea, instead of one of those quack vials of a mixture dipped from Acheron and the Dead Sea, which come out of those long shallow black-schooner looking wagons which we sometimes see made to carry bottles, let me have a draught of undiluted morning air. Morning air! If men will not drink of this at the fountain-head of the day, why, then, we must even bottle up some and sell it in the shops, for the benefit of those who have lost their subscription ticket to morning time in this world. But remember, it will not keep quite till noonday even in the coolest cellar, but drive out the stopples long ere that and follow westward the steps of Aurora. I am no worshipper of Hygeia, who was the daughter of that old herb-doctor Aesculapius, and who is represented on monuments holding a serpent in one hand, and in the other a cup out of which the serpent sometimes drinks; but rather of Hebe, cup-bearer to Jupiter, who was the daughter of Juno and wild lettuce, and who had the power of restoring gods and men to the vigor of youth. She was probably the only thoroughly sound-conditioned, healthy, and robust young lady that ever walked the globe, and wherever she came it was spring.

1   T is probably thinking of Morrison's Pill, which Carlyle describes in the chapter of that name in *Past and Present*.

2   Thomas Parr, reputedly born in 1483, who died in Salop, England, in 1635 at the age of 152.

3   Patent medicines of the day, hawked from village to village in covered wagons.

4   The modern Souli River, which according to Greek mythology was in communication with the realms of Pluto.

5   A Roman goddess, the forerunner of the sun.

6   The Greek goddess of health.

7   The "blameless physician" of the *Iliad*.

8   According to some ancient authorities, Juno conceived Hebe after eating lettuce. As Eddleman demonstrates, T is quoting almost word for word from Lemprière's *Classical Dictionary*.

VISITORS

1   For an analysis of the structure of this chapter, see Ross (1970).

2   Although it may seem that this would crowd his ten-by-fifteen-foot cabin, it was found by experimenting at the 1992 annual Thoreau Society meeting that thirty people could easily fit into that space and still leave room for a cot, a desk, a fireplace, and three chairs — as long as everyone stood up.

3   Three well-known hotels in T's day, in Boston, New York, and Concord, respectively.

4   "Mountains will labor, to bring forth a ridiculous mouse" (Horace, De Arte Poetica, I, 139).

I THINK THAT I love society as much as most, and am ready enough to fasten myself like a bloodsucker for the time to any full-blooded man that comes in my way. I am naturally no hermit, but might possibly sit out the sturdiest frequenter of the bar-room, if my business called me thither.

I had three chairs in my house; one for solitude, two for friendship, three for society. When visitors came in larger and unexpected numbers there was but the third chair for them all, but they generally economized the room by standing up. It is surprising how many great men and women a small house will contain. I have had twenty-five or thirty souls, with their bodies, at once under my roof, and yet we often parted without being aware that we had come very near to one another. Many of our houses, both public and private, with their almost innumerable apartments, their huge halls and their cellars for the storage of wines and other munitions of peace, appear to be extravagantly large for their inhabitants. They are so vast and magnificent that the latter seem to be only vermin which infest them. I am surprised when the herald blows his summons before some Tremont or Astor or Middlesex House, to see come creeping out over the piazza for all inhabitants a ridiculous mouse, which soon again slinks into some hole in the pavement.

One inconvenience I sometimes experienced in so small a house, the difficulty of getting to a sufficient distance from my guest when we began to utter the big thoughts in big words. You want room for your thoughts to get into sailing trim and run a course or two before they make their port. The bullet of your thought must have overcome its lateral and ricochet motion and fallen into its [1] last and steady course before it reaches the ear of the hearer, else it may plow out again through the side of his head. Also, our sentences wanted room to unfold and form their columns in the interval. Individuals, like nations, must have suitable broad and natural boundaries, even a considerable neutral ground, between them. I have found it a singular luxury to talk across the pond to a companion on the opposite side. In my house we were so near that we could not begin to hear — we could not speak low enough to be heard; as when you throw two stones into calm water so near that they break each other's undulations. If we are merely loquacious and loud talkers, then we can afford to stand very near together, cheek by jowl, and feel each other's breath; but if we speak reservedly and thoughtfully, we want to be farther apart, that all animal heat and moisture may have a chance to evaporate. If we would enjoy the most intimate society with that in each of us which is without, or above, being spoken to, we must not only be silent, but commonly so far apart bodily that we cannot possibly hear each other's voice in any case. Referred to this standard, speech is for the convenience of those who are hard of hearing; but there are many fine things which we cannot say if we have to shout. As the conversation began to assume a loftier and grander tone, we gradually shoved our chairs farther apart till they touched the wall in opposite corners, and then commonly there was not room enough.

My 'best' room, however, my withdrawing room, al-[2] ways ready for company, on whose carpet the sun rarely fell, was the pine wood behind my house. Thither in summer days, when distinguished guests came, I took them, and a priceless domestic swept the floor and dusted the furniture and kept the things in order.

1 T here shows a surprising technical knowledge of ballistic science. He refers to the fact that a bullet travels several yards after leaving the muzzle before overcoming its wobble and achieving gyrostatic stability (Tate).

2 Originally the drawing room was the room to which ladies withdrew after dinner so that the men remaining behind might drink and smoke.

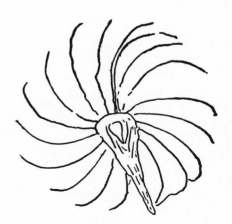

A pine cone blossoms out now fully in about three days, in the house. (January 25, 1855)

1   Indian-meal mush, a popular New England breakfast dish.

2   T is referring to the parable of the loaves and the fishes (Matthew 15).

3   Pluto's three-headed dog, who stood watch at the entrance to hell.

4   Edmund Spenser, *The Faerie Queene*, I, i, 35.

If one guest came he sometimes partook of my frugal meal, and it was no interruption to conversation to be stirring a hasty-pudding, or watching the rising and maturing of a loaf of bread in the ashes, in the meanwhile. But if twenty came and sat in my house there was nothing said about dinner, though there might be bread enough for two, more than if eating were a forsaken habit; but we naturally practised abstinence; and this was never felt to be an offence against hospitality, but the most proper and considerate course. The waste and decay of physical life, which so often needs repair, seemed miraculously retarded in such a case, and the vital vigor stood its ground. I could entertain thus a thousand as well as twenty; and if any ever went away disappointed or hungry from my house when they found me at home, they may depend upon it that I sympathized with them at least. So easy is it, though many housekeepers doubt it, to establish new and better customs in the place of the old. You need not rest your reputation on the dinners you give. For my own part, I was never so effectually deterred from frequenting a man's house, by any kind of Cerberus whatever, as by the parade one made about dining me, which I took to be a very polite and roundabout hint never to trouble him so again. I think I shall never revisit those scenes. I should be proud to have for the motto of my cabin those lines of Spenser which one of my visitors inscribed on a yellow walnut leaf for a card:

> 'Arrivèd there, the little house they fill,
>   Ne looke for entertainment where none was;
> Rest is their feast, and all things at their will:
>   The noblest mind the best contentment has.'

When Winslow, afterward governor of the Plymouth Colony, went with a companion on a visit of ceremony to

Massasoit on foot through the woods, and arrived tired and hungry at his lodge, they were well received by the king, but nothing was said about eating that day. When the night arrived, to quote their own words — 'He laid us on the bed with himself and his wife, they at the one end and we at the other, it being only planks laid a foot from the ground and a thin mat upon them. Two more of his chief men, for want of room, pressed by and upon us; so that we were worse weary of our lodging than of our journey.' At one o'clock the next day Massasoit 'brought **1** two fishes that he had shot,' about thrice as big as a bream. 'These being boiled, there were at least forty looked for a share in them; the most eat of them. This meal only we had in two nights and a day; and had not one of us bought a partridge, we had taken our journey fasting.' Fearing that they would be light-headed for want of food and also sleep, owing to 'the savages' barbarous singing, (for they use to sing themselves asleep,)' and that they might get home while they had strength to travel, they departed. As for lodging, it is true they were but poorly entertained, though what they found an inconvenience was no doubt intended for an honor; but as far as eating was concerned, I do not see how the Indians could have done better. They had nothing to eat themselves, and they were wiser than to think that apologies could supply the place of food to their guests; so they drew their belts tighter and said nothing about it. Another time when Winslow visited them, it being a season of plenty with them, there was no deficiency in this respect.

As for men, they will hardly fail one anywhere. I had more visitors while I lived in the woods than at any other period of my life; I mean that I had some. I met several there under more favorable circumstances than I could anywhere else. But fewer came to see me on trivial busi-

1 *A Relation or Journall of the Beginning and Proceedings of the English Plantation at Plimouth in New England* (London, 1622, part II). As Gottesman (1621) points out, T modernizes and regularizes his text frequently, and while "bought" is in his original, it seems likely that it should have read "brought."

Aboak-henjo [?], a birch-bark vessel for water. Can boil meat in it with hot stones; takes a long time. (November 26, 1850)

1   Paphlagonia: an ancient region of northern Asia Minor. Since the mountainous interior was heavily forested, many of its people were woodsmen. The man was Alex Therien, a French Canadian (Shanley, 1957, 170). For a discussion of T's friendship with Therien, see Bradford and see Harding (1991).

2   Significantly Achilles, in the *Iliad*, cultivates the friendship of Patroclus just as T was cultivating that of the woodcutter.

3   The *Iliad*, beginning of book XVI.

4   A powerful astringent frequently used in folk medicine.

ness. In this respect, my company was winnowed by my mere distance from town. I had withdrawn so far within the great ocean of solitude, into which the rivers of society empty, that for the most part, so far as my needs were concerned, only the finest sediment was deposited around me. Beside, there were wafted to me evidences of unexplored and uncultivated continents on the other side.

Who should come to my lodge this morning but a true Homeric or Paphlagonian man — he had so suitable and poetic a name that I am sorry I cannot print it here — a Canadian, a woodchopper and postmaker, who can hole fifty posts in a day, who made his last supper on a woodchuck which his dog caught. He, too, has heard of Homer, and, 'if it were not for books,' would 'not know what to do rainy days,' though perhaps he has not read one wholly through for many rainy seasons. Some priest who could pronounce the Greek itself taught him to read his verse in the Testament in his native parish far away; and now I must translate to him, while he holds the book, Achilles' reproof to Patroclus for his sad countenance. — 'Why are you in tears, Patroclus, like a young girl?'

'Or have you alone heard some news from Phthia?
They say that Menoetius lives yet, son of Actor,
And Peleus lives, son of Aeacus, among the Myrmidons,
Either of whom having died, we should greatly grieve.'

He says, 'That's good.' He has a great bundle of white oak bark under his arm for a sick man, gathered this Sunday morning. 'I suppose there's no harm in going after such a thing today,' says he. To him Homer was a great writer, though what his writing was about he did not know. A more simple and natural man it would be hard to find. Vice and disease, which cast such a sombre moral hue over the world, seemed to have hardly any existence for

him. He was about twenty-eight years old, and had left [1]
Canada and his father's house a dozen years before to
work in the States, and earn money to buy a farm with at
last, perhaps in his native country. He was cast in the
coarsest mould; a stout but sluggish body, yet gracefully
carried, with a thick sunburnt neck, dark bushy hair, and
dull sleepy blue eyes, which were occasionally lit up with
expression. He wore a flat gray cloth cap, a dingy wool-
colored greatcoat, and cow-hide boots. He was a great
consumer of meat, usually carrying his dinner to his work
a couple of miles past my house — for he chopped all
summer — in a tin pail; cold meats, often cold woodchucks, and coffee in a stone bottle which dangled by a
string from his belt; and sometimes he offered me a drink.
He came along early, crossing my bean-field, though without anxiety or haste to get to his work, such as Yankees
exhibit. He wasn't a-going to hurt himself. He didn't care
if he only earned his board. Frequently he would leave
his dinner in the bushes, when his dog had caught a
woodchuck by the way, and go back a mile and a half to
dress it and leave it in the cellar of the house where he
boarded, after deliberating first for half an hour whether
he could not sink it in the pond safely till night fall —
loving to dwell long upon these themes. He would say, as
he went by in the morning, 'How thick the pigeons are! If [2]
working every day were not my trade, I could get all the
meat I should want by hunting — pigeons, woodchucks,
rabbits, partridges — by gosh! I could get all I should
want for a week in one day.'

He was a skilful chopper, and indulged in some flourishes and ornaments in his art. He cut his trees level and
close to the ground, that the sprouts which came up
afterward might be more vigorous and a sled might slide
over the stumps; and instead of leaving a whole tree to

[1]   According to Concord town records,
Therien was born in 1811 and so would have
been thirty-four when T went to Walden.
[2]   The passenger pigeons, which were common in T's day, are now extinct.

Dense flocks of pigeons hurry-skurry over the hill.
Pass near Brooks's pigeon-stands. There was a
flock perched on his poles, and they sat so still and
in such regular order there, being also the color of
the wood, that I thought they were wooden figures
at first. (September 15, 1859)

support his corded wood, he would pare it away to a slender stake or splinter which you could break off with your hand at last.

He interested me because he was so quiet and solitary and so happy withal; a well of good humor and contentment which overflowed at his eyes. His mirth was without alloy. Sometimes I saw him at his work in the woods, felling trees, and he would greet me with a laugh of inexpressible satisfaction, and a salutation in Canadian French, though he spoke English as well. When I approached him he would suspend his work, and with half-suppressed mirth lie along the trunk of a pine which he had felled, and, peeling off the inner bark, roll it up into a ball and chew it while he laughed and talked. Such an exuberance of animal spirits had he that he sometimes tumbled down and rolled on the ground with laughter at anything which made him think and tickled him. Looking round upon the trees he would exclaim — 'By George! I can enjoy myself well enough here chopping; I want no better sport.' Sometimes, when at leisure, he amused himself all day in the woods with a pocket pistol, firing salutes to himself at regular intervals as he walked. In the winter he had a fire by which at noon he warmed his coffee in a kettle; and as he sat on a log to eat his dinner the chickadees would sometimes come round and alight on his arm and peck at the potato in his fingers; and he said that he 'liked to have the little *fellers* about him.'

In him the animal man chiefly was developed. In physical endurance and contentment he was cousin to the pine and the rock. I asked him once if he was not sometimes tired at night, after working all day; and he answered, with a sincere and serious look, 'Gorrappit, I never was tired in my life.' But the intellectual and what is called spiritual man in him were slumbering as in an

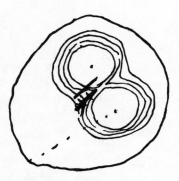

They have cut and sawed off the butt of the great elm at nine and a half feet from the ground, and I counted the annual rings there with the greatest ease and accuracy. . . . There were thirteen distinct rings about each centre, before they united and one ring inclosed both. (January 25, 1856)

infant. He had been instructed only in that innocent and ineffectual way in which the Catholic priests teach the aborigines, by which the pupil is never educated to the degree of consciousness, but only to the degree of trust and reverence, and a child is not made a man, but kept a child. When Nature made him, she gave him a strong body and contentment for his portion, and propped him on every side with reverence and reliance, that he might live out his threescore years and ten a child. He was so **1** genuine and unsophisticated that no introduction would serve to introduce him, more than if you introduced a woodchuck to your neighbor. He had got to find him out as you did. He would not play any part. Men paid him wages for work, and so helped to feed and clothe him; but he never exchanged opinions with them. He was so simply and naturally humble — if he can be called humble who never aspires — that humility was no distinct quality in him, nor could he conceive of it. Wiser men were demigods to him. If you told him that such a one was coming, he did as if he thought that anything so grand would expect nothing of himself, but take all the responsibility on itself, and let him be forgotten still. He never heard the sound of praise. He particularly reverenced the writer and the preacher. Their performances were miracles. When I told him that I wrote considerably, he thought for a long time that it was merely the handwriting which I meant, for he could write a remarkably good hand himself. I sometimes found the name of his native parish handsomely written in the snow by the highway, with the proper French accent, and knew that he had passed. I asked him if he ever wished to write his thoughts. He said that he had read and written letters for those who could not, but he never tried to write thoughts — no, he could not, he could not tell what to put first, it would kill

1 "The days of our years are three-score years and ten" (Psalms 90:10).

The white or sap wood averaged about two inches thick. The bark was from one to two inches thick, and in the last case I could count from twelve to fifteen distinct rings in it, as if it were regularly shed after that period. (January 26, 1856)

1 Probably Emerson.
2 Again, probably Emerson.
3 Homespun manufactured in Vermont.
4 He is referring to the hemlock tree (*Tsuga canadensis*) and not the hemlock plant (*Cicuta maculata*), which is the deadly poison Socrates drank.

him, and then there was spelling to be attended to at the same time!

1 I heard that a distinguished wise man and reformer asked him if he did not want the world to be changed; but he answered with a chuckle of surprise in his Canadian accent, not knowing that the question had ever been entertained before, 'No, I like it well enough.' It would have suggested many things to a philosopher to have dealings with him. To a stranger he appeared to know nothing of things in general; yet I sometimes saw in him a man whom I had not seen before, and I did not know whether he was as wise as Shakespeare or as simply ignorant as a child, whether to suspect him of a fine poetic conscious- **2** ness or of stupidity. A townsman told me that when he met him sauntering through the village in his small close-fitting cap, and whistling to himself, he reminded him of a prince in disguise.

His only books were an almanac and an arithmetic, in which last he was considerably expert. The former was a sort of cyclopaedia to him, which he supposed to contain an abstract of human knowledge, as indeed it does to a considerable extent. I loved to sound him on the various reforms of the day, and he never failed to look at them in the most simple and practical light. He had never heard of such things before. Could he do without factories? I **3** asked. He had worn the home-made Vermont gray, he said, and that was good. Could he dispense with tea and coffee? Did this country afford any beverage beside water? **4** He had soaked hemlock leaves in water and drank it, and thought that was better than water in warm weather. When I asked him if he could do without money, he showed the convenience of money in such a way as to suggest and coincide with the most philosophical accounts of the origin of this institution, and the very derivation of the word

pecunia. If an ox were his property, and he wished to get 1
needles and thread at the store, he thought it would be
inconvenient and impossible soon to go on mortgaging
some portion of the creature each time to that amount.
He could defend many institutions better than any philosopher, because, in describing them as they concerned
him, he gave the true reason for their prevalence, and
speculation had not suggested to him any other. At another time, hearing Plato's definition of a man — a biped
without feathers — and that one exhibited a cock plucked 2
and called it Plato's man, he thought it an important
difference that the *knees* bent the wrong way. He would
sometimes exclaim, 'How I love to talk! By George, I
could talk all day!' I asked him once, when I had not seen
him for many months, if he had got a new idea this
summer. 'Good Lord,' said he, 'a man that has to work as
I do, if he does not forget the ideas he has had, he will do
well. May be the man you hoe with is inclined to race;
then, by gorry, your mind must be there; you think of
weeds.' He would sometimes ask me first on such occasions, if I had made any improvement. One winter day I
asked him if he was always satisfied with himself, wishing
to suggest a substitute within him for the priest without,
and some higher motive for living. 'Satisfied!' said he;
'some men are satisfied with one thing, and some with
another. One man, perhaps, if he has got enough, will be
satisfied to sit all day with his back to the fire and his belly
to the table, by George!' Yet I never, by any manoeuvring,
could get him to take the spiritual view of things; the
highest that he appeared to conceive of was a simple
expediency, such as you might expect an animal to appreciate; and this, practically, is true of most men. If I suggested any improvement in his mode of life, he merely
answered, without expressing any regret, that it was too

1   The Latin word for money, *pecunia,* is derived from *pecus,* cattle.
2   "Man is the plume-less genus of bipeds"
(Plato, *Politicus,* 266).

How snug and warm a hemlock looks in the
winter! That by the azalea looks thus: There is a
tendency in the limbs to arrange themselves
ray-wise about a point one third from the base to
the top. What singular regularity in the outline of a
tree! (December 14, 1855)

1　For more on Walden's bottom, see "The Pond in Winter."

2　In his *Journal* (III, 198) T tells an anecdote of two young women who borrowed his dipper and failed to return it. He then adds, "They were a disgrace to their sex and to humanity. Pariahs of the moral world."

3　The Concord almshouse (poorhouse), on Walden Street, was just across the fields from Emerson's house.

4　In many small New England towns, the offices of overseers of the poor and selectmen were combined.

late. Yet he thoroughly believed in honesty and the like virtues.

There was a certain positive originality, however slight, to be detected in him, and I occasionally observed that he was thinking for himself and expressing his own opinion, a phenomenon so rare that I would any day walk ten miles to observe it, and it amounted to the re-origination of many of the institutions of society. Though he hesitated, and perhaps failed to express himself distinctly, he always had a presentable thought behind. Yet his thinking was so primitive and immersed in his animal life, that, though more promising than a merely learned man's, it rarely ripened to anything which can be reported. He suggested that there might be men of genius in the lowest grades of life, however permanently humble and illiterate, who take their own view always, or do not pretend to see at all; who are as bottomless even as Walden Pond was thought to be, though they may be dark and muddy.

Many a traveller came out of his way to see me and the inside of my house, and, as an excuse for calling, asked for a glass of water. I told them that I drank at the pond, and pointed thither, offering to lend them a dipper. Far off as I lived, I was not exempted from the annual visitation which occurs, methinks, about the first of April, when everybody is on the move; and I had my share of good luck, though there were some curious specimens among my visitors. Half-witted men from the almshouse and elsewhere came to see me; but I endeavored to make them exercise all the wit they had, and make their confessions to me; in such cases making wit the theme of our conversation; and so was compensated. Indeed, I found some of them to be wiser than the so-called *overseers* of the poor and selectmen of the town, and thought it was time that the tables were turned. With respect to wit, I learned that there was not much difference between the half and the whole. One day, in particular, an inoffensive, simple-minded pauper, whom with others I had often seen used **1** as fencing stuff, standing or sitting on a bushel in the fields to keep cattle and himself from straying, visited me, and expressed a wish to live as I did. He told me, with the utmost simplicity and truth, quite superior, or rather *inferior*, to anything that is called humility, that he was 'deficient in intellect.' These were his words. The Lord had made him so, yet he supposed the Lord cared as much for him as for another. 'I have always been so,' said he, 'from my childhood; I never had much mind; I was not like other children; I am weak in the head. It was the Lord's will, I suppose.' And there he was to prove the truth of his words. He was a metaphysical puzzle to me. I have rarely met a fellow-man on such promising ground — it was so simple and sincere and so true all that he said. And, true enough, in proportion as he appeared to humble himself was he exalted. I did not know at first but it was the result **2** of a wise policy. It seemed that from such a basis of truth and frankness as the poor weak-headed pauper had laid, our intercourse might go forward to something better than the intercourse of sages.

I had some guests from those not reckoned commonly among the town's poor, but who should be; who are among the world's poor, at any rate; guests who appeal, not to your hospitality, but to your *hospitalality*; who earnestly wish to be helped, and preface their appeal with the information that they are resolved, for one thing, never to help themselves. I require of a visitor that he be not actually starving, though he may have the very best appetite in the world, however he got it. Objects of charity are not guests. Men who did not know when their visit had terminated, though I went about my business again, answering them

1 Channning suggests that this might have been one David Flint. A David Flint is listed in the Concord Register with the birth date of March 28, 1791.

2 "He that shall humble himself shall be exalted" (Matthew 23:12).

1 While T unquestionably aided many escaped slaves on their way to freedom in Canada, he rarely if ever used his Walden cabin for this purpose, since it was too tiny and exposed to be used for hiding slaves (Harding, 1992). Rather, he used his parents' house on Main Street, which was much larger. Conway (I, 141) gives a vivid account of T's aiding a slave there.

2 Aesop, "The Cock and the Fox."

3 "The hounds are baying on my track, / O Christian! Will you send me back?" (Elizur Wright, "The Fugitive Slave to the Christian," in George W. Clark, *The Liberty Minstrel* [New York, 1845]). Note that T quotes the first line outside of quotation marks.

4 Escaped slaves traditionally used the North Star to guide their way to Canada and freedom.

5 It was common in those days for tourist sites to keep a register in which visitors signed their names. One could be found at the top of Mount Washington, in New Hampshire's White Mountains, as early as 1824.

6 Willis (91–4), a friend of the Alcotts, describes his visit, as a child, with T in his cabin.

7 In the first edition this was misspelled "occcasionally."

from greater and greater remoteness. Men of almost every degree of wit called on me in the migrating season. Some who had more wits than they knew what to do with; 1 run-away slaves with plantation manners, who listened 2 from time to time, like the fox in the fable, as if they heard the hounds a-baying on their track, and looked at me beseechingly, as much as to say,

3 'O Christian, will you send me back?'

One real runaway slave, among the rest, whom I helped 4 to forward toward the north star. Men of one idea, like a hen with one chicken, and that a duckling; men of a thousand ideas, and unkempt heads, like those hens which are made to take charge of a hundred chickens, all in pursuit of one bug, a score of them lost in every morning's dew — and become frizzled and mangy in consequence; men of ideas instead of legs, a sort of intellectual centipede that made you crawl all over. One man proposed a 5 book in which visitors should write their names, as at the White Mountains; but, alas! I have too good a memory to make that necessary.

I could not but notice some of the peculiarities of my 6 visitors. Girls and boys and young women generally seemed glad to be in the woods. They looked in the pond and at the flowers, and improved their time. Men of business, even farmers, thought only of solitude and employment, and of the great distance at which I dwelt from something or other; and though they said that they loved a ramble in 7 the woods occasionally, it was obvious that they did not. Restless committed men, whose time was all taken up in getting a living or keeping it; ministers who spoke of God as if they enjoyed a monopoly of the subject, who could not bear all kinds of opinions; doctors, lawyers, uneasy housekeepers who pried into my cupboard and bed when I was out — how came Mrs. —— to know that my sheets were not as clean as hers? — young men who had ceased to be young, and had concluded that it was safest to follow the beaten track of the professions — all these generally said that it was not possible to do so much good in my position. Ay! there was the rub. The old and infirm and **1** the timid, of whatever age or sex, thought most of sickness, and sudden accident and death; to them life seemed full of danger — what danger is there if you don't think of any? — and they thought that a prudent man would carefully select the safest position, where Dr. B. might be on **2** hand at a moment's warning. To them the village was literally a *com-munity*, a league for mutual defence, and you would suppose that they would not go a-huckleberrying without a medicine chest. The amount of it is, if a man is alive, there is always *danger* that he may die, though the danger must be allowed to be less in proportion as he is dead-and-alive to begin with. A man sits as many risks as he runs. Finally, there were the self-styled reformers, the **3** greatest bores of all, who thought that I was forever singing,

> This is the house that I built;
> This is the man that lives in the house that I built;

4

but they did not know that the third line was,

> These are the folks that worry the man
> That lives in the house that I built.

I did not fear the hen-harriers, for I kept no chickens; but **5**
I feared the men-harriers rather.   **6**

I had more cheering visitors than the last. Children come a-berrying, railroad men taking a Sunday morning walk in clean shirts, fishermen and hunters, poets and

1 "Ay, there's the rub" (*Hamlet,* III, l).

2 Dr. Josiah Bartlett was a Concord physician for over half a century.

3 Emerson's home in Concord was a mecca for reformers from all over the world, and T frequently met many there. T gives a vivid account of three such reformers in his *Journal* for June 17, 1853 (V, 263).

4 T's parody of the familiar nursery rhyme "The House That Jack Built."

5 Various hawks, particularly the red-tailed hawk, that occasionally raided farmers' flocks.

6 Federal marshals searching for fugitive slaves.

View of White Mountains *proper* from town house and store in Jefferson. Other mountains and Franconia Mountains further to the right. N.B.—Oakes puts Jefferson next to Washington, but makes it lower than the third. (July 13, 1858)

1   Samoset's greeting to the Pilgrim fathers upon their arrival in Plymouth. Cooper suggests that T was referring to his English friend Thomas Cholmondeley, but he did not meet Cholmondeley until the fall of 1854, after W was published.

philosophers; in short, all honest pilgrims, who came out to the woods for freedom's sake, and really left the village behind, I was ready to greet with — 'Welcome, Englishmen! welcome, Englishmen!' for I had had communication with that race. [1]

Few mortals ever look down on the tail coverts of a young hen-hawk, yet these are not only beautiful but of a peculiar beauty, being differently marked and colored . . . from those of the old bird. (November 11, 1858)

The Bean-Field

MEANWHILE MY BEANS, the length of whose rows, added together, was seven miles already planted, were impatient to be hoed, for the earliest had grown considerably before the latest were in the ground; indeed they were not easily to be put off. What was the meaning of this so steady and self-respecting, this small Herculean labor, I knew not. I came to love my rows, my beans, though so many more than I wanted. They attached me to the earth, and so I got strength like Antaeus. But why should I raise them? Only Heaven knows. This was my curious labor all summer — to make this portion of the earth's surface, which had yielded only cinquefoil, blackberries, johnswort, and the like, before, sweet wild fruits and pleasant flowers, produce instead this pulse. What shall I learn of beans or beans of me? I cherish them, I hoe them, early and late I have an eye to them; and this is my day's work. It is a fine broad leaf to look on. My auxiliaries are the dews and rains which water this dry soil, and what fertility is in the soil itself, which for the most part is lean and effete. My enemies are worms, cool days, and most of all woodchucks. The last have nibbled for me a quarter of an acre clean. But what right had I to oust johnswort and the rest, and break up their ancient herb garden? Soon, however, the remaining beans will be too tough for them, and go forward to meet new foes.

When I was four years old, as I well remember, I was brought from Boston to this my native town, through these very woods and this field, to the pond. It is one of the oldest scenes stamped on my memory. And now tonight my flute has waked the echoes over that very water. The pines still stand here older than I; or, if some have

1 Gross (1985) describes this chapter as "a wonderfully malicious parody of agricultural reform literature" and points out that beans were never an important money crop in Concord.

Matthews asserts that "careful reading shows that T put W together with the consummate skill of a master craftsman." Domina sees this chapter as a miniature of the whole book.

2 In his *Journal* for June 3, 1851, T identifies them as a variety of bush bean known as "Phaseolus vulgaris"; later in this chapter he identifies them as "common small white bush beans." His beanfield was located on the level land just north of the cabin. In 1857 when he and Emerson were walking in the area, T said he thought the ground barren and offered to replant it for Emerson. It was two years before he did it, when he planted four hundred white pines, as well as oaks, birches, and larch trees. The result was a beautiful grove that became a popular picnic site. In 1872 a spark from a passing locomotive started a fire that burned part of it. But a good deal of the grove lasted well into this century, though the great hurricane of 1938 felled most of what was left. One can still identify the beanfield site by the rows of stumps of the pine trees felled by the hurricane.

3 This is not Thoreauvian hyperbole. He tells us later in the chapter that he planted $2\frac{1}{2}$ acres of beans in rows 15 rods long and 3 feet apart, which means approximately 146 rows. Their total length would be approximately 36,000 feet, or just short of seven miles.

4 Hercules was forced by Zeus to perform twelve labors for Eurystheus, among them the cleaning of the Augean stables and destruction of the Lernean Hydra.

5 In Greek mythology, a giant who became stronger whenever he touched his mother, the Earth. Hercules defeated Antaeus by lifting him up in the air and squeezing him to death in his arms.

6 Pulse: edible seeds of plants having pods.

7 According to legend, T could not bear to kill an offending woodchuck, so he caught it in a box trap, releasing it several miles away to feed on someone else's garden (Canby, 219).

(Notes to page 151 continued on next page)

(Notes to page 151 continued)

8   In his *Journal* for August 1845 (I, 380), T says he was five at the time of this visit.

9   Thoreau was born in Concord. In 1818 his family moved to Chelmsford, and then in 1821 to Boston, returning to Concord to settle permanently in 1823.

10   T's flute can be seen in the Concord Museum.

PAGE 152

1   T had a lifelong interest in Indians and assembled a large collection of Indian artifacts that is now in the Fruitlands Museum in Harvard, Massachusetts (Sayre). Ellery Channing tells a story: "In his walk, his companion, a citizen, said, 'I do not see where you find your Indian arrowheads.' Stooping to the ground, Henry picked one up, and presented it to him, crying, 'Here is one.'" T tells a somewhat similar anecdote in his *Journal* for October 29, 1837 (I, 7).

2   Myers analyzes this paragraph at length to explain T's methods and purposes.

3   The farmers knew more about this than T did, as Paul Williams (1977) points out. Most gardening books say that if bean plants are bruised when wet, they are likely to spread disease.

4   "And sprinkled dust upon their heads towards heaven" (Job 2:12).

fallen, I have cooked my supper with their stumps, and a new growth is rising all around, preparing another aspect for new infant eyes. Almost the same johnswort springs from the same perennial root in this pasture, and even I have at length helped to clothe that fabulous landscape of my infant dreams, and one of the results of my presence and influence is seen in these bean leaves, corn blades, and potato vines.

I planted about two acres and a half of upland; and as it was only about fifteen years since the land was cleared, and I myself had got out two or three cords of stumps, I did not give it any manure; but in the course of the sum-
1 mer it appeared by the arrowheads which I turned up in hoeing, that an extinct nation had anciently dwelt here and planted corn and beans ere white men came to clear the land, and so, to some extent, had exhausted the soil for this very crop.

2   Before yet any woodchuck or squirrel had run across the road, or the sun had got above the shrub oaks, while all the dew was on, though the farmers warned me against
3 it — I would advise you to do all your work if possible while the dew is on — I began to level the ranks of haughty
4 weeds in my bean-field and throw dust upon their heads. Early in the morning I worked barefooted, dabbling like a plastic artist in the dewy and crumbling sand, but later in the day the sun blistered my feet. There the sun lighted me to hoe beans, pacing slowly backward and forward over that yellow gravelly upland, between the long green rows, fifteen rods, the one end terminating in a shrub oak copse where I could rest in the shade, the other in a blackberry field where the green berries deepened their tints by the time I had made another bout. Removing the weeds, putting fresh soil about the bean stems, and encouraging this weed which I had sown, making the yel-

low soil express its summer thought in bean leaves and blossoms rather than in wormwood and piper and millet grass, making the earth say beans instead of grass — this was my daily work. As I had little aid from horses or cattle, or hired men or boys, or improved implements of husbandry, I was much slower, and became much more intimate with my beans than usual. But labor of the hands, [1] even when pursued to the verge of drudgery, is perhaps never the worst form of idleness. It has a constant and imperishable moral, and to the scholar it yields a classic result. A very *agricola laboriosus* was I to travellers bound [2] westward through Lincoln and Wayland to nobody knows [3] where; they sitting at their ease in gigs, with elbows on [4] knees, and reins loosely hanging in festoons; I the home-staying, laborious native of the soil. But soon my homestead was out of their sight and thought. It was the only open and cultivated field for a great distance on either side of the road, so they made the most of it; and sometimes the man in the field heard more of travellers' gossip and comment than was meant for his ear: 'Beans so late! peas so late!' — for I continued to plant when others had begun to hoe — the ministerial husbandman had not sus- [5] pected it. 'Corn, my boy, for fodder; corn for fodder.' 'Does he *live* there?' asks the black bonnet of the gray coat; and the hard-featured farmer reins up his grateful dobbin to inquire what you are doing where he sees no [6] manure in the furrow, and recommends a little chip dirt, [7] or any little waste stuff, or it may be ashes or plaster. But here were two acres and a half of furrows, and only a hoe for cart and two hands to draw it — there being an aversion to other carts and horses — and chip dirt far away. Fellow-travellers as they rattled by compared it aloud with the fields which they had passed, so that I came to know how I stood in the agricultural world. This was one field

1   Each year T planted and cultivated a vegetable garden at his parents' home.

2   Hard-working farmer.

3   The road past Walden Pond leads from Concord to Lincoln and thence to Wayland (Gleason).

4   A light, two-wheeled, horse-drawn carriage.

5   The Reverend Henry Colman [*sic*] (1785–1849) published for the state a series of four agricultural surveys of Massachusetts, from 1838 to 1841. T misspelled the name throughout the chapter, and Shanley (1971, 399) has corrected it in each case.

6   Common pet name for a horse.

7   Sweepings from an area where wood has been chopped.

1 The various grass crops grown for fodder in New England were not native but imported, and were known as English hay to distinguish them from meadow hay harvested for bedding.

2 Hirsh suggests that T was thinking of Friedrich von Schiller's "Ranz des Vaches," the opening song of *Wilhelm Tell* (1804). A *ranz des vaches* is a Swiss pastoral song for calling cows home. Shanley (1971, 399) corrects T's first edition misspelling of "Rans."

3 Nicolò Paganini (1782–1840), perhaps the most famous violinist of all time, was noted for his ability to play entire passages on a single string.

not in Mr. Colman's report. And, by the way, who estimates the value of the crop which nature yields in the still wilder fields unimproved by man? The crop of *English* **1** hay is carefully weighed, the moisture calculated, the silicates and the potash; but in all dells and pond-holes in the woods and pastures and swamps grows a rich and various crop only unreaped by man. Mine was, as it were, the connecting link between wild and cultivated fields; as some states are civilized, and others half-civilized, and others savage or barbarous, so my field was, though not in a bad sense, a half-cultivated field. They were beans cheerfully returning to their wild and primitive state that I **2** cultivated, and my hoe played the *Ranz des Vaches* for them.

Near at hand, upon the topmost spray of a birch, sings the brown thrasher — or red mavis, as some love to call him — all the morning, glad of your society, that would find out another farmer's field if yours were not here. While you are planting the seed, he cries — 'Drop it, drop it — cover it up, cover it up — pull it up, pull it up, pull it up.' But this was not corn, and so it was safe from such enemies as he. You may wonder what his rigmarole, **3** his amateur Paganini performances on one string or on twenty, have to do with your planting, and yet prefer it to leached ashes or plaster. It was a cheap sort of top dressing in which I had entire faith.

As I drew a still fresher soil about the rows with my hoe, I disturbed the ashes of unchronicled nations who in primeval years lived under these heavens, and their small implements of war and hunting were brought to the light of this modern day. They lay mingled with other natural stones, some of which bore the marks of having been burned by Indian fires, and some by the sun, and also bits of pottery and glass brought hither by the recent cultivators of the soil. When my hoe tinkled against the stones,

The birches have been steadily changing and falling for a long, long time. The lowermost leaves turn golden and fall first; so their autumn change is like a fire which has steadily burned up higher and higher, consuming the fuel below, till now it has nearly reached their tops. (October 22, 1858)

that music echoed to the woods and the sky, and was an accompaniment to my labor which yielded an instant and immeasurable crop. It was no longer beans that I hoed, nor I that hoed beans; and I remembered with as much pity as pride, if I remembered at all, my acquaintances who had gone to the city to attend the oratorios. The nighthawk circled overhead in the sunny afternoons [1] — for I sometimes made a day of it — like a mote in the [2] eye, or in heaven's eye, falling from time to time with a swoop and a sound as if the heavens were rent, torn at last to very rags and tatters, and yet a seamless cope remained; small imps that fill the air and lay their eggs on the ground on bare sand or rocks on the tops of hills, where few have found them; graceful and slender like ripples caught up from the pond, as leaves are raised by the wind to float in the heavens; such kindredship is in nature. The hawk is aerial brother of the wave which he sails over and surveys, those his perfect air-inflated wings answering to the elemental unfledged pinions of the sea. Or sometimes I watched a pair of hen-hawks circling high in the sky, al- [3] ternately soaring and descending, approaching and leaving one another, as if they were the embodiment of my own thoughts. Or I was attracted by the passage of wild pigeons from this wood to that, with a slight quivering winnowing sound and carrier haste; or from under a rotten stump my hoe turned up a sluggish portentous and outlandish spotted salamander, a trace of Egypt and the [4] Nile, yet our contemporary. When I paused to lean on my hoe, these sounds and sights I heard and saw anywhere in the row, a part of the inexhaustible entertainment which the country offers.

On gala days the town fires its great guns, which echo like popguns to these woods, and some waifs of martial music occasionally penetrate thus far. To me, away there

[1] Not a hawk at all but a member of the goatsucker family and a relative of the whippoorwill.

[2] "Why beholdest thou the mote that is in thy brother's eye?" (Matthew 7:3).

[3] Common name for any large hawk, but especially the red-tailed hawk.

[4] A common amphibian, black with bright yellow spots.

On the wall, at the brook behind Cyrus Hosmer's barn, I start a nighthawk within a rod or two. It alights again on his barn-yard board fence, sitting diagonally. (May 29, 1860)

1   A common fungus that, when ripe, bursts open when touched, spreading its spores in all directions.

2   Scarlatina: now known as scarlet fever. Emerson's son died of it in 1842.

3   Canker-rash: a form of malignant sore throat.

4   All young men were required to turn out for military training and were known as trainers.

5   Most of T's references to bees are negative, rejecting them as automatons (Swanson).

6   The nearest that Virgil seems to have come to that word is in his *Georgics,* where in book IV he uses the word *tinnitusque.*

7   A folk belief that swarming bees could be called back to their hive.

8   Concord is in Middlesex County.

9   "And the trumpet that sings of fame" (Felicia Hemans, "The Landing of the Pilgrims"). Hemans was one of T's favorite poets.

10   The United States was at war with Mexico during T's stay at Walden. Need it be pointed out that T is using irony here?

11   In T's day, elm trees lined most of Concord's streets. They have long since been killed off by Dutch elm disease.

in my bean-field at the other end of the town, the big guns sounded as if a puffball had burst; and when there was a military turnout of which I was ignorant, I have sometimes had a vague sense all the day of some sort of itching and disease in the horizon, as if some eruption would break out there soon, either scarlatina or canker-rash, until at length some more favorable puff of wind, making haste over the fields and up the Wayland road, brought me information of the 'trainers.' It seemed by the distant hum as if somebody's bees had swarmed, and that the neighbors, according to Virgil's advice, by a faint *tintinnabulum* upon the most sonorous of their domestic utensils, were endeavoring to call them down into the hive again. And when the sound died quite away, and the hum had ceased, and the most favorable breezes told no tale, I knew that they had got the last drone of them all safely into the Middlesex hive, and that now their minds were bent on the honey with which it was smeared.

I felt proud to know that the liberties of Massachusetts and of our fatherland were in such safe keeping; and as I turned to my hoeing again I was filled with an inexpressible confidence, and pursued my labor cheerfully with a calm trust in the future.

When there were several bands of musicians, it sounded as if all the village was a vast bellows and all the buildings expanded and collapsed alternately with a din. But sometimes it was a really noble and inspiring strain that reached these woods, and the trumpet that sings of fame, and I felt as if I could spit a Mexican with a good relish — for why should we always stand for trifles? — and looked round for a woodchuck or a skunk to exercise my chivalry upon. These martial strains seemed as far away as Palestine, and reminded me of a march of crusaders in the horizon, with a slight tantivy and tremulous motion of the elm tree tops which overhang the village. This was one of the *great* days; though the sky had from my clearing only the same everlastingly great look that it wears daily, and I saw no difference in it.

It was a singular experience that long acquaintance which I cultivated with beans, what with planting, and hoeing, and harvesting, and threshing, and picking over and selling them — the last was the hardest of all — I might add eating, for I did taste. I was determined to know **1** beans. When they were growing, I used to hoe from five o'clock in the morning till noon, and commonly spent the rest of the day about other affairs. Consider the intimate and curious acquaintance one makes with various kinds of weeds — it will bear some iteration in the account, for there was no little iteration in the labor — disturbing their delicate organizations so ruthlessly, and making such invidious distinctions with his hoe, levelling whole ranks of one species, and sedulously cultivating another. That's Roman wormwood — that's pigweed — that's sorrel — that's piper-grass — have at him, chop him up, turn his roots upward to the sun, don't let him have a fibre in the shade, if you do he'll turn himself t'other side up and be as green as a leek in two days. A long war, not **2** with cranes, but with weeds, those Trojans who had sun **3** and rain and dews on their side. Daily the beans saw me come to their rescue armed with a hoe, and thin the ranks of their enemies, filling up the trenches with weedy dead. Many a lusty crest-waving Hector, that towered a whole **4** foot above his crowding comrades, fell before my weapon and rolled in the dust.

Those summer days which some of my contemporaries devoted to the fine arts in Boston or Rome, and others to contemplation in India, and others to trade in London or New York, I thus, with the other farmers of New England,

1 A common expression in New England still is "He doesn't know beans," meaning the person is ignorant.
2 A reference to the simile in the opening lines of *Iliad* III.
3 The enemies of the Greeks in the *Iliad.*
4 The son of King Priam and Hecuba, he was the most valiant of the Trojan warriors. The falling and rolling in the dust is described in the *Iliad* (22.330).

Chenopodium album, pigweed. The common form of the arrowhead, with larger, clear-white flowers. Also another arrowhead, with a leaf shaped (July 14, 1852).

 not

1 Pythagoras, an ancient Greek philosopher and mathematician, forbade his disciples to eat beans because he supposed them to have been produced from the same putrefied matter from which, at the creation of the world, man was formed.

2 In the ancient world beans were often used as voting tallies.

3 John Evelyn, *Terra: A Philosophical Discourse of Earth* (London, 1729, 14–6).

4 Laetation: manure.

5 Repastination: a second digging.

6 Succedaneous: employed as a substitute.

7 English writer (1603–1665). "Vital spirits" is all T quotes from Digby, and even that he derives from Evelyn (West, 1971; Pebworth).

8 T was probably the largest bean grower in Concord that year, for beans were not an important Concord crop (Gross, 1985).

9 T actually paid only about half the going rate at that time (Gross, 1985).

10 Crow fence: a scarecrow device.

devoted to husbandry. Not that I wanted beans to eat, for I am by nature a Pythagorean, so far as beans are concerned, whether they mean porridge or voting, and exchanged them for rice; but, perchance, as some must work in fields if only for the sake of tropes and expression, to serve a parable-maker one day. It was on the whole a rare amusement, which, continued too long, might have become a dissipation. Though I gave them no manure, and did not hoe them all once, I hoed them unusually well as far as I went, and was paid for it in the end, 'there being in truth,' as Evelyn says, 'no compost or laetation whatsoever comparable to this continual motion, repastination, and turning of the mould with the spade.' 'The earth,' he adds elsewhere, 'especially if fresh, has a certain magnetism in it, by which it attracts the salt, power, or virtue (call it either) which gives it life, and is the logic of all the labor and stir we keep about it, to sustain us; all dungings and other sordid temperings being but the vicars succedaneous to this improvement.' Moreover, this being one of those 'worn-out and exhausted lay fields which enjoy their sabbath,' had perchance, as Sir Kenelm Digby thinks likely, attracted 'vital spirits' from the air. I harvested twelve bushels of beans.

But to be more particular, for it is complained that Mr. Colman has reported chiefly the expensive experiments of gentlemen farmers, my outgoes were,

For a hoe	$0	54
Plowing, harrowing, and furrowing	7	50 Too much.
Beans for seed	3	12 ½
Potatoes "	1	33
Peas "	0	40
Turnip seed	0	06
White line for crow fence	0	02
Horse cultivator and boy three hours	1	00

Horse and cart to get crop . . . .   o 75
In all . . . . $14 72 ½

My income was (patremfamilias vendacem, non **1**
emacem esse oportet), from

Nine bushels and twelve quarts of beans sold $16 94
Five " large potatoes 2 50
Nine " small 2 25
Grass 1 00
Stalks . . . .   o 75
In all $23 44
Leaving a pecuniary profit, as I have   **2**
   elsewhere said, of . . . . $08 71 ½

This is the result of my experience in raising beans:
Plant the common small white bush bean about the first
of June, in rows three feet by eighteen inches apart, being
careful to select fresh round and unmixed seed. First look **3**
out for worms, and supply vacancies by planting anew.
Then look out for woodchucks, if it is an exposed place,
for they will nibble off the earliest tender leaves almost
clean as they go; and again, when the young tendrils
make their appearance, they have notice of it, and will
shear them off with both buds and young pods, sitting
erect like a squirrel. But above all harvest as early as
possible, if you would escape frosts and have a fair and
salable crop; you may save much loss by this means.

This further experience also I gained: I said to myself, I
will not plant beans and corn with so much industry
another summer, but such seeds, if the seed is not lost, as
sincerity, truth, simplicity, faith, innocence, and the like,
and see if they will not grow in this soil, even with less toil
and manurance, and sustain me, for surely it has not been
exhausted for these crops. Alas! I said this to myself; but
now another summer is gone, and another, and another,
and I am obliged to say to you, Reader, that the seeds

1   "The master should have the selling
habit, not the buying habit" (Cato, *De Agri Cultura* 2.7).

2   Elsewhere: in "Economy," p. 55.

3   An account of Squanto teaching the
Pilgrims how to plant corn can be found in
Alexander Young, *Chronicles of the Pilgrim
Fathers* (Boston, 1841, 231).

1   It was a popular custom in T's day for congressmen to distribute free seeds to their constituents.

2   Gozzi (1966) points out that T is too elliptical here, and we must insert after "earth" the words "rather we would deal with him as" to make sense of the sentence — which Shanley (1971, 399) does.

which I planted, if indeed they *were* the seeds of those virtues, were wormeaten or had lost their vitality, and so did not come up. Commonly men will only be brave as their fathers were brave, or timid. This generation is very sure to plant corn and beans each new year precisely as the Indians did centuries ago and taught the first settlers to do, as if there were a fate in it. I saw an old man the other day, to my astonishment, making the holes with a hoe for the seventieth time at least, and not for himself to lie down in! But why should not the New Englander try new adventures, and not lay so much stress on his grain, his potato and grass crop, and his orchards — raise other crops than these? Why concern ourselves so much about our beans for seed, and not be concerned at all about a new generation of men? We should really be fed and cheered if when we met a man we were sure to see that some of the qualities which I have named, which we all prize more than those other productions, but which are for the most part broadcast and floating in the air, had taken root and grown in him. Here comes such a subtile and ineffable quality, for instance, as truth or justice, though the slightest amount or new variety of it, along the road. Our ambassadors should be instructed to send home

1 such seeds as these, and Congress help to distribute them over all the land. We should never stand upon ceremony with sincerity. We should never cheat and insult and banish one another by our meanness, if there were present the kernel of worth and friendliness. We should not meet thus in haste. Most men I do not meet at all, for they seem not to have time; they are busy about their beans. We would not deal with a man thus plodding ever, leaning on a hoe or a spade as a staff between his work, not as a

2 mushroom, but partially risen out of the earth, something

more than erect, like swallows alighted and walking on the ground:

> 'And as he spake, his wings would now and then
> Spread, as he meant to fly, then close again — '   **1**

so that we should suspect that we might be conversing with an angel. Bread may not always nourish us; but it always does us good, it even takes stiffness out of our joints, and makes us supple and buoyant, when we knew not what ailed us, to recognize any generosity in man or Nature, to share any unmixed and heroic joy.

Ancient poetry and mythology suggest, at least, that **2** husbandry was once a sacred art; but it is pursued with irreverent haste and heedlessness by us, our object being to have large farms and large crops merely. We have no festival, nor procession, nor ceremony, not excepting our cattle-shows and so-called Thanksgivings, by which the **3** farmer expresses a sense of the sacredness of his calling, or is reminded of its sacred origin. It is the premium and the feast which tempt him. He sacrifices not to Ceres and **4** the Terrestrial Jove, but to the infernal Plutus rather. By **5, 6** avarice and selfishness, and a grovelling habit, from which none of us is free, of regarding the soil as property, or the means of acquiring property chiefly, the landscape is deformed, husbandry is degraded with us, and the farmer leads the meanest of lives. He knows Nature but as a robber. Cato says that the profits of agriculture are particularly pious or just (*maximeque pius quaestus*), and **7** according to Varro the old Romans 'called the same earth **8** Mother and Ceres, and thought that they who cultivated it led a pious and useful life, and that they alone were left of the race of King Saturn.'

We are wont to forget that the sun looks on our culti- **9**

1   Francis Quarles, "The Shepherd's Oracles," eclogue V.

2   Cook (1971, 41–2) relates this passage to a primitive use of magic.

3   Middlesex County held a cattle show, or county fair, in Concord every year. T delivered his "The Succession of Forest Trees" lecture there in 1860.

4   The Roman goddess of corn and harvests.

5   Terrestrial Jove: Jupiter, the Roman god of the earth.

6   Plutus, the Greek god of agricultural prosperity, is often confused with Pluto, the god of the underworld. Albanese (313) suggests that T referred to Plutus as infernal because he supposedly corrupted farmers into acquiring wealth.

7   "At best the most respected" (Cato, *De Agri Cultura*, introduction).

8   "It was not without reason that they called the same earth 'Mother' and 'Ceres'" (M. Terenti Varronis [Varro], Rerum Rusticarum [*On Agriculture*], 3.1.5). Saturn was the Greek god of agriculture. When he was banished from his throne by Jupiter, he fled to Italy and taught the natives there the art of agriculture.

9   "For he maketh his sun to rise on the evil and on the good, and sendeth rain on the just and unjust" (Matthew 5:45).

"The grain is so called from *gerere;* for the seed is planted that the ear may 'bear' (*gerat*) the grain. . . . The ear, however, which the peasants, in their old-fashioned way, call *speca,* seems to have got its name from *spes:* for it is because they hope (*sperant*) to have this grow that they plant" (Varro, *Rerum Rusticarum,* I.48.2–3).

2 Referring to the Old Testament law that a man sacrifice to God the first fruits of his crops (Exodus 22:29).

vated fields and on the prairies and forests without distinction. They all reflect and absorb his rays alike, and the former make but a small part of the glorious picture which he beholds in his daily course. In his view the earth is all equally cultivated like a garden. Therefore we should receive the benefit of his light and heat with a corresponding trust and magnanimity. What though I value the seed of these beans, and harvest that in the fall of the year? This broad field which I have looked at so long looks not to me as the principal cultivator, but away from me to influences more genial to it, which water and make it green. These beans have results which are not harvested by me. Do they not grow for woodchucks partly? The ear **1** of wheat (in Latin *spica,* obsoletely *speca,* from *spe,* hope) should not be the only hope of the husbandman; its kernel or grain (*granum* from *gerendo,* bearing) is not all that it bears. How, then, can our harvest fail? Shall I not rejoice also at the abundance of the weeds whose seeds are the granary of the birds? It matters little comparatively whether the fields fill the farmer's barns. The true husbandman will cease from anxiety, as the squirrels manifest no concern whether the woods will bear chestnuts this year or not, and finish his labor with every day, relinquishing all claim to the produce of his fields, and sac- **2** rificing in his mind not only his first but his last fruits also.

The Village

AFTER HOEING, OR perhaps reading and writing, in the
forenoon, I usually bathed again in the pond, swimming
across one of its coves for a stint, and washed the dust of **2**
labor from my person, or smoothed out the last wrinkle
which study had made, and for the afternoon was absolutely free. Every day or two I strolled to the village to
hear some of the gossip which is incessantly going on
there, circulating either from mouth to mouth, or from
newspaper to newspaper, and which, taken in homeo- **3**
pathic doses, was really as refreshing in its way as the
rustle of leaves and the peeping of frogs. As I walked in
the woods to see the birds and squirrels, so I walked in the
village to see the men and boys; instead of the wind
among the pines I heard the carts rattle. In one direction
from my house there was a colony of muskrats in the river
meadows; under the grove of elms and buttonwoods in
the other horizon was a village of busy men, as curious to
me as if they had been prairie-dogs, each sitting at the
mouth of its burrow, or running over to a neighbor's to
gossip. I went there frequently to observe their habits.
The village appeared to me a great news room; and on
one side, to support it, as once at Redding & Company's **4**
on State Street, they kept nuts and raisins, or salt and
meal and other groceries. Some have such a vast appetite
for the former commodity, that is, the news, and such
sound digestive organs, that they can sit forever in public
avenues without stirring, and let it simmer and whisper
through them like the Etesian winds, or as if inhaling **5**
ether, it only producing numbness and insensibility to **6**
pain — otherwise it would often be painful to hear —
without affecting the consciousness. I hardly ever failed,

1 This is the shortest chapter in the book,
implying village matters are of little importance
to T.

2 When M. Fabulet was translating W into
French, he had difficulty with "stint." Finding
that in England the word was also the name of
a small sandpiper, he translated "for a stint" as
"en chasse d'une bécassine," that is, "in pursuit
of a snipe" (Allen, 1952).

3 Homeopathic remedies are taken in minute doses.

4 Redding & Company were booksellers at
8 State Street, Boston.

5 A Mediterranean summer wind from the
north, frequently mentioned by classical writers.

6 Ether came into general use in Boston in
the late 1840s. Emerson's brother-in-law, Dr.
Charles Jackson and Oliver Wendell Holmes,
Sr., were early proponents of the use of ether.

1 Caryatid: a female figure used as a supporting column in Greek architecture.

2 A punishment formerly used on sailing ships. The crew, provided with rope ends, were lined up in two rows, and the delinquent sailor had to run between them as the crew delivered as many lashes as they could.

3 In colonial times, houses were taxed according to the number of windows.

when I rambled through the village, to see a row of such worthies, either sitting on a ladder sunning themselves, with their bodies inclined forward and their eyes glancing along the line this way and that, from time to time, with a voluptuous expression, or else leaning against a barn with

1 their hands in their pockets, like caryatides, as if to prop it up. They, being commonly out of doors, heard whatever was in the wind. These are the coarsest mills, in which all gossip is first rudely digested or cracked up before it is emptied into finer and more delicate hoppers within doors. I observed that the vitals of the village were the grocery, the bar-room, the post-office, and the bank; and, as a necessary part of the machinery, they kept a bell, a big gun, and a fire engine, at convenient places; and the houses were so arranged as to make the most of mankind, in lanes and fronting one another, so that every traveller

2 had to run the gauntlet, and every man, woman, and child might get a lick at him. Of course, those who were stationed nearest to the head of the line, where they could most see and be seen, and have the first blow at him, paid the highest prices for their places; and the few straggling inhabitants in the outskirts, where long gaps in the line began to occur, and the traveller could get over walls or turn aside into cow-paths, and so escape, paid a very slight

3 ground or window tax. Signs were hung out on all sides to allure him; some to catch him by the appetite, as the tavern and victualling cellar; some by the fancy, as the dry goods store and the jeweller's; and others by the hair or the feet or the skirts, as the barber, the shoemaker, or the tailor. Besides, there was a still more terrible standing invitation to call at every one of these houses, and company expected about these times. For the most part I escaped wonderfully from these dangers, either by proceeding at once boldly and without deliberation to the

In 1677 the town's "brandmarke" as fixed by the State was ⌐ℓ ⌐. (August 14, 1859)

goal, as is recommended to those who run the gauntlet, or by keeping my thoughts on high things, like Orpheus, who, 'loudly singing the praises of the gods to his lyre, drowned the voices of the Sirens, and kept out of danger.' **1** Sometimes I bolted suddenly, and nobody could tell my whereabouts, for I did not stand much about gracefulness, and never hesitated at a gap in a fence. I was even accustomed to make an irruption into some houses, where I **2** was well entertained, and after learning the kernels and very last sieveful of news — what had subsided, the prospects of war and peace, and whether the world was likely to hold together much longer — I was let out through the rear avenues, and so escaped to the woods again.

It was very pleasant, when I stayed late in town, to launch myself into the night, especially if it was dark and tempestuous, and set sail from some bright village parlor or lecture room, with a bag of rye or Indian meal upon my shoulder, for my snug harbor in the woods, having made all tight without and withdrawn under hatches with a merry crew of thoughts, leaving only my outer man at the helm, or even tying up the helm when it was plain sailing. I had many a genial thought by the cabin fire 'as I **3** sailed.' I was never cast away nor distressed in any weather, though I encountered some severe storms. It is darker in the woods, even in common nights, than most suppose. I frequently had to look up at the opening between the trees above the path in order to learn my route, and, where there was no cart-path, to feel with my feet the faint track which I had worn, or steer by the known relation of particular trees which I felt with my hands, passing between two pines for instance, not more than eighteen inches apart, in the midst of the woods, invariably, in the **4** darkest night. Sometimes, after coming home thus late in a dark and muggy night, when my feet felt the path which

1 Sir Francis Bacon, *De Sapienta Veterum,* chap. 31; apparently T's translation (Woodson, 1975).

2 T was likely thinking of Emerson here, for it was but a short walk from Emerson's back door, through the fields and woods, to the Walden cabin.

3 The refrain of the old American "Ballad of Captain Robert Kidd."

4 In his copy of W, T inserted the comma after "invariably."

1   As Thomas Blanding has suggested to me, these were quite probably George William Curtis and his brother Burrill, who lived for a time on the Hosmer farm on Lincoln Road and who had helped T build his cabin (Gleason).

my eyes could not see, dreaming and absent-minded all the way, until I was aroused by having to raise my hand to lift the latch, I have not been able to recall a single step of my walk, and I have thought that perhaps my body would find its way home if its master should forsake it, as the hand finds its way to the mouth without assistance. Several times, when a visitor chanced to stay into evening, and it proved a dark night, I was obliged to conduct him to the cart-path in the rear of the house, and then point out to him the direction he was to pursue, and in keeping which he was to be guided rather by his feet than his eyes. One very dark night I directed thus on their way two young men who had been fishing in the pond. They lived about a mile off through the woods, and were quite used to the route. A day or two after one of them told me that they wandered about the greater part of the night, close by their own premises, and did not get home till toward morning, by which time, as there had been several heavy showers in the meanwhile, and the leaves were very wet, they were drenched to their skins. I have heard of many going astray even in the village streets, when the darkness was so thick that you could cut it with a knife, as the saying is. Some who live in the outskirts, having come to town a-shopping in their wagons, have been obliged to put up for the night; and gentlemen and ladies making a call have gone half a mile out of their way, feeling the sidewalk only with their feet, and not knowing when they turned. It is a surprising and memorable, as well as valuable experience, to be lost in the woods any time. Often in a snowstorm, even by day, one will come out upon a well-known road and yet find it impossible to tell which way leads to the village. Though he knows that he has travelled it a thousand times, he cannot recognize a feature in it, but it is as strange to him as if it were a road in

Siberia. By night, of course, the perplexity is infinitely greater In our most trivial walks, we are constantly, though unconsciously, steering like pilots by certain well-known beacons and headlands, and if we go beyond our usual course we still carry in our minds the bearing of some neighboring cape; and not till we are completely lost, or turned round — for a man needs only to be turned round once with his eyes shut in this world to be lost — do we appreciate the vastness and strangeness of nature. Every man has to learn the points of compass again as often as he awakes, whether from sleep or any abstraction. Not till we are lost, in other words not till we have lost the world, do we begin to find ourselves, and realize where we are **1** and the infinite extent of our relations.

One afternoon, near the end of the first summer, when I went to the village to get a shoe from the cobbler's, I was seized and put into jail, because, as I have elsewhere **2** related, I did not pay a tax to, or recognize the authority of, the State which buys and sells men, women, and children, like cattle, at the door of its senate-house. I had gone down to the woods for other purposes. But, wherever a man goes, men will pursue and paw him with their dirty institutions, and, if they can, constrain him to belong to their desperate odd-fellow society. It is true, I might have **3** resisted forcibly with more or less effect, might have run 'amok' against society; but I preferred that society should run 'amok' against me, it being the desperate party. However, I was released the next day, obtained my mended shoe, and returned to the woods in season to get my dinner of huckleberries on Fair Haven Hill. I was never **4** molested by any person but those who represented the State. I had no lock nor bolt but for the desk which held my papers, not even a nail to put over my latch or windows. I never fastened my door night or day, though I was

1 "He that findeth his life shall lose it; and he that loseth his life for my sake shall find it" (Matthew 10:39).

2 T has told in further detail the story of his personal rebellion against slavery in "Resistance to Civil Government" (better known as "Civil Disobedience"), which has had a worldwide impact on such people as Gandhi and Martin Luther King and their followers.

3 A pun on the Independent Order of Odd Fellows, a fraternal organization.

4 A short distance southwest of Walden, on the shore of the Sudbury River (Gleason).

1 T left Walden for Maine on August 31, 1846. His account of this excursion can be found in the first chapter ("Ktaadn") of *The Maine Woods*.

2 It was the first volume of the Pope translation of the *Iliad* (Baltimore, 1812; Harding, 1983). It was apparently "borrowed" by the French-Canadian woodcutter Alex Therien, for it was found in his family's possession more than a century later (Harding, 1993, 190–1). It has since disappeared again. Therien was apparently attracted to it by T's reading to him from it (see "Visitors"). Interestingly, in his chapter "Reading" T denounces the use of translations of the great books, but he kept Pope's translation in his Walden cabin.

3 In the "Sayings of Confucius," which T edited for the *Dial* (III, 494), he quotes, "A soldier of the kingdom of Ci lost his buckler; and having sought after it a long time in vain, he comforted himself with this reflection: 'A soldier has lost his buckler, but a soldier in our camp will find it; he will use it.'" He had apparently found this fable in *The Phenix: A Collection of Old and Rare Fragments* (New York, 1836, 83), where it is printed as one of the "Morals of Confucius."

4 "Nev bella fuerant, Faginus abstabat quum [*sic*] scyphus ante dapes" (*Elegies of Tibullus* 3.11.7–8). It is interesting to note that John Evelyn quotes these two lines and gives almost exactly the same translation in *Silva; or, A Discourse of Forest-Trees* (London, 1679, 46), so it is quite possible that T derived the quotation from this secondary source.

5 *Confucian Analects*, XII, xix.

1 to be absent several days; not even when the next fall I spent a fortnight in the woods of Maine. And yet my house was more respected than if it had been surrounded by a file of soldiers. The tired rambler could rest and warm himself by my fire, the literary amuse himself with the few books on my table, or the curious, by opening my closet door, see what was left of my dinner, and what prospect I had of a supper. Yet, though many people of every class came this way to the pond, I suffered no serious inconvenience from these sources, and I never missed 2 anything but one small book, a volume of Homer, which perhaps was improperly gilded, and this I trust a soldier of 3 our camp has found by this time. I am convinced, that if all men were to live as simply as I then did, thieving and robbery would be unknown. These take place only in communities where some have got more than is sufficient while others have not enough. The Pope's Homers would soon get properly distributed.

4

'Nec bella fuerunt,
Faginus astabat dum scyphus ante dapes.'

'Nor wars did men molest,
When only beechen bowls were in request.'

'You who govern public affairs, what need have you to employ punishments? Love virtue, and the people will be virtuous. The virtues of a superior man are like the wind; the virtues of a common man are like the grass; the grass, 5 when the wind passes over it, bends.'

THE PONDS

SOMETIMES, HAVING HAD a surfeit of human society and gossip, and worn out all my village friends, I rambled still farther westward than I habitually dwell, into yet more unfrequented parts of the town, 'to fresh woods and pastures new,' or, while the sun was setting, made my supper of huckleberries and blueberries on Fair Haven Hill, and laid up a store for several days. The fruits do not yield their true flavor to the purchaser of them, nor to him who raises them for the market. There is but one way to obtain it, yet few take that way. If you would know the flavor of huckleberries, ask the cow-boy or the partridge. It is a vulgar error to suppose that you have tasted huckleberries who never plucked them. A huckleberry never reaches Boston; they have not been known there since they grew on her three hills. The ambrosial and essential part of the fruit is lost with the bloom which is rubbed off in the market cart, and they become mere provender. As long as Eternal Justice reigns, not one innocent huckleberry can be transported thither from the country's hills.

Occasionally, after my hoeing was done for the day, I joined some impatient companion who had been fishing on the pond since morning, as silent and motionless as a duck or a floating leaf, and, after practising various kinds of philosophy, had concluded commonly, by the time I arrived, that he belonged to the ancient sect of Coenobites. There was one older man, an excellent fisher and skilled in all kinds of woodcraft, who was pleased to look upon my house as a building erected for the convenience of fishermen; and I was equally pleased when he sat in my doorway to arrange his lines. Once in a while we sat together on the pond, he at one end of the boat, and I at

---

1 Woodruff argues that T in this chapter imparts to Walden Pond "a cosmological significance which places it simultaneously both within and outside space and time."
For an analysis of the structure of this chapter in relation to the book as a whole, see Baker.

2 Milton, "Lycidas," line 193.

3 Again, on the shore of the Sudbury River, south of Walden (Gleason).

4 "Would you know the ripest cherries? Ask the boys and blackbirds" (Goethe, "Sprichwortlich," lines 458–9).

5 A boy who tends cows in the local pastures, as distinct from the cowboy of the western ranges.

6 Copp's, Fort, and Beacon Hills, where the city was first founded.

7 Huckleberries and blueberries are often confused. It is the blueberry that has a bloom, not the huckleberry.

8 Members of a religious order, but here used as one of T's best — or worst — puns, that is, "See, no bites."

1　George William Curtis tells of a very similar incident involving himself and T on the Concord River. Presumably T simply transferred the incident to Walden, and Curtis is the companion mentioned.

the other; but not many words passed between us, for he had grown deaf in his later years, but he occasionally hummed a psalm, which harmonized well enough with my philosophy. Our intercourse was thus altogether one of unbroken harmony, far more pleasing to remember than if it had been carried on by speech. When, as was commonly the case, I had none to commune with, I used to raise the echoes by striking with a paddle on the side of my boat, filling the surrounding woods with circling and dilating sound, stirring them up as the keeper of a menagerie his wild beasts, until I elicited a growl from every wooded vale and hillside.

In warm evenings I frequently sat in the boat playing the flute, and saw the perch, which I seem to have charmed, hovering around me, and the moon travelling over the ribbed bottom, which was strewed with the wrecks of the forest. Formerly I had come to this pond adventurously, from time to time, in dark summer nights, with a **1** companion, and, making a fire close to the water's edge, which we thought attracted the fishes, we caught pouts with a bunch of worms strung on a thread, and when we had done, far in the night, threw the burning brands high into the air like skyrockets, which, coming down into the pond, were quenched with a loud hissing, and we were suddenly groping in total darkness. Through this, whistling a tune, we took our way to the haunts of men again. But now I had made my home by the shore.

Sometimes, after staying in a village parlor till the family had all retired, I have returned to the woods, and, partly with a view to the next day's dinner, spent the hours of midnight fishing from a boat by moonlight, serenaded by owls and foxes, and hearing, from time to time, the creaking note of some unknown bird close at hand. These experiences were very memorable and valuable to me —

With Russell to Fair Haven by boat. (August 16, 1854)

anchored in forty feet of water, and twenty or thirty rods from the shore, surrounded sometimes by thousands of small perch and shiners, dimpling the surface with their tails in the moonlight, and communicating by a long flaxen line with mysterious nocturnal fishes which had their dwelling forty feet below, or sometimes dragging sixty feet of line about the pond as I drifted in the gentle night breeze, now and then feeling a slight vibration along it, indicative of some line prowling about its extremity, of dull uncertain blundering purpose there, and slow to make up its mind. At length you slowly raise, pulling hand over hand, some horned pout squeaking and squirming to the upper air. It was very queer, especially in dark nights, when your thoughts had wandered to vast and cosmogonal themes in other spheres, to feel this faint jerk, which came to interrupt your dreams and link you to Nature again. It seemed as if I might next cast my line upward into the air, as well as downward into this element, which was scarcely more dense. Thus I caught two fishes as it were with one hook.

The scenery of Walden is on a humble scale, and, **1** though very beautiful, does not approach to grandeur, nor can it much concern one who has not long frequented it or lived by its shore; yet this pond is so remarkable for its depth and purity as to merit a particular description. It is a clear and deep green well, half a mile long and a mile and three quarters in circumference, and contains about sixty-one and a half acres; a perennial spring in the midst of pine and oak woods, without any visible inlet or outlet except by the clouds and evaporation. The surrounding hills rise abruptly from the water to the height of forty to eighty feet, though on the southeast and east they attain

1 Over the years, Emerson and his family and friends bought up the land around Walden Pond as it became available. In 1922 the family gave the land to the Commonwealth of Massachusetts, to be preserved forever as it was in the days of Emerson and T. Unfortunately, although there are many other ponds in the vicinity, Walden is the only one accessible to the public, and it has become inundated with swarms of people, who use it for swimming and hiking. Added to these are the tourists making their pilgrimage to see where T had once lived. The stress has been too much for Walden's environment. As a result, limitations on access to the pond have been imposed on summer weekends. Tourists should try to limit their visits to off-season times if they want to see Walden at its best.

1   James D. Forbes, *Travels Through the Alps of Savoy* (Edinburgh, 1843, 71).

to about one hundred and one hundred and fifty feet respectively, within a quarter and a third of a mile. They are exclusively woodland. All our Concord waters have two colors at least; one when viewed at a distance, and another, more proper, close at hand. The first depends more on the light, and follows the sky. In clear weather, in summer, they appear blue at a little distance, especially if agitated, and at a great distance all appear alike. In stormy weather they are sometimes of a dark slate-color. The sea, however, is said to be blue one day and green another without any perceptible change in the atmosphere. I have seen our river, when, the landscape being covered with snow, both water and ice were almost as green as grass. Some consider blue 'to be the color of pure water, whether liquid or solid.' But, looking directly down into our waters from a boat, they are seen to be of very different colors. Walden is blue at one time and green at another, even from the same point of view. Lying between the earth and the heavens, it partakes of the color of both. Viewed from a hilltop it reflects the color of the sky; but near at hand it is of a yellowish tint next the shore where you can see the sand, then a light green, which gradually deepens to a uniform dark green in the body of the pond. In some lights, viewed even from a hilltop, it is of a vivid green next the shore. Some have referred this to the reflection of the verdure; but it is equally green there against the railroad sandbank, and in the spring, before the leaves are expanded, and it may be simply the result of the prevailing blue mixed with the yellow of the sand. Such is the color of its iris. This is that portion, also, where in the spring, the ice being warmed by the heat of the sun reflected from the bottom, and also transmitted through the earth, melts first and forms a narrow canal about the still frozen middle. Like the rest

When, returning at 5 o'clock, I pass the pond in the road, I see the sun, which is about entering the grosser hazy atmosphere above the western horizon, brilliantly reflected in the pond,—a dazzling sheen, a bright golden shimmer. His broad sphere extended stretches the whole length of the pond toward me. (October 19, 1855)

of our waters, when much agitated, in clear weather, so that the surface of the waves may reflect the sky at the right angle, or because there is more light mixed with it, it appears at a little distance of a darker blue than the sky itself; and at such a time, being on its surface, and looking with divided vision, so as to see the reflection, I have discerned a matchless and indescribable light blue, such as watered or changeable silks and sword blades suggest, more cerulean than the sky itself, alternating with the original dark green on the opposite sides of the waves, which last appeared but muddy in comparison. It is a vitreous greenish blue, as I remember it, like those patches of the winter sky seen through cloud vistas in the west before sundown. Yet a single glass of its water held up to the light is as colorless as an equal quantity of air. It is well known that a large plate of glass will have a green tint, owing, as the makers say, to its 'body,' but a small piece of the same will be colorless. How large a body of Walden water would be required to reflect a green tint I have never proved. The water of our river is black or a very dark brown to one looking directly down on it, and, like that of most ponds, imparts to the body of one bathing in it a yellowish tinge; but this water is of such crystalline purity that the body of the bather appears of an alabaster whiteness, still more unnatural, which, as the limbs are magnified and distorted withal, produces a monstrous effect, making fit studies for a Michael Angelo.   **1**

The water is so transparent that the bottom can easily be discerned at the depth of twenty-five or thirty feet. Paddling over it, you may see, many feet beneath the surface, the schools of perch and shiners, perhaps only an inch long, yet the former easily distinguished by their transverse bars, and you think that they must be ascetic fish that find a subsistence there. Once, in the winter, **2**

1 One characteristic of the male figures in Michelangelo's paintings is their overdeveloped muscles.

2 T's telling of this incident seems to echo II Kings 6:1–7 (Paul Williams, 1963, 2).

Observed the reflection of the snow on Pine Hill from Walden, extending far beyond the true limits of a reflection, quite across the pond. (December 14, 1852)

1   In the first edition, this reads "neighhor-hood," an obvious typographical error.

2   The whereabouts of these stones is now a mystery. I have searched for them many times without success. I have been told by others that they have succeeded in finding a few small ones by diving in deeper water, but otherwise they seem to have disappeared. Probably some have been carted away and others have drifted farther out in the pond.

3   Seemingly every community in New England has its "bottomless pond." I am familiar with a number of them, and T mentions some of them in his *Journal,* such as at II, 68.

many years ago, when I had been cutting holes through the ice in order to catch pickerel, as I stepped ashore I tossed my axe back on to the ice, but, as if some evil genius had directed it, it slid four or five rods directly into one of the holes, where the water was twenty-five feet deep. Out of curiosity, I lay down on the ice and looked through the hole, until I saw the axe a little on one side, standing on its head, with its helve erect and gently swaying to and fro with the pulse of the pond; and there it might have stood erect and swaying till in the course of time the handle rotted off, if I had not disturbed it. Making another hole directly over it with an ice chisel which I had, and cutting down the longest birch which I could **1** find in the neighborhood with my knife, I made a slip-noose, which I attached to its end, and, letting it down carefully, passed it over the knob of the handle, and drew it by a line along the birch, and so pulled the axe out again.

The shore is composed of a belt of smooth rounded **2** white stones like paving-stones, excepting one or two short sand beaches, and is so steep that in many places a single leap will carry you into water over your head; and were it not for its remarkable transparency, that would be the last to be seen of its bottom till it rose on the opposite side. **3** Some think it is bottomless. It is nowhere muddy, and a casual observer would say that there were no weeds at all in it; and of noticeable plants, except in the little meadows recently overflowed, which do not properly belong to it, a closer scrutiny does not detect a flag nor a bulrush, nor even a lily, yellow or white, but only a few small heart-leaves and potamogetons, and perhaps a water-target or two; all which however a bather might not perceive; and these plants are clean and bright like the element they grow in. The stones extend a rod or two into the water, and then the bottom is pure sand, except in the deepest parts, where there is usually a little sediment, probably from the decay of the leaves which have been wafted on to it so many successive falls, and a bright green weed is brought up on anchors even in midwinter.

We have one other pond just like this, White Pond, in Nine Acre Corner, about two and a half miles westerly; [1] but, though I am acquainted with most of the ponds within a dozen miles of this centre, I do not know a third of this pure and well-like character. Successive nations perchance have drank at, admired, and fathomed it, and passed away, and still its water is green and pellucid as ever. Not an intermitting spring! Perhaps on that spring morning when Adam and Eve were driven out of Eden Walden Pond was already in existence, and even then breaking up in a gentle spring rain accompanied with mist and a southerly wind, and covered with myriads of ducks and geese, which had not heard of the fall, when still such pure lakes sufficed them. Even then it had commenced to rise and fall, and had clarified its waters and colored them of the hue they now wear, and obtained a patent of Heaven to be the only Walden Pond in the world and distiller of celestial dews. Who knows in how many unremembered nations' literatures this has been the Castalian Fountain? or what nymphs presided [2] over it in the Golden Age? It is a gem of the first water [3] which Concord wears in her coronet.

Yet perchance the first who came to this well have left some trace of their footsteps. I have been surprised to detect encircling the pond, even where a thick wood has just been cut down on the shore, a narrow shelf-like path [4] in the steep hillside, alternately rising and falling, approaching and receding from the water's edge, as old probably as the race of man here, worn by the feet of

1 Nine Acre Corner is a little over a mile southwest of Walden Pond, near the Sudbury town line (Gleason).

2 A spring sacred to the Muses, flowing from the slope of Parnassus.

3 The reign of Saturn is usually considered the Golden Age in mythological history. Saturn was king of the Titans and was overthrown by Jupiter.

4 The path is still visible and has, in fact, been worn much deeper by visitors to the pond over the years.

There is so fine a ripple on White Pond that it amounts to a mere imbrication, very regular. (May 6, 1860)

1   Sculpture that stands out in relief.

2   Presumably Walden Pond has been preserved from such a fate, for in 1922 the Emerson family and some of their friends donated the land surrounding the pond to the Commonwealth of Massachusetts and it is now a state park.

3   Walker (1971) gives the first scientific explanation of this. He points out that the rising and falling coincide with fluctuations of the area's water table and that the pond is a kind of natural well, having been carved out by glaciers down to the water table. Walden needs no hidden water source, for its watershed is ample to supply the pond. Note that earlier in this chapter T himself refers to the pond as a well. Incidentally, in 1956, when the pond was at so high a level that the beaches had to be closed, officials attempted to lower its level by pumping the water, at the rate of 4,000 gallons a minute, into the Sudbury River. They pumped all summer and did not succeed in lowering the level one inch!

4   The cove is now known as Wyman's Meadow. It still shifts from meadow to cove, depending on the water level of the pond. The cove is a few rods southeast of T's cabin site.

5   One of the many indications that a large part of W was written in the seven years between his leaving Walden and the publication of the book in 1854.

aboriginal hunters, and still from time to time unwittingly trodden by the present occupants of the land. This is particularly distinct to one standing on the middle of the pond in winter, just after a light snow has fallen, appearing as a clear undulating white line, unobscured by weeds and twigs, and very obvious a quarter of a mile off in many places where in summer it is hardly distinguishable close at hand. The snow reprints it, as it were, in clear white

1   type alto-relievo. The ornamented grounds of villas which

2   will one day be built here may still preserve some trace of this.

3   The pond rises and falls, but whether regularly or not, and within what period, nobody knows, though, as usual, many pretend to know. It is commonly higher in the winter and lower in the summer, though not corresponding to the general wet and dryness. I can remember when it was a foot or two lower, and also when it was at least five feet higher, than when I lived by it. There is a narrow sand-bar running into it, with very deep water on one side, on which I helped boil a kettle of chowder, some six rods from the main shore, about the year 1824, which it has not been possible to do for twenty-five years; and, on the other hand, my friends used to listen with incredulity when I told them, that a few years later I was accustomed

4   to fish from a boat in a secluded cove in the woods, fifteen rods from the only shore they knew, which place was long since converted into a meadow. But the pond has risen

5   steadily for two years, and now, in the summer of '52, is just five feet higher than when I lived there, or as high as it was thirty years ago, and fishing goes on again in the meadow. This makes a difference of level, at the outside, of six or seven feet; and yet the water shed by the surrounding hills is insignificant in amount, and this overflow must be referred to causes which affect the deep

springs. This same summer the pond has begun to fall
again. It is remarkable that this fluctuation, whether peri-
odical or not, appears thus to require many years for its
accomplishment. I have observed one rise and a part of
two falls, and I expect that a dozen or fifteen years hence
the water will again be as low as I have ever known it.
Flint's Pond, a mile eastward, allowing for the disturbance **1**
occasioned by its inlets and outlets, and the smaller intermediate ponds also, sympathize with Walden, and recently attained their greatest height at the same time with
the latter. The same is true, as far as my observation goes,
of White Pond.

This rise and fall of Walden at long intervals serves this
use at least; the water standing at this great height for a
year or more, though it makes it difficult to walk round it,
kills the shrubs and trees which have sprung up about its
edge since the last rise — pitch pines, birches, alders,
aspens, and others — and, falling again, leaves an unob-
structed shore; for, unlike many ponds and all waters
which are subject to a daily tide, its shore is cleanest when
the water is lowest. On the side of the pond next my
house a row of pitch pines, fifteen feet high, has been
killed and tipped over as if by a lever, and thus a stop put
to their encroachments; and their size indicates how many
years have elapsed since the last rise to this height. By this
fluctuation the pond asserts its title to a shore, and thus
the *shore* is *shorn*, and the trees cannot hold it by right of
possession. These are the lips of the lake, on which no
beard grows. It licks its chaps from time to time. When
the water is at its height, the alders, willows, and maples
send forth a mass of fibrous red roots several feet long
from all sides of their stems in the water, and to the height
of three or four feet from the ground, in the effort to
maintain themselves; and I have known the high blue-

1   Known for many years as Sandy Pond, its
name was recently changed back to Flint's Pond
at the request of the Flint family (*Lincoln Journal*). It is in the town of Lincoln, about a mile
southeast of Walden (Gleason), and is now used
as a reservoir. T's college classmate Charles
Stearns Wheeler built a hut there in 1836,
where he stayed during vacations for the next
six years. T spent some time there with him,
and perhaps this was a source for the idea of
building his own cabin at Walden.

1   In T's copy of W, he has noted that this tale is told of Alexander's Lake in Killingly, Connecticut, in Barber's *Connecticut Historical Collections* (New Haven, 1838, 431). But Cameron (1956) cites an article in the *Middlesex Gazette* for August 11, 1821, that attributes this legend to Walden Pond itself.

Hanley quotes the geologist Joseph Hartshorn as saying, "Walden Pond could have been a high hill, covered with an earth crust and supporting growing trees. And it could have collapsed into a pond, because the heart of the hill would have been a huge ice pocket left by the glacier. When the ice melted, the thin earth crust would have sunk to become the bottom of Walden Pond." Skehan (50) advances a similar theory.

2   See "Solitude."

3   Again, a forked stick used to find underground sources of water.

4   Glaciers.

5   According to a note in his own copy of W, T got this name from Evelyn's diary, but the Concord Minot family, which was related to T by marriage, originally came from Saffron Walden, a suburb of London, and it seems likely T heard the name in family tradition. T himself speaks of this tradition in his *Journal* for December 2, 1857 (X, 219). Yet in an unpublished manuscript in the Huntington Library (HM 924) he points out that the Minot family did not come to Concord until after Walden was named. The earliest known reference to Walden Pond is a Concord property record of 1652 or 1653.

Walden is a fairly common place name in England. There is, for example, a King's Walden, a St. Paul's Walden, and a Walden Bury. Hudson suggests the pond may have been named for Richard Walden, the speaker of the General Court of Massachusetts from 1666 to 1679 and an associate of Major Simon Willard, one of the pioneers of Concord. Olhoff points out that in Old English the word "walden" (also spelled "wealand") means lord or ruler, and had T been aware of that, he might have expanded greatly on his puns. See also Walker (1972).

(Notes to page 178 continued on next page)

berry bushes about the shore, which commonly produce no fruit, bear an abundant crop under these circumstances.

Some have been puzzled to tell how the shore became so regularly paved. My townsmen have all heard the tradition — the oldest people tell me that they heard it in their youth — that anciently the Indians were holding a pow-wow upon a hill here, which rose as high into the heavens as the pond now sinks deep into the earth, and they used much profanity, as the story goes, though this vice is one of which the Indians were never guilty, and while they were thus engaged the hill shook and suddenly sank, and only one old squaw, named Walden, escaped, and from her the pond was named. It has been conjectured that when the hill shook these stones rolled down its side and became the present shore. It is very certain, at any rate, that once there was no pond here, and now there is one; and this Indian fable does not in any respect conflict with the account of that ancient settler whom I have mentioned, who remembers so well when he first came here with his divining-rod, saw a thin vapor rising from the sward, and the hazel pointed steadily downward, and he concluded to dig a well here. As for the stones, many still think that they are hardly to be accounted for by the action of the waves on these hills; but I observe that the surrounding hills are remarkably full of the same kind of stones, so that they have been obliged to pile them up in walls on both sides of the railroad cut nearest the pond; and, moreover, there are most stones where the shore is most abrupt; so that, unfortunately, it is no longer a mystery to me. I detect the paver. If the name was not derived from that of some English locality — Saffron Walden, for instance — one might suppose that it was called originally *Walled-in* Pond.

The pond was my well ready dug. For four months in

the year its water is as cold as it is pure at all times; and I think that it is then as good as any, if not the best, in the town. In the winter, all water which is exposed to the air is colder than springs and wells which are protected from it. The temperature of the pond water which had stood in **1** the room where I sat from five o'clock in the afternoon till noon the next day, the sixth of March, 1846, the thermometer having been up to 65° or 70° some of the time, owing partly to the sun on the roof, was 42°, or one degree colder than the water of one of the coldest wells in the village just drawn. The temperature of the Boiling Spring **2** the same day was 45°, or the warmest of any water tried, though it is the coldest that I know of in summer, when, beside, shallow and stagnant surface water is not mingled with it. Moreover, in summer, Walden never becomes so warm as most water which is exposed to the sun, on account of its depth. In the warmest weather I usually placed a pailful in my cellar, where it became cool in the night, and remained so during the day; though I also resorted to a spring in the neighborhood. It was as good **3** when a week old as the day it was dipped, and had no taste of the pump. Whoever camps for a week in summer by the shore of a pond, needs only bury a pail of water a few feet deep in the shade of his camp to be independent of the luxury of ice.

There have been caught in Walden pickerel, one weigh- **4** ing seven pounds — to say nothing of another which carried off a reel with great velocity, which the fisherman safely set down at eight pounds because he did not see him — perch and pouts, some of each weighing over two pounds, shiners, chivins or roach (*Leuciscus pulchellus*), a very few breams, and a couple of eels, one weighing **5** four pounds — I am thus particular because the weight of a fish is commonly its only title to fame, and these are

(Notes to page 178 continued)

Since in German *wald* means woods, T's book in Germany is occasionally mistaken for a book on forestry, a fact that would probably have amused T.

6   Cameron (1956) cites a reference, in the Concord *Yeoman's Gazette* for August 21, 1830, to Walden as "Wall'd in," so T obviously did not coin this pun. It is said in England that the word "walden" might be derived from "walled-in," as an estate surrounded by a wall.

PAGE 179

1   These seemingly unimportant facts, so carefully recorded by T, occasionally bore the modern reader — as do the measurements of whales in *Moby-Dick* — but they indicate the growing interest in scientific research in mid-nineteenth-century America. In later years T sometimes bewailed the fact that the recording of such minutiae was gradually usurping his time and leaving him little for philosophical speculation. See, for example, his *Journal* (II, 406).

2   Slightly west of Walden Pond (Gleason). A boiling spring is not a hot spring, but merely one in which the water can be seen bubbling up from the bottom.

3   Brister's Spring, northeast of Walden. It feeds what T called the Fairyland Pond, in what is now the Town Forest.

4   For an excellent account of the fish of Walden Pond, see Ted Williams. According to local legend, at about the turn of the century a local fisherman started adding to Walden Pond specimens of fish T mentioned in his works. Many of these were river fish rather than pond fish, and they upset the ecological balance of the pond. Later, to correct the problem, state officials had all the fish killed off with poison. But then they restocked the pond only with species such as trout and bass, which made fishermen happy but which were not necessarily native species. Today, the pond is restocked every spring, and on the first day of fishing season it is surrounded by hundreds of fishermen pulling out the fish. Incidentally, it has been said that there were no fish at all in Walden

(Notes to page 179 continued on next page)

Pond until they were transplanted there by man (Shattuck, 200).

5   In his own copy of W, after the word "breams" T inserted "Pomotis obesus [Nov. 26–58] one trout weighing a little over 5 lbs — (Nov. 14–57)." In his *Journal* entry for the latter date, he records the catching of a trout by Gardiner Heywood (X, 180), and for the former date discusses various types of fresh-water fish (XI, 344–7).

PAGE 180

1   Netlike.

2   Speckled.

3   In the first edition, spelled "muscles," fresh-water bivalves.

4   In his copy of W, T inserted the words "kingfisher dart away from its coves" after the word "it."

5   Osprey.

the only eels I have heard of here; — also, I have a faint recollection of a little fish some five inches long, with silvery sides and a greenish back, somewhat dace-like in its character, which I mention here chiefly to link my facts to fable. Nevertheless, this pond is not very fertile in fish. Its pickerel, though not abundant, are its chief boast. I have seen at one time lying on the ice pickerel of at least three different kinds: a long and shallow one, steel-colored, most like those caught in the river; a bright golden kind, with greenish reflections and remarkably deep, which is the most common here; and another, golden-colored, and shaped like the last, but peppered on the sides with small dark brown or black spots, intermixed with a few faint blood-red ones, very much like a trout. The specific

1 name *reticulatus* would not apply to this; it should be
2 *guttatus* rather. These are all very firm fish, and weigh more than their size promises. The shiners, pouts, and perch also, and indeed all the fishes which inhabit this pond, are much cleaner, handsomer, and firmer-fleshed than those in the river and most other ponds, as the water is purer, and they can easily be distinguished from them. Probably many ichthyologists would make new varieties of some of them. There are also a clean race of frogs and
3 tortoises, and a few mussels in it; muskrats and minks leave their traces about it, and occasionally a travelling mud-turtle visits it. Sometimes, when I pushed off my boat in the morning, I disturbed a great mud-turtle which had secreted himself under the boat in the night. Ducks and geese frequent it in the spring and fall, the white-bel-
4 lied swallows (*Hirundo bicolor*) skim over it, and the peet-weets (*Trotanus macularius*) 'teeter' along its stony shores
5 all summer. I have sometimes disturbed a fish hawk sitting on a white pine over the water; but I doubt if it is ever

profaned by the wing of a gull, like Fair Haven. At most, it **1**
tolerates one annual loon. These are all the animals of
consequence which frequent it now.

You may see from a boat, in calm weather, near the
sandy eastern shore, where the water is eight or ten feet
deep, and also in some other parts of the pond, some
circular heaps half a dozen feet in diameter by a foot in
height, consisting of small stones less than a hen's egg in
size, where all around is bare sand. At first you wonder if
the Indians could have formed them on the ice for any
purpose, and so, when the ice melted, they sank to the
bottom; but they are too regular and some of them plainly
too fresh for that. They are similar to those found in rivers;
but as there are no suckers nor lampreys here, I know not
by what fish they could be made. Perhaps they are the
nests of the chivin. These lend a pleasing mystery to the **2**
bottom.

The shore is irregular enough not to be monotonous. I
have in my mind's eye the western, indented with deep
bays, the bolder northern, and the beautifully scalloped
southern shore, where successive capes overlap each other
and suggest unexplored coves between. The forest has
never so good a setting, nor is so distinctly beautiful, as
when seen from the middle of a small lake amid hills
which rise from the water's edge; for the water in which it
is reflected not only makes the best foreground in such a
case, but, with its winding shore, the most natural and
agreeable boundary to it. There is no rawness nor imperfection in its edge there, as where the axe has cleared a
part, or a cultivated field abuts on it. The trees have ample
room to expand on the water side, and each sends forth its
most vigorous branch in that direction. There Nature has
woven a natural selvage, and the eye rises by just grada-

1 A widening of the Sudbury River about a
mile southwest of Walden Pond.

2 T's guess was correct. An account of this
fish and its nest-building habits will be found in
*The Fishes of the Connecticut Lakes and Neigh-
boring Waters,* by W. C. Kendall and E. L.
Goldsborough, published as Document No. 633
of the U.S. Bureau of Fisheries.

1 It was a habit of T's to bend over and peer at the landscape through his legs, providing a novel view — a device sometimes used by artists.

2 T inserted "(Hydrometer)" after "insects" in his copy of W.

Close under the lee of the button-bushes which skirt the pond, as I look south, there is a narrow smooth strip of water, silvery and contrasting with the darker rippled body of the pond. Its edge, or the separation between this, which I will call the polished silvery border of the pond, and the dark and ruffled body, is not a straight line or film, but an ever-varying, irregularly and finely serrated or fringed border, ever changing as the breeze falls over the bushes at an angle more or less steep, so that this moment it is a rod wide, the next not half so much. Every feature is thus fluent in the landscape. (May 14, 1853)

tions from the low shrubs of the shore to the highest trees. There are few traces of man's hand to be seen. The water laves the shore as it did a thousand years ago.

A lake is the landscape's most beautiful and expressive feature. It is earth's eye; looking into which the beholder measures the depth of his own nature. The fluviatile trees next the shore are the slender eyelashes which fringe it, and the wooded hills and cliffs around are its overhanging brows.

Standing on the smooth sandy beach at the east end of the pond, in a calm September afternoon, when a slight haze makes the opposite shore-line indistinct, I have seen whence came the expression, 'the glassy surface of a lake.'
1 When you invert your head, it looks like a thread of finest gossamer stretched across the valley, and gleaming against the distant pine woods, separating one stratum of the atmosphere from another. You would think that you could walk dry under it to the opposite hills, and that the swallows which skim over might perch on it. Indeed, they sometimes dive below the line, as it were by mistake, and are undeceived. As you look over the pond westward you are obliged to employ both your hands to defend your eyes against the reflected as well as the true sun, for they are equally bright; and if, between the two, you survey its surface critically, it is literally as smooth as glass, except
2 where the skater insects, at equal intervals scattered over its whole extent, by their motions in the sun produce the finest imaginable sparkle on it, or, perchance, a duck plumes itself, or, as I have said, a swallow skims so low as to touch it. It may be that in the distance a fish describes an arc of three or four feet in the air, and there is one bright flash where it emerges, and another where it strikes the water; sometimes the whole silvery arc is revealed; or here and there, perhaps, is a thistle-down floating on its

surface, which the fishes dart at and so dimple it again. It is like molten glass cooled but not congealed, and the few motes in it are pure and beautiful like the imperfections in glass. You may often detect a yet smoother and darker water, separated from the rest as if by an invisible cobweb, boom of the water nymphs, resting on it. From a hilltop you can see a fish leap in almost any part; for not a pickerel or shiner picks an insect from this smooth surface but it manifestly disturbs the equilibrium of the whole lake. It is wonderful with what elaborateness this simple fact is advertised — this piscine murder will out — and [1] from my distant perch I distinguish the circling undulations when they are half a dozen rods in diameter. You can even detect a water-bug (*Gyrinus*) ceaselessly progressing over the smooth surface a quarter of a mile off; for they furrow the water slightly, making a conspicuous ripple bounded by two diverging lines, but the skaters glide over it without rippling it perceptibly. When the surface is considerably agitated there are no skaters nor water-bugs on it, but apparently, in calm days, they leave their havens and adventurously glide forth from the shore by short impulses till they completely cover it. It is a soothing employment, on one of those fine days in the fall when all the warmth of the sun is fully appreciated, to sit on a stump on such a height as this, overlooking the pond, and study the dimpling circles which are incessantly inscribed on its otherwise invisible surface amid the reflected skies and trees. Over this great expanse there is no disturbance but it is thus at once gently smoothed away and assuaged, as, when a vase of water is jarred, the trembling circles seek the shore and all is smooth again. Not a fish can leap or an insect fall on the pond but it is thus reported in circling dimples, in lines of beauty, as it were the constant welling up of its fountain, the gentle

[1] "Mordre wol out" (Chaucer, "The Prioress's Tale," i.1766).

1 The shortest sentence in W.

pulsing of its life, the heaving of its breast. The thrills of joy and thrills of pain are undistinguishable. How peaceful the phenomena of the lake! Again the works of man shine as in the spring. Ay, every leaf and twig and stone and cobweb sparkles now at mid-afternoon as when covered with dew in a spring morning. Every motion of an oar or an insect produces a flash of light; and if an oar falls, how sweet the echo!

In such a day, in September or October, Walden is a perfect forest mirror, set round with stones as precious to my eye as if fewer or rarer. Nothing so fair, so pure, and at the same time so large, as a lake, perchance, lies on the **1** surface of the earth. Sky water. It needs no fence. Nations come and go without defiling it. It is a mirror which no stone can crack, whose quicksilver will never wear off, whose gilding Nature continually repairs; no storms, no dust, can dim its surface ever fresh; — a mirror in which all impurity presented to it sinks, swept and dusted by the sun's hazy brush — this the light dust-cloth — which retains no breath that is breathed on it, but sends its own to float as clouds high above its surface, and be reflected in its bosom still.

A field of water betrays the spirit that is in the air. It is continually receiving new life and motion from above. It is intermediate in its nature between land and sky. On land only the grass and trees wave, but the water itself is rippled by the wind. I see where the breeze dashes across it by the streaks or flakes of light. It is remarkable that we can look down on its surface. We shall, perhaps, look down thus on the surface of air at length, and mark where a still subtler spirit sweeps over it.

The skaters and water-bugs finally disappear in the latter part of October, when the severe frosts have come; and then and in November, usually, in a calm day, there

Looking from the Cliffs, the sun being as before invisible, I saw far more light in the reflected sky in the neighborhood of the sun than I could see in the heavens from my position, and it occurred to me that the reason was that there was reflected to me from the river the view I should have got if I had stood there on the water in a more favorable position. (March 8, 1855)

is absolutely nothing to ripple the surface. One November afternoon, in the calm at the end of a rain-storm of several days' duration, when the sky was still completely overcast and the air was full of mist, I observed that the pond was remarkably smooth, so that it was difficult to distinguish its surface; though it no longer reflected the bright tints of October, but the sombre November colors of the surrounding hills. Though I passed over it as gently as possible, the slight undulations produced by my boat extended almost as far as I could see, and gave a ribbed appearance to the reflections. But, as I was looking over the surface, I saw here and there at a distance a faint glimmer, as if some skater insects which had escaped the frosts might be collected there, or, perchance, the surface, being so smooth, betrayed where a spring welled up from the bottom. Paddling gently to one of these places, I was surprised to find myself surrounded by myriads of small perch, about five inches long, of a rich bronze color in the green water, sporting there, and constantly rising to the surface and dimpling it, sometimes leaving bubbles on it. In such transparent and seemingly bottomless water, reflecting the clouds, I seemed to be floating through the air as in a balloon, and their swimming impressed me as a kind of flight or hovering, as if they were a compact flock of birds passing just beneath my level on the right or left, their fins, like sails, set all around them. There were many such schools in the pond, apparently improving the short season before winter would draw an icy shutter over their broad skylight, sometimes giving to the surface an appearance as if a slight breeze struck it, or a few rain-drops fell there. When I approached carelessly and alarmed them, they made a sudden plash and rippling with their tails, as if one had struck the water with a brushy bough, and instantly took refuge in the depths. At length the wind

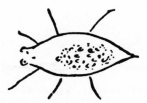

I see running on the muddy shore under the pontederia a large flat and thin-edged brown bug (with six legs), some seven eighths of an inch long, pointed behind; with apparently its eggs, fifty or sixty in number, large and dark-colored, standing side by side on their ends and forming a very conspicuous patch which covers about a third of its flat upper surface. (July 27, 1860)

1　1852, according to his *Journal* (IV, 424).

2　Tommy Wyman, whose pottery was at the northeast end of the pond. T recounts Wyman's story in his *Journal* for June 16, 1853 (V, 260).

3　D'Avanzo (1979) expounds at length on biblical echoes of this image.

rose, the mist increased, and the waves began to run, and the perch leaped much higher than before, half out of water, a hundred black points, three inches long, at once above the surface. Even as late as the fifth of December, one year, I saw some dimples on the surface, and thinking it was going to rain hard immediately, the air being full of mist, I made haste to take my place at the oars and row homeward; already the rain seemed rapidly increasing, though I felt none on my cheek, and I anticipated a **1** thorough soaking. But suddenly the dimples ceased, for they were produced by the perch, which the noise of my oars had scared into the depths, and I saw their schools dimly disappearing; so I spent a dry afternoon after all.

An old man who used to frequent this pond nearly sixty years ago, when it was dark with surrounding forests, tells me that in those days he sometimes saw it all alive with ducks and other water-fowl, and that there were many eagles about it. He came here a-fishing, and used an old log canoe which he found on the shore. It was made of two white pine logs dug out and pinned together, and was cut off square at the ends. It was very clumsy, but lasted a great many years before it became water-logged and perhaps sank to the bottom. He did not know whose it was; it belonged to the pond. He used to make a cable for his anchor of strips of hickory bark tied together. An old man, **2** a potter, who lived by the pond before the Revolution, **3** told him once that there was an iron chest at the bottom, and that he had seen it. Sometimes it would come floating up to the shore; but when you went toward it, it would go back into deep water and disappear. I was pleased to hear of the old log canoe, which took the place of an Indian one of the same material but more graceful construction, which perchance had first been a tree on the bank, and then, as it were, fell into the water, to float

Saw my white-headed eagle again, first at the same place, the outlet of Fair Haven Pond. . . . When I observed him edgewise I noticed that the tips of his wings curved upward slightly the more, like a stereotyped undulation. He rose very high at last, till I almost lost him in the clouds, circling or rather *looping* along westward, high over river and wood and farm, effectually concealed in the sky. We who live this plodding life here below never know how many eagles fly over us. (April 23, 1854)

there for a generation, the most proper vessel for the lake. I remember that when I first looked into these depths there were many large trunks to be seen indistinctly lying on the bottom, which had either been blown over formerly, or left on the ice at the last cutting, when wood was cheaper; but now they have mostly disappeared.

When I first paddled a boat on Walden, it was completely surrounded by thick and lofty pine and oak woods, and in some of its coves grapevines had run over the trees next the water and formed bowers under which a boat could pass. The hills which form its shores are so steep, and the woods on them were then so high, that, as you looked down from the west end, it had the appearance of an amphitheatre for some kind of sylvan spectacle. I have spent many an hour, when I was younger, floating over its surface as the zephyr willed, having paddled my boat to the middle, and lying on my back across the seats, in a summer forenoon, dreaming awake, until I was aroused by the boat touching the sand, and I arose to see what shore my fates had impelled me to; days when idleness was the most attractive and productive industry. Many a forenoon have I stolen away, preferring to spend thus the most valued part of the day; for I was rich, if not in money, in sunny hours and summer days, and spent them lavishly; nor do I regret that I did not waste more of them in the workshop or the teacher's desk. But since I left those **1** shores the woodchoppers have still further laid them waste, **2** and now for many a year there will be no more rambling through the aisles of the wood, with occasional vistas through which you see the water. My Muse may be excused if she is silent henceforth. How can you expect the birds to sing when their groves are cut down?

Now the trunks of trees on the bottom, and the old log canoe, and the dark surrounding woods, are gone, and

1   T had been previously employed as a schoolteacher and as a worker in his father's pencil factory.

2   Now, thanks to the fact that Walden Pond is a state reservation, the woods have returned to its shores, though the great hurricane of 1938 and a misguided attempt by park commissioners in 1957 to put in a new parking lot destroyed many of the trees.

Behind one house, an Indian had nearly finished one canoe and was just beginning another, outdoors. (September 22, 1853)

Canoe is nearly straight on bottom—straight in principle—and not so rounded the other way as is supposed. *Vide* this section in middle. (September 22, 1853)

1 That plan was never carried out, and Concord now gets its water from Nagog Pond in Acton.

2 Locomotive, which in T's day needed regularly to replenish its water and wood for its steam engine.

3 The Greeks were finally able to pierce Troy's defenses by hiding in a wooden horse and persuading the Trojans to drag it into the city as a god.

4 "But More of More-Hall, with nothing at all, / He slew the dragon of Wantley" (Bishop Percy, "The Dragon of Wantley," *Reliques of Ancient English Poetry*).

5 Just northwest of Walden Pond, the earth was cut away to some depth to permit the railroad to proceed on a level track.

6 Another reference to the Irish railroad workers' shanties about half a mile northwest of T's cabin site.

7 "Behold an Israelite indeed, in whom is no guile!" (John 1:47).

the villagers, who scarcely know where it lies, instead of going to the pond to bathe or drink, are thinking to bring its water, which should be as sacred as the Ganges at least, to the village in a pipe, to wash their dishes with! — to earn their Walden by the turning of a cock or drawing of a plug! That devilish Iron Horse, whose ear-rending neigh is heard throughout the town, has muddied the Boiling Spring with his foot, and he it is that has browsed off all the woods on Walden shore, that Trojan horse, with a thousand men in his belly, introduced by mercenary Greeks! Where is the country's champion, the Moore of Moore Hall, to meet him at the Deep Cut and thrust an avenging lance between the ribs of the bloated pest?

Nevertheless, of all the characters I have known, perhaps Walden wears best, and best preserves its purity. Many men have been likened to it, but few deserve that honor. Though the woodchoppers have laid bare first this shore and then that, and the Irish have built their sties by it, and the railroad has infringed on its border, and the ice-men have skimmed it once, it is itself unchanged, the same water which my youthful eyes fell on; all the change is in me. It has not acquired one permanent wrinkle after all its ripples. It is perennially young, and I may stand and see a swallow dip apparently to pick an insect from its surface as of yore. It struck me again tonight, as if I had not seen it almost daily for more than twenty years — Why, here is Walden, the same woodland lake that I discovered so many years ago; where a forest was cut down last winter another is springing up by its shore as lustily as ever; the same thought is welling up to its surface that was then; it is the same liquid joy and happiness to itself and its Maker, ay, and it *may* be to me. It is the work of a brave man surely, in whom there was no guile!

He rounded this water with his hand, deepened and clarified it in his thought, and in his will bequeathed it to
Concord. I see by its face that it is visited by the same
reflection; and I can almost say, Walden, is it you?

> It is no dream of mine,
> To ornament a line;
> I cannot come nearer to God and Heaven
> Than I live to Walden even.
> I am its stony shore,
> And the breeze that passes o'er
> In the hollow of my hand
> Are its water and its sand,
> And its deepest resort
> Lies high in my thought.   1

The cars never pause to look at it; yet I fancy that the
engineers and firemen and brakemen, and those passengers who have a season ticket and see it often, are better
men for the sight. The engineer does not forget at night,
or his nature does not, that he has beheld this vision of
serenity and purity once at least during the day. Though
seen but once, it helps to wash out State Street and the 2
engine's soot. One proposes that it be called 'God's Drop.' 3
I have said that Walden has no visible inlet nor outlet,
but it is on the one hand distantly and indirectly related to
Flint's Pond, which is more elevated, by a chain of small
ponds coming from that quarter, and on the other directly
and manifestly to Concord River, which is lower, by a
similar chain of ponds through which in some other geo-
logical period it may have flowed, and by a little digging,
which God forbid, it can be made to flow thither again. If
by living thus reserved and austere, like a hermit in the 4
woods, so long, it has acquired such wonderful purity,

1 T's own poem. Critics vary widely in
their interpretation of it, though most agree that
he is speaking of his own identity with Walden
Pond. For further explication see Paul Williams
(1964) and see Bode.

2 The financial district in Boston.

3 Emerson thus refers to Walden Pond in
his *Journal* for April 9, 1840 (V, 381). Benoit
suggests the term was derived from the Hindu
concept of Bindu.

4 "He lived reserved and austere" (Andrew
Marvell, "An Horatian Ode," line 30).

1   "And waste its sweetness on the desert air" (Thomas Gray, "Elegy in a Country Churchyard").

2   Although the American chestnut had been one of the commonest trees in T's day, it was almost completely obliterated by a blight early in this century.

3   These balls are a green alga of the genus *Cladophora*. A detailed description of them can be found in Smith (424–31).

who would not regret that the comparatively impure waters of Flint's Pond should be mingled with it, or itself 1 should ever go to waste its sweetness in the ocean wave?

Flint's, or Sandy Pond, in Lincoln, our greatest lake and inland sea, lies about a mile east of Walden. It is much larger, being said to contain one hundred and ninety-seven acres, and is more fertile in fish; but it is comparatively shallow, and not remarkably pure. A walk through the woods thither was often my recreation. It was worth the while, if only to feel the wind blow on your cheek freely, and see the waves run, and remember the life of 2 mariners. I went a-chestnutting there in the fall, on windy days, when the nuts were dropping into the water and were washed to my feet; and one day, as I crept along its sedgy shore, the fresh spray blowing in my face, I came upon the mouldering wreck of a boat, the sides gone, and hardly more than the impression of its flat bottom left amid the rushes; yet its model was sharply defined, as if it were a large decayed pad, with its veins. It was as impressive a wreck as one could imagine on the seashore, and had as good a moral. It is by this time mere vegetable mould and undistinguishable pond shore, through which rushes and flags have pushed up. I used to admire the ripple marks on the sandy bottom, at the north end of this pond, made firm and hard to the feet of the wader by the pressure of the water, and the rushes which grew in Indian file, in waving lines, corresponding to these marks, rank behind rank, as if the waves had planted them. There also 3 I have found, in considerable quantities, curious balls, composed apparently of fine grass or roots, of pipewort perhaps, from half an inch to four inches in diameter, and perfectly spherical. These wash back and forth in shallow water on a sandy bottom, and are sometimes cast on the shore. They are either solid grass, or have a little sand in the middle. At first you would say that they were formed by the action of the waves, like a pebble; yet the smallest are made of equally coarse materials, half an inch long, and they are produced only at one season of the year. Moreover, the waves, I suspect, do not so much construct as wear down a material which has already acquired consistency. They preserve their form when dry for an indefinite period.

Flint's Pond! Such is the poverty of our nomenclature. What right had the unclean and stupid farmer, whose **1** farm abutted on this sky water, whose shores he has ruthlessly laid bare, to give his name to it? Some skin-flint, who loved better the reflecting surface of a dollar, or a bright cent, in which he could see his own brazen face; who regarded even the wild ducks which settled in it as trespassers; his fingers grown into crooked and horny talons from the long habit of grasping harpy-like; — so it is **2** not named for me. I go not there to see him nor to hear of him; who never *saw* it, who never bathed in it, who never loved it, who never protected it, who never spoke a good word for it, nor thanked God that He had made it. Rather let it be named from the fishes that swim in it, the wild fowl or quadrupeds which frequent it, the wild flowers which grow by its shores, or some wild man or child the thread of whose history is interwoven with its own; not from him who could show no title to it but the deed which a like-minded neighbor or legislature gave him — him who thought only of its money value; whose presence perchance cursed all the shores; who exhausted the land around it, and would fain have exhausted the waters within it; who regretted only that it was not English hay or cranberry meadow — there was nothing to redeem it, forsooth, in his eyes — and would have drained and sold it

1 T had originally hoped to build his cabin on the shore of Flint's Pond but had been thwarted by the owner, Mr. Flint — which explains his anger (Eidson, 53).

2 In Greek mythology, a harpy is a filthy, hideous winged monster.

1 Landowners in New England were required to obtain a written "privilege" from the
community before they could dam up a stream
for water power.

2 The part of the Aegean Sea where Icarus
was drowned.

3 "For still the shore my brave attempt resounds" (William Drummond of Hawthornden,
"Icarus").

4 Originally two tiny ponds just east of Walden. One has in recent years been filled in by
the Concord town dump.

5 England's scenic Lake District, made famous by Wordsworth.

for the mud at its bottom. It did not turn his mill, and it
1 was no *privilege* to him to behold it. I respect not his
labors, his farm where everything has its price, who would
carry the landscape, who would carry his God, to market,
if he could get anything for him; who goes to market *for*
his god as it is; on whose farm nothing grows free, whose
fields bear no crops, whose meadows no flowers, whose
trees no fruits, but dollars; who loves not the beauty of his
fruits, whose fruits are not ripe for him till they are turned
to dollars. Give me the poverty that enjoys true wealth.
Farmers are respectable and interesting to me in proportion as they are poor — poor farmers. A model farm! where
the house stands like a fungus in a muckheap, chambers
for men, horses, oxen, and swine, cleansed and unclean-
sed, all contiguous to one another! Stocked with men! A
great grease-spot, redolent of manures and buttermilk!
Under a high state of cultivation, being manured with the
hearts and brains of men! As if you were to raise your
potatoes in the churchyard! Such is a model farm.

No, no; if the fairest features of the landscape are to be
named after men, let them be the noblest and worthiest
men alone. Let our lakes receive as true names at least as
2 the Icarian Sea, where 'still the shore' a 'brave attempt
3 resounds.'

4 Goose Pond, of small extent, is on my way to Flint's;
Fair Haven, an expansion of Concord River, said to contain some seventy acres, is a mile southwest; and White
Pond, of about forty acres, is a mile and a half beyond Fair
5 Haven. This is my lake country. These, with Concord
River, are my water privileges; and night and day, year in
year out, they grind such grist as I carry to them.

Since the wood-cutters, and the railroad, and I myself

have profaned Walden, perhaps the most attractive, if not the most beautiful, of all our lakes, the gem of the woods, is White Pond; — a poor name from its commonness, whether derived from the remarkable purity of its waters or the color of its sands. In these as in other respects, however, it is a lesser twin of Walden. They are so much alike that you would say they must be connected under ground. It has the same stony shore, and its waters are of the same hue. As at Walden, in sultry dogday weather, looking down through the woods on some of its bays which are not so deep but that the reflection from the bottom tinges them, its waters are of a misty bluish-green or glaucous color. Many years since I used to go there to collect the sand by cartloads, to make sandpaper with, **1** and I have continued to visit it ever since. One who frequents it proposes to call it Virid Lake. Perhaps it might **2** be called Yellow Pine Lake, from the following circumstance. About fifteen years ago you could see the top of a pitch pine, of the kind called yellow pine hereabouts, though it is not a distinct species, projecting above the surface in deep water, many rods from the shore. It was even supposed by some that the pond had sunk, and this was one of the primitive forest that formerly stood there. I find that even so long ago as 1792, in a 'Topographical **3** Description of the Town of Concord,' by one of its citizens, in the Collections of the Massachusetts Historical Society, the author, after speaking of Walden and White Ponds, adds, 'In the middle of the latter may be seen, when the water is very low, a tree which appears as if it grew in the place where it now stands, although the roots are fifty feet below the surface of the water; the top of this tree is broken off, and at that place measures fourteen inches in diameter.' In the spring of '49 I talked with the man who lives nearest the pond in Sudbury, who told me **4**

1   Part of the Thoreau family business was the manufacture of sandpaper, no piece of which, to my knowledge, now exists.

2   Sanborn (1909, II, 323) suggests that it was Ellery Channing who gave White Pond this name.

3   William Jones, "A Topographical Description of Concord," *Massachusetts Historical Society Collections* (I, 1792, 238).

4   A Mr. Haynes. His grandson, Adrian Hayward, gives an amusing account of the pulling out of the tree. Haynes later commented to his son, "T was as anxious for all the particulars as if apples of gold had grown on it."

1   Usually spelled "but-end."

that it was he who got out this tree ten or fifteen years before. As near as he could remember, it stood twelve or fifteen rods from the shore, where the water was thirty or forty feet deep. It was in the winter, and he had been getting out ice in the forenoon, and had resolved that in the afternoon, with the aid of his neighbors, he would take out the old yellow pine. He sawed a channel in the ice toward the shore, and hauled it over and along and out on to the ice with oxen; but, before he had gone far in his work, he was surprised to find that it was wrong end upward, with the stumps of the branches pointing down, and the small end firmly fastened in the sandy bottom. It was about a foot in diameter at the big end, and he had expected to get a good saw-log, but it was so rotten as to be fit only for fuel, if for that. He had some of it in his shed then. There were marks of an axe and of woodpeckers on the butt. He thought that it might have been a dead tree on the shore, but was finally blown over into the pond, and after the top had become water-logged, while the
1   butt-end was still dry and light, had drifted out and sunk wrong end up. His father, eighty years old, could not remember when it was not there. Several pretty large logs may still be seen lying on the bottom, where, owing to the undulation of the surface, they look like huge water snakes in motion.

This pond has rarely been profaned by a boat, for there is little in it to tempt a fisherman. Instead of the white lily, which requires mud, or the common sweet flag, the blue flag (*Iris versicolor*) grows thinly in the pure water, rising from the stony bottom all around the shore, where it is visited by hummingbirds in June; and the color both of its bluish blades and its flowers and especially their reflections, is in singular harmony with the glaucous water.

White Pond and Walden are great crystals on the sur-

Observed a large mass of white lily root with the mud washed up, the woolly steel-blue root, with singular knobs for offshoots and long, large, succulent white roots from all sides, the leaf-buds yellow and lightly rolled up on each side. (April 17, 1856)

face of the earth, Lakes of Light. If they were permanently congealed, and small enough to be clutched, they would, perchance, be carried off by slaves, like precious stones, to adorn the heads of emperors; but being liquid, and ample, and secured to us and our successors forever, we disregard them, and run after the diamond of Kohinoor. **1** They are too pure to have a market value; they contain no muck. How much more beautiful than our lives, how much more transparent than our characters, are they! We never learned meanness of them. How much fairer than the pool before the farmer's door, in which his ducks swim! Hither the clean wild ducks come. Nature has no human inhabitant who appreciates her. The birds with their plumage and their notes are in harmony with the flowers, but what youth or maiden conspires with the wild luxuriant beauty of Nature? She flourishes most alone, far from the towns where they reside. Talk of heaven! ye disgrace earth.

1 One of the world's largest diamonds — 109 carats — first discovered in India and now part of the British crown jewels.

There is a fine vapor, twice as high as a house, over the flooded meadows, through which I see the whiter dense smoke columns or streaks from the chimneys of the village, a cheerful scene. (October 31, 1853)

That lichen with a white elastic thread for core is like a tuft of hair on the trees, sometimes springing from the centre of another, larger, flat lichen.
(February 9, 1854)

BAKER FARM

Sometimes I rambled to pine groves, standing like temples, or like fleets at sea, full-rigged, with wavy boughs, and rippling with light, so soft and green and shady that the Druids would have forsaken their oaks to worship in them; or to the cedar wood beyond Flint's Pond, where the trees, covered with hoary blue berries, spiring higher and higher, are fit to stand before Valhalla, and the creeping juniper covers the ground with wreaths full of fruit; or to swamps where the usnea lichen hangs in festoons from the black-spruce trees, and toadstools, round tables of the swamp gods, cover the ground, and more beautiful fungi adorn the stumps, like butterflies or shells, vegetable winkles; where the swamp-pink and dogwood grow, the red alder berry glows like eyes of imps, the waxwork grooves and crushes the hardest woods in its folds, and the wild holly berries make the beholder forget his home with their beauty, and he is dazzled and tempted by nameless other wild forbidden fruits, too fair for mortal taste. Instead of calling on some scholar, I paid many a visit to particular trees, of kinds which are rare in this neighborhood, standing far away in the middle of some pasture, or in the depths of a wood or swamp, or on a hilltop; such as the black birch, of which we have some handsome specimens two feet in diameter; its cousin, the yellow birch, with its loose golden vest, perfumed like the first; the beech, which has so neat a bole and beautifully lichen-painted, perfect in all its details, of which, excepting scattered specimens, I know but one small grove of sizable trees left in the township, supposed by some to have been planted by the pigeons that were once baited with beech-nuts near by; it is worth the while to see the silver grain sparkle when you split this wood; the bass; the hornbeam; the *Celtis occidentalis*, or false elm, of which we have but one well-grown; some taller mast of a pine, a shingle tree, **1** or a more perfect hemlock than usual, standing like a pagoda in the midst of the woods; and many others I could mention. These were the shrines I visited both summer and winter.

Once it chanced that I stood in the very abutment of a rainbow's arch, which filled the lower stratum of the **2** atmosphere, tinging the grass and leaves around, and dazzling me as if I looked through colored crystal. It was a lake of rainbow light, in which, for a short while, I lived like a dolphin. If it had lasted longer it might have tinged my employments and life. As I walked on the railroad causeway, I used to wonder at the halo of light around my shadow, and would fain fancy myself one of the elect. One who visited me declared that the shadows **3** of some Irishmen before him had no halo about them, that it was only natives that were so distinguished. Benvenuto Cellini tells us in his memoirs, that, after a cer- **4** tain terrible dream or vision which he had during his confinement in the castle of St. Angelo a resplendent **5** light appeared over the shadow of his head at morning and evening, whether he was in Italy or France, and it was particularly conspicuous when the grass was moist with dew. This was probably the same phenomenon to which I have referred, which is especially observed in the morning, but also at other times, and even by moonlight. Though a constant one, it is not commonly noticed, and, in the case of an excitable imagination like Cellini's, it **6** would be basis enough for superstition. Beside, he tells us that he showed it to very few. But are they not in-

1 A tree with wood especially good for making shingles.

2 Technically it is impossible to stand in the abutment of a rainbow's arch, since rainbows are optical illusions and always appear directly ahead of a viewer, but T claims in his *Journal* (II, 382–3, and IV, 288) to have done this twice. Stewart claims it would have been possible.

3 T is here poking fun at the Puritan belief in God's choosing certain individuals for redemption.

4 Noted Italian sculptor, artist, and autobiographer (1500–1571).

5 A castle in Rome that was originally the tomb of the emperor Hadrian.

6 Cellini, *Autobiography* (book 1, chap. 128). This light is a phenomenon known as *Heiligenschein* and is explained in Minnaert (230–3).

1   Directly south of Walden Pond, on the shore of Fair Haven Bay (Gleason).

2   Ellery Channing, "Baker Farm," *Thoreau, the Poet-Naturalist* (Boston, 1902, 225), which gives slight variations in the lines.

3   Hooked: stole.

4   The Indian name for muskrat.

deed distinguished who are conscious that they are regarded at all?

✤

1 I set out one afternoon to go a-fishing to Fair Haven, through the woods, to eke out my scanty fare of vegetables. My way led through Pleasant Meadow, an adjunct of the Baker Farm, that retreat of which a poet has since sung, beginning,

> 'Thy entry is a pleasant field,
> Which some mossy fruit trees yield
> Partly to a ruddy brook,
> By gliding musquash undertook,
> And mercurial trout,
2 > Darting about.'

3 I thought of living there before I went to Walden. I 'hooked'
4 the apples, leaped the brook, and scared the musquash and the trout. It was one of those afternoons which seem indefinitely long before one, in which many events may happen, a large portion of our natural life, though it was already half spent when I started. By the way there came up a shower, which compelled me to stand half an hour under a pine, piling boughs over my head, and wearing my handkerchief for a shed; and when at length I had made one cast over the pickerelweed, standing up to my middle in water, I found myself suddenly in the shadow of a cloud, and the thunder began to rumble with such emphasis that I could do no more than listen to it. The gods must be proud, thought I, with such forked flashes to rout a poor unarmed fisherman. So I made haste for shelter to the nearest hut, which stood half a mile from any road, but so much the nearer to the pond, and had long been uninhabited:

Some boys brought me to-night a singular kind of spawn found attached to a pole floating in Fair Haven Pond. (July 1, 1854)

"And here a poet builded,
    In the completed years,
For behold a trivial cabin
    That to destruction steers."

      1

So the Muse fables. But therein, as I found, dwelt now John Field, an Irishman, and his wife, and several chil-**2** dren, from the broad-faced boy who assisted his father at his work, and now came running by his side from the bog to escape the rain, to the wrinkled, sibyl-like, cone-**3** headed infant that sat upon its father's knee as in the palaces of nobles,and looked out from its home in the midst of wet and hunger inquisitively upon the stranger, with the privilege of infancy, not knowing but it was the last of a noble line, and the hope and cynosure of the world, instead of John Field's poor starveling brat. There we sat together under that part of the roof which leaked the least, while it showered and thundered without. I had sat there many times of old before the ship was built that floated his family to America. An honest, hard-working, but shiftless man plainly was John Field; and his wife, she too was brave to cook so many successive dinners in the recesses of that lofty stove; with round greasy face and bare breast, still thinking to improve her condition one day; with the never absent mop in one hand, and yet no effects of it visible anywhere. The chickens, which had also taken shelter here from the rain, stalked about the room like members of the family, too humanized, methought, to roast well. They stood and looked in my eye or pecked at my shoe significantly. Meanwhile my host told me his story, how hard he worked 'bogging' for a neighboring farmer, turning up a meadow with a spade or bog hoe at the rate of ten dollars an acre and the use of the land with manure for one year, and his little broad-faced son

1 Again, Channing's "Baker Farm" (371), with slight variations.

2 John Field was a real person. The birth of his daughter, mentioned just below, is recorded in the vital records of Lincoln for May 1844. T's rather snide comments about Field reflects the typical stance of Concord Yankees then toward new immigrants. T, once he got to know the Irish better, changed his attitude completely and became their friend and protector. Since this all happened before W was published, Bridgman (107) quite legitimately asks why T did not modify his criticisms of the Irish in his text.

3 In Greek mythology, a Sibyl was granted as many years of life as she had grains of sand in her hand. The older she grew, the more decrepit and haggard she looked.

1   "As broad as long." An English proverb that can be traced back at least as far as John Ray's *English Proverbs* (1678).

2   T has an unwarranted reputation for wishing to abandon civilization. He states here that he would favor such an abandonment *only* if it redeemed men's character — and he obviously believes that that would not be the result.

worked cheerfully at his father's side the while, not knowing how poor a bargain the latter had made. I tried to help him with my experience, telling him that he was one of my nearest neighbors, and that I too, who came a-fishing here, and looked like a loafer, was getting my living like himself; that I lived in a tight, light, and clean house, which hardly cost more than the annual rent of such a ruin as his commonly amounts to; and how, if he chose, he might in a month or two build himself a palace of his own; that I did not use tea, nor coffee, nor butter, nor milk, nor fresh meat, and so did not have to work to get them; again, as I did not work hard, I did not have to eat hard, and it cost me but a trifle for my food; but as he began with tea, and coffee, and butter, and milk, and beef, he had to work hard to pay for them, and when he had worked hard he had to eat hard again to repair the

1 waste of his system — and so it was as broad as it was long, indeed it was broader than it was long, for he was discontented and wasted his life into the bargain; and yet he had rated it as a gain in coming to America, that here you could get tea, and coffee, and meat every day. But the only true America is that country where you are at liberty to pursue such a mode of life as may enable you to do without these, and where the state does not endeavor to compel you to sustain the slavery and war and other superfluous expenses which directly or indirectly result from the use of such things. For I purposely talked to him as if he were a philosopher, or desired to be one. I should be glad if all the meadows on the earth were left in a wild state, if that were the consequence of men's beginning to

2 redeem themselves. A man will not need to study history to find out what is best for his own culture. But alas! the culture of an Irishman is an enterprise to be undertaken

with a sort of moral bog hoe. I told him, that as he worked so hard at bogging, he required thick boots and stout clothing, which yet were soon soiled and worn out, but I wore light shoes and thin clothing, which cost not half so much, though he might think that I was dressed like a gentleman (which, however, was not the case), and in an hour or two, without labor, but as a recreation, I could, if I wished, catch as many fish as I should want for two days, or earn enough money to support me a week. If he and his family would live simply, they might all go a-huckleberrying in the summer for their amusement. John heaved a sigh at this, and his wife stared with arms a-kimbo, and both appeared to be wondering if they had capital enough to begin such a course with, or arithmetic enough to carry it through. It was sailing by dead reckoning to them, and they saw not clearly how to make their port so; therefore I suppose they still take life bravely, after their fashion, face to face, giving it tooth and nail, 1 not having skill to split its massive columns with any fine entering wedge, and rout it in detail; — thinking to deal with it roughly, as one should handle a thistle. But they fight at an overwhelming disadvantage — living, John Field, alas! without arithmetic, and failing so.

'Do you ever fish?' I asked. 'Oh yes, I catch a mess now and then when I am lying by; good perch I catch.' 'What's your bait?' 'I catch shiners with fishworms, and bait the perch with them.' 'You'd better go now, John,' said his wife, with glistening and hopeful face; but John demurred.

The shower was now over, and a rainbow above the eastern woods promised a fair evening; so I took my departure. When I had got without I asked for a drink, hoping to get a sight of the well bottom, to complete my survey of the premises; but there, alas! are shallows and

1 Tooth and nail: a common phrase that can be traced as far back as *Andria* (I, 161) by Terence (c. 185–159 B.C.).

Examining those minnows by day, I find that they are one and one sixth inches long by two fifths of an inch wide (this my largest); in form like a bream; of a very pale golden like a perch, or more bluish. . . . They have about seven transverse dusky bars like a perch (!). Yet, from their form and single dorsal fin, I think they are breams. Are they not a new species? (November 26, 1858)

1 Many of T's contemporaries disparaged him for wasting his time at Walden after having obtained a college education.

2 "Remember now thy Creator in the days of thy youth" (Ecclesiastes 12:1). See D'Avanzo (1982) for an extended analysis of this allusion.

3 An imported crop used to feed cattle and horses, and which will grow here only when cultivated.

quicksands, and rope broken withal, and bucket irrecoverable. Meanwhile the right culinary vessel was selected, water was seemingly distilled, and after consultation and long delay passed out to the thirsty one — not yet suffered to cool, not yet to settle. Such gruel sustains life here, I thought; so, shutting my eyes, and excluding the motes by a skilfully directed undercurrent, I drank to genuine hospitality the heartiest draught I could. I am not squeamish in such cases when manners are concerned.

As I was leaving the Irishman's roof after the rain, bending my steps again to the pond, my haste to catch pickerel, wading in retired meadows, in sloughs and bog-holes, in forlorn and savage places, appeared for an instant trivial

1 to me who had been sent to school and college; but as I ran down the hill toward the reddening west, with the rainbow over my shoulder, and some faint tinkling sounds borne to my ear through the cleansed air, from I know not what quarter, my Good Genius seemed to say — Go fish and hunt far and wide day by day — farther and wider — and rest thee by many brooks and hearth-sides without

2 misgiving. Remember thy Creator in the days of thy youth. Rise free from care before the dawn, and seek adventures. Let the noon find thee by other lakes, and the night overtake thee everywhere at home. There are no larger fields than these, no worthier games than may here be played. Grow wild according to thy nature, like these

3 sedges and brakes, which will never become English hay. Let the thunder rumble; what if it threaten ruin to farmers' crops? that is not its errand to thee. Take shelter under the cloud, while they flee to carts and sheds. Let not to get a living be thy trade, but thy sport. Enjoy the land, but own it not. Through want of enterprise and faith men are where they are, buying and selling, and spending their lives like serfs.

O Baker Farm!

'Landscape where the richest element
Is a little sunshine innocent.'. . .

'No one runs to revel
On thy rail-fenced lea.' . . .

'Debate with no man hast thou,
    With questions art never perplexed,
As tame at the first sight as now,
    In thy plain russet gabardine dressed.'. . .

'Come ye who love,
    And ye who hate,
Children of the Holy Dove,
    And Guy Faux of the state,   **1**
And hang conspiracies
From the tough rafters of the trees!'   **2**

Men come tamely home at night only from the next field or street, where their household echoes haunt, and their life pines because it breathes its own breath over again; their shadows, morning and evening, reach farther than their daily steps. We should come home from far, from adventures, and perils, and discoveries every day, with new experience and character.

Before I had reached the pond some fresh impulse had brought out John Field, with altered mind, letting go 'bogging' ere this sunset. But he, poor man, disturbed only a couple of fins while I was catching a fair string, and he said it was his luck; but when we changed seats in the boat luck changed seats too. Poor John Field! — I trust he does not read this, unless he will improve by it — thinking to live by some derivative old-country mode in this primitive new country — to catch perch with shiners. It is good bait sometimes, I allow. With his horizon all his

1 Guy Fawkes (1570–1606), who was hanged for conspiring to blow up the houses of Parliament.

2 Ellery Channing, "Baker Farm" (370, 372), again with slight variations.

1 Field was following the customs of times so ancient they seemed to date back even further than Adam.

2 The winged sandals worn by several minor Greek gods, giving them swift and unimpeded flight through space.

own, yet he a poor man, born to be poor, with his inherited Irish poverty or poor life, his Adam's grandmother **1** and boggy ways, not to rise in this world, he nor his posterity, till their wading webbed bog-trotting feet get **2** *talaria* to their heels.

In the zenith or apparently about in the zenith, was an arc of a distinct rainbow. A rainbow right overhead. (February 2, 1860)

Higher Laws

As I came home through the woods with my string of fish, trailing my pole, it being now quite dark, I caught a glimpse of a woodchuck stealing across my path, and felt a strange thrill of savage delight, and was strongly tempted **2** to seize and devour him raw; not that I was hungry then, except for that wildness which he represented. Once or **3** twice, however, while I lived at the pond, I found myself ranging the woods, like a half-starved hound, with a strange abandonment, seeking some kind of venison which I might devour, and no morsel could have been too savage for me. The wildest scenes had become unaccountably familiar. I found in myself, and still find, an instinct toward a higher, or, as it is named, spiritual life, as do most men, and another toward a primitive rank and savage one, and I reverence them both. I love the wild not less than the good. The wildness and adventure that are in fishing still **4** recommended it to me. I like sometimes to take rank hold on life and spend my day more as the animals do. Perhaps I have owed to this employment and to hunting, when quite young, my closest acquaintance with Nature. They early introduce us to and detain us in scenery with which otherwise, at that age, we should have little acquaintance. Fishermen, hunters, woodchoppers, and others, spending their lives in the fields and woods, in a peculiar sense a part of Nature themselves, are often in a more favorable mood for observing her, in the intervals of their pursuits, than philosophers or poets even, who approach her with expectation. She is not afraid to exhibit herself to them. The traveller on the prairie is naturally a hunter, on the head waters of the Missouri and Columbia a trapper, and at the Falls of St. Mary a fisherman. He **5**

1 The phrase "Higher Laws" was very popular in the years prior to the Civil War, particularly among transcendentalists and abolitionists in their fight against the proslavery laws passed by Congress. As Theodore Parker once said, "To say that there is no law higher than what the State can make is practical atheism" (Commager, 208). Higher laws, then, are the laws of one's conscience. For an extended exposition of the term contemporary to Thoreau, see Hosmer. For a modern evaluation of the movement, see Madden. T's most important discussion of the idea is in his essay "Civil Disobedience." Pickard stresses that while the religious beliefs expressed in this chapter are highly unconventional by Christian standards, they contain the essentials of all religious experience. For more on the place of religion in this chapter, see Wolf. Rose discusses the humor in this chapter.

2 "Cynics may be inclined to suspect that an almost exclusive diet of rice, Indian meal, and molasses might reasonably be expected to make even woodchuck look strangely attractive to any man" (Krutch, 83).

3 T had a strong belief, as he said in his essay "Walking, or the Wild," that "In wildness is the preservation of the world," and this has become the motto of the present-day conservation movement (Burroughs; Oelschlaeger).

4 Boudreau (1992) discusses T's changing attitudes toward hunting, fishing, and trapping. In general T grew more ill at ease regarding these activities.

5 The falls of the St. Mary River, in southeastern British Columbia.

1   Most New England towns have an area near the center of town that was originally owned in common for the pasturing of farm animals. Nowadays town commons are used as public parks.

2   A generic term for charitable organizations formed to protect domestic animals from cruel treatment.

3   T developed a life-long interest in the study of birds and was one of the earliest to advocate studying them in the wild rather than shooting them and studying their carcasses. He made a number of contributions to our knowledge of birds (Thoreau, 1993; Griscom).

who is only a traveller learns things at second-hand and by the halves, and is poor authority. We are most interested when science reports what those men already know practically or instinctively, for that alone is a true *humanity*, or account of human experience.

They mistake who assert that the Yankee has few amusements, because he has not so many public holidays, and men and boys do not play so many games as they do in England, for here the more primitive but solitary amusements of hunting, fishing, and the like have not yet given place to the former. Almost every New England boy among my contemporaries shouldered a fowling-piece between the ages of ten and fourteen; and his hunting and fishing grounds were not limited, like the preserves of an English nobleman, but were more boundless even than those of a savage. No wonder, then, that he did not oftener stay to play on the common. But already a change is taking place, owing, not to an increased humanity, but to an increased scarcity of game, for perhaps the hunter is the greatest friend of the animals hunted, not excepting the Humane Society.

Moreover, when at the pond, I wished sometimes to add fish to my fare for variety. I have actually fished from the same kind of necessity that the first fishers did. Whatever humanity I might conjure up against it was all factitious, and concerned my philosophy more than my feelings. I speak of fishing only now, for I had long felt differently about fowling, and sold my gun before I went to the woods. Not that I am less humane than others, but I did not perceive that my feelings were much affected. I did not pity the fishes nor the worms. This was habit. As for fowling, during the last years that I carried a gun my excuse was that I was studying ornithology, and sought only new or rare birds. But I confess that I am now inclined to think that there is a finer way of studying ornithology than this. It requires so much closer attention to the habits of the birds, that, if for that reason only, I have been willing to omit the gun. Yet notwithstanding the objection on the score of humanity, I am compelled to doubt if equally valuable sports are ever substituted for these; and when some of my friends have asked me anxiously about their boys, whether they should let them hunt, I have answered, yes — remembering that it was one of the best parts of my education — *make* them hunters, though sportsmen only at first, if possible, mighty hunters at last, so that they shall not find game large enough for them in this or any vegetable wilderness — hunters as well as fishers of men. Thus far I am of the **1** opinion of Chaucer's nun, who

> 'yave not of the text a pulled hen
> That saith that hunters ben not holy men.'   **2**

There is a period in the history of the individual, as of the race, when the hunters are the 'best men,' as the Algon- **3** quins called them. We cannot but pity the boy who has never fired a gun; he is no more humane, while his education has been sadly neglected. This was my answer with respect to those youths who were bent on this pursuit, trusting that they would soon outgrow it. No humane being, past the thoughtless age of boyhood, will wantonly murder any creature which holds its life by the same tenure that he does. The hare in its extremity cries like a child. I warn you, mothers, that my sympathies do not always make the usual phil*anthropic* distinctions.   **4**

Such is oftenest the young man's introduction to the forest, and the most original part of himself. He goes thither at first as a hunter and fisher, until at last, if he has the seeds of a better life in him, he distinguishes his

1 "And Jesus said unto them, Come after me, and I will make you to become fishers of men" (Mark 1:17).

2 "He yaf nat of that text a pulled hen. / That seith that hunters beth nat hooly men" (Chaucer, Prologue to *Canterbury Tales*, II, 178–9). But this is said of the monk, rather than the nun.

3 Indians of northeastern North America.

4 Literally, "love of man." T is merely pointing out that his love is wider than that.

1   "I am the good shepherd" (John 10:11).

2   In Massachusetts, a Governor's Council is elected to advise the governor in affairs of state.

3   Limiting the number of hooks on a fishing line was a conservation measure.

proper objects, as a poet or naturalist it may be, and leaves the gun and fish-pole behind. The mass of men are still and always young in this respect. In some countries a hunting parson is no uncommon sight. Such a one might make a good shepherd's dog, but is far from being the 1 Good Shepherd. I have been surprised to consider that the only obvious employment, except wood-chopping, ice-cutting, or the like business, which ever to my knowledge detained at Walden Pond for a whole half-day any of my fellow-citizens, whether fathers or children of the town, with just one exception, was fishing. Commonly they did not think that they were lucky, or well paid for their time, unless they got a long string of fish, though they had the opportunity of seeing the pond all the while. They might go there a thousand times before the sediment of fishing would sink to the bottom and leave their purpose pure; but no doubt such a clarifying process would be going on 2 all the while. The Governor and his Council faintly remember the pond, for they went a-fishing there when they were boys; but now they are too old and dignified to go a-fishing, and so they know it no more forever. Yet even they expect to go to heaven at last. If the legislature re-3 gards it, it is chiefly to regulate the number of hooks to be used there; but they know nothing about the hook of hooks with which to angle for the pond itself, impaling the legislature for a bait. Thus, even in civilized communities, the embryo man passes through the hunter stage of development.

I have found repeatedly, of late years, that I cannot fish without falling a little in self-respect. I have tried it again and again. I have skill at it, and, like many of my fellows, a certain instinct for it, which revives from time to time, but always when I have done I feel that it would have been better if I had not fished. I think that I do not mis-

Their spear very serviceable. The inner, pointed part, of a hemlock knot; the side spring pieces, of hickory. Spear salmon, pickerel, trout, chub, etc.; also by birch-bark light at night, using the other end of spear as pole. (November 26, 1850)

take. It is a faint intimation, yet so are the first streaks of morning. There is unquestionably this instinct in me which belongs to the lower orders of creation; yet with every year I am less a fisherman, though without more humanity or even wisdom; at present I am no fisherman at all. But I see that if I were to live in a wilderness I should again be tempted to become a fisher and hunter in earnest. Beside, there is something essentially unclean about this diet and all flesh, and I began to see where house-work commences, and whence the endeavor, which costs so much, to wear a tidy and respectable appearance each day, to keep the house sweet and free from all ill odors and sights. Having been my own butcher and scullion and cook, as well as the gentleman for whom the dishes were served up, I can speak from an unusually complete experience. The practical objection to animal food in my 1 case was its uncleanness; and besides, when I had caught and cleaned and cooked and eaten my fish, they seemed not to have fed me essentially. It was insignificant and unnecessary, and cost more than it came to. A little bread or a few potatoes would have done as well, with less trouble and filth. Like many of my contemporaries, I had rarely for many years used animal food, or tea, or coffee, etc.; not so much because of any ill effects which I had traced to them, as because they were not agreeable to my imagination. The repugnance to animal food is not the effect of experience, but is an instinct. It appeared more beautiful to live low and fare hard in many respects; and though I never did so, I went far enough to please my imagination. I believe that every man who has ever been earnest to preserve his higher or poetic faculties in the best condition has been particularly inclined to abstain from animal food, and from much food of any kind. It is a significant fact, stated by entomologists — I find it in

1   In the 1840s and 1850s, vegetarians and food faddists — Dr. Sylvester Graham among them — called for radical changes in diet. Adams and Hutter gives an amusing account of some of the food reforms suggested. Seybold (42) suggests that some of T's vegetarian ideas were derived from his reading of Porphyry's "On Abstinence from Animal Food."

1   William Kirby and William Spence, *An Introduction to Entomology (Philadelphia, 1846, 258).*

2   T misspelled this as "carniverous" in the first edition.

1 Kirby and Spence — that 'some insects in their perfect state, though furnished with organs of feeding, make no use of them;' and they lay it down as 'a general rule, that almost all insects in this state eat much less than in that of larvae. The voracious caterpillar when transformed into a butterfly. . . and the gluttonous maggot when become a fly' content themselves with a drop or two of honey or some other sweet liquid. The abdomen under the wings of the butterfly still represents the larva. This is the tidbit which tempts his insectivorous fate. The gross feeder is a man in the larva state; and there are whole nations in that condition, nations without fancy or imagination, whose vast abdomens betray them.

It is hard to provide and cook so simple and clean a diet as will not offend the imagination; but this, I think, is to be fed when we feed the body; they should both sit down at the same table. Yet perhaps this may be done. The fruits eaten temperately need not make us ashamed of our appetites, nor interrupt the worthiest pursuits. But put an extra condiment into your dish, and it will poison you. It is not worth the while to live by rich cookery. Most men would feel shame if caught preparing with their own hands precisely such a dinner, whether of animal or vege-table food, as is every day prepared for them by others. Yet till this is otherwise we are not civilized, and, if gentle-men and ladies, are not true men and women. This cer-tainly suggests what change is to be made. It may be vain to ask why the imagination will not be reconciled to flesh and fat. I am satisfied that it is not. Is it not a reproach that

2 man is a carnivorous animal? True, he can and does live, in a great measure, by preying on other animals; but this is a miserable way — as any one who will go to snaring rabbits, or slaughtering lambs, may learn — and he will be regarded as a benefactor of his race who shall teach

Ed. Emerson shows me his aquarium. He has two minnows from the brook, which I think must be the banded minnow; a little more than an inch long with very conspicuous broad black transverse bars. Some *Rana sylvatica* spawn just begun to flatout. Also several kinds of larvae in the water. (April 18, 1859)

man to confine himself to a more innocent and wholesome diet. Whatever my own practice may be, I have no doubt that it is a part of the destiny of the human race, in its gradual improvement, to leave off eating animals, as **1** surely as the savage tribes have left off eating each other when they came in contact with the more civilized.

If one listens to the faintest but constant suggestions of his genius, which are certainty true, he sees not to what extremes, or even insanity, it may lead him; and yet that way, as he grows more resolute and faithful, his road lies. The faintest assured objection which one healthy man feels will at length prevail over the arguments and customs of mankind. No man ever followed his genius till it **2** misled him. Though the result were bodily weakness, yet perhaps no one can say that the consequences were to be regretted, for these were a life in conformity to higher principles. If the day and the night are such that you greet them with joy, and life emits a fragrance like flowers and sweet-scented herbs, is more elastic, more starry, more immortal — that is your success. All nature is your congratulation, and you have cause momentarily to bless yourself. The greatest gains and values are farthest from being appreciated. We easily come to doubt if they exist. We soon forget them. They are the highest reality. Perhaps the facts most astounding and most real are never communicated by man to man. The true harvest of my daily life is somewhat as intangible and indescribable as the tints of morning or evening. It is a little star-dust caught, a segment of the rainbow which I have clutched.

Yet, for my part, I was never unusually squeamish; I could sometimes eat a fried rat with a good relish, if it **3** were necessary. I am glad to have drunk water so long, for the same reason that I prefer the natural sky to an opium- **4** eater's heaven. I would fain keep sober always; and there

1 Although T generally practiced vegetarianism, he did not confine himself wholly to that diet. For a discussion of his vegetarianism, see Joseph Jones, 1957.

2 See Emerson's "Self-Reliance" for the most noted exposition of this theme, an idea central to transcendentalism.

3 T was probably referring here to the muskrat, which by some is considered edible (Bridgman, 295).

4 Opium addiction was common in T's day. Witness Thomas De Quincey's *Confessions of an English Opium Eater.*

1 Rajah Rammohun Roy, *Translation of Several . . . of the Veds* (London, 1832, 21).

2 Confucius, *The Great Learning*, "Commentary of the Philosopher Tsang" (chap. VII, 2).

are infinite degrees of drunkenness. I believe that water is the only drink for a wise man; wine is not so noble a liquor; and think of dashing the hopes of a morning with a cup of warm coffee, or of an evening with a dish of tea! Ah, how low I fall when I am tempted by them! Even music may be intoxicating. Such apparently slight causes destroyed Greece and Rome, and will destroy England and America. Of all ebriosity, who does not prefer to be intoxicated by the air he breathes? I have found it to be the most serious objection to coarse labors long continued, that they compelled me to eat and drink coarsely also. But to tell the truth, I find myself at present somewhat less particular in these respects. I carry less religion to the table, ask no blessing; not because I am wiser than I was, but, I am obliged to confess, because, however much it is to be regretted, with years I have grown more coarse and indifferent. Perhaps these questions are entertained only in youth, as most believe of poetry. My practice is 'nowhere,' my opinion is here. Nevertheless I am far from regarding myself as one of those privileged ones

1 to whom the Ved refers when it says, that 'he who has true faith in the Omnipresent Supreme Being may eat all that exists,' that is, is not bound to inquire what is his food, or who prepares it; and even in their case it is to be observed, as a Hindoo commentator has remarked, that the Vedant limits this privilege to 'the time of distress.'

Who has not sometimes derived an inexpressible satisfaction from his food in which appetite had no share? I have been thrilled to think that I owed a mental perception to the commonly gross sense of taste, that I have been inspired through the palate, that some berries which I had eaten on a hillside had fed my genius. 'The soul not

2 being mistress of herself,' says Thseng-tseu, 'one looks, and one does not see; one listens, and one does not hear;

one eats, and one does not know the savor of food.' He who distinguishes the true savor of his food can never be a glutton; he who does not cannot be otherwise. A puritan may go to his brown-bread crust with as gross an appetite as ever an alderman to his turtle. Not that food which **1** entereth into the mouth defileth a man, but the appetite **2** with which it is eaten. It is neither the quality nor the quantity, but the devotion to sensual savors; when that which is eaten is not a viand to sustain our animal, or inspire our spiritual life, but food for the worms that possess us. If the hunter has a taste for mud-turtles, muskrats, and other such savage tidbits, the fine lady indulges a taste for jelly made of a calf's foot, or for sardines from over the sea, and they are even. He goes to the mill-pond, she to her preserve-pot. The wonder is how they, how you and I, can live this slimy, beastly life, eating and drinking.

Our whole life is startlingly moral. There is never an instant's truce between virtue and vice. Goodness is the only investment that never fails. In the music of the harp which trembles round the world it is the insisting on this which thrills us. The harp is the travelling patterer for the Universe's Insurance Company, recommending its laws, and our little goodness is all the assessment that we pay. Though the youth at last grows indifferent, the laws of the universe are not indifferent, but are forever on the side of the most sensitive. Listen to every zephyr for some reproof, for it is surely there, and he is unfortunate who does not hear it. We cannot touch a string or move a stop but the charming moral transfixes us. Many an irksome noise, go a long way off, is heard as music, a proud, sweet satire on the meanness of our lives.

We are conscious of an animal in us, which awakens in **3** proportion as our higher nature slumbers. It is reptile and sensual, and perhaps cannot be wholly expelled; like the

1 Aldermen are often depicted as lovers of exotic foods.

2 "But those things which proceed out of the mouth come forth from the heart; and they defile the man" (Matthew 15:18).

3 T is probably thinking of Hawthorne's short story "Egotism, or the Bosom Serpent" (Davidson, 1947).

At Dugan Desert many fresh turtle-tracks. They generally steer for some more elevated and perhaps bushy place. The tail makes a serpentine track, the tracks of the flippers and claws quite distinct, and you see where the turtle rested on its shell, flatting the sand, from time to time. (June 14, 1860)

1 T describes this incident in his *Journal* for June 9, 1850 (II, 36). A later discovery of a hog's jawbones is discussed by Sanborn (1909, I, 320).

2 Mencius, *Works* (book IV ["Le Low"], part II, chap. XIX, p. 1).

3 Rajah Rammohun Roy, *Translation of Several . . . of the Veds* (London, 1832, 21).

4 T's views on sexuality were even more conservative than those of most of his fellow Victorians and seem outlandish today. For a discussion of his sexuality, see Harding (1991).

5 In Roman mythology, a class of deities part human and part goat.

worms which, even in life and health, occupy our bodies. Possibly we may withdraw from it, but never change its nature. I fear that it may enjoy a certain health of its own; that we may be well, yet not pure. The other day I picked **1** up the lower jaw of a hog, with white and sound teeth and tusks, which suggested that there was an animal health and vigor distinct from the spiritual. This creature succeeded by other means than temperance and purity. 'That **2** in which men differ from brute beasts,' says Mencius, 'is a thing very inconsiderable; the common herd lose it very soon; superior men preserve it carefully.' Who knows what sort of life would result if we had attained to purity? If I knew so wise a man as could teach me purity I would go to seek him forthwith. 'A command over our passions, and over the external senses of the body, and good acts, **3** are declared by the Ved to be indispensable in the mind's approximation to God.' Yet the spirit can for the time pervade and control every member and function of the body, and transmute what in form is the grossest sensual-**4** ity into purity and devotion. The generative energy, which, when we are loose, dissipates and makes us unclean, when we are continent invigorates and inspires us. Chastity is the flowering of man; and what are called Genius, Heroism, Holiness, and the like, are but various fruits which succeed it. Man flows at once to God when the channel of purity is open. By turns our purity inspires and our impurity casts us down. He is blessed who is assured that the animal is dying out in him day by day, and the divine being established. Perhaps there is none but has cause for shame on account of the inferior and brutish nature to which he is allied. I fear that we are such gods or demi-**5** gods only as fauns and satyrs, the divine allied to beasts, the creatures of appetite, and that, to some extent, our very life is our disgrace.

'How happy's he who hath due place assigned
To his beasts and disafforested his mind!
. . . .

Can use his horse, goat, wolf, and ev'ry beast,
And is not ass himself to all the rest!
Else man not only is the herd of swine,
But he's those devils too which did incline
Them to a headlong rage, and made them worse.' **1**

All sensuality is one, though it takes many forms; all purity is one. It is the same whether a man eat, or drink, or cohabit, or sleep sensually. They are but one appetite, and we only need to see a person do any one of these things to know how great a sensualist he is. The impure can neither stand nor sit with purity. When the reptile is attacked at one mouth of his burrow, he shows himself at another. If you would be chaste, you must be temperate. What is chastity? How shall a man know if he is chaste? He shall not know it. We have heard of this virtue, but we know not what it is. We speak conformably to the rumor which we have heard. From exertion come wisdom and purity; from sloth ignorance and sensuality. In the student sensuality is a sluggish habit of mind. An unclean person is universally a slothful one, one who sits by a stove, whom the sun shines on prostrate, who reposes without being fatigued. If you would avoid uncleanness, and all the sins, work earnestly, though it be at cleaning a **2** stable. Nature is hard to be overcome, but she must be overcome. What avails it that you are Christian, if you are not purer than the heathen, if you deny yourself no more, if you are not more religious? I know of many systems **3** of religion esteemed heathenish whose precepts fill the reader with shame, and provoke him to new endeavors, though it be to the performance of rites merely.

I hesitate to say these things, but it is not because of the

1 John Donne, "To Sr Edward Herbert at Iulyers."

2 That T practiced what he preached is evident in his *Journal* entry for April 20, 1841 (I, 250–1): "To-day I earned seventy-five cents heaving manure out of a pen."

3 T was undoubtedly thinking of the Hindu *Laws of Menu, or the Vishnu Purana,* which he had read in the H. H. Wilson translation (London, 1840).

1   "Ye are the temple of God" (I Corinthians 3:16).

2   Farmer is used as a type name, rather than referring to a specific individual. In the original manuscript it read "John Spaulding" (Stern). Spaulding was a common name in Concord in those days, though there seems to be no John Spaulding listed in the town records.

3   In the first edition, this word came at the end of a line of type and was broken into "recreate." In T's own copy, he corrected the syllabification, and a hyphen has crept into the word in some editions.

4   T himself often loved to play his flute, particularly when in his rowboat on the pond.

subject — I care not how obscene my *words* are — but because I cannot speak of them without betraying my impurity. We discourse freely without shame of one form of sensuality, and are silent about another. We are so degraded that we cannot speak simply of the necessary functions of human nature. In earlier ages, in some countries, every function was reverently spoken of and regulated by law. Nothing was too trivial for the Hindoo lawgiver, however offensive it may be to modern taste. He teaches how to eat, drink, cohabit, void excrement and urine, and the like, elevating what is mean, and does not falsely excuse himself by calling these things trifles.

1   Every man is the builder of a temple, called his body, to the god he worships, after a style purely his own, nor can he get off by hammering marble instead. We are all sculptors and painters, and our material is our own flesh and blood and bones. Any nobleness begins at once to refine a man's features, any meanness or sensuality to imbrute them.

2   John Farmer sat at his door one September evening, after a hard day's work, his mind still running on his labor
3   more or less. Having bathed, he sat down to re-create his intellectual man. It was a rather cool evening, and some of his neighbors were apprehending a frost. He had not attended to the train of his thoughts long when he heard
4   some one playing on a flute, and that sound harmonized with his mood. Still he thought of his work; but the burden of his thought was, that though this kept running in his head, and he found himself planning and contriving it against his will, yet it concerned him very little. It was no more than the scurf of his skin, which was constantly shuffled off. But the notes of the flute came home to his ears out of a different sphere from that he worked in, and suggested work for certain faculties which slumbered in

him. They gently did away with the street, and the village, and the state in which he lived. A voice said to him — Why do you stay here and live this mean moiling life, when a glorious existence is possible for you? Those same stars twinkle over other fields than these. — But how to come out of this condition and actually migrate thither? All that he could think of was to practise some new austerity, to let his mind descend into his body and redeem it, and treat himself with ever increasing respect.

In the reflection you have an infinite number of eyes to see for you and report the aspect of things each from its point of view. The statue in the meadow which actually is seen obscurely against the meadow, in the reflection appears dark and distinct against the sky. (October 16, 1858)

Brute Neighbors

1 Brenner suggests that in this chapter, "One can observe the animal cosmos in its comparative levels of natural, unnatural, preternatural, and supernatural."

2 Ellery Channing, T's closest friend and first biographer. In the dialogue that follows, T is the hermit and Channing the poet. Charles Anderson (1968, 179) thinks, instead, that they represent two facets of T's own personality. Shanley (1957, 80) suggests that T introduced this dialogue as a comic interlude because he felt the need of a descent from the level of "Higher Laws" to "Brute Neighbors." Hodges suggests that the dialogue "has dramatized a state of spiritual emptiness and fraud, an unhappy possibility of following literally T's 'Higher Laws'" (I am not convinced). Blanding thinks this seems to have been modeled on the dialogues of the Angler, the Falconer, and the Hunter in Izaac Walton's *Compleat Angler*.

3 This is one of the rare times when T refers to himself as a hermit. Actually there was hardly a day when he did not either walk into town or have friends come out to visit him. His aunt Maria complained that everyone in Concord thought he had the right to picnic on the cabin doorstep. And the county women's anti-slavery society (of which his mother was an officer) once held its annual meeting at the cabin.

4 Farmers often rang a bell or sounded a horn to call their hired hands in from the fields for meals.

5 Bread made of corn meal.

6 T is here reversing John Smith's charge to his fellow colonists in Virginia (Smith, *Travels and Works* [Edinburgh, 1910, part I, 194]).

7 A then popular name for a pet dog.

8 Charles Anderson (1968, 180) suggests that T was referring to Saint Bavo (c. 655), who lived in a hollow tree. George Fox, the Quaker theologian, is also said to have lived in a tree.

9 Channing had sailed along the coast of Spain on his way to Italy in 1846.

2 SOMETIMES I HAD a companion in my fishing, who came through the village to my house from the other side of the town, and the catching of the dinner was as much a social exercise as the eating of it.

3 *Hermit.* I wonder what the world is doing now. I have not heard so much as a locust over the sweet-fern these three hours. The pigeons are all asleep upon their roosts **4** — no flutter from them. Was that a farmer's noon horn which sounded from beyond the woods just now? The hands are coming in to boiled salt beef and cider and **5** Indian bread. Why will men worry themselves so? He that **6** does not eat need not work. I wonder how much they have reaped. Who would live there where a body can **7** never think for the barking of Bose? And oh, the housekeeping! to keep bright the devil's door-knobs, and scour his tubs this bright day! Better not keep a house. Say, **8** some hollow tree; and then for morning calls and dinner-parties! Only a woodpecker tapping. Oh, they swarm; the sun is too warm there; they are born too far into life for me. I have water from the spring, and a loaf of brown bread on the shelf. — Hark! I hear a rustling of the leaves. Is it some ill-fed village hound yielding to the instinct of the chase? or the lost pig which is said to be in these woods, whose tracks I saw after the rain? It comes on apace; my sumachs and sweetbriers tremble. — Eh, Mr. Poet, is it you? How do you like the world today?

Poet. See those clouds; how they hang! That's the greatest thing I have seen today. There's nothing like it in old paintings, nothing like it in foreign lands — unless when **9** we were off the coast of Spain. That's a true Mediterranean sky. I thought, as I have my living to get, and have not eaten today, that I might go a-fishing. That's the true industry for poets. It is the only trade I have learned. Come, let's along.

Hermit. I cannot resist. My brown bread will soon be **1** gone. I will go with you gladly soon, but I am just concluding a serious meditation. I think that I am near the end of it. Leave me alone, then, for a while. But that we may not be delayed, you shall be digging the bait meanwhile. Angleworms are rarely to be met with in these parts, where the soil was never fattened with manure; the race is nearly extinct. The sport of digging the bait is nearly equal to that of catching the fish, when one's appetite is not too keen; and this you may have all to yourself today. I would advise you to set in the spade down yonder among the ground-nuts, where you see the johnswort **2** waving. I think that I may warrant you one worm to every three sods you turn up, if you look well in among the roots of the grass, as if you were weeding. Or, if you choose to go farther, it will not be unwise, for I have found the increase of fair bait to be very nearly as the squares of the distances.

Hermit alone. Let me see; where was I? Methinks I was nearly in this frame of mind; the world lay about at this angle. Shall I go to heaven or a-fishing? If I should soon bring this meditation to an end, would another so sweet occasion be likely to offer? I was as near being resolved into the essence of things as ever I was in my life. I fear my thoughts will not come back to me. If it would do any good, I would whistle for them. When they make us an offer, is it wise to say, We will think of it? My thoughts have left no track, and I cannot find the path again. What was it that I was thinking of? It was a very hazy day. I will just try these three sentences of Confut-see; they may **3** fetch that state about again. I know not whether it was the

1 Bread sweetened with molasses and raisins, usually served with baked beans.

2 A common plant (*Apios americana*) of the area, which has edible tubers.

3 A variant spelling of Confucius.

The johnswort and the larger pinweed are conspicuous above the snow. (December 4, 1856)

1 Abbreviation for memorandum.

2 A New England term for any small fresh-water fish.

3 Pilpay, known also as Bidpai, was the reputed author of a collection of fables of East Indian origin. T was familiar with them in the Charles Wilkins translation, and Emerson had used some of them in the *Dial* (III, 1842, 82–5).

4 The Latin name, *Mus Leucupus* did not appear in the first edition, but T added it in his own copy.

5 Louis Agassiz (1807–1873). In the late 1840s T collected various specimens of fish, reptiles, and mammals for Agassiz, who was working on the classification of species at Harvard.

1 dumps or a budding ecstasy. Mem. There never is but one opportunity of a kind.

Poet. How now, Hermit, is it too soon? I have got just thirteen whole ones, beside several which are imperfect or undersized; but they will do for the smaller fry; they do not cover up the hook so much. Those village worms are 2 quite too large; a shiner may make a meal off one without finding the skewer.

Hermit. Well, then, let's be off. Shall we to the Concord? There's good sport there if the water be not too high.

Why do precisely these objects which we behold make a world? Why has man just these species of animals for his neighbors; as if nothing but a mouse could have filled this 3 crevice? I suspect that Pilpay & Co. have put animals to their best use, for they are all beasts of burden, in a sense, made to carry some portion of our thoughts.

The mice which haunted my house were not the common ones, which are said to have been introduced into 4 the country, but a wild native kind not found in the vil-5 lage. I sent one to a distinguished naturalist, and it interested him much. When I was building, one of these had its nest underneath the house, and before I had laid the second floor, and swept out the shavings, would come out regularly at lunch time and pick up the crumbs at my feet. It probably had never seen a man before; and it soon became quite familiar, and would run over my shoes and up my clothes. It could readily ascend the sides of the room by short impulses, like a squirrel, which it resembled in its motions. At length, as I leaned with my elbow on the bench one day, it ran up my clothes, and along my sleeve, and round and round the paper which held my dinner, while I kept the latter close, and dodged and

played at bopeep with it; and when at last I held still a **1**
piece of cheese between my thumb and finger, it came
and nibbled it, sitting in my hand, and afterward cleaned
its face and paws, like a fly, and walked away.

A phoebe soon built in my shed, and a robin for protection in a pine which grew against the house. In June the
partridge (*Tetrao umbellus*), which is so shy a bird, led her
brood past my windows, from the woods in the rear to the
front of my house, clucking and calling to them like a
hen, and in all her behavior proving herself the hen of the
woods. The young suddenly disperse on your approach,
at a signal from the mother, as if a whirlwind had swept
them away, and they so exactly resemble the dried leaves
and twigs that many a traveller has placed his foot in the
midst of a brood, and heard the whir of the old bird as she
flew off, and her anxious calls and mewing, or seen her
trail her wings to attract his attention, without suspecting
their neighborhood. The parent will sometimes roll and
spin round before you in such a dishabille, that you cannot, for a few moments, detect what kind of creature it is.
The young squat still and flat, often running their heads
under a leaf, and mind only their mother's directions
given from a distance, nor will your approach make them
run again and betray themselves. You may even tread on
them, or have your eyes on them for a minute, without
discovering them. I have held them in my open hand at
such a time, and still their only care, obedient to their
mother and their instinct, was to squat there without fear
or trembling. So perfect is this instinct, that once, when I
had laid them on the leaves again, and one accidentally
fell on its side, it was found with the rest in exactly the
same position ten minutes afterward. They are not callow
like the young of most birds, but more perfectly developed and precocious even than chickens. The remarkably

1   A children's game also known as peekaboo.

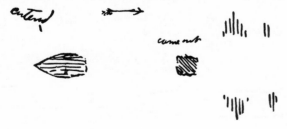

Their tracks, when perfectly distinct, are seen to
be almost in one straight line thus, trailing the
middle toe: about five inches apart. (February 13,
1855)

1   Again, the transcendentalist belief in the superior moral sense of the uncorrupted child.

2   A small elevation about a quarter mile north of Walden (Gleason).

adult yet innocent expression of their open and serene eyes is very memorable. All intelligence seems reflected in them. They suggest not merely the purity of infancy, but a wisdom clarified by experience. Such an eye was not born when the bird was, but is coeval with the sky it reflects. The woods do not yield another such a gem. The traveller does not often look into such a limpid well. The ignorant or reckless sportsman often shoots the parent at such a time, and leaves these innocents to fall a prey to some prowling beast or bird, or gradually mingle with the decaying leaves which they so much resemble. It is said that when hatched by a hen they will directly disperse on some alarm, and so are lost, for they never hear the mother's call which gathers them again. These were my hens and chickens.

It is remarkable how many creatures live wild and free though secret in the woods, and still sustain themselves in the neighborhood of towns, suspected by hunters only. How retired the otter manages to live here! He grows to be four feet long, as big as a small boy, perhaps without any human being getting a glimpse of him. I formerly saw the raccoon in the woods behind where my house is built, and probably still heard their whinnering at night. Commonly I rested an hour or two in the shade at noon, after planting, and ate my lunch, and read a little by a spring which was the source of a swamp and of a brook, oozing from under Brister's Hill, half a mile from my field. The approach to this was through a succession of descending grassy hollows, full of young pitch pines, into a larger wood about the swamp. There, in a very secluded and shaded spot, under a spreading white pine, there was yet a clean, firm sward to sit on. I had dug out the spring and made a well of clear gray water, where I could dip up a pailful without roiling it, and thither I went for this

See a broad and distinct otter-trail, made last night or yesterday. (February 20, 1856)

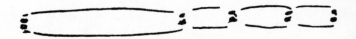

purpose almost every day in midsummer, when the pond was warmest. Thither, too, the woodcock led her brood, to probe the mud for worms, flying but a foot above them down the bank, while they ran in a troop beneath; but at last, spying me, she would leave her young and circle round and round me, nearer and nearer till within four or five feet, pretending broken wings and legs, to attract my attention, and get off her young, who would already have taken up their march, with faint, wiry peep, single file through the swamp, as she directed. Or I heard the peep of the young when I could not see the parent bird. There too the turtle doves sat over the spring, or fluttered from **1** bough to bough of the soft white pines over my head; or the red squirrel, coursing down the nearest bough, was particularly familiar and inquisitive. You only need sit still long enough in some attractive spot in the woods that all its inhabitants may exhibit themselves to you by turns.

I was witness to events of a less peaceful character. One **2** day when I went out to my wood-pile, or rather my pile of stumps, I observed two large ants, the one red, the other much larger, nearly half an inch long, and black, fiercely contending with one another. Having once got hold they never let go, but struggled and wrestled and rolled on the chips incessantly. Looking farther, I was surprised to find that the chips were covered with such combatants, that it was not a *duellum*, but a *bellum*, a war between two races of ants, the red always pitted against the black, and frequently two red ones to one black. The legions of these Myrmidons covered all the hills and vales in my wood- **3** yard, and the ground was already strewn with the dead and dying, both red and black. It was the only battle which I have ever witnessed, the only battle-field I ever trod while the battle was raging; internecine war; the red republicans on the one hand, and the black imperialists

1 Now more commonly known as mourning doves.

2 The battle of the ants, which follows, is one of the best-known passages in W. T uses the technique of the mock heroic, describing the battle in terms of a major engagement of nations (Adams, 1955). Francis Ross examines the rhetorical procedures and the use of point of view in this section. For a detailed analysis of this section, see O'Connell.

3 The warlike people of ancient Thessaly who accompanied Achilles, their king, to the Trojan War. They are popularly identified with the descendants of the transformed ants of the legend referred to in "Where I Lived, and What I Lived For" (see Hahn).

Saw two red squirrels on the fence, one on each side of his house, particularly red along their backs and top of head and tail. They are remarkably tame. One sits twirling apparently a dried apple in his paws, with his tail curled close over his back as if to keep it warm, fitting its curve. (December 16, 1855)

1 Literally, to fall overboard.

2 The motto of the Duke of Kent. It was also emblazoned on the flag of the Bedford Minutemen at the battle of Concord (O'Connell).

3 "Another [Spartan woman], as she handed her son his shield, exhorted him, saying, 'Either this or upon this'" (Plutarch, *Sayings of Spartan Women*, 16).

4 Achilles, filled with resentment against Agamemnon, refused to participate in the Trojan War. But when his friend Patroclus was killed, he went forth to battle.

on the other. On every side they were engaged in deadly combat, yet without any noise that I could hear, and human soldiers never fought so resolutely. I watched a couple that were fast locked in each other's embraces, in a little sunny valley amid the chips, now at noonday prepared to fight till the sun went down, or life went out. The smaller red champion had fastened himself like a vice to his adversary's front, and through all the tumblings on that field never for an instant ceased to gnaw at one of his feelers near the root, having already caused the other to

1 go by the board; while the stronger black one dashed him from side to side, and, as I saw on looking nearer, had already divested him of several of his members. They fought with more pertinacity than bulldogs. Neither manifested the least disposition to retreat. It was evident that

2 their battle-cry was 'Conquer or die.' In the meanwhile there came along a single red ant on the hillside of this valley, evidently full of excitement, who either had despatched his foe, or had not yet taken part in the battle; probably the latter, for he had lost none of his limbs;

3 whose mother had charged him to return with his shield

4 or upon it. Or perchance he was some Achilles, who had nourished his wrath apart, and had now come to avenge or rescue his Patroclus. He saw this unequal combat from afar — for the blacks were nearly twice the size of the red — he drew near with rapid pace till he stood on his guard within half an inch of the combatants; then, watching his opportunity, he sprang upon the black warrior, and commenced his operations near the root of his right fore leg, leaving the foe to select among his own members; and so there were three united for life, as if a new kind of attraction had been invented which put all other locks and cements to shame. I should not have wondered by this time to find that they had their respective musical bands

stationed on some eminent chip, and playing their national airs the while, to excite the slow and cheer the dying combatants. I was myself excited somewhat even as if they had been men. The more you think of it, the less the difference. And certainly there is not the fight recorded in Concord history, at least, if in the history of **1** America, that will bear a moment's comparison with this, whether for the numbers engaged in it, or for the patriotism and heroism displayed. For numbers and for carnage it was an Austerlitz or Dresden. Concord Fight! Two killed **2** on the patriots' side, and Luther Blanchard wounded! Why here every ant was a Buttrick — 'Fire! for God's sake fire!' — and thousands shared the fate of Davis and Hosmer. There was not one hireling there. I have no doubt **3** that it was a principle they fought for, as much as our ancestors, and not to avoid a three-penny tax on their tea; **4** and the results of this battle will be as important and memorable to those whom it concerns as those of the battle of Bunker Hill, at least. **5**

I took up the chip on which the three I have particularly described were struggling, carried it into my house, and placed it under a tumbler on my window-sill, in order to see the issue. Holding a microscope to the first-mentioned red ant, I saw that, though he was assiduously gnawing at the near fore leg of his enemy, having severed his remaining feeler, his own breast was all torn away, exposing what vitals he had there to the jaws of the black warrior, whose breastplate was apparently too thick for him to pierce; and the dark carbuncles of the sufferer's eyes shone with ferocity such as war only could excite. They struggled half an hour longer under the tumbler, and when I looked again the black soldier had severed the heads of his foes from their bodies, and the still living heads were hanging on either side of him like ghastly

1 The battle of Concord, of April 19, 1775, was of course one of the most famous in American history. The names and quotations given are familiar to any student of that battle.

2 The sites of two of Napoleon's bloodiest battles.

3 The Americans much resented the use of Hessian mercenaries by the British.

4 It was this tax by the British on the colonists that helped arouse much of their resentment, which led to the Revolution.

5 In Charlestown, Massachusetts, on June 17, 1775.

1 The arched front part of a saddle.

2 A huge hospital for disabled veterans in Paris, built by Louis XIV.

3 William Kirby and William Spence, *An Introduction to Entomology*, (Philadelphia, 1846, 361–2). Tripp shows how T made use of the Kirby and Spence text, changing the tone from heroic to mock heroic.

4 Pierre Huber, *Recherches sur les Moeurs des Fournis Indigenes* (Paris, 1810, chap. V), gives the account paraphrased by Kirby and Spence (Woodson, 1975).

5 Pseudonym of Pope Pius II (1405–1464).

6 Pope Eugene IV (1383–1447).

7 Swedish archbishop (1490–1558).

8 A Danish king (1481–1559) who imposed himself on Sweden with great cruelty, but who was eventually driven off.

9 James Polk was president from 1845 to 1849.

10 Daniel Webster was not the author of the fugitive slave bill, which authorized the arrest of escaping slaves by federal marshals, but he was roundly condemned by abolitionists for his part in its passage.

11 Course: pursue.

1 trophies at his saddle-bow, still apparently as firmly fastened as ever, and he was endeavoring with feeble struggles, being without feelers and with only the remnant of a leg, and I know not how many other wounds, to divest himself of them; which at length, after half an hour more, he accomplished. I raised the glass, and he went off over the window-sill in that crippled state. Whether he finally survived that combat, and spent the remainder of his days **2** in some Hôtel des Invalides, I do not know; but I thought that his industry would not be worth much thereafter. I never learned which party was victorious, nor the cause of the war; but I felt for the rest of that day as if I had had my feelings excited and harrowed by witnessing the struggle, the ferocity and carnage, of a human battle before my door.

3 Kirby and Spence tell us that the battles of ants have long been celebrated and the date of them recorded, **4** though they say that Huber is the only modern author **5** who appears to have witnessed them. 'Aeneas Sylvius,' say they, 'after giving a very circumstantial account of one contested with great obstinacy by a great and small species on the trunk of a pear tree,' adds that ' "this action was **6** fought in the pontificate of Eugenius the Fourth, in the presence of Nicholas Pistoriensis, an eminent lawyer, who related the whole history of the battle with the greatest fidelity." A similar engagement between great and small **7** ants is recorded by Olaus Magnus, in which the small ones, being victorious, are said to have buried the bodies of their own soldiers, but left those of their giant enemies a prey to the birds. This event happened previous to the **8** expulsion of the tyrant Christiern the Second from Sweden.' The battle which I witnessed took place in the Presi- **9** dency of Polk, five years before the passage of Webster's **10** Fugitive-Slave Bill.

11 Many a village Bose, fit only to course a mud-turtle in a victualling cellar, sported his heavy quarters in the woods, without the knowledge of his master, and ineffectually smelled at old fox burrows and woodchucks' holes; led perchance by some slight cur which nimbly threaded the wood, and might still inspire a natural terror in its denizens; — now far behind his guide, barking like a canine bull toward some small squirrel which had treed itself for scrutiny, then, cantering off, bending the bushes with his weight, imagining that he is on the track of some stray member of the gerbille family. Once I was surprised to see **1** a cat walking along the stony shore of the pond, for they rarely wander so far from home. The surprise was mutual. Nevertheless the most domestic cat, which has lain on a rug all her days, appears quite at home in the woods, and, by her sly and stealthy behavior, proves herself more native there than the regular inhabitants. Once, when berrying, I met with a cat with young kittens in the woods, quite wild, and they all, like their mother, had their backs up and were fiercely spitting at me. A few years before I lived in the woods there was what was called a 'winged **2** cat' in one of the farm-houses in Lincoln nearest the pond, Mr. Gilian Baker's. When I called to see her in **3** June, 1842, she was gone a-hunting in the woods, as was her wont (I am not sure whether it was a male or female, **4** and so use the more common pronoun), but her mistress told me that she came into the neighborhood a little more than a year before, in April, and was finally taken into their house; that she was of a dark brownish-gray color, with a white spot on her throat, and white feet, and had a large bushy tail like a fox; that in the winter the fur grew thick and flatted out along her sides, forming stripes ten or twelve inches long by two and a half wide, and under her chin like a muff, the upper side loose, the under matted like felt, and in the spring these append-

1 A member of the mouse family.

2 A similar cat was found in West Virginia in 1959 (*Thoreau Society Bulletin* 68 [1959, 1]).

3 According to Richard O'Connor, Gilian Baker is not listed either in Concord's or Lincoln's *Births, Deaths, and Marriages* or in county records. It is possible that T is giving a false name. As on other occasions, perhaps he thought the person would be unhappy about having his name in print.

4 Most hybrids are sterile.

1 Pegasus, the winged horse of Greek mythology, was a favorite of the Muses, and so has come to be considered the steed of poets.

2 Again, in the center of Concord.

3 Two-wheeled, open carriages.

ages dropped off. They gave me a pair of her 'wings,' which I keep still. There is no appearance of a membrane about them. Some thought it was part flying squirrel or some other wild animal, which is not impossible, for, according to naturalists, prolific hybrids have been produced by the union of the marten and domestic cat. This would have been the right kind of cat for me to keep, if I had kept any; for why should not a poet's cat be winged as 1 well as his horse?

In the fall the loon (*Colymbus glacialis*) came, as usual, to moult and bathe in the pond, making the woods ring with his wild laughter before I had risen. At rumor of 2 his arrival all the Mill-dam sportsmen are on the alert, in 3 gigs and on foot, two by two and three by three, with patent rifles and conical balls and spy-glasses. They come rustling through the woods like autumn leaves, at least ten men to one loon. Some station themselves on this side of the pond, some on that, for the poor bird cannot be omnipresent; if he dive here he must come up there. But now the kind October wind rises, rustling the leaves and rippling the surface of the water, so that no loon can be heard or seen, though his foes sweep the pond with spy-glasses, and make the woods resound with their discharges. The waves generously rise and dash angrily, taking sides with all water-fowl, and our sportsmen must beat a retreat to town and shop and unfinished jobs. But they were too often successful. When I went to get a pail of water early in the morning I frequently saw this stately bird sailing out of my cove within a few rods. If I endeavored to overtake him in a boat, in order to see how he would manoeuvre, he would dive and be completely lost, so that I did not discover him again, sometimes, till the latter part of the day. But I was more than a match for him on the surface. He commonly went off in a rain.

As I was paddling along the north shore one very calm October afternoon, for such days especially they settle on [1] to the lakes, like the milkweed down, having looked in vain over the pond for a loon, suddenly one, sailing out from the shore toward the middle a few rods in front of me, set up his wild laugh and betrayed himself. I pursued with a paddle and he dived, but when he came up I was nearer than before. He dived again, but I miscalculated [2] the direction he would take, and we were fifty rods apart when he came to the surface this time, for I had helped to widen the interval; and again he laughed long and loud, and with more reason than before. He manoeuvred so cunningly that I could not get within half a dozen rods of him. Each time, when he came to the surface, turning his head this way and that, he coolly surveyed the water and the land, and apparently chose his course so that he might come up where there was the widest expanse of water and at the greatest distance from the boat. It was surprising how quickly he made up his mind and put his resolve into execution. He led me at once to the widest part of the pond, and could not be driven from it. While he was thinking one thing in his brain, I was endeavoring to divine his thought in mine. It was a pretty game, played on the smooth surface of the pond, a man against a loon. Suddenly your adversary's checker disappears beneath the board, and the problem is to place yours nearest to where his will appear again. Sometimes he would come up unexpectedly on the opposite side of me, having apparently passed directly under the boat. So long-winded was he and so unweariable, that when he had swum farthest he would immediately plunge again, nevertheless; and then no wit could divine where in the deep pond, beneath the smooth surface, he might be speeding his way like a fish, for he had time and ability to visit the bottom of the pond

---

1   T notes in his *Journal* (IV, 380) that this happened on October 8, 1852, well after he had left Walden.

2   The Ojibway Indians did learn how to predict where a loon would surface, and thus they could keep tracking it until it was winded, making it easy to capture (Sayre, 85).

The outer part of the down of the upper seeds is blown loose, while they are still retained by the ends of the middle portion in loops attached to the core. (October 19, 1856)

1 "Not long since we saw one of those birds, loons of usual size . . . it had been caught in Seneca Lake [in upstate New York] on the hook of what fishermen call a set-line, dropped to the depth of ninety-five feet, the birds having dived that distance to reach the bait. Several others have been caught in the same manner in Seneca Lake upon lines sunk from eighty to one hundred feet" (Susan Fenimore Cooper, *Rural Hours* [New York, 1850, 10]). T, in his *Journal* for October 8, 1852 (IV, 380), says he also found this information in a newspaper.

Saw two white-throated, black-beaked divers fly off swiftly low over the water, with black tips of wings curved short downward. Afterward saw one scoot along out from the shore upon the water and dive; and that was the last I could see of him, though I watched four or five minutes. (March 29, 1854)

in its deepest part. It is said that loons have been caught in

1 the New York lakes eighty feet beneath the surface, with hooks set for trout — though Walden is deeper than that. How surprised must the fishes be to see this ungainly visitor from another sphere speeding his way amid their schools! Yet he appeared to know his course as surely under water as on the surface, and swam much faster there. Once or twice I saw a ripple where he approached the surface, just put his head out to reconnoitre, and instantly dived again. I found that it was as well for me to rest on my oars and wait his reappearing as to endeavor to calculate where he would rise; for again and again, when I was straining my eyes over the surface one way, I would suddenly be startled by his unearthly laugh behind me. But why, after displaying so much cunning, did he invariably betray himself the moment he came up by that loud laugh? Did not his white breast enough betray him? He was indeed a silly loon, I thought. I could commonly hear the plash of the water when he came up, and so also detected him. But after an hour he seemed as fresh as ever, dived as willingly, and swam yet farther than at first. It was surprising to see how serenely he sailed off with unruffled breast when he came to the surface, doing all the work with his webbed feet beneath. His usual note was this demoniac laughter, yet somewhat like that of a waterfowl; but occasionally, when he had balked me most successfully and come up a long way off, he uttered a long-drawn unearthly howl, probably more like that of a wolf than any bird; as when a beast puts his muzzle to the ground and deliberately howls. This was his looning — perhaps the wildest sound that is ever heard here, making the woods ring far and wide. I concluded that he laughed in derision of my efforts, confident of his own resources. Though the sky was by this time overcast, the pond was so smooth that I could see where he broke the surface when I did not hear him. His white breast, the stillness of the air, and the smoothness of the water were all against him. At length having come up fifty rods off, he uttered one of those prolonged howls, as if calling on the god of loons to aid him, and immediately there came a wind from the east and rippled the surface, and filled the whole air with misty rain, and I was impressed as if it were the prayer of the loon answered, and his god was angry with me; and so I left him disappearing far away on the tumultuous surface.

For hours, in fall days, I watched the ducks cunningly tack and veer and hold the middle of the pond, far from the sportsman; tricks which they will have less need to practise in Louisiana bayous. When compelled to rise they would sometimes circle round and round and over the pond at a considerable height, from which they could easily see to other ponds and the river, like black motes in the sky; and, when I thought they had gone off thither long since, they would settle down by a slanting flight of a quarter of a mile on to a distant part which was left free; but what beside safety they got by sailing in the middle of Walden I do not know, unless they love its water for the same reason that I do.

The hill and opposite woods are dark with fine effect. The little peepers have much the greatest apparatus for peeping of any frogs that I know. Frogs are the birds of the night. (May 3, 1852)

1 To treat with special care.
2 Chestnuts have long since virtually disappeared from the area because of the chestnut blight.
3 Again, T is punning on "sleeper," the old name for a railroad tie.

HOUSE-WARMING

IN OCTOBER I went a-graping to the river meadows, and loaded myself with clusters more precious for their beauty and fragrance than for food. There, too, I admired, though I did not gather, the cranberries, small waxen gems, pendants of the meadow grass, pearly and red, which the farmer plucks with an ugly rake, leaving the smooth meadow in a snarl, heedlessly measuring them by the bushel and the dollar only, and sells the spoils of the meads to Boston and New York; destined to be *jammed*, to satisfy the tastes of lovers of Nature there. So butchers rake the tongues of bison out of the prairie grass, regardless of the torn and drooping plant. The barberry's brilliant fruit was likewise food for my eyes merely; but I **1** collected a small store of wild apples for coddling, which the proprietor and travellers had overlooked. When chest- **2** nuts were ripe I laid up half a bushel for winter. It was very exciting at that season to roam the then boundless **3** chestnut woods of Lincoln — they now sleep their long sleep under the railroad — with a bag on my shoulder, and a stick to open burs with in my hand, for I did not always wait for the frost, amid the rustling of leaves and the loud reproofs of the red squirrels and the jays, whose half-consumed nuts I sometimes stole, for the burs which they had selected were sure to contain sound ones. Occasionally I climbed and shook the trees. They grew also behind my house, and one large tree, which almost overshadowed it, was, when in flower, a bouquet which scented the whole neighborhood, but the squirrels and the jays got most of its fruit; the last coming in flocks early in the morning and picking the nuts out of the burs before they

I still pick chestnuts. Some larger ones proved to contain double meats, divided, as it were arbitrarily, as with a knife, each part having the common division without the brown skin transverse to this. (January 25, 1853)

fell. I relinquished these trees to them and visited the more distant woods composed wholly of chestnut. These nuts, as far as they went, were a good substitute for bread. Many other substitutes might, perhaps, be found. Digging one day for fishworms, I discovered the ground-nut (*Apios tuberosa*) on its string, the potato of the aborigines, a sort of fabulous fruit, which I had begun to doubt if I had ever dug and eaten in childhood, as I had told, and **1** had not dreamed it. I had often since seen its crumpled red velvety blossom supported by the stems of other plants without knowing it to be the same. Cultivation has wellnigh exterminated it. It has a sweetish taste, much like that of a frost-bitten potato, and I found it better boiled than roasted. This tuber seemed like a faint promise of Nature to rear her own children and feed them simply here at some future period. In these days of fatted cattle and waving grain-fields this humble root, which was once the *totem* of an Indian tribe, is quite forgotten, or known **2** only by its flowering vine; but let wild Nature reign here once more, and the tender and luxurious English grains will probably disappear before a myriad of foes, and without the care of man the crow may carry back even the last seed of corn to the great cornfield of the Indian's God in **3** the southwest, whence he is said to have brought it; but the now almost exterminated ground-nut will perhaps revive and flourish in spite of frosts and wildness, prove itself indigenous, and resume its ancient importance and dignity as the diet of the hunter tribe. Some Indian Ceres **4** or Minerva must have been the inventor and bestower of it; and when the reign of poetry commences here, its leaves and string of nuts may be represented on our works **5** of art.

Already, by the first of September, I had seen two or

1 Bickman (86) suggests that the word "been" was inadvertently dropped from between "had" and "told," and since T seems not to have mentioned earlier his eating groundnuts in childhood, it is possible that that happened. However, Clapper (638) does not indicate a previous reference in any of the early drafts.

2 T found this information in E. B. O'Callaghan, *The Documentary History of the State of New York* (Albany, 1849, I, 10).

3 T read of this in the *Collections of the Massachusetts Historical Society for the Year 1794* (III, 219), where it says, "The crow brought them at first an Indian grain of corn . . . from the great God Cawantowwit's field in the southwest."

4 Roman goddesses: Ceres, of harvests and corn; Minerva, of wisdom.

5 This has, on occasion, been done, as in the cornices and columns of the Department of Agriculture building in Washington, D.C.

1   "Those evening bells! those evening bells! /
How many a tale their music tells" (Thomas
Moore, "Those Evening Bells"). T later wrote
an extensive essay on "Autumnal Tints."

2   "Avoiding winter and unspeakable cold"
(*Iliad,* 3.4).

3   The period after "masonry" was inadvertently omitted in the first edition.

three small maples turned scarlet across the pond, beneath where the white stems of three aspens diverged, at the point of a promontory, next the water. Ah, many a tale their color told! And gradually from week to week the character of each tree came out, and it admired itself reflected in the smooth mirror of the lake. Each morning the manager of this gallery substituted some new picture, distinguished by more brilliant or harmonious coloring, for the old upon the walls.

The wasps came by thousands to my lodge in October, as to winter quarters, and settled on my windows within and on the walls overhead, sometimes deterring visitors from entering. Each morning, when they were numbed with cold, I swept some of them out, but I did not trouble myself much to get rid of them; I even felt complimented by their regarding my house as a desirable shelter. They never molested me seriously, though they bedded with me; and they gradually disappeared, into what crevices I do not know, avoiding winter and unspeakable cold.

Like the wasps, before I finally went into winter quarters in November, I used to resort to the northeast side of Walden, which the sun, reflected from the pitch pine woods and the stony shore, made the fireside of the pond; it is so much pleasanter and wholesomer to be warmed by the sun while you can be, than by an artificial fire. I thus warmed myself by the still glowing embers which the summer, like a departed hunter, had left.

When I came to build my chimney I studied masonry. My bricks, being second-hand ones, required to be cleaned with a trowel, so that I learned more than usual of the qualities of bricks and trowels. The mortar on them was fifty years old, and was said to be still growing harder; but this is one of those sayings which men love to repeat whether they are true or not. Such sayings themselves grow harder and adhere more firmly with age, and it would take many blows with a trowel to clean an old wiseacre of them. Many of the villages of Mesopotamia **1** are built of second-hand bricks of a very good quality, obtained from the ruins of Babylon, and the cement on them is older and probably harder still. However that may be, I was struck by the peculiar toughness of the steel which bore so many violent blows without being worn out. As my bricks had been in a chimney before, though I did not read the name of Nebuchadnezzar on them, I **2** picked out as many fireplace bricks as I could find, to save work and waste, and I filled the spaces between the bricks about the fireplace with stones from the pond shore, and also made my mortar with the white sand from the same place. I lingered most about the fireplace, as the most vital part of the house. Indeed, I worked so deliberately, that though I commenced at the ground in the morning, a course of bricks raised a few inches above the floor served for my pillow at night; yet I did not get a stiff neck **3, 4** for it that I remember; my stiff neck is of older date. I took a poet to board for a fortnight about those times, which **5** caused me to be put to it for room. He brought his own knife, though I had two, and we used to scour them by thrusting them into the earth. He shared with me the labors of cooking. I was pleased to see my work rising so square and solid by degrees, and reflected, that, if it proceeded slowly, it was calculated to endure a long time. The chimney is to some extent an independent structure, standing on the ground, and rising through the house to the heavens; even after the house is burned it still stands

1 T was much interested in the excavations that were going on in the Middle East during his lifetime and read widely the various reports about them.

2 T is referring to the handwriting on the wall (Daniel 5).

3 T is undoubtedly referring to Jacob's pillow (Genesis 28:11) (D'Avanzo, 1977).

4 T is alluding to the many references in the Bible to the Jewish people as stiff-necked (Doudna).

5 Ellery Channing, who slept on the floor under T's cot.

1   Painting with watercolor on wet plaster.
2   Andirons.
3   Keeping-room: New England term for a sitting room.
4   Cato, *De Agri Cultura* 3.2.

sometimes, and its importance and independence are apparent. This was toward the end of summer. It was now November.

❧

The north wind had already begun to cool the pond, though it took many weeks of steady blowing to accomplish it, it is so deep. When I began to have a fire at evening, before I plastered my house, the chimney carried smoke particularly well, because of the numerous chinks between the boards. Yet I passed some cheerful evenings in that cool and airy apartment, surrounded by the rough brown boards full of knots, and rafters with the bark on high overhead. My house never pleased my eye so much after it was plastered, though I was obliged to confess that it was more comfortable. Should not every apartment in which man dwells be lofty enough to create some obscurity overhead, where flickering shadows may play at evening about the rafters? These forms are more agreeable to the fancy and imagination than fresco paint-
1 ings or other the most expensive furniture. I now first began to inhabit my house, I may say, when I began to use it for warmth as well as shelter. I had got a couple of
2 old fire-dogs to keep the wood from the hearth, and it did me good to see the soot form on the back of the chimney which I had built, and I poked the fire with more right and more satisfaction than usual. My dwelling was small, and I could hardly entertain an echo in it; but it seemed larger for being a single apartment and remote from neighbors. All the attractions of a house were concentrated in one room; it was kitchen, chamber, parlor, and keeping-
3 room; and whatever satisfaction parent or child, master or servant, derive from living in a house, I enjoyed it all.
4 Cato says, the master of a family (*patremfamilias*) must

The old Woods place, a quarter of a mile off the road, looked like this. (October 3, 1855) have in his rustic villa 'cellam oleariam, vinariam, dolia multa, uti lubeat caritatem expectare, et rei, et virtuti, et gloriae erit,' that is, 'an oil and wine cellar, many casks, so that it may be pleasant to expect hard times; it will be for his advantage, and virtue, and glory.' I had in my cellar a firkin of potatoes, about two quarts of peas with the weevil **1** in them, and on my shelf a little rice, a jug of molasses, and of rye and Indian meal a peck each.

I sometimes dream of a larger and more populous house, **2** standing in a golden age, of enduring materials, and without gingerbread work, which shall still consist of only one **3** room, a vast, rude, substantial, primitive hall, without ceiling or plastering, with bare rafters and purlins sup- **4** porting a sort of lower heaven over one's head — useful to keep off rain and snow, where the king and queen posts **5** stand out to receive your homage, when you have done reverence to the prostrate Saturn of an older dynasty on **6** stepping over the sill; a cavernous house, wherein you must reach up a torch upon a pole to see the roof; where some may live in the fireplace, some in the recess of a window, and some on settles, some at one end of the hall, some at another, and some aloft on rafters with the spiders, if they choose; a house which you have got into when you have opened the outside door, and the ceremony is over; where the weary traveller may wash, and eat, and converse, and sleep, without further journey; such a shelter as you would be glad to reach in a tempestuous night, containing all the essentials of a house, and nothing for house-keeping; where you can see all the treasures of the house at one view, and everything hangs upon its peg that a man should use; at once kitchen, pantry, parlor, chamber, storehouse, and garret; where you can see so necessary a thing as a barrel or a ladder, so convenient a thing as a cupboard, and hear the pot boil,

1   A small wooden vessel with the capacity of a quarter of a barrel.

2   The longest sentence in W — 341 words! Although this is, of course, a description of T's Walden cabin, many Japanese students of T have pointed out that it is also an almost perfect description of a typical Japanese house — which T could not have known, since Japan was not opened to the Western world until 1853, and Perry's report on this was not published until 1856, two years after W.

3   The rococo scrollwork so popular in the outside decoration of houses in T's day.

4   A piece of timber laid horizontally to support the rafters of a roof.

5   Two different types of support for a peaked roof. A king post is a vertical member connecting the apex of a triangular truss with its base. Queen posts, also vertical, connect the midpoints of the sides with the base.

6   A Roman god who was worshiped by uncovering the head.

The end showed the great stone chimney, all stone to top, except about hearth. The upper story overlapped about eighteen inches, with the ornamental points of timbers dropping from it. Above this, in front, the shingles were rounded, scale-like. (October 3, 1855)

1   There is an apocryphal story that T and Channing once set their compass toward a distant mountain peak, determining to walk to it in a straight line. Midway on their journey they came to a farmhouse in their path, but since the front and back doors (connected, as usual, by a long hall) were open and no one was in evidence, the two proceeded directly through the house.

2   According to court etiquette, one should never turn one's back on royalty.

and pay your respects to the fire that cooks your dinner, and the oven that bakes your bread, and the necessary furniture and utensils are the chief ornaments; where the washing is not put out, nor the fire, nor the mistress, and perhaps you are sometimes requested to move from off the trap-door, when the cook would descend into the cellar, and so learn whether the ground is solid or hollow beneath you without stamping. A house whose inside is as open and manifest as a bird's nest, and you cannot go in 1 at the front door and out at the back without seeing some of its inhabitants; where to be a guest is to be presented with the freedom of the house, and not to be carefully excluded from seven eighths of it, shut up in a particular cell, and told to make yourself at home there — in solitary confinement. Nowadays the host does not admit you to *his* hearth, but has got the mason to build one for yourself somewhere in his alley, and hospitality is the art of *keeping* you at the greatest distance. There is as much secrecy about the cooking as if he had a design to poison you. I am aware that I have been on many a man's premises, and might have been legally ordered off, but I am not aware that I have been in many men's houses. I might visit in my old clothes a king and queen who lived simply in such a house as I have described, if I were going their 2 way; but backing out of a modern palace will be all that I shall desire to learn, if ever I am caught in one.

It would seem as if the very language of our parlors would lose all its nerve and degenerate into *palaver* wholly, our lives pass at such remoteness from its symbols, and its metaphors and tropes are necessarily so far fetched, through slides and dumb-waiters, as it were; in other words, the parlor is so far from the kitchen and workshop. The dinner even is only the parable of a dinner, commonly. As if only the savage dwelt near enough to Nature and Truth to borrow a trope from them. How can the scholar, who dwells away in the North West Territory or the Isle of **1** Man, tell what is parliamentary in the kitchen?   **2**

However, only one or two of my guests were ever bold enough to stay and eat a hasty-pudding with me; but **3** when they saw that crisis approaching they beat a hasty retreat rather, as if it would shake the house to its foundations. Nevertheless, it stood through a great many hasty-puddings.

I did not plaster till it was freezing weather. I brought **4** over some whiter and cleaner sand for this purpose from the opposite shore of the pond in a boat, a sort of conveyance which would have tempted me to go much farther if necessary. My house had in the meanwhile been shingled down to the ground on every side. In lathing I was pleased to be able to send home each nail with a single blow of the hammer, and it was my ambition to transfer the plaster from the board to the wall neatly and rapidly. I remembered the story of a conceited fellow, who, in fine clothes, was wont to lounge about the village once, giving advice to workmen. Venturing one day to substitute deeds for words, he turned up his cuffs, seized a plasterer's board, and having loaded his trowel without mishap, with a complacent look toward the lathing overhead, made a bold gesture thitherward; and straightway, to his complete discomfiture, received the whole contents in his ruffled bosom. I admired anew the economy and convenience of plastering, which so effectually shuts out the cold and takes a handsome finish, and I learned the various casualties to which the plasterer is liable. I was surprised to see how thirsty the bricks were which drank up all the moisture in my plaster before I had smoothed it, and how many pailfuls of water it takes to christen a new hearth. I had the previous winter made a small quantity of lime by

1 The area northwest of the Ohio River, set aside by the Continental Congress in 1787 for new states when the land was sufficiently populated. Out of it were formed Ohio, Michigan, Illinois, Indiana, and Wisconsin.

2 A British island in the Irish Sea.

3 A cornmeal mush then popular in New England as a breakfast food.

4 According to his *Journal* (I, 387), T "Left house on account of plastering, Wednesday, November 12th, at night; returned Saturday, December 6th." As Robbins (52) points out, T showed poor judgment in waiting until freezing weather, for a freeze could have damaged the drying plaster.

1 The common fresh-water clam.
2 There is still a pit where limestone was mined in the Easterbrook country north of Concord center (Gleason).

1 burning the shells of the *Unio fluviatilis*, which our river affords, for the sake of the experiment; so that I knew where my materials came from. I might have got good
2 limestone within a mile or two and burned it myself, if I had cared to do so.

❧

The pond had in the meanwhile skimmed over in the shadiest and shallowest coves, some days or even weeks before the general freezing. The first ice is especially interesting and perfect, being hard, dark, and transparent, and affords the best opportunity that ever offers for examining the bottom where it is shallow; for you can lie at your length on ice only an inch thick, like a skater insect on the surface of the water, and study the bottom at your leisure, only two or three inches distant, like a picture behind a glass, and the water is necessarily always smooth then. There are many furrows in the sand where some creature has travelled about and doubled on its tracks; and, for wrecks, it is strewn with the cases of caddis-worms made of minute grains of white quartz. Perhaps these have creased it, for you find some of their cases in the furrows, though they are deep and broad for them to make. But the ice itself is the object of most interest, though you must improve the earliest opportunity to study it. If you examine it closely the morning after it freezes, you find that the greater part of the bubbles, which at first appeared to be within it, are against its under surface, and that more are continually rising from the bottom; while the ice is as yet comparatively solid and dark, that is, you see the water through it. These bubbles are from an eightieth to an eighth of an inch in diameter, very clear and beautiful, and you see your face reflected in them through the ice. There may be thirty or forty of them to a

About an old boat frozen in, I see a great many little gyrinus-shaped bugs swimming about in the water above the ice. (February 8, 1860)

square inch. There are also already within the ice narrow oblong perpendicular bubbles about half an inch long, sharp cones with the apex upward; or oftener, if the ice is quite fresh, minute spherical bubbles one directly above another, like a string of beads. But these within the ice are not so numerous nor obvious as those beneath. I sometimes used to cast on stones to try the strength of the ice, and those which broke through carried in air with them, which formed very large and conspicuous white bubbles beneath. One day when I came to the same place forty-eight hours afterward, I found that those large bubbles were still perfect, though an inch more of ice had formed, as I could see distinctly by the seam in the edge of a cake. But as the last two days had been very warm, like an Indian summer, the ice was not now transparent, showing the dark green color of the water, and the bottom, but opaque and whitish or gray, and though twice as thick was hardly stronger than before, for the air bubbles had greatly expanded under this heat and run together, and lost their regularity; they were no longer one directly over another, but often like silvery coins poured from a bag, one overlapping another, or in thin flakes, as if occupying slight cleavages. The beauty of the ice was gone, and it was too late to study the bottom. Being curious to know what position my great bubbles occupied with regard to the new ice, I broke out a cake containing a middling sized one, and turned it bottom upward. The new ice had formed around and under the bubble, so that it was included between the two ices. It was wholly in the lower ice, but close against the upper, and was flattish, or perhaps slightly lenticular, with a rounded edge, a quarter of an inch deep by four inches in diameter; and I was surprised to find that directly under the bubble the ice was melted with great regularity in the form of a saucer re-

The finest grasses support the most wonderful burdens of ice and most branched on their minute threads. These weeds are spread and arched over into the snow again,—countless little arches a few inches high, each cased in ice, which you break with a tinkling crash at each step. (December 26, 1855)

versed, to the height of five eighths of an inch in the middle, leaving a thin partition there between the water and the bubble, hardly an eighth of an inch thick; and in many places the small bubbles in this partition had burst out downward, and probably there was no ice at all under the largest bubbles, which were a foot in diameter. I inferred that the infinite number of minute bubbles which I had first seen against the under surface of the ice were now frozen in likewise, and that each, in its degree, had operated like a burning-glass on the ice beneath to melt and rot it. These are the little air-guns which contribute to make the ice crack and whoop.

❧

At length the winter set in in good earnest, just as I had finished plastering, and the wind began to howl around the house as if it had not had permission to do so till then. Night after night the geese came lumbering in in the dark with a clangor and a whistling of wings, even after the ground was covered with snow, some to alight in Walden, and some flying low over the woods toward Fair Haven, bound for Mexico. Several times, when returning from the village at ten or eleven o'clock at night, I heard the tread of a flock of geese, or else ducks, on the dry leaves in the woods by a pond-hole behind my dwelling, where they had come up to feed, and the faint honk or quack of their leader as they hurried off. In 1845 Walden froze entirely over for the first time on the night of the 22nd of December, Flint's and other shallower ponds and the river having been frozen ten days or more; in '46, the 16th; in '49, about the 31st; and in '50, about the 27th of December; in '52, the 5th of January; in '53, the 31st of December. The snow had already covered the ground since the 25th of November, and surrounded me sud-

All along the ice belt or shelf—for the river has fallen more than a foot—countless white figures stand crowded, their minute cores of sedge or twigs being concealed. Some are like beaks of birds,—cranes or herons. (February 13, 1860)

denly with the scenery of winter. I withdrew yet farther into my shell, and endeavored to keep a bright fire both within my house and within my breast. My employment out of doors now was to collect the dead wood in the forest, bringing it in my hands or on my shoulders, or sometimes trailing a dead pine tree under each arm to my shed. An old forest fence which had seen its best days was a great haul for me. I sacrificed it to Vulcan, for it was past **1** serving the god Terminus. How much more interesting an event is that man's supper who has just been forth in the snow to hunt, nay, you might say, steal, the fuel to **2** cook it with! His bread and meat are sweet. There are **3** enough fagots and waste wood of all kinds in the forests of most of our towns to support many fires, but which at present warm none, and, some think, hinder the growth of the young wood. There was also the driftwood of the pond. In the course of the summer I had discovered a raft of pitch pine logs with the bark on, pinned together by the Irish when the railroad was built. This I hauled up partly on the shore. After soaking two years and then lying high six months it was perfectly sound, though water-logged past drying. I amused myself one winter day with sliding this piecemeal across the pond, nearly half a mile, skating behind with one end of a log fifteen feet long on my shoulder, and the other on the ice; or I tied several logs together with a birch withe, and then, with a longer birch or alder which had a hook at the end, dragged them across. Though completely waterlogged and almost as heavy as lead, they not only burned long, but made a very hot fire; nay, I thought that they burned better for the soaking, as if the pitch, being confined by the water, burned longer, as in a lamp.

Gilpin, in his account of the forest borderers of Eng- **4** land, says that 'the encroachments of trespassers, and the

1 The Roman god of fire (Vulcan) and of boundaries (Terminus). In other words, the wood was no longer good for fencing, so he burned it.

2 In his *Journal* (III, 308), T tells us that this comment was inspired by seeing the Irishman Patrick Riordan carrying home an armful of faggots.

3 "Stolen waters are sweet, and bread eaten in secret is pleasant" (Proverbs 9:17).

4 William Gilpin, *Remarks on Forest Scenery* (Edinburgh, 1834, II, 122) (Templeman; Boudreau, 1973).

On the ice at Walden are very beautiful great leaf crystals in great profusion. (January 1, 1856)

1   Vert: forest vegetation used as food by deer.

2   William Gilpin, *Remarks on Forest Scenery* (II, 101ff). T comments at length on these passages in his *Journal* (III, 407–8).

A lord warden in England is in charge of protecting the wildlife and greenery of a forest.

3   Again T is referring to the time he and Edward Hoar accidentally set fire to the woods on Fair Haven Bay. Haddin makes a comprehensive study of the fire imagery and particularly its psychological impact on T after letting this fire get away from him.

4   "The following is the Roman formula to be observed in thinning a grove. A pig is to be sacrificed, and [a] . . . prayer uttered" (Cato, *De Agri Cultura* 139).

5   Francois André Michaux, *Voyage a l'ouest des monts Alleghanys* . . . (Paris, 1808) (Christie, 288).

houses and fences thus raised on the borders of the forest,' were 'considered as great nuisances by the old forest law, and were severely punished under the name of *purprestures*, as tending *ad terrorem ferarum — ad nocumentum forestae*, etc.,' to the frightening of the game and the detriment of the forest. But I was interested in the preservation of the venison and the vert more than the hunters or woodchoppers, and as much as though I had been the Lord Warden himself; and if any part was burned, though I burned it myself by accident, I grieved with a grief that lasted longer and was more inconsolable than that of the proprietors; nay, I grieved when it was cut down by the proprietors themselves. I would that our farmers when they cut down a forest felt some of that awe which the old Romans did when they came to thin, or let in the light to, a consecrated grove (*lucum conlucare*), that is, would believe that it is sacred to some god. The Roman made an expiatory offering, and prayed, Whatever god or goddess thou art to whom this grove is sacred, be propitious to me, my family, and children, etc.

It is remarkable what a value is still put upon wood even in this age and in this new country, a value more permanent and universal than that of gold. After all our discoveries and inventions no man will go by a pile of wood. It is as precious to us as it was to our Saxon and Norman ancestors. If they made their bows of it, we make our gunstocks of it. Michaux, more than thirty years ago, says that the price of wood for fuel in New York and Philadelphia 'nearly equals, and sometimes exceeds, that of the best wood in Paris, though this immense capital annually requires more than three hundred thousand cords, and is surrounded to the distance of three hundred miles by cultivated plains.' In this town the price of wood rises almost steadily, and the only question is, how much higher it is to be this year than it was the last. Mechanics and tradesmen who come in person to the forest on no other errand, are sure to attend the wood auction, and even pay a high price for the privilege of gleaning after the wood-chopper. It is now many years that men have resorted to the forest for fuel and the materials of the arts: the New Englander and the New Hollander, the Parisian and the Celt, the farmer and Robin Hood, Goody Blake and Harry **1** Gill; in most parts of the world the prince and the peasant, the scholar and the savage, equally require still a few sticks from the forest to warm them and cook their food. Neither could I do without them.

Every man looks at his wood-pile with a kind of affection. I love to have mine before my window, and the more chips the better to remind me of my pleasing work. I had an old axe which nobody claimed, with which by spells in winter days, on the sunny side of the house, I played about the stumps which I had got out of my bean-field. As my driver prophesied when I was plowing, they warmed me twice — once while I was splitting them, and again when they were on the fire, so that no fuel could give out more heat. As for the axe, I was advised to get the village blacksmith to 'jump' it; but I jumped him, and, putting a **2** hickory helve from the woods into it, made it do. If it was dull, it was at least hung true.

A few pieces of fat pine were a great treasure. It is interesting to remember how much of this food for fire is still concealed in the bowels of the earth. In previous years I had often gone 'prospecting' over some bare hill-side, where a pitch pine wood had formerly stood, and got out the fat pine roots. They are almost indestructible. Stumps thirty or forty years old, at least, will still be sound at the core, though the sapwood has all become vegetable mould, as appears by the scales of the thick bark forming

1 In Wordsworth's poem "Goody Blake and Harry Gill," Gill seizes Blake for taking sticks from a hedge for fuel. For Wordsworth's impact on T, and particularly on this section of W, see Moldenhauer (1990).

2 If an ax becomes blunt and some cutting steel remains, its edge can be improved by heating and hammering it, to thin the head and lengthen it.

1 Icarus, in Greek mythology, was the son of Daedalus, who made him wings to fly, but Icarus flew too close to the sun, melted the wax that held his wings in place, and plunged to his death.

2 T's poem. For extensive analyses see Matthiessen (165–6) and Cook (1971). Cook discusses the mythological background.

a ring level with the earth four or five inches distant from the heart. With axe and shovel you explore this mine, and follow the marrowy store, yellow as beef tallow, or as if you had struck on a vein of gold, deep into the earth. But commonly I kindled my fire with the dry leaves of the forest, which I had stored up in my shed before the snow came. Green hickory finely split makes the woodchopper's kindlings, when he has a camp in the woods. Once in a while I got a little of this. When the villagers were lighting their fires beyond the horizon, I too gave notice to the various wild inhabitants of Walden vale, by a smoky streamer from my chimney, that I was awake.

1   Light-winged Smoke, Icarian bird,
         Melting thy pinions in thy upward flight,
         Lark without song, and messenger of dawn,
         Circling above the hamlets as thy nest;
         Or else, departing dream, and shadowy form
         Of midnight vision, gathering up thy skirts;
         By night star-veiling, and by day
         Darkening the light and blotting out the sun;
         Go thou my incense upward from this
               hearth,
2   And ask the gods to pardon this clear flame.

Hard green wood just cut, though I used but little of that, answered my purpose better than any other. I sometimes left a good fire when I went to take a walk in a winter afternoon; and when I returned, three or four hours afterward, it would be still alive and glowing. My house was not empty though I was gone. It was as if I had left a cheerful housekeeper behind. It was I and Fire that lived there; and commonly my housekeeper proved trustworthy. One day, however, as I was splitting wood, I thought that I would just look in at the window and see if the house was not on fire; it was the only time I remember to have been particularly anxious on this score; so I looked and saw that a spark had caught my bed, and I went in **1** and extinguished it when it had burned a place as big as my hand. But my house occupied so sunny and sheltered a position, and its roof was so low, that I could afford to let the fire go out in the middle of almost any winter day.

The moles nested in my cellar, nibbling every third **2** potato, and making a snug bed even there of some hair left after plastering and of brown paper; for even the wildest animals love comfort and warmth as well as man, and they survive the winter only because they are so careful to secure them. Some of my friends spoke as if I was coming to the woods on purpose to freeze myself. The animal merely makes a bed, which he warms with his body, in a sheltered place; but man, having discovered fire, boxes up some air in a spacious apartment, and warms that, instead of robbing himself, makes that his bed, in which he can move about divested of more cumbrous clothing, maintain a kind of summer in the midst of winter, and by means of windows even admit the light, and with a lamp lengthen out the day. Thus he goes a step or two beyond instinct, and saves a little time for the fine arts. Though, when I had been exposed to the rudest blasts a long time, my whole body began to grow torpid, when I reached the genial atmosphere of my house I soon recovered my faculties and prolonged my life. But the most luxuriously housed has little to boast of in this respect, nor need we trouble ourselves to speculate how the human race may be at last destroyed. It would be easy to cut their threads **3** any time with a little sharper blast from the north. We go on dating from Cold Fridays and Great Snows; but a little **4, 5** colder Friday, or greater snow would put a period to man's existence on the globe.

1 Hellenbrand thinks he sees in the associated images of fire, bed, and hand a cryptic reference to masturbation.

2 Teale points out that since moles are completely carnivorous, it was undoubtedly the meadow mouse that was nibbling T's potatoes.

3 A reference to the three Parcae (Fates) of Greek mythology: the first held the distaff of life, the second spun out the thread, and the third cut it.

4 The Cold Friday was January 19, 1810. T collects reminiscences of it in his *Journal* for January 22, 1857 (IX, 230).

5 The Great Snow was that of December 10, 1717, a famous description of which, by Cotton Mather, T quotes in his *Journal* for February 3, 1856 (VIII, 163–5).

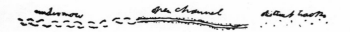

I see such mice or mole tracks as these. (February 24, 1854)

1 These lines are from a poem by Ellen Hooper, published in the transcendentalist *Dial* (I, 1840, 193). T omits the first portion of the poem and changes the stanza breaks of the portion he prints. The poet's name did not appear in the first edition, but T added it in his own copy.

The next winter I used a small cooking-stove for economy, since I did not own the forest; but it did not keep fire so well as the open fireplace. Cooking was then, for the most part, no longer a poetic, but merely a chemic process. It will soon be forgotten, in these days of stoves, that we used to roast potatoes in the ashes, after the Indian fashion. The stove not only took up room and scented the house, but it concealed the fire, and I felt as if I had lost a companion. You can always see a face in the fire. The laborer, looking into it at evening, purifies his thoughts of the dross and earthiness which they have accumulated during the day. But I could no longer sit and look into the fire, and the pertinent words of a poet recurred to me with new force.

'Never, bright flame, may be denied to me
Thy dear, life imaging, close sympathy.
What but my hopes shot upward e'er so bright?
What but my fortunes sunk so low in night?
Why art thou banished from our hearth and hall,
Thou who art welcomed and beloved by all?
Was thy existence then too fanciful
For our life's common light, who are so dull?
Did thy bright gleam mysterious converse hold
With our congenial souls? secrets too bold?

'Well, we are safe and strong, for now we sit
Beside a hearth where no dim shadows flit,
Where nothing cheers nor saddens, but a fire
Warms feet and hands — nor does to more aspire;
By whose compact utilitarian heap
The present may sit down and go to sleep,
Nor fear the ghosts who from the dim past
    walked,
And with us by the unequal light of the old wood
    fire talked.'

ELLEN HOOPER

Former Inhabitants; and Winter Visitors

I WEATHERED SOME merry snow-storms, and spent some cheerful winter evenings by my fireside, while the snow whirled wildly without, and even the hooting of the owl was hushed. For many weeks I met no one in my walks but those who came occasionally to cut wood and sled it to the village. The elements, however, abetted me in making a path through the deepest snow in the woods, for when I had once gone through the wind blew the oak leaves into my tracks, where they lodged, and by absorbing the rays of the sun melted the snow, and so not only made a dry bed for my feet, but in the night their dark line was my guide. For human society I was obliged to conjure up the former occupants of these woods. Within the memory of many of my townsmen the road near which **1** my house stands resounded with the laugh and gossip of inhabitants, and the woods which border it were notched and dotted here and there with their little gardens and dwellings, though it was then much more shut in by the forest than now. In some places, within my own remembrance, the pines would scrape both sides of a chaise at once, and women and children who were compelled to go this way to Lincoln alone and on foot did it with fear, and often ran a good part of the distance. Though mainly but a humble route to neighboring villages, or for the woodman's team, it once amused the traveller more than now by its variety, and lingered longer in his memory. Where now firm open fields stretch from the village to the woods, it then ran through a maple swamp on a foundation of logs, the remnants of which, doubtless, still underlie the present dusty highway, from the Stratton, now the Alms-House, Farm, to Brister's Hill. **2**

1 The road nearest T's cabin led from Concord to Lincoln (Gleason).

2 The Concord Alms House, formerly the Stratton farm, was on Walden Street, across from the present-day fire station. Brister's Hill is now cut by Walden Street (Gleason).

This morning it has begun to snow apparently in earnest. The air is quite thick and the view confined. It is quite still, yet some flakes come down from one side and some from another, crossing each other like woof and warp apparently, is they are falling in different eddies and currents of air.

1 Cato worked as a day laborer. He and his wife apparently kept a guest room for transients. He died in 1804, when slavery was still legal in Massachusetts. His cellar hole, according to Channing in his own copy of W, was "at the opening of the path from the Walden Road to Goose Pond."

2 Duncan Ingraham was Concord's wealthiest citizen in the late eighteenth century, having made a good part of his fortune in the slave trade.

3 Cato Uticensis, a grandson of M. Porcius Cato, whom T quotes so frequently in this book, was so named from his death at Utica.

4 The grave.

5 Zilpha White had formerly been a slave. Although she attended church regularly, she was generally considered at least somewhat deranged. She died on April 16, 1820, and her obituary, which appeared in the *Middlesex Gazette* for April 22, 1820, has been reprinted in the *Concord Saunterer* 14 (Spring, 1979), 27.

6 Captured English soldiers were sometimes paroled to Concord until they could be exchanged.

7 T has here confused Sippio Brister with Brister Freeman. The former was a resident of Lincoln and the slave of the Hoar family there. Brister Freeman was a Concord resident and died there on January 31, 1822, at the age of seventy-eight. He worked as a barber and a nurse.

8 A Concord physician of Scottish parentage who died in 1788 (Sanborn, 1909, II, 154).

9 It reads: "In memory of Sippio Brister, a man of Colour who died Nov. 1, 1820. Et. 61."

1 East of my bean-field, across the road, lived Cato Ingra-
2 ham, slave of Duncan Ingraham, Esquire, gentleman, of Concord village, who built his slave a house, and gave him permission to live in Walden Woods; — Cato, not
3 Uticensis, but Concordiensis. Some say that he was a Guinea Negro. There are a few who remember his little patch among the walnuts, which he let grow up till he should be old and need them; but a younger and whiter speculator got them at last. He too, however, occupies an
4 equally narrow house at present. Cato's half-obliterated cellar-hole still remains, though known to few, being concealed from the traveller by a fringe of pines. It is now filled with the smooth sumach (*Rhus glabra*), and one of the earliest species of goldenrod (*Solidago stricta*) grows there luxuriantly.

Here, by the very corner of my field, still nearer to
5 town, Zilpha, a colored woman, had her little house, where she spun linen for the townsfolk, making the Walden Woods ring with her shrill singing, for she had a loud and notable voice. At length, in the war of 1812, her dwell-
6 ing was set on fire by English soldiers, prisoners on parole, when she was away, and her cat and dog and hens were all burned up together. She led a hard life, and somewhat inhumane. One old frequenter of these woods remembers, that as he passed her house one noon he heard her muttering to herself over her gurgling pot — 'Ye are all bones, bones!' I have seen bricks amid the oak copse there.

Down the road, on the right hand, on Brister's Hill,
7 lived Brister Freeman, 'a handy Negro,' slave of Squire
8 Cummings once — there where grow still the apple trees which Brister planted and tended; large old trees now, but their fruit still wild and ciderish to my taste. Not
9 long since I read his epitaph in the old Lincoln burying-

ground, a little on one side, near the unmarked graves of some British grenadiers who fell in the retreat from Concord — where he is styled 'Sippio Brister' — Scipio Africanus he had some title to be called — 'a man of color,' as if he were discolored. It also told me, with staring emphasis, when he died; which was but an indirect way of informing me that he ever lived. With him dwelt Fenda, his hospitable wife, who told fortunes, yet pleasantly — large, round, and black, blacker than any of the children of night, such a dusky orb as never rose on Concord before or since. **1**

Farther down the hill, on the left, on the old road in the woods, are marks of some homestead of the Stratton family; whose orchard once covered all the slope of Brister's Hill, but was long since killed out by pitch pines, excepting a few stumps, whose old roots furnish still the wild stocks of many a thrifty village tree. **2** **3**

Nearer yet to town, you come to Breed's location, on the other side of the way, just on the edge of the wood; ground famous for the pranks of a demon not distinctly named in old mythology, who has acted a prominent and astounding part in our New England life, and deserves, as much as any mythological character, to have his biography written one day; who first comes in the guise of a friend or hired man, and then robs and murders the whole family — New-England Rum. But history must not yet tell the tragedies enacted here; let time intervene in some measure to assuage and lend an azure tint to them. Here the most indistinct and dubious tradition says that once a tavern stood; the well the same, which tempered the traveller's beverage and refreshed his steed. Here then men saluted one another, and heard and told the news, and went their ways again. **4**

Breed's hut was standing only a dozen years ago, though

1 The battle of April 19, 1775.

2 In his copy of W, T corrected this from "Stratten." At the end of the seventeenth century, the Stratton family owned most of the land on the west side of Walden Street, from the edge of Concord center to Walden Pond. The homestead T speaks of stood near the present intersection of Walden Street and Brister's Hill Road. It was destroyed about 1770.

3 In his copy of W, T adds at the end of this paragraph: "Surveying for Cyrus Jarvis Dec. 23 '56 — he shows me a deed of this lot containing 6 A. 52 rods all on the W. of the Wayland Road — & 'consisting of plowland, orcharding & woodland' — sold by Joseph Stratton to Samuel Swan of Concord In holder Aug. 11th 1777."

4 According to T's *Journal* for 1850 (II, 20), John C. Breed was a Concord barber. Byron Rees quotes a manuscript in the Concord Free Public Library: "John C. Breed. barber and drunkard, found dead in the road at last, in 1824 . . . an extreme instance of the power of appetite for rum . . . was its complete slave. He was all absorbed in it; he had no other want, no other affection. If he had opportunity to earn six cents by shaving, he would spend one cent for a cracker and five cents for his rum." His cellar hole can still be found a few yards into the woods from the northern end of the Fairyland Woods parking lot on Walden Street (Gleason). Note that virtually all the "former inhabitants" of the Walden Pond area were social outcasts. Many of Concord's residents of T's time would thus have thought it an appropriate area for T to have settled in.

1   According to the *Concord Republican* for May 28, 1841, it had been set on fire the previous Wednesday "by some graceless scamps" and burned to the ground. Election nights were often the occasion for mischief making on the part of the town's young men. Since the fire alarm had not been rung until midnight, T was up late reading.

2   T was then living with the Emersons, and the brook he speaks later of jumping was the Mill Brook, which runs between the Emerson and Breed properties (Gleason).

3   William Davenant, *Gondibert: An Heroick Poem* (London, 1651).

4   T's maternal uncle Charles Dunbar. T tells many tales of this eccentric uncle in his *Journal* (for example, VIII, 229–46).

5   Alexander Chalmers, *The Works of the English Poets from Chaucer to Cowper* (21 vols., London, 1810). T is said to have read the entire set in his "spare" time while attending Harvard.

6   "That day he overcame the Nervii" (Julius Caesar, III, ii, 178). The Nervii, a mixed Celto-Germanic tribe occupying Flanders, were defeated by Caesar in 57 B.C.

7   Both Jacob and James Baker lived south of Walden Pond. It is probably Jacob's barn that is referred to here (Gleason).

8   The home of Lincoln's wealthiest family, a magnificent mansion still standing west of the Lincoln railroad station.

9   The Middlesex Mutual Fire Insurance Company was established in Concord in 1826.

it had long been unoccupied. It was about the size of
1   mine. It was set on fire by mischievous boys, one Election
2   night, if I do not mistake. I lived on the edge of the village
3   then, and had just lost myself over Davenant's 'Gondibert,' that winter that I labored with a lethargy — which, by the way, I never knew whether to regard as a family com-
4   plaint, having an uncle who goes to sleep shaving himself, and is obliged to sprout potatoes in a cellar Sundays, in order to keep awake and keep the Sabbath, or as the
5   consequence of my attempt to read Chalmers' collection of English poetry without skipping. It fairly overcame my
6   Nervii. I had just sunk my head on this when the bells rung fire, and in hot haste the engines rolled that way, led by a straggling troop of men and boys, and I among the foremost, for I had leaped the brook. We thought it was far south over the woods — we who had run to fires before — barn, shop, or dwelling-house, or all together. 'It's
7, 8 Baker's barn,' cried one. 'It is the Codman place,' affirmed another. And then fresh sparks went up above the wood, as if the roof fell in, and we all shouted 'Concord to the rescue!' Wagons shot past with furious speed and crushing loads, bearing, perchance, among the rest, the
9   agent of the Insurance Company, who was bound to go however far; and ever and anon the engine bell tinkled behind, more slow and sure; and rearmost of all, as it was afterward whispered, came they who set the fire and gave the alarm. Thus we kept on like true idealists, rejecting the evidence of our senses, until at a turn in the road we heard the crackling and actually felt the heat of the fire from over the wall, and realized, alas! that we were there. The very nearness of the fire but cooled our ardor. At first we thought to throw a frog-pond on to it; but concluded to let it burn, it was so far gone and so worthless. So we stood round our engine, jostled one another, expressed

our sentiments through speaking-trumpets, or in lower tone referred to the great conflagrations which the world has witnessed, including Bascom's shop, and, between [1] ourselves, we thought that, were we there in season with our 'tub,' and a full frog-pond by, we could turn that [2] threatened last and universal one into another flood. We finally retreated without doing any mischief — returned to sleep and 'Gondibert.' But as for 'Gondibert,' I would except that passage in the preface about wit being the [3] soul's powder — 'but most of mankind are strangers to wit, as Indians are to powder.'

It chanced that I walked that way across the fields the following night, about the same hour, and hearing a low moaning at this spot, I drew near in the dark, and discovered the only survivor of the family that I know, the heir of both its virtues and its vices, who alone was interested in this burning, lying on his stomach and looking over the cellar wall at the still smouldering cinders beneath, muttering to himself, as is his wont. He had been working far off in the river meadows all day, and had improved the first moments that he could call his own to visit the home of his fathers and his youth. He gazed into the cellar from all sides and points of view by turns, always lying down to it, as if there was some treasure, which he remembered, concealed between the stones, where there was absolutely nothing but a heap of bricks and ashes. The house being gone, he looked at what there was left. He was soothed by the sympathy which my mere presence implied, and showed me, as well as the darkness permitted, where the well was covered up; which, thank Heaven, could never be burned; and he groped long about the wall to find the well-sweep which his father had cut and mounted, feeling for the iron hook or staple by which a burden had been fastened to the heavy end — all that he could now

1 According to the *Yeoman's Gazette* for May 3, 1828, Bascom & Cole English and West Indian Shop, on Concord's Mill Dam, burned down on the night of April 25, 1828, in one of the more spectacular fires in Concord's business district.

2 In T's day, fires were fought with little hand-drawn vehicles, usually referred to as tubs. Incidentally, T's father was long active in the Concord fire company.

3 Davenant, *Gondibert*, "The Author's Preface."

1 Stephen Nutting (1768–?) on April 1, 1792, purchased here a house, barn, and 113 acres of land. He was a bachelor.

2 Francis Le Grosse (176?–1809) rented a house, barn, and small plot of land from Peter Wheeler. He, like T's grandfather, was from the isle of Jersey.

3 John Wyman, or Wayman (1730?–1800), in 1787 built his house at what is now the entrance to the Walden Pond State Reservation parking lot, on land then owned by Dr. Abel Prescott. He apparently stopped making pottery by 1810. As recently as the 1940s pottery shards could be picked up, but the land was regraded when the parking lot was put in, and they can no longer be found.

4 An old custom in which a sheriff symbolically attached a chip of wood if there was no other possession to place a lien on.

5 Thomas Wyman (?–1843), John's son, died at the age of sixty-nine. It was in the settlement of his estate that Emerson purchased the land at Walden upon which T built his cabin.

6 In his copy of W, T apparently deleted the words "clay and" and inserted a "?" after the word "use" in the next line.

7 "Behold, as the clay is in the potter's hand" (Jeremiah 18:6).

8 A brief account of the death of Hugh Coyle [sic], from the *Concord Freeman* of October 3, 1845, is reprinted in *Thoreau Society Bulletin* 33 (1950, 3). T writes at great length on Quoil in his *Journal* (I, 414ff). There is further description of Quoil's hut in T's "A Winter Walk."

cling to — to convince me that it was no common 'rider.' I felt it, and still remark it almost daily in my walks, for by it hangs the history of a family.

Once more, on the left, where are seen the well and lilac bushes by the wall, in the now open field, lived **1, 2** Nutting and Le Grosse. But to return toward Lincoln.

Farther in the woods than any of these, where the road **3** approaches nearest to the pond, Wyman the potter squatted, and furnished his townsmen with earthenware, and left descendants to succeed him. Neither were they rich in worldly goods, holding the land by sufferance while they lived; and there often the sheriff came in vain to **4** collect the taxes, and 'attached a chip,' for form's sake, as I have read in his accounts, there being nothing else that he could lay his hands on. One day in midsummer, when I was hoeing, a man who was carrying a load of pottery to market stopped his horse against my field and inquired **5** concerning Wyman the younger. He had long ago bought a potter's wheel of him, and wished to know what had **6** become of him. I had read of the potter's clay and wheel **7** in Scripture, but it had never occurred to me that the pots we use were not such as had come down unbroken from those days, or grown on trees like gourds somewhere, and I was pleased to hear that so fictile an art was ever practiced in my neighborhood.

The last inhabitant of these woods before me was an **8** Irishman, Hugh Quoil (if I have spelt his name with coil enough), who occupied Wyman's tenement — Col. Quoil, he was called. Rumor said that he had been a soldier at Waterloo. If he had lived I should have made him fight his battles over again. His trade here was that of a ditcher. Napoleon went to St. Helena; Quoil came to Walden Woods. All I know of him is tragic. He was a man of manners, like one who had seen the world, and was capable of more civil speech than you could well attend to. He wore a greatcoat in midsummer, being affected with the trembling delirium, and his face was the color of carmine. He died in the road at the foot of Brister's Hill shortly after I came to the woods, so that I have not remembered him as a neighbor. Before his house was pulled down, when his comrades avoided it as 'an unlucky castle,' I visited it. There lay his old clothes curled up by use, as if they were himself, upon his raised plank bed. His pipe lay broken on the hearth, instead of a bowl broken at the fountain. **1** The last could never have been the symbol of his death, for he confessed to me that, though he had heard of Brister's Spring, he had never seen it; and soiled cards, kings of diamonds, spades, and hearts, were scattered over the floor. One black chicken which the administrator could not catch, black as night and as silent, not even croaking, awaiting Reynard, still went to roost in the next **2** apartment. In the rear there was the dim outline of a garden, which had been planted but had never received its first hoeing, owing to those terrible shaking fits, though it was now harvest time. It was overrun with Roman wormwood and beggar-ticks, which last stuck to my clothes for **3** all fruit. The skin of a woodchuck was freshly stretched upon the back of the house, a trophy of his last Waterloo; but no warm cap or mittens would he want more.

Now only a dent in the earth marks the site of these dwellings, with buried cellar stones, and strawberries, raspberries, thimble-berries, hazel-bushes, and sumachs growing in the sunny sward there; some pitch pine or gnarled oak occupies what was the chimney nook, and a sweet-scented black birch, perhaps, waves where the door-stone was. Sometimes the well dent is visible, where once a spring oozed; now dry and tearless grass; or it was covered deep — not to be discovered till some late day — with a

1   "The golden bowl be broken, or the pitcher be broken at the fountain" (Ecclesiastes 12:6).

2   The traditional literary name for a fox.

3   Beggar-tick: a pestilent weed whose seeds, when ripe, catch on the clothes of passersby.

By the railroad against Walden I heard the lisping of a chickadee, and saw it on a sumach. It repeatedly hopped to a bunch of berries, took one, and, hopping to a more horizontal twig, placed it under one foot and hammered at it with its bill. (January 30, 1856)

1 "Fix'd fate, free-will, foreknowledge absolute" (Milton, *Paradise Lost,* II, 560).

2 They were hired to scrape the wool from
hides in the tanning process.

3 "Only the ashes of the just / Smell sweet
and blossom in their dust" (James Shirley, "The
Lady of Pleasure").

4 The right to dam up a stream for water
power.

flat stone under the sod, when the last of the race departed. What a sorrowful act must that be — the covering up of wells! coincident with the opening of wells of tears. These cellar dents, like deserted fox burrows, old holes, are all that is left where once were the stir and bustle of human life, and 'fate, free will, foreknowledge absolute,' in some form and dialect or other were by turns discussed. But all I can learn of their conclusions amounts to just this, that 'Cato and Brister pulled wool;' which is about as edifying as the history of more famous schools of philosophy.

Still grows the vivacious lilac a generation after the door and lintel and the sill are gone, unfolding its sweet-scented flowers each spring, to be plucked by the musing traveller; planted and tended once by children's hands, in front-yard plots — now standing by wallsides in retired pastures, and giving place to new-rising forests; — the last of that stirp, sole survivor of that family. Little did the dusky children think that the puny slip with its two eyes only, which they stuck in the ground in the shadow of the house and daily watered, would root itself so, and outlive them, and house itself in the rear that shaded it, and grown man's garden and orchard, and tell their story faintly to the lone wanderer a half-century after they had grown up and died — blossoming as fair, and smelling as sweet, as in that first spring. I mark its still tender, civil, cheerful lilac colors.

But this small village, germ of something more, why did it fail while Concord keeps its ground? Were there no natural advantages — no water privileges, forsooth? Ay, the deep Walden Pond and cool Brister's Spring — privilege to drink long and healthy draughts at these, all unimproved by these men but to dilute their glass. They were universally a thirsty race. Might not the basket, stable-broom, mat-making, corn-parching, linen-spinning, and pottery business have thrived here, making the wilderness to blossom like the rose, and a numerous posterity have [1] inherited the land of their fathers? The sterile soil would at least have been proof against a lowland degeneracy. Alas! how little does the memory of these human inhabitants enhance the beauty of the landscape! Again, perhaps, Nature will try, with me for a first settler, and my house raised last spring to be the oldest in the hamlet.

I am not aware that any man has ever built on the spot which I occupy. Deliver me from a city built on the site of [2] a more ancient city, whose materials are ruins, whose gardens cemeteries. The soil is blanched and accursed there, and before that becomes necessary the earth itself will be destroyed. With such reminiscences I repeopled the woods and lulled myself asleep.

At this season I seldom had a visitor. When the snow lay deepest no wanderer ventured near my house for a week or fortnight at a time, but there I lived as snug as a meadow mouse, or as cattle and poultry which are said to have survived for a long time buried in drifts, even without food; or like that early settler's family in the town of Sutton, in this State, whose cottage was completely covered by the great snow of 1717 when he was absent, and an [3] Indian found it only by the hole which the chimney's breath made in the drift, and so relieved the family. But no friendly Indian concerned himself about me; nor needed he, for the master of the house was at home The Great Snow! How cheerful it is to hear of! When the farmers could not get to the woods and swamps with their teams, and were obliged to cut down the shade trees before their houses, and, when the crust was harder, cut off the trees

1 "The wilderness and the solitary place shall be glad for them; and the desert shall rejoice, and blossom as the rose" (Isaiah 35:1).

2 In the fall of 1853 T read Austen Henry Layard's *Ninevah and Its Remains* (New York, 1849) with its account of the discovery of numerous layers of archeological remains. See his *Journal* (VI, 11, 15).

3 Here T is quoting extensively from Cotton Mather's description of the Great Snow, as referred to in previous chapters.

A compass used for measuring distances
on maps.

in the swamps, ten feet from the ground, as it appeared
the next spring.

In the deepest snows, the path which I used from the
highway to my house, about half a mile long, might have
been represented by a meandering dotted line, with wide
intervals between the dots. For a week of even weather I
took exactly the same number of steps, and of the same
length, coming and going, stepping deliberately and with
the precision of a pair of dividers in my own deep tracks
— to such routine the winter reduces us — yet often they
were filled with heaven's own blue. But no weather inter-
fered fatally with my walks, or rather my going abroad, for
I frequently tramped eight or ten miles through the deepest snow to keep an appointment with a beech tree, or a
yellow birch, or an old acquaintance among the pines;
when the ice and snow causing their limbs to droop, and
so sharpening their tops, had changed the pines into fir
trees; wading to the tops of the highest hills when the snow
was nearly two feet deep on a level, and shaking down
another snow-storm on my head at every step; or sometimes creeping and floundering thither on my hands and
knees, when the hunters had gone into winter quarters.
One afternoon I amused myself by watching a barred owl
(*Strix nebulosa*) sitting on one of the lower dead limbs of
a white pine, close to the trunk, in broad daylight, I standing within a rod of him. He could hear me when I moved
and cronched the snow with my feet, but could not plainly
see me. When I made most noise he would stretch out his
neck, and erect his neck feathers, and open his eyes wide;
but their lids soon fell again, and he began to nod. I too
felt a slumberous influence after watching him half an
hour, as he sat thus with his eyes half open, like a cat,
winged brother of the cat. There was only a narrow slit
left between their lids, by which he preserved a peninsu-

It is certain, then, that a sudden strong wind when
the snow is moist but light (it had fallen the
afternoon previous) will catch and roll it up as a
boy rolls up his ball. These white balls are seen far
off over the fields. (December 13, 1859)

lar relation to me; thus, with half-shut eyes, looking out from the land of dreams, and endeavoring to realize me, vague object or mote that interrupted his visions. At length, on some louder noise or my nearer approach, he would grow uneasy and sluggishly turn about on his perch, as if impatient at having his dreams disturbed; and when he launched himself off and flapped through the pines, spreading his wings to unexpected breadth, I could not hear the slightest sound from them. Thus, guided amid the pine boughs rather by a delicate sense of their neighborhood than by sight, feeling his twilight way, as it were, with his sensitive pinions, he found a new perch, where he might in peace await the dawning of his day.

As I walked over the long causeway made for the railroad through the meadows, I encountered many a blustering and nipping wind, for nowhere has it freer play; and when the frost had smitten me on one cheek, heathen as I was, I turned to it the other also. **1** Nor was it much better by the carriage road from Brister's Hill. For I came to town still, like a friendly Indian, when the contents of the broad open fields were all piled up between the walls of the Walden road, and half an hour sufficed to obliterate the tracks of the last traveller. And when I returned new drifts would have formed, through which I floundered, where the busy northwest wind had been depositing the powdery snow round a sharp angle in the road, and not a rabbit's track, nor even the fine print, the small type, of a meadow mouse was to be seen. Yet I rarely failed to find, even in midwinter, some warm and springy swamp where the grass and the skunk-cabbage still put forth with perennial verdure, and some hardier bird occasionally awaited the return of spring.

Sometimes, notwithstanding the snow, when I returned from my walk at evening I crossed the deep tracks of a

1 "Whomsoever shall smite thee on thy right cheek, turn to him the other also" (Matthew 5:39).

The small white pines stand thus, the lower branches loaded and bent down the ground, while the upper are commonly free and erect. (January 4, 1859)

1   Alex Therien, who was described at length in the "Visitors" chapter.

2   Sanborn (1909, II, 167) identifies him as Edmund Hosmer. A detailed account of their friendship may be found in Brown (88–111).

3   Emerson, "The American Scholar" (Gottesman, 1697).

4   William Ellery Channing the Younger then lived on Punkatasset Hill on the opposite side of Concord.

5   More commonly, "brand new" — that is, so fresh from the furnace that it is still burning. Neufeldt (1989, 96) suggests T was punning here on Sylvester Graham's health-food theories, but I doubt it, since this was the form he regularly used.

6   Amos Bronson Alcott, father of Louisa May Alcott, the author of *Little Women*. T makes the identification in his *Journal* for May 9, 1853 (V, 130). In his youth Alcott had been a peddler in the South. T was one of the first to recognize his strange genius, and Alcott one of the first to recognize T's.

On the north side of the Cut, above the crossing, the jutting edges of the drift are quite handsome upon the bank. The snow is raised twelve feet above the track, and it is all scalloped with projecting eaves or copings, like turtle-shells. They project from three to five feet, and I can stand under them. They are in three or four great layers, one lapping over another like the coarse edge of a shell. Looking along it, they appear somewhat thus. (January 6, 1856)

1 woodchopper leading from my door, and found his pile of whittlings on the hearth, and my house filled with the odor of his pipe. Or on a Sunday afternoon, if I chanced to be at home, I heard the cronching of the snow made by **2** the step of a long-headed farmer, who from far through the woods sought my house, to have a social 'crack;' one **3** of the few of his vocation who are 'men on their farms;' who donned a frock instead of a professor's gown, and is as ready to extract the moral out of church or state as to haul a load of manure from his barn-yard. We talked of rude and simple times, when men sat about large fires in cold, bracing weather, with clear heads; and when other dessert failed, we tried our teeth on many a nut which wise squirrels have long since abandoned, for those which have the thickest shells are commonly empty.

    The one who came from farthest to my lodge, through **4** deepest snows and most dismal tempests, was a poet. A farmer, a hunter, a soldier, a reporter, even a philosopher, may be daunted; but nothing can deter a poet, for he is actuated by pure love. Who can predict his comings and goings? His business calls him out at all hours, even when doctors sleep. We made that small house ring with boisterous mirth and resound with the murmur of much sober talk, making amends then to Walden vale for the long silences. Broadway was still and deserted in comparison. At suitable intervals there were regular salutes of laughter, which might have been referred indifferently to the last-uttered or the forth-coming jest. We made many a **5** 'bran new' theory of life over a thin dish of gruel, which combined the advantages of conviviality with the clear-headedness which philosophy requires.

    I should not forget that during my last winter at the **6** pond there was another welcome visitor, who at one time

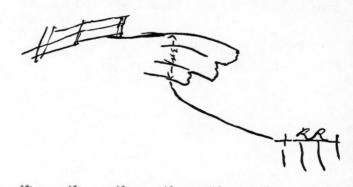

came through the village, through snow and rain and darkness, till he saw my lamp through the trees, and shared with me some long winter evenings. One of the last of the philosophers — Connecticut gave him to the world — he peddled first her wares, afterwards, as he declares, his brains. These he peddles still, prompting God and disgracing man, bearing for fruit his brain only, like the nut its kernel. I think that he must be the man of the most faith of any alive. His words and attitude always suppose a better state of things than other men are acquainted with, and he will be the last man to be disappointed as the ages revolve. He has no venture in the present. But though comparatively disregarded now, when his day comes, laws unsuspected by most will take effect, and masters of families and rulers will come to him for advice.

'How blind that cannot see serenity!'   1

A true friend of man; almost the only friend of human progress. An Old Mortality, say rather an Immortality, 2 with unwearied patience and faith making plain the image engraven in men's bodies, the God of whom they are but defaced and leaning monuments. With his hospitable intellect he embraces children, beggars, insane, and scholars, and entertains the thought of all, adding to it commonly some breadth and elegance. I think that he should keep a caravansary on the world's highway, where philosophers of all nations might put up, and on his sign should be printed, 'Entertainment for man, but not for 3 his beast. Enter ye that have leisure and a quiet mind, who earnestly seek the right road.' He is perhaps the sanest man and has the fewest crotchets of any I chance to know; the same yesterday and tomorrow. Of yore we had sauntered and talked, and effectually put the world be-

1   Thomas Storer, "Wolseius Triumphans," in *The Life and Death of Thomas Wolsey, Cardinall* (1599).
2   The title character in a novel by Sir Walter Scott. As Gottesman (1698) suggests, it was particularly appropriate because Old Mortality went from churchyard to churchyard cleaning and rechiseling old gravestones.
3   Inns in those days were accustomed to advertising "Entertainment for man and beast."

As the current rises to go over the wall, it produces a lull in the angle made by the wall and ground, and accordingly just enough snow is deposited there to fill the triangular calm, but the greater part passes over and is deposited in the larger calm. (February 23, 1854)

1   Indigenous.

2   Charles Anderson (73) points out that T has taken this passage almost word for word from his *Journal* for May 9, 1853 (V, 130–1), describing a conversation that took place years after he left Walden.

3   First growth white pine, so called from the yellowish color of its wood.

4   A play on *Arabian Nights' Entertainment.*

5   In "Solitude."

6   T put a question mark in the margin of his copy of W after "of."

7   Ralph Waldo Emerson.

8   H. H. Wilson, trans., *The Vishnu Purana* (London, 1840), 305.

1   hind us; for he was pledged to no institution in it, free-born, *ingenuus*. Whichever way we turned, it seemed that the heavens and the earth had met together, since he enhanced the beauty of the landscape. A blue-robed man, whose fittest roof is the overarching sky which reflects his serenity. I do not see how he can ever die; Nature cannot spare him.

2   Having each some shingles of thought well dried, we sat and whittled them, trying our knives, and admiring the
3   clear yellowish grain of the pumpkin pine. We waded so gently and reverently, or we pulled together so smoothly, that the fishes of thought were not scared from the stream, nor feared any angler on the bank, but came and went grandly, like the clouds which float through the western sky, and the mother-o'-pearl flocks which sometimes form and dissolve there. There we worked, revising mythology, rounding a fable here and there, and building castles in the air for which earth offered no worthy foundation. Great Looker! Great Expecter! to converse with whom
4   was a New England Night's Entertainment. Ah! such discourse we had, hermit and philosopher, and the old
5, 6   settler I have spoken of — we three — it expanded and racked my little house; I should not dare to say how many pounds' weight there was above the atmospheric pressure on every circular inch; it opened its seams so that they had to be calked with much dulness thereafter to stop the consequent leak; — but I had enough of that kind of oakum already picked.

7   There was one other with whom I had 'solid seasons,' long to be remembered, at his house in the village, and who looked in upon me from time to time; but I had no more for society there.

There too, as everywhere, I sometimes expected the
8   Visitor who never comes. The Vishnu Purana says, 'The

house-holder is to remain at eventide in his courtyard as long as it takes to milk a cow, or longer if he pleases, to await the arrival of a guest.' I often performed this duty of hospitality, waited long enough to milk a whole herd of cows, but did not see the man approaching from the town.   **1**

1   "But never more could see the man / Approaching from the town" ("The Children in the Wood," an old English ballad).

I skated up as far as the boundary between Wayland and Sudbury just above Pelham's Pond, to a point which a woman called about one and a half miles from Saxonville, about twelve miles, between 10 A.M. and one, quite leisurely. There I found the river open unexpectedly, as if there were a rapid there, and as I walked up it some three quarters of a mile, it was still open before me a half-mile further at least, or probably to the falls. Somewhat like this. (January 31, 1855)

Winter Animals

WHEN THE PONDS were firmly frozen, they afforded not only new and shorter routes to many points, but new views from their surfaces of the familiar landscape around them. When I crossed Flint's Pond, after it was covered with snow, though I had often paddled about and skated over it, it was so unexpectedly wide and so strange that I could think of nothing but Baffin's Bay. The Lincoln hills rose up around me at the extremity of a snowy plain, in which I did not remember to have stood before; and the fishermen, at an indeterminable distance over the ice, moving slowly about with their wolfish dogs, passed for sealers or Esquimaux, or in misty weather loomed like fabulous creatures, and I did not know whether they were giants or pygmies. I took this course when I went to lecture in Lincoln in the evening, travelling in no road and passing no house between my own hut and the lecture room. In Goose Pond, which lay in my way, a colony of muskrats dwelt, and raised their cabins high above the ice, though none could be seen abroad when I crossed it. Walden, being like the rest usually bare of snow, or with only shallow and interrupted drifts on it, was my yard where I could walk freely when the snow was nearly two feet deep on a level elsewhere and the villagers were confined to their streets. There, far from the village street, and except at very long intervals, from the jingle of sleigh-bells, I slid and skated, as in a vast moose-yard well trodden, overhung by oak woods and solemn pines bent down with snow or bristling with icicles.

For sounds in winter nights, and often in winter days, I heard the forlorn but melodious note of a hooting owl indefinitely far; such a sound as the frozen earth would

---

1 Charles Anderson (183) points out that there are more than seven hundred references to animals in W.

2 Baffin Bay, a part of the Arctic Ocean between Greenland and the Canadian arctic islands. T had a particular interest in the arctic regions and read widely about them.

3 Now generally spelled "Eskimo."

4 In his *Journal* for January 7, 1852 (III, 177), T describes walking to Lincoln in a snow-storm to lecture. He lectured professionally most of his adult life, and W, like many of his other works, was in large part first heard by his lecture audiences (Harding, 1948).

5 Although many people refer to the building at Walden as a hut, T uses that term only twice in the whole book, once here and again eight paragraphs below. Robbins (10) points out that T refers to it as a house eighty-odd times, a lodge three times, a dwelling twice, and a homestead once.

6 Strangely enough, Goose Pond is about a quarter of a mile northeast of Walden, while Lincoln is southeast.

7 In wintertime, moose tramp out an area in the woods where they herd together. A few lines above, T has tramped out his own yard.

yield if struck with a suitable plectrum, the very *lingua* **1**
vernacula of Walden Wood, and quite familiar to me at
last, though I never saw the bird while it was making it. I
seldom opened my door in a winter evening without hearing it; *Hoo hoo hoo, hoorer hoo*, sounded sonorously, and
the first three syllables accented somewhat like *how der
do*; or sometimes *hoo hoo* only. One night in the beginning of winter, before the pond froze over, about nine
o'clock, I was startled by the loud honking of a goose,
and, stepping to the door, heard the sound of their wings
like a tempest in the woods as they flew low over my
house. They passed over the pond toward Fair Haven,
seemingly deterred from settling by my light, their com-
modore honking all the while with a regular beat. Suddenly an unmistakable cat owl from very near me, with **2**
the most harsh and tremendous voice I ever heard from
any inhabitant of the woods, responded at regular intervals to the goose, as if determined to expose and disgrace
this intruder from Hudson's Bay by exhibiting a greater
compass and volume of voice in a native, and *boo-hoo*
him out of Concord horizon. What do you mean by
alarming the citadel at this time of night consecrated to **3**
me? Do you think I am ever caught napping at such an
hour, and that I have not got lungs and a larynx as well as
yourself? *Boo-hoo, boo-hoo, boo-hoo!* It was one of the
most thrilling discords I ever heard. And yet, if you had a
discriminating ear, there were in it the elements of a
concord such as these plains never saw nor heard.

I also heard the whooping of the ice in the pond, my **4**
great bedfellow in that part of Concord, as if it were
restless in its bed and would fain turn over, were troubled
with flatulency and bad dreams; or I was waked by the
cracking of the ground by the frost, as if some one had
driven a team against my door, and in the morning would

1   The native language of an area.
2   Great horned owl.
3   T is undoubtedly referring to the incident of the geese alarming the citadel when the
Gauls took Rome in 390 B.C. See Livy, *History
of Rome* 5.47.
4   Caused by expansion and contraction of
the ice. See "The Pond in Winter."

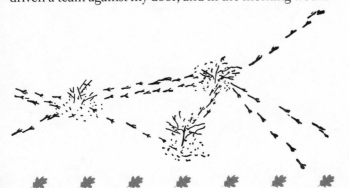

I see a flock of snow buntings. They are feeding
exclusively on that ragged weed which I take to be
Roman wormwood. (January 6, 1859)

1   T tells of this incident in his *Journal* for November 3, 1852 (IV, 409).
2   Hind legs.
3   Old spelling of somersault.

1 find a crack in the earth a quarter of a mile long and a third of an inch wide.

Sometimes I heard the foxes as they ranged over the snow-crust, in moonlight nights, in search of a partridge or other game, barking raggedly and demoniacally like forest dogs, as if laboring with some anxiety, or seeking expression, struggling for light and to be dogs outright and run freely in the streets; for if we take the ages into our account, may there not be a civilization going on among brutes as well as men? They seemed to me to be rudimental, burrowing men, still standing on their defence, awaiting their transformation. Sometimes one came near to my window, attracted by my light, barked a vulpine curse at me, and then retreated.

Usually the red squirrel (*Sciurus Hudsonius*) waked me in the dawn, coursing over the roof and up and down the sides of the house, as if sent out of the woods for this purpose. In the course of the winter I threw out half a bushel of ears of sweet corn, which had not got ripe, on to the snow-crust by my door, and was amused by watching the motions of the various animals which were baited by it. In the twilight and the night the rabbits came regularly and made a hearty meal. All day long the red squirrels came and went, and afforded me much entertainment by their manoeuvres. One would approach at first warily through the shrub oaks, running over the snow-crust by fits and starts like a leaf blown by the wind, now a few paces this way, with wonderful speed and waste of energy,

2 making inconceivable haste with his 'trotters,' as if it were for a wager, and now as many paces that way, but never getting on more than half a rod at a time; and then suddenly pausing with a ludicrous expression and a gratui-

3 tous somerset, as if all the eyes in the universe were fixed on him — for all the motions of a squirrel, even in the

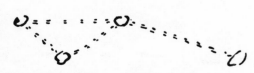

Under the hill, on the southeast side of R. W. E.'s lot, where the hemlock stands, I see many tracks of squirrels. (December 17, 1859)

most solitary recesses of the forest, imply spectators as much as those of a dancing girl — wasting more time in **1** delay and circumspection than would have sufficed to walk the whole distance — I never saw one walk — and then suddenly, before you could say Jack Robinson, he **2** would be in the top of a young pitch pine, winding up his clock and chiding all imaginary spectators, soliloquizing **3** and talking to all the universe at the same time — for no reason that I could ever detect, or he himself was aware of, I suspect. At length he would reach the corn, and selecting a suitable ear, frisk about in the same uncertain **4** trigonometrical way to the topmost stick of my wood-pile, before my window, where he looked me in the face, and there sit for hours, supplying himself with a new ear from time to time, nibbling at first voraciously and throwing the half-naked cobs about; till at length he grew more dainty still and played with his food, tasting only the inside of the kernel, and the ear, which was held balanced over the stick by one paw, slipped from his careless grasp and fell to the ground, when he would look over at it with a ludicrous expression of uncertainty, as if suspecting that it had life, with a mind not made up whether to get it again, or a new one, or be off; now thinking of corn, then listening to hear what was in the wind. So the little impudent fellow would waste many an ear in a forenoon; till at last, seizing some longer and plumper one, considerably bigger than himself, and skilfully balancing it, he would set out with it to the woods, like a tiger with a buffalo, by the same zigzag course and frequent pauses, scratching along with it as if it were too heavy for him and falling all the while, making its fall a diagonal between a perpendicular and horizontal, being determined to put it through at any rate; — a singularly frivolous and whimsical fellow; — and so he would get off with it to where he

1 Dhawan (75) sees this as an allusion to Maya-Shakti, the creative activity of Brahma, but I doubt if T had this in mind.

2 Bartlett says this phrase is derived from a popular song written by a London tobacconist by the name of Hudson.

3 The squirrel when angry makes a chattering noise much like a noisy clock.

4 In his copy of W, T corrected "brisk" to "frisk."

lived, perhaps carry it to the top of a pine tree forty or fifty rods distant, and I would afterwards find the cobs strewn about the woods in various directions.

At length the jays arrive, whose discordant screams were heard long before, as they were warily making their approach an eighth of a mile off, and in a stealthy and sneaking manner they flit from tree to tree, nearer and nearer, and pick up the kernels which the squirrels have dropped. Then, sitting on a pitch pine bough, they attempt to swallow in their haste a kernel which is too big for their throats and chokes them; and after great labor they disgorge it, and spend an hour in the endeavor to crack it by repeated blows with their bills. They were manifestly thieves, and I had not much respect for them; but the squirrels, though at first shy, went to work as if they were taking what was their own.

Meanwhile also came the chickadees in flocks, which, picking up the crumbs the squirrels had dropped, flew to the nearest twig, and, placing them under their claws, hammered away at them with their little bills, as if it were an insect in the bark, till they were sufficiently reduced for their slender throats. A little flock of these titmice came daily to pick a dinner out of my wood-pile, or the crumbs at my door, with faint flitting lisping notes, like the tinkling of icicles in the grass, or else with sprightly *day day day*, or more rarely, in springlike days, a wiry summery *phe-be* from the woodside. They were so familiar that at length one alighted on an armful of wood which I was carrying in, and pecked at the sticks without fear. I once had a sparrow alight upon my shoulder for a moment while I was hoeing in a village garden, and I felt that I was more distinguished by that circumstance than I should have been by any epaulet I could have worn. The squirrels also grew at last to be quite familiar, and occa-

They have gnawed off the cones which were perfectly closed. I see where one has taken one of a pair and left the other partly off. He had first sheared off the needles that were in the way, and then gnawed off the sides or cheeks of the twig to come at the stem of the cone, which as usual was cut by successive cuts as with a knife, while bending it. (January 22, 1856)

sionally stepped upon my shoe, when that was the nearest way.

When the ground was not yet quite covered, and again near the end of winter, when the snow was melted on my south hillside and about my wood-pile, the partridges came out of the woods morning and evening to feed there. Whichever side you walk in the woods the partridge bursts away on whirring wings, jarring the snow from the dry leaves and twigs on high, which comes sifting down in the sunbeams like golden dust, for this brave bird is not to be scared by winter. It is frequently covered up by drifts, and, it is said, 'sometimes plunges from on wing into the soft snow, where it remains concealed for a day or two.' I used to start them in the open land also, **1** where they had come out of the woods at sunset to 'bud' **2** the wild apple trees. They will come regularly every evening to particular trees, where the cunning sportsman lies in wait for them, and the distant orchards next the woods suffer thus not a little. I am glad that the partridge gets fed, at any rate. It is Nature's own bird which lives on buds and diet-drink. **3**

In dark winter mornings, or in short winter afternoons, I sometimes heard a pack of hounds threading all the woods with hounding cry and yelp, unable to resist the instinct of the chase, and the note of the hunting-horn at intervals, proving that man was in the rear. The woods ring again, and yet no fox bursts forth on to the open level of the pond, nor following pack pursuing their Actaeon. **4** And perhaps at evening I see the hunters returning with a single brush trailing from their sleigh for a trophy, seeking **5** their inn. They tell me that if the fox would remain in the bosom of the frozen earth he would be safe, or if he would run in a straight line away no foxhound could overtake him; but, having left his pursuers far behind, he

1 Although T, in one of the W drafts, attributes this quotation to Audubon, I have been unable to find it in any of Audubon's writings.

2 To feed on the tree's buds.

3 T was hardly thinking of our present-day diet sodas, but of some nineteenth-century health food.

4 An ancient Greek hunter who, when he saw Artemis bathing, was changed into a stag and then devoured by his own dogs.

5 Brush: foxtail.

Came across a fox's track, which I think was made last night or since. The tracks were about two inches long, or a little less, by one and a half wide, shaped thus where the snow was only half an inch deep on ice. (February 5, 1854)

His tracks when running, as I have described, were like this:—being about two by five inches, as if he slid a little, no marks of toes being seen in that shallow snow; the greatest interval above, one foot.

1 T gives the detailed conversation with this man in his *Journal* (I, 398–9).

2 Woodson (1975, 554) argues convincingly that this is T's old friend George Minott.

3 As T knew only too well, the hunter with his one bath a year was probably outdoing many of his neighbors. In his *Journal* for July 8, 1852 (IV, 202), T says, "One farmer, who came to bathe in Walden one Sunday while I lived there, told me it was the first bath he had had for fifteen years."

4 A small town south of Concord.

stops to rest and listen till they come up, and when he runs he circles round to his old haunts, where the hunters await him. Sometimes, however, he will run upon a wall many rods, and then leap off far to one side, and he appears to know that water will not retain his scent. A 1 hunter told me that he once saw a fox pursued by hounds burst out on to Walden when the ice was covered with shallow puddles, run part way across, and then return to the same shore. Ere long the hounds arrived, but here they lost the scent. Sometimes a pack hunting by themselves would pass my door, and circle round my house, and yelp and hound without regarding me, as if afflicted by a species of madness, so that nothing could divert them from the pursuit. Thus they circle until they fall upon the recent trail of a fox, for a wise hound will forsake everything else for this. One day a man came to my hut from Lexington to inquire after his hound that made a large track, and had been hunting for a week by himself. But I fear that he was not the wiser for all I told him, for every time I attempted to answer his questions he interrupted me by asking, 'What do you do here?' He had lost a dog, but found a man.

2 One old hunter who has a dry tongue, who used to 3 come to bathe in Walden once every year when the water was warmest, and at such times looked in upon me, told me that many years ago he took his gun one afternoon and went out for a cruise in Walden Wood; and as he 4 walked the Wayland road he heard the cry of hounds approaching, and ere long a fox leaped the wall into the road, and as quick as thought leaped the other wall out of the road, and his swift bullet had not touched him. Some way behind came an old hound and her three pups in full pursuit, hunting on their own account, and disappeared again in the woods. Late in the afternoon, as he was

Soon after, thus: The greatest interval sometimes four feet even.

resting in the thick woods south of Walden, he heard the voice of the hounds far over toward Fair Haven still pursuing the fox; and on they came, their hounding cry which made all the woods ring sounding nearer and nearer, now from Well Meadow, now from the Baker Farm. For a long **1** time he stood still and listened to their music, so sweet to a hunter's ear, when suddenly the fox appeared, threading the solemn aisles with an easy coursing pace, whose sound was concealed by a sympathetic rustle of the leaves, swift and still, keeping the ground, leaving his pursuers far behind; and, leaping upon a rock amid the woods, he sat erect and listening, with his back to the hunter. For a moment compassion restrained the latter's arm; but that was a short-lived mood, and as quick as thought can follow thought his piece was levelled, and *whang!* — the fox, rolling over the rock, lay dead on the ground. The hunter still kept his place and listened to the hounds. Still on they came, and now the near woods resounded through all their aisles with their demoniac cry. At length the old hound burst into view with muzzle to the ground, and snapping the air as if possessed, and ran directly to the rock; but, spying the dead fox, she suddenly ceased her hounding, as if struck dumb with amazement, and walked round and round him in silence; and one by one her pups arrived, and, like their mother, were sobered into silence by the mystery. Then the hunter came forward and stood in their midst, and the mystery was solved. They waited in silence while he skinned the fox, then followed the brush a while, and at length turned off into the woods again. That evening a Weston squire came to **2** the Concord hunter's cottage to inquire for his hounds, and told how for a week they had been hunting on their own account from Weston woods. The Concord hunter told him what he knew and offered him the skin; but the

1   Well-Meadow was on the shore of Fair Haven Bay, about a mile southwest of Walden (Gleason).

2   T is probably punning on Squire Weston, a character in Henry Fielding's novel *Tom Jones*. Weston is a village a few miles southeast of Concord.

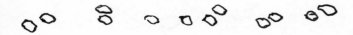

Sometimes the three tracks merged together where the crust broke.

1 In his *Journal* for March 10, 1853 (V, 16), T calls him "Old Fox" Nutting and records that he had killed moose as well as bear. T also says that he lived in Jacob Baker's house in Lincoln (Gleason).

2 On Fair Haven Hill, southwest of Walden (Gleason).

3 After a lapse of nearly two centuries, moose have occasionally wandered down to Concord from the New Hampshire mountains in recent years.

4 This old record book was found in Deacon Brown's attic, and T quotes at length from it in his *Journal* for January 27, 1854 (VI, 77-9). Channing says it was Ephraim Jones's book.

5 Catt: in his copy of W, T queried whether this should be "calf" and adds "v. Mott ledger near beginning." But various types of wildcat have been caught in Concord, and on October 15, 1860, T wrote a letter to the Boston Society of Natural History, presenting it with the skin of a Canada lynx killed in nearby Carlisle.

6 The French and Indian War of 1754 to 1763.

7 Deer nowadays overrun the area. With the return of forests, Concord is much wilder today than it was in T's day.

8 "Nimrod, the mighty hunter before the Lord" (Genesis 10:9).

other declined it and departed. He did not find his hounds that night, but the next day learned that they had crossed the river and put up at a farmhouse for the night, whence, having been well fed, they took their departure early in the morning.

The hunter who told me this could remember one Sam **1, 2** Nutting, who used to hunt bears on Fair Haven Ledges, and exchange their skins for rum in Concord village; **3** who told him, even, that he had seen a moose there. Nutting had a famous foxhound named Burgoyne — he pronounced it Bugine — which my informant used to **4** borrow. In the 'Wast Book' of an old trader of this town, who was also a captain, town-clerk, and representative, I find the following entry. Jan. 18th, 1742-3, 'John Melven Cr. by 1 Grey Fox 0 — 2 — 3;' they are not now found here; and in his ledger, Feb. 7th, 1743, Hezekiah Stratton **5** has credit 'by ½ a Catt skin 0 — 1 — 4½;' of course, a wild-cat, for Stratton was a sergeant in the old French **6** war, and would not have got credit for hunting less noble game. Credit is given for deerskins also, and they were daily sold. One man still preserves the horns of the last **7** deer that was killed in this vicinity, and another has told me the particulars of the hunt in which his uncle was engaged. The hunters were formerly a numerous and **8** merry crew here. I remember well one gaunt Nimrod who would catch up a leaf by the roadside and play a strain on it wilder and more melodious, if my memory serves me, than any hunting-horn.

At midnight, when there was a moon, I sometimes met with hounds in my path prowling about the woods, which would skulk out of my way, as if afraid, and stand silent amid the bushes till I had passed.

Squirrels and wild mice disputed for my store of nuts. There were scores of pitch pines around my house, from

When walking at ease, before he saw me his tracks were more round and nearer together,—about two inches by two and a half, thus. (February 10, 1856)

one to four inches in diameter, which had been gnawed by mice the previous winter — a Norwegian winter for them, for the snow lay long and deep, and they were obliged to mix a large proportion of pine bark with their other diet. These trees were alive and apparently flourishing at midsummer, and many of them had grown a foot, though completely girdled; but after another winter such were without exception dead. It is remarkable that a single mouse should thus be allowed a whole pine tree for its dinner, gnawing round instead of up and down it; but perhaps it is necessary in order to thin these trees, which are wont to grow up densely.

The hares (*Lepus Americanus*) were very familiar. One had her form under my house all winter, separated from **1** me only by the flooring, and she startled me each morning by her hasty departure when I began to stir — thump, thump, thump, striking her head against the floor timbers in her hurry. They used to come round my door at dusk to nibble the potato parings which I had thrown out, and were so nearly the color of the ground that they could hardly be distinguished when still. Sometimes in the twilight I alternately lost and recovered sight of one sitting motionless under my window. When I opened my door in the evening, off they would go with a squeak and a bounce. Near at hand they only excited my pity. One evening one sat by my door two paces from me, at first trembling with fear, yet unwilling to move; a poor wee thing, lean and bony, with ragged ears and sharp nose, scant tail and slender paws. It looked as if Nature no longer contained the breed of nobler bloods, but stood on **2** her last toes. Its large eyes appeared young and unhealthy, almost dropsical. I took a step, and lo, away it scud with an elastic spring over the snow-crust, straightening its body and its limbs into graceful length, and soon put the forest

1   Form: the resting place of a hare.
2   "Rome, thou hast lost the breed of noble bloods" (Julius Caesar, I, ii).

The tracks of the mice suggest extensive hopping in the night and going a-gadding. They commence and terminate in the most insignificant little holes by the side of a twig or tuft, and occasionally they give us the type of their tails very distinctly, even sidewise to the course on a bank-side, thus. (January 31, 1856)

1 "Lucius Aelius thought that the hare received its name *lepus* because of its swiftness, being *levipes,* nimblefoot" (Varro, *Rerum Rusticarum* 3.12).

2 Small fence built of twigs and placed across a rabbit's run to divert it into a snare.

3 Not in the modern sense of the word, but a boy who attends cows.

between me and itself — the wild free venison, asserting its vigor and the dignity of Nature. Not without reason was its slenderness. Such then was its nature. (*Lepus, levipes,* light-foot, some think.)

1

What is a country without rabbits and partridges? They are among the most simple and indigenous animal products; ancient and venerable families known to antiquity as to modern times; of the very hue and substance of Nature, nearest allied to leaves and to the ground — and to one another; it is either winged or it is legged. It is hardly as if you had seen a wild creature when a rabbit or a partridge bursts away, only a natural one, as much to be expected as rustling leaves. The partridge and the rabbit are still sure to thrive, like true natives of the soil, whatever revolutions occur. If the forest is cut off, the sprouts and bushes which spring up afford them concealment, and they become more numerous than ever. That must be a poor country indeed that does not support a hare. Our woods teem with them both, and around every swamp may be seen the partridge or rabbit walk, beset

2
3

with twiggy fences and horse-hair snares, which some cow-boy tends.

I found myself walking in one of those shelf-like hillside paths made by Indians, hunters, cows, or what-not, and it was beset with fresh snares for partridges, this wise: Upright twigs are stuck in the ground across the path, a foot or more in height and just close enough together to turn a partridge aside, leaving a space about four inches wide in the middle, and some twigs are stretched across above to prevent the birds hopping over. (November 28, 1857)

The Pond in Winter

AFTER A STILL winter night I awoke with the impression that some question had been put to me, which I had been endeavoring in vain to answer in my sleep, as what — how — when — where? But there was dawning Nature, in whom all creatures live, looking in at my broad windows with serene and satisfied face, and no question on *her* lips. I awoke to an answered question, to Nature and daylight. The snow lying deep on the earth dotted with young pines, and the very slope of the hill on which my house is placed, seemed to say, Forward! Nature puts no question and answers none which we mortals ask. She has long ago taken her resolution. 'O Prince, our eyes contemplate with admiration and transmit to the soul the wonderful and varied spectacle of this universe. The night veils without doubt a part of this glorious creation; but day comes to reveal to us this great work, which extends from earth even into the plains of the ether.' 2

Then to my morning work. First I take an axe and pail and go in search of water, if that be not a dream. After a cold and snowy night it needed a divining-rod to find it. Every winter the liquid and trembling surface of the pond, which was so sensitive to every breath, and reflected every light and shadow, becomes solid to the depth of a foot or a foot and a half, so that it will support the heaviest teams, and perchance the snow covers it to an equal depth, and it is not to be distinguished from any level field. Like the marmots in the surrounding hills, it closes its eyelids and 3 becomes dormant for three months or more. Standing on the snow-covered plain, as if in a pasture amid the hills, I cut my way first through a foot of snow, and then a foot of

1 Borck and Rothschild discuss this chapter, showing that it is carrying out the philosophy of the book as a whole.

2 *Harivansa, ou Histoire de la Famille de Hari* (Paris, 1834, II, 361).

3 Woodchucks.

The skater can afford to follow all the windings of a stream, and yet soon leaves far behind and out of sight the walker who cuts across. Distance is hardly an obstacle to him. I observe that my ordinary track is like this. (December 29, 1858)

1   Heavy woolen coats.

ice, and open a window under my feet, where, kneeling to drink, I look down into the quiet parlor of the fishes, pervaded by a softened light as through a window of ground glass, with its bright sanded floor the same as in summer; there a perennial waveless serenity reigns as in the amber twilight sky, corresponding to the cool and even temperament of the inhabitants. Heaven is under our feet as well as over our heads.

Early in the morning, while all things are crisp with frost, men come with fishing-reels and slender lunch, and let down their fine lines through the snowy field to take pickerel and perch; wild men, who instinctively follow other fashions and trust other authorities than their townsmen, and by their goings and comings stitch towns together in parts where else they would be ripped. They sit 1 and eat their luncheon in stout fear-naughts on the dry oak leaves on the shore, as wise in natural lore as the citizen is in artificial. They never consulted with books, and know and can tell much less than they have done. The things which they practice are said not yet to be known. Here is one fishing for pickerel with grown perch for bait. You look into his pail with wonder as into a summer pond, as if he kept summer locked up at home, or knew where she had retreated. How, pray, did he get these in midwinter? Oh, he got worms out of rotten logs since the ground froze, and so he caught them. His life itself passes deeper in nature than the studies of the naturalist penetrate; himself a subject for the naturalist. The latter raises the moss and bark gently with his knife in search of insects; the former lays open logs to their core with his axe, and moss and bark fly far and wide. He gets his living by barking trees. Such a man has some right to fish, and I love to see nature carried out in him. The perch swallows the grub-worm, the pickerel swallows the

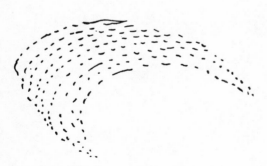

At Cardinal Shore, as usual, there is a great crescent of hobbly ice, where, two or three days ago, the northwest wind drove the waves back up-stream and broke up the edge of the ice. (December 7, 1856)

perch, and the fisherman swallows the pickerel; and so all the chinks in the scale of being are filled.   1

When I strolled around the pond in misty weather I was sometimes amused by the primitive mode which some ruder fisherman had adopted. He would perhaps have placed alder branches over the narrow holes in the ice, which were four or five rods apart and an equal distance from the shore, and having fastened the end of the line to a stick to prevent its being pulled through, have passed the slack line over a twig of the alder, a foot or more above the ice, and tied a dry oak leaf to it, which, being pulled down, would show when he had a bite. These alders loomed through the mist at regular intervals as you walked half way round the pond.

Ah, the pickerel of Walden! when I see them lying on   2 the ice, or in the well which the fisherman cuts in the ice, making a little hole to admit the water, I am always surprised by their rare beauty, as if they were fabulous fishes, they are so foreign to the streets, even to the woods, foreign as Arabia to our Concord life. They possess a quite dazzling and transcendent beauty which separates them by a wide interval from the cadaverous cod and haddock whose fame is trumpeted in our streets. They are not   3 green like the pines, nor gray like the stones, nor blue like the sky; but they have, to my eyes, if possible, yet rarer colors, like flowers and precious stones, as if they were the pearls, the animalized *nuclei* or crystals of the Walden water. They, of course, are Walden all over and all through; are themselves small Waldens in the animal kingdom, Waldenses. It is surprising that they are caught here — 4 that in this deep and capacious spring, far beneath the rattling teams and chaises and tinkling sleighs that travel the Walden road, this great gold and emerald fish swims. I never chanced to see its kind in any market; it would be

1   The idea of the "great chain of being" was popular particularly in eighteenth-century England. See Arthur O. Lovejoy, *The Great Chain of Being* (Cambridge, 1933).

2   For a good discussion of the fish native to Walden Pond, see Ted Williams. There is a legend that some years ago a T admirer introduced into the pond every species of fish that T mentioned in his works. Many of these were trash fish, which soon crowded out the better fish. In 1968 the state deliberately poisoned the entire pond, killing off all the fish, and since then each year restocking the pond with game fish, many of them not natives, to please the "sportsmen" of the area.

Boudreau (1974) gives an extended analysis of the creation of this paragraph, showing the impact of the philologist Richard Trent on T.

3   In T's day, fish peddlers blew horns to announce their presence as they walked through the streets.

4   Waldenses were a group of fifteenth-century Christian heretics whose purity and spirituality reflect morally the physical beauty of the pickerel (D'Avanzo, 1971). The pun on Walden hardly needs amplification.

1 David Cooper has a most interesting analysis of this paragraph from a humanist and a poststructuralist point of view.

2 For an extended discussion of T's use of pond bottoms as a metaphor, see Michaels. See also Boone.

3 In 1939 Edward S. Deevey rechecked T's survey and analysis of Walden Pond with the latest scientific instruments and concluded that T was amazingly accurate in his observations, when one considers he was using the crudest of instruments, and that his contribution to the science of limnology was original and genuine. (Deevey).

4 New England has many traditions of "bottomless" ponds. In his *Journal* for September 15, 1850 (II, 68), T records visiting such ponds in Sudbury and beyond.

5 I have heard people theorize that Walden connects underground with a spring in the White Mountains, with Lake Winnipesaukee in New Hampshire, or with a pond on Cape Cod. Some present-day Concordians even assert that once the body of a man who had drowned in Walden eventually surfaced in nearby White Pond. Suggestions have been made for adding a dye to these other bodies of water to see if it comes out in Walden. To my knowledge, none of these experiments have ever been attempted, but some people still believe these old folktales.

6 According to the ancient Greeks, the river that flows around Hades.

7 A fifty-six-pound weight.

8 See map on page 330.

the cynosure of all eyes there. Easily, with a few convulsive quirks, they give up their watery ghosts, like a mortal translated before his time to the thin air of heaven.

❦

1 As I was desirous to recover the long lost bottom of
2 Walden Pond, I surveyed it carefully, before the ice broke
3 up, early in '46, with compass and chain and sounding line. There have been many stories told about the bottom, or rather no bottom, of this pond, which certainly had no foundation for themselves. It is remarkable how long men will believe in the bottomlessness of a pond without taking the trouble to sound it. I have visited two
4 such Bottomless Ponds in one walk in this neighborhood.
5 Many have believed that Walden reached quite through to the other side of the globe. Some who have lain flat on the ice for a long time, looking down through the illusive medium, perchance with watery eyes into the bargain, and driven to hasty conclusions by the fear of catching cold in their breasts, have seen vast holes 'into which a load of hay might be driven,' if there were anybody to
6 drive it, the undoubted source of the Styx and entrance to the Infernal Regions from these parts. Others have gone
7 down from the village with a 'fifty-six' and a wagon load of inch rope, but yet have failed to find any bottom; for while the 'fifty-six' was resting by the way, they were paying out the rope in the vain attempt to fathom their truly immeasurable capacity for marvellousness. But I can assure my readers that Walden has a reasonably tight bottom at a not unreasonable, though at an unusual, depth. I
8 fathomed it easily with a cod-line and a stone weighing about a pound and a half, and could tell accurately when the stone left the bottom, by having to pull so much harder before the water got underneath to help me. The

greatest depth was exactly one hundred and two feet; to **1**
which may be added the five feet which it has risen since,
making one hundred and seven. This is a remarkable
depth for so small an area; yet not an inch of it can be
spared by the imagination. What if all ponds were shallow? Would it not react on the minds of men? I am
thankful that this pond was made deep and pure for a
symbol. While men believe in the infinite some ponds
will be thought to be bottomless.

A factory-owner, hearing what depth I had found, **2**
thought that it could not be true, for, judging from his
acquaintance with dams, sand would not lie at so steep an
angle. But the deepest ponds are not so deep in proportion to their area as most suppose, and, if drained, would
not leave very remarkable valleys. They are not like cups
between the hills; for this one, which is so unusually deep
for its area, appears in a vertical section through its centre
not deeper than a shallow plate. Most ponds, emptied,
would leave a meadow no more hollow than we frequently
see. William Gilpin, who is so admirable in all that re- **3**
lates to landscapes, and usually so correct, standing at the
head of Loch Fyne, in Scotland, which he describes as 'a
bay of salt water, sixty or seventy fathoms deep, four miles
in breadth,' and about fifty miles long, surrounded by
mountains, observes, 'If we could have seen it immediately after the diluvian crash, or whatever convulsion of
nature occasioned it, before the waters gushed in, what a
horrid chasm must it have appeared!

> 'So high as heaved the tumid hills, so low
> Down sunk a hollow bottom broad and deep,
> Capacious bed of waters.'   **4**

But if, using the shortest diameter of Loch Fyne, we apply
these proportions to Walden, which, as we have seen,

1 On September 28, 1968, the New England chapter of the Marine Technology Society,
using the latest oceanographic instruments,
confirmed precisely this measurement (*Concord
Journal,* October 3, 1968).

2 Probably Calvin Damon, who in 1834
had established a factory in West Concord that
prospered for many years.

3 William Gilpin, *Observations on . . . the
High-lands of Scotland,* (London, 1808, II, 4).

4 Milton, *Paradise Lost,* VII, 288–90.

1 The first edition reads "have been."

appears already in a vertical section only like a shallow plate, it will appear four times as shallow. So much for the *increased* horrors of the chasm of Loch Fyne when emptied. No doubt many a smiling valley with its stretching cornfields occupies exactly such a 'horrid chasm,' from which the waters have receded, though it requires the insight and the far sight of the geologist to convince the unsuspecting inhabitants of this fact. Often an inquisitive eye may detect the shores of a primitive lake in the low horizon hills, and no subsequent elevation of the plain **1** has been necessary to conceal their history. But it is easiest, as they who work on the highways know, to find the hollows by the puddles after a shower. The amount of it is, the imagination, give it the least license, dives deeper and soars higher than Nature goes. So, probably, the depth of the ocean will be found to be very inconsiderable compared with its breadth.

As I sounded through the ice I could determine the shape of the bottom with greater accuracy than is possible in surveying harbors which do not freeze over, and I was surprised at its general regularity. In the deepest part there are several acres more level than almost any field which is exposed to the sun, wind, and plow. In one instance, on a line arbitrarily chosen, the depth did not vary more than one foot in thirty rods; and generally, near the middle, I could calculate the variation for each one hundred feet in any direction beforehand within three or four inches. Some are accustomed to speak of deep and dangerous holes even in quiet sandy ponds like this, but the effect of water under these circumstances is to level all inequalities. The regularity of the bottom and its conformity to the shores and the range of the neighboring hills were so perfect that a distant promontory betrayed itself in the soundings quite across the pond, and its direction could

This spray had improved the least core—as the
dead and slender rushes drooping over the
water—and formed larger icicles about them,
shaped exactly like horns. (January 26, 1853)

be determined by observing the opposite shore. Cape becomes bar, and plain shoal, and valley and gorge deep water and channel.

When I had mapped the pond by the scale of ten rods to an inch, and put down the soundings, more than a hundred in all, I observed this remarkable coincidence. Having noticed that the number indicating the greatest depth was apparently in the centre of the map, I laid a rule on the map lengthwise, and then breadthwise, and found, to my surprise, that the line of greatest length intersected the line of greatest breadth *exactly* at the point of greatest depth, notwithstanding that the middle is so nearly level, the outline of the pond far from regular, and the extreme length and breadth were got by measuring into the coves; and I said to myself, Who knows but this hint would conduct to the deepest part of the ocean as well as of a pond or puddle? Is not this the rule also for the height of mountains, regarded as the opposite of valleys? We know that a hill is not highest at its narrowest part.

Of five coves, three, or all which had been sounded, **1** were observed to have a bar quite across their mouths and deeper water within, so that the bay tended to be an expansion of water within the land not only horizontally but vertically, and to form a basin or independent pond, the direction of the two capes showing the course of the bar. Every harbor on the sea-coast, also, has its bar at its entrance. In proportion as the mouth of the cove was wider compared with its length, the water over the bar was deeper compared with that in the basin. Given, then, the length and breadth of the cove, and the character of the surrounding shore, and you have almost elements enough to make out a formula for all cases.

In order to see how nearly I could guess, with this experience, at the deepest point in a pond, by observing

1 Meigs names, describes, and maps each of these coves.

Looking down on it.

A form like this would project over the water: six inches deep by four or five in width and a foot long, held by the rocks, but with a slight weed for core. You could take off the incrustations on the rocks, turn them up, and they were perfect shells. (January 26, 1853)

the outlines of a surface and the character of its shores alone, I made a plan of White Pond, which contains about forty-one acres, and, like this, has no island in it, nor any visible inlet or outlet; and as the line of greatest breadth fell very near the line of least breadth, where two opposite capes approached each other and two opposite bays receded, I ventured to mark a point a short distance from the latter line, but still on the line of greatest length, as the deepest. The deepest part was found to be within one hundred feet of this, still farther in the direction to which I had inclined, and was only one foot deeper, namely, sixty feet. Of course, a stream running through, or an island in the pond, would make the problem much more complicated.

If we knew all the laws of Nature, we should need only one fact, or the description of one actual phenomenon, to infer all the particular results at that point. Now we know only a few laws, and our result is vitiated, not, of course, by any confusion or irregularity in Nature, but by our ignorance of essential elements in the calculation. Our notions of law and harmony are commonly confined to those instances which we detect; but the harmony which results from a far greater number of seemingly conflicting, but really concurring, laws, which we have not detected, is still more wonderful. The particular laws are as our points of view, as, to the traveller, a mountain outline varies with every step, and it has an infinite number of profiles, though absolutely but one form. Even when cleft or bored through it is not comprehended in its entireness.

What I have observed of the pond is no less true in ethics. It is the law of average. Such a rule of the two diameters not only guides us toward the sun in the system and the heart in man, but draw lines through the length and breadth of the aggregate of a man's particular daily

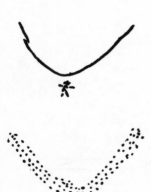

As usual, I now see, walking on the river and river-meadow ice, thus thinly covered with the fresh snow, that conical rainbow, or parabola of rainbow-colored reflections, from the myriad reflecting crystals of the snow, *i.e.*, as I walk toward the sun, —always a little in advance of me, of course, angle of reflection being equal to that of incidence. (January 29, 1860)

behaviors and waves of life into his coves and inlets, and where they intersect will be the height or depth of his character. Perhaps we need only to know how his shores trend and his adjacent country or circumstances, to infer his depth and concealed bottom. If he is surrounded by mountainous circumstances, an Achillean shore, whose **1** peaks overshadow and are reflected in his bosom, they suggest a corresponding depth in him. But a low and smooth shore proves him shallow on that side. In our bodies, a bold projecting brow falls off to and indicates a corresponding depth of thought. Also there is a bar across **2** the entrance of our every cove, or particular inclination; each is our harbor for a season, in which we are detained and partially landlocked. These inclinations are not whimsical usually, but their form, size, and direction are determined by the promontories of the shore, the ancient axes of elevation. When this bar is gradually increased by storms, tides, or currents, or there is a subsidence of the waters, so that it reaches to the surface, that which was at first but an inclination in the shore in which a thought was harbored becomes an individual lake, cut off from the ocean, wherein the thought secures its own conditions — changes, perhaps, from salt to fresh, becomes a sweet sea, dead sea, or a marsh. At the advent of each individual into this life, may we not suppose that such a bar has risen to the surface somewhere? It is true, we are such poor navigators that our thoughts, for the most part, stand off and on upon a harborless coast, are conversant only with the bights of the bays of poesy, or steer for the public ports of entry, and go into the dry docks of science, where they merely refit **3** for this world, and no natural currents concur to individualize them.

As for the inlet or outlet of Walden, I have not discovered any but rain and snow and evaporation, though per-

1 Achilles was born in Thessaly, according to tradition. T is probably referring to a rugged, mountainous shore.

2 T here refers to one of the beliefs of phrenology, a popular pseudoscience of his day that claimed a relationship between one's character and the shape of one's head.

3 In his copy of W, T placed a "?" in the margin by these lines.

Walking over Hubbard's broad meadow on the softened ice, I admire the markings in it. . . . a sort of fibrous structure of waving lines, hair-like or rather flame-like,—call it *phlogistic:*—only far more regular and beautiful than I can draw. Sometimes like perhaps a cassowary's feathers, the branches being very long and fine. (February 8, 1860)

1 Frederic Tudor, the "ice king" of the nine-teenth-century New England ice industry, and his former partner, Nathaniel Jarvis Wyeth, engaged in a trade war in the mid-1840s. Rather than be forced to buy ice from Wyeth, who had a monopoly of the sources, Tudor, who shipped ice all over the world, did his own harvesting at Walden Pond. When Tudor won the war, he had no need for the Walden ice, so it was left to melt on the shores of the pond (Cummings). Harding (1968) reproduces Tudor's memo of agreement with the Fitchburg Railroad on the ice rights for Walden Pond.

2 Jacobs points out that in the use of "un-dulated" T anticipates by half a century the continental-drift theories of the early twentieth century.

I see some old holes, now smoothly frozen over, where these rays have flowed from all sides into the hole in the midst of the checked ice, making a circular figure which reminded me of a jellyfish: only far more beautiful than this. (February 8, 1860)

haps, with a thermometer and a line, such places may be found, for where the water flows into the pond it will probably be coldest in summer and warmest in winter.

1 When the ice-men were at work here in '46–7, the cakes sent to the shore were one day rejected by those who were stacking them up there, not being thick enough to lie side by side with the rest; and the cutters thus discovered that the ice over a small space was two or three inches thinner than elsewhere, which made them think that there was an inlet there. They also showed me in another place what they thought was a 'leach-hole,' through which the pond leaked out under a hill into a neighboring meadow, pushing me out on a cake of ice to see it. It was a small cavity under ten feet of water; but I think that I can warrant the pond not to need soldering till they find a worse leak than that. One has suggested, that if such a 'leach-hole' should be found, its connection with the meadow, if any existed, might be proved by conveying some colored powder or sawdust to the mouth of the hole, and then putting a strainer over the spring in the meadow, which would catch some of the particles carried through by the current.

While I was surveying, the ice, which was sixteen inches thick, undulated under a slight wind like water. It is well known that a level cannot be used on ice. At one rod from the shore its greatest fluctuation, when observed by means of a level on land directed toward a graduated staff on the ice, was three quarters of an inch, though the ice appeared firmly attached to the shore. It was probably greater in the middle. Who knows but if our instruments

2 were delicate enough we might detect an undulation in the crust of the earth? When two legs of my level were on the shore and the third on the ice, and the sights were directed over the latter, a rise or fall of the ice of an almost

infinitesimal amount made a difference of several feet on a tree across the pond. When I began to cut holes for sounding there were three or four inches of water on the ice under a deep snow which had sunk it thus far; but the water began immediately to run into these holes, and continued to run for two days in deep streams, which wore away the ice on every side, and contributed essentially, if not mainly, to dry the surface of the pond; for, as the water ran in, it raised and floated the ice. This was somewhat like cutting a hole in the bottom of a ship to let the water out. When such holes freeze, and a rain succeeds, and finally a new freezing forms a fresh smooth ice over all, it is beautifully mottled internally by dark figures, shaped somewhat like a spider's web, what you may call ice rosettes, produced by the channels worn by the water flowing from all sides to a centre. Sometimes, also, when the ice was covered with shallow puddles, I saw a double shadow of myself, one standing on the head of the other, one on the ice, the other on the trees or hillside.

🍂

While yet it is cold January, and snow and ice are thick and solid, the prudent landlord comes from the village to get ice to cool his summer drink; impressively, even pathetically, wise, to foresee the heat and thirst of July now in January — wearing a thick coat and mittens! when so many things are not provided for. It may be that he lays up no treasures in this world which will cool his summer **1** drink in the next. He cuts and saws the solid pond, unroofs the house of fishes, and carts off their very element and air, held fast by chains and stakes like corded wood, through the favoring winter air, to wintry cellars, to underlie the summer there. It looks like solidified azure, as, far off, it is drawn through the streets. These ice-cutters

1   "But lay up for yourselves treasures in heaven" (Matthew 6:20).

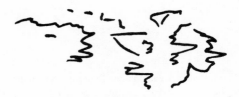

I see some quite thin ice which had formed on puddles on the ice, now soaked through, and in these are very interesting figures bounded by straight and crinkled particularly white lines. (February 8, 1860)

1 According to Greek legend, a people who lived in a land of plenty and perpetual sunshine beyond the north wind. T may have read of them in Diodorus (2.47).

2 The *New England Farmer* was an agricultural journal published at Quincy Hall in Boston. There was a *New England Cultivator* and a *Boston Cultivator*, both published in Boston.

3 Sanborn (1909, II, 205) says T identifies this farmer as Mr. Tudor.

are a merry race, full of jest and sport, and when I went among them they were wont to invite me to saw pit-fashion with them, I standing underneath.

In the winter of '46-7 there came a hundred men of 1 Hyperborean extraction swoop down on to our pond one morning, with many carloads of ungainly-looking farming tools — sleds, plows, drill-barrows, turf-knives, spades, saws, rakes, and each man was armed with a double-pointed pike-staff, such as is not described in the New-2 England Farmer or the Cultivator. I did not know whether they had come to sow a crop of winter rye, or some other kind of grain recently introduced from Iceland. As I saw no manure, I judged that they meant to skim the land, as I had done, thinking the soil was deep and had lain fallow 3 long enough. They said that a gentleman farmer, who was behind the scenes, wanted to double his money, which, as I understood, amounted to half a million already; but in order to cover each one of his dollars with another, he took off the only coat, ay, the skin itself, of Walden Pond in the midst of a hard winter. They went to work at once, plowing, harrowing, rolling, furrowing, in admirable order, as if they were bent on making this a model farm; but when I was looking sharp to see what kind of seed they dropped into the furrow, a gang of fellows by my side suddenly began to hook up the virgin mould itself, with a peculiar jerk, clean down to the sand, or rather the water — for it was a very springy soil — indeed all the *terra firma* there was — and haul it away on sleds, and then I guessed that they must be cutting peat in a bog. So they came and went every day, with a peculiar shriek from the locomotive, from and to some point of the polar regions, as it seemed to me, like a flock of arctic snowbirds. But sometimes Squaw Walden had her revenge, and a hired man, walking behind his team, slipped through a crack in

Then there is occasionally, where puddles on the ice have frozen, that triangular rib-work of crystals,—a beautiful casting in alto*[sic]*-relievo of low crystal prisms with one edge up,—so meeting and crossing as to form triangular and other figures. Shining splinters in the sun. Giving a rough hold to the feet. (February 8, 1860)

the ground down toward Tartarus, and he who was so **1**
brave before suddenly became but the ninth part of a **2**
man, almost gave up his animal heat, and was glad to take
refuge in my house, and acknowledged that there was
some virtue in a stove; or sometimes the frozen soil took a
piece of steel out of a plowshare, or a plow got set in the
furrow and had to be cut out.

To speak literally, a hundred Irishmen, with Yankee
overseers, came from Cambridge every day to get out the **3**
ice. They divided it into cakes by methods too well known
to require description, and these, being sledded to the
shore, were rapidly hauled off on to an ice platform, and
raised by grappling irons and block and tackle, worked by
horses, on to a stack, as surely as so many barrels of flour,
and there placed evenly side by side, and row upon row,
as if they formed the solid base of an obelisk designed to
pierce the clouds. They told me that in a good day they
could get out a thousand tons, which was the yield of
about one acre. Deep ruts and 'cradle-holes' were worn in **4**
the ice, as on *terra firma*, by the passage of the sleds over
the same track, and the horses invariably ate their oats out
of cakes of ice hollowed out like buckets. They stacked
up the cakes thus in the open air in a pile thirty-five feet
high on one side and six or seven rods square, putting hay
between the outside layers to exclude the air; for when
the wind, though never so cold, finds a passage through,
it will wear large cavities, leaving slight supports or studs
only here and there, and finally topple it down. At first it
looked like a vast blue fort or Valhalla; but when they **5**
began to tuck the coarse meadow hay into the crevices,
and this became covered with rime and icicles, it looked
like a venerable moss-grown and hoary ruin, built of az-
ure-tinted marble, the abode of Winter, that old man we
see in the almanac — his shanty, as if he had a design to **6**

1 In Greek mythology, the lowest region of
the underworld.
2 An old proverb that can be traced back
at least as far as John Ray's *English Proverbs*
(1678): "Nine tailors make but one man."
3 About fifteen miles east of Concord on
the Fitchburg Railroad.
4 Small depressions in a roadway that ob-
struct traffic.
5 In Scandinavian mythology, the hall of immortality.
6 In the 1850s, issues of the *Old Farmer's
Almanac*, on the January page, depict winter as
an old man.

Where the open water comes within half a dozen
feet of the shore, the spray has blown over the
intervening ice and covered the grass and stubble,
looking like a glaze,—countless loby fingers and
horns over some fine stubble core,—and when the
grass or stem is horizontal you have a rake.
(February 10, 1860)

1   The real reason is given in note 2, page 292.
2   The Goose Ponds just east of Walden.
3   In Cambridge.

estivate with us. They calculated that not twenty-five per cent of this would reach its destination, and that two or three per cent would be wasted in the cars. However, a still greater part of this heap had a different destiny from what was intended; for, either because the ice was found not to keep so well as was expected, containing more air than usual, or for some other reason, it never got to market. This heap, made in the winter of '46–7 and estimated to contain ten thousand tons, was finally covered with hay and boards; and though it was unroofed the following July, and a part of it carried off, the rest remaining exposed to the sun, it stood over that summer and the next winter, and was not quite melted till September, 1848. Thus the pond recovered the greater part.

Like the water, the Walden ice, seen near at hand, has a green tint, but at a distance is beautifully blue, and you can easily tell it from the white ice of the river, or the merely greenish ice of some ponds, a quarter of a mile off. Sometimes one of those great cakes slips from the iceman's sled into the village street, and lies there for a week like a great emerald, an object of interest to all passers. I have noticed that a portion of Walden which in the state of water was green will often, when frozen, appear from the same point of view blue. So the hollows about this pond will, sometimes, in the winter, be filled with a greenish water somewhat like its own, but the next day will have frozen blue. Perhaps the blue color of water and ice is due to the light and air they contain, and the most transparent is the bluest. Ice is an interesting subject for contemplation. They told me that they had some in the icehouses at Fresh Pond five years old which was as good as ever. Why is it that a bucket of water soon becomes putrid, but frozen remains sweet forever? It is commonly

Those great organ-pipe icicles that drip from rocks have an annular structure growing downward. (February 10, 1860)

said that this is the difference between the affections and the intellect.

Thus for sixteen days I saw from my window a hundred men at work like busy husbandmen, with teams and horses and apparently all the implements of farming, such a picture as we see on the first page of the almanac; and as **1** often as I looked out I was reminded of the fable of the **2** lark and the reapers, or the parable of the sower, and the **3** like; and now they are all gone, and in thirty days more, probably, I shall look from the same window on the pure sea-green Walden water there, reflecting the clouds and the trees, and sending up its evaporations in solitude, and no traces will appear that a man has ever stood there. Perhaps I shall hear a solitary loon laugh as he dives and plumes himself, or shall see a lonely fisher in his boat, like a floating leaf, beholding his form reflected in the waves, where lately a hundred men securely labored.

Thus it appears that the sweltering inhabitants of Char- **4** leston and New Orleans, of Madras and Bombay and **5** Calcutta, drink at my well. In the morning I bathe my intellect in the stupendous and cosmogonal philosophy of the Bhagvat-Geeta, since whose composition years of **6** the gods have elapsed, and in comparison with which our **7** modern world and its literature seem puny and trivial; and I doubt if that philosophy is not to be referred to a previous state of existence, so remote is its sublimity from our conceptions. I lay down the book and go to my well for water, and lo! there I meet the servant of the Bramin, priest of Brahma and Vishnu and Indra, who still sits in his temple on the Ganges reading the Vedas, or dwells at **8** the root of a tree with his crust and water jug. I meet his servant come to draw water for his master, and our buckets as it were grate together in the same well. The pure

1   T was probably again thinking of the *Old Farmer's Almanac,* which featured these illustrations on the front cover.

2   He is probably referring to La Fontaine's fable (IV, 22) "The Lark and Her Young Ones with the Owner of the Field," which Emerson speaks of at some length under the title "The Lark and the Reaper" in the *Dial* (III, 414). In his manuscript commonplace book, now in the Library of Congress, T mentions reading this fable in J. Payne Collier, *Old Ballads* (London, 1843).

3   The parable as told by Jesus (Matthew 13).

4   Van Doren (81) feels that this final paragraph of the chapter shows the direct influence of Sir Thomas Browne in its style.

5   Ice harvesting was a major industry in nineteenth-century New England, and ice was shipped to all these and many other ports.

6   One of the major Hindu sacred writings, and one particularly admired by T.

7   According to Albanese (327), the Hindus equate 360 human years to one "year of the Gods": "In the *Rig Veda,* Vishnu was only a minor sun deity, but later, merging his identity with that of two other gods, he attained cosmic importance as the preserver of the world. . . . Indra figures prominently in earlier Indian religion but then loses most of his importance. The ascendancy of Brahma and Vishnu belongs to a later period."

8   The sacred scriptures of the Hindus. T would be pleased to know that the Hindus received not only ice from Walden Pond, but his own writings as well. His works had a profound influence on Gandhi and his followers. And W has been officially translated into fifteen Indian languages by the government of India.

Then there is the thickened edge of the ice, like a cliff, on the southeast sides of openings against which the wind has dashed the waves, especially on the southeast side of broad meadows. (February 10, 1860)

1   A fabled land now supposedly at the bottom of the Atlantic Ocean.

2   Legendary Greek islands at the western extremity of the world.

3   Hanno, a Carthaginian explorer, went to West Africa in 480 B.C. His report, "The Periplus of Hanno," is considered the earliest extant eyewitness report of an explorer.

4   "Of Ternate and Tidor, whence merchants bring / Their spicy drugs" (Milton, *Paradise Lost,* II, 639). They are two of the Spice Islands in the Dutch East Indies.

5   Alexander the Great became the most widely traveled man of his time.

Walden water is mingled with the sacred water of the Ganges. With favoring winds it is wafted past the site
1, 2 of the fabulous islands of Atlantis and the Hesperides,
3 makes the periplus of Hanno, and, floating by Ternate
4 and Tidore and the mouth of the Persian Gulf, melts in the tropic gales of the Indian seas, and is landed in ports
5 of which Alexander only heard the names.

I tread on ice in which are traced all kinds of characters, Coptic and Syriac, etc. (February 12, 1860)

Spring

THE OPENING OF large tracts by the ice-cutters commonly causes a pond to break up earlier; for the water, agitated by the wind, even in cold weather, wears away the surrounding ice. But such was not the effect on Walden that year, for she had soon got a thick new garment to take the place of the old. This pond never breaks up so soon as the others in this neighborhood, on account both of its greater depth and its having no stream passing through it to melt or wear away the ice. I never knew it to open in the course of a winter, not excepting that of '52–3, which gave the ponds so severe a trial. It commonly opens **2** about the first of April, a week or ten days later than Flint's Pond and Fair Haven, beginning to melt on the north side and in the shallower parts where it began to freeze. It indicates better than any water hereabouts the absolute progress of the season, being least affected by transient changes of temperature. A severe cold of a few days' duration in March may very much retard the opening of the former ponds, while the temperature of Walden increases almost uninterruptedly. A thermometer thrust into the middle of Walden on the 6th of March, 1847, stood at 32°, or freezing point; near the shore at 33°; in the middle of Flint's Pond, the same day, at 32 ½°; at a dozen rods from the shore, in shallow water, under ice a foot thick, at 36°. This difference of three and a half degrees between the temperature of the deep water and the shallow in the latter pond, and the fact that a great proportion of it is comparatively shallow, show why it should break up so much sooner than Walden. The ice in the shallowest part was at this time several inches thinner than in the middle. In midwinter the middle had been the warmest

1 For a discussion of the spring and rebirth imagery throughout the book, and particularly in this chapter, see Richard Adams (424–8). Hume gives a detailed analysis of this chapter as a psychological preparation for the advent of spring. Sweeney discusses the particular influence of Oriental philosophies on this chapter.

2 T here reflects the mid-nineteenth-century fascination with scientific phenomena almost for their own sake — an interest that Melville parodied in portions of *Moby-Dick*. To his dismay, T found that as he grew older he became more interested in merely recording statistics and less interested in interpreting those statistics for a better understanding of life.

1 The *Concord Freeman* for September 30, 1842, announced that "they are building a reservoir on a very large scale at Fresh Pond, for the purpose of *manufacturing ice,* the coming winter. It is intended to pump up the water into the basin and allow it to freeze, which it will more readily do, than in the pond, as the depth will be but little, and it can be but slightly disturbed."

and the ice thinnest there. So, also, every one who has waded about the shores of a pond in summer must have perceived how much warmer the water is close to the shore, where only three or four inches deep, than a little distance out, and on the surface where it is deep, than near the bottom. In spring the sun not only exerts an influence through the increased temperature of the air and earth, but its heat passes through ice a foot or more thick, and is reflected from the bottom in shallow water, and so also warms the water and melts the under side of the ice, at the same time that it is melting it more directly above, making it uneven, and causing the air bubbles which it contains to extend themselves upward and downward until it is completely honeycombed, and at last disappears suddenly in a single spring rain. Ice has its grain as well as wood, and when a cake begins to rot or 'comb,' that is, assume the appearance of honeycomb, whatever may be its position, the air cells are at right angles with what was the water surface. Where there is a rock or a log rising near to the surface the ice over it is much thinner, and is frequently quite dissolved by this reflected heat; and I have been told that in the experiment at Cambridge to freeze water in a shallow wooden pond, though the cold air circulated underneath, and so had access to both sides, the reflection of the sun from the bottom more than counterbalanced this advantage. When a warm rain in the middle of the winter melts off the snow ice from Walden, and leaves a hard dark or transparent ice on the middle, there will be a strip of rotten though thicker white ice, a rod or more wide, about the shores, created by this reflected heat. Also, as I have said, the bubbles themselves within the ice operate as burning-glasses to melt the ice beneath.

When lately the open parts of the river froze more or less in the night after that windy day, they froze by stages, as it were, many feet wide, and the water dashed and froze against the edge of each successive strip of ice, leaving so many parallel ridges. (February 15, 1860)

The phenomena of the year take place every day in a **1** pond on a small scale. Every morning, generally speaking, the shallow water is being warmed more rapidly than the deep, though it may not be made so warm after all, and every evening it is being cooled more rapidly until the morning. The day is an epitome of the year. The night is the winter, the morning and evening are the spring and fall, and the noon is the summer. The cracking and booming of the ice indicate a change of temperature. One pleasant morning after a cold night, February 24th, 1850, having gone to Flint's Pond to spend the day, I noticed with surprise, that when I struck the ice with the head of my axe, it resounded like a gong for many rods around, or as if I had struck on a tight drum-head. The pond began to boom about an hour after sunrise, when it felt the influence of the sun's rays slanted upon it from over the hills; it stretched itself and yawned like a waking man with a gradually increasing tumult, which was kept up three or four hours. It took a short siesta at noon, and boomed once more toward night, as the sun was withdrawing his influence. In the right stage of the weather a pond fires its evening gun with great regularity. But in the middle of the day, being full of cracks, and the air also being less elastic, it had completely lost its resonance, and probably fishes and muskrats could not then have been stunned by a blow on it. The fishermen say that the 'thundering of the pond' scares the fishes and prevents their biting. The pond does not thunder every evening, and I cannot tell surely when to expect its thundering; but though I may perceive no difference in the weather, it does. Who would have suspected so large and cold and thick-skinned a thing to be so sensitive? Yet it has its law to which it thunders obedience when it should as surely as

1 It was a favorite fancy of T's to see the world in microcosm — the Atlantic Ocean as Walden Pond, etc.

The various figures in the partially rotted ice are very interesting . . . parallel waving lines, with sometimes very slight intervals, on the under side of sloping white ice, marking the successive levels at which the water has stood. (March 1, 1855)

1 Tiny protruding cells.

2 Since in his *Journal* for March 28, 1854 (VI, 176), T notes that he has received the first proofs of W, this last entry must have been inserted into the final text, which means that he kept revising the book up to the last moment. In his *Journal* for April 9, 1854 (VI, 191), he records his discovery that Walden had opened several days before.

the buds expand in the spring. The earth is all alive and covered with papillae. The largest pond is as sensitive to atmospheric changes as the globule of mercury in its tube.

One attraction in coming to the woods to live was that I should have leisure and opportunity to see the Spring come in. The ice in the pond at length begins to be honeycombed, and I can set my heel in it as I walk. Fogs and rains and warmer suns are gradually melting the snow; the days have grown sensibly longer; and I see how I shall get through the winter without adding to my wood-pile, for large fires are no longer necessary. I am on the alert for the first signs of spring, to hear the chance note of some arriving bird, or the striped squirrel's chirp, for his stores must be now nearly exhausted, or see the wood-chuck venture out of his winter quarters. On the 13th of March, after I had heard the bluebird, song sparrow, and red-wing, the ice was still nearly a foot thick. As the weather grew warmer it was not sensibly worn away by the water, nor broken up and floated off as in rivers, but, though it was completely melted for half a rod in width about the shore, the middle was merely honeycombed and saturated with water, so that you could put your foot through it when six inches thick; but by the next day evening, perhaps, after a warm rain followed by fog, it would have wholly disappeared, all gone off with the fog, spirited away. One year I went across the middle only five days before it disappeared entirely. In 1845 Walden was first completely open on the 1st of April; in '46, the 25th of March; in '47, the 8th of April; in '51, the 28th of March; in '52, the 18th of April; in '53, the 23d of March; in '54, about the 7th of April.

Every incident connected with the breaking up of the rivers and ponds and the settling of the weather is particularly interesting to us who live in a climate of so great

As I paddle or push along by the edge of the thick ice which lines the shore, sometimes pushing against it, I observe that is curiously worn by the water into this form: the dotted line being the water's edge. (March 19, 1855)

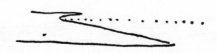

extremes. When the warmer days come, they who dwell near the river hear the ice crack at night with a startling whoop as loud as artillery, as if its icy fetters were rent from end to end, and within a few days see it rapidly going out. So the alligator comes out of the mud with quakings of the earth. One old man, who has been a close observer of Nature, and seems as thoroughly wise in regard to all her operations as if she had been put upon the stocks when he was a boy, and he had helped to lay her keel — who has come to his growth, and can hardly acquire more of natural lore if he should live to the age of Methuselah **1** — told me — and I was surprised to hear him express wonder at any of Nature's operations, for I thought that there were no secrets between them — that one spring day he took his gun and boat, and thought that he would have a little sport with the ducks. There was ice still on the meadows, but it was all gone out of the river, and he dropped down without obstruction from Sudbury, where **2** he lived, to Fair Haven Pond, which he found, unexpectedly, covered for the most part with a firm field of ice. It was a warm day, and he was surprised to see so great a body of ice remaining. Not seeing any ducks, he hid his boat on the north or back side of an island in the pond, and then concealed himself in the bushes on the south side, to await them. The ice was melted for three or four rods from the shore, and there was a smooth and warm sheet of water, with a muddy bottom, such as the ducks love, within, and he thought it likely that some would be along pretty soon. After he had lain still there about an hour he heard a low and seemingly very distant sound, but singularly grand and impressive, unlike anything he had ever heard, gradually swelling and increasing as if it would have a universal and memorable ending, a sullen rush and roar, which seemed to him all at once like the

1 "All the days of Methuselah were 969 years" (Genesis 5:27).

2 The next town southwest of Concord (Gleason).

1 Few passages in W have been analyzed with more frequency and at greater length than these paragraphs. Bigelow cites them as an outstanding early example of "how the modern symbolist mind works." Saucerman discusses it in the light of contemporary theories of geology. Perhaps the best general discussion can be found in Paul (1958, 346–9).

2 Just northwest of Walden Pond, where the earth was cut away to some depth to avoid too great an incline on the railroad (Gleason).

sound of a vast body of fowl coming in to settle there, and, seizing his gun, he started up in haste and excited; but he found, to his surprise, that the whole body of the ice had started while he lay there, and drifted in to the shore, and the sound he had heard was made by its edge grating on the shore — at first gently nibbled and crumbled off, but at length heaving up and scattering its wrecks along the island to a considerable height before it came to a standstill.

At length the sun's rays have attained the right angle, and warm winds blow up mist and rain and melt the snowbanks, and the sun, dispersing the mist, smiles on a checkered landscape of russet and white smoking with incense, through which the traveller picks his way from islet to islet, cheered by the music of a thousand tinkling rills and rivulets whose veins are filled with the blood of winter which they are bearing off.

1 Few phenomena gave me more delight than to observe the forms which thawing sand and clay assume in flowing
2 down the sides of a deep cut on the railroad through which I passed on my way to the village, a phenomenon not very common on so large a scale, though the number of freshly exposed banks of the right material must have been greatly multiplied since railroads were invented. The material was sand of every degree of fineness and of various rich colors, commonly mixed with a little clay. When the frost comes out in the spring, and even in a thawing day in the winter, the sand begins to flow down the slopes like lava, sometimes bursting out through the snow and overflowing it where no sand was to be seen before. Innumerable little streams overlap and interlace one with another, exhibiting a sort of hybrid product, which obeys half way the law of currents, and half way that of vegetation. As it flows it takes the forms of sappy leaves or vines, making heaps of pulpy sprays a foot or

more in depth, and resembling, as you look down on them, the laciniated, lobed, and imbricated thalluses of some lichens; or you are reminded of coral, of leopard's paws or birds' feet, of brains or lungs or bowels, and excre- **1** ments of all kinds. It is a truly *grotesque* vegetation, whose forms and color we see imitated in bronze, a sort of architectural foliage more ancient and typical than acanthus, **2** chiccory, ivy, vine, or any vegetable leaves; destined perhaps, under some circumstances, to become a puzzle to future geologists. The whole cut impressed me as if it were a cave with its stalactites laid open to the light. The various shades of the sand are singularly rich and agreeable, embracing the different iron colors, brown, gray, yellowish, and reddish. When the flowing mass reaches the drain at the foot of the bank it spreads out flatter into *strands*, the separate streams losing their semicylindrical form and gradually becoming more flat and broad, running together as they are more moist, till they form an almost flat *sand*, still variously and beautifully shaded, but in which you can trace the original forms of vegetation; till at length, in the water itself, they are converted into *banks*, like those formed off the mouths of rivers, and the forms of vegetation are lost in the ripple-marks on the bottom.

The whole bank, which is from twenty to forty feet high, is sometimes overlaid with a mass of this kind of foliage, or sandy rupture, for a quarter of a mile on one or both sides, the produce of one spring day. What makes this sand foliage remarkable is its springing into existence thus suddenly. When I see on the one side the inert bank — for the sun acts on one side first — and on the other this luxuriant foliage, the creation of an hour, I am affected as if in a peculiar sense I stood in the laboratory of the Artist who made the world and me — had come to

1 Many have suggested that T's comments here indicate the psychological orientation that Freud called anal. West (1974), in fact, finds scattered throughout W, particularly in some of T's puns, many scatological references.

2 All of these leaves have been used as decorative motifs in various schools of architecture.

The surface of the snow was diversified by those slight drifts, or perhaps cliffs, which are left a few inches high (like the fracture of slate rocks), with a waved outline, and all the sand was collected in waving lines just on the edge of these little drifts, in ridges, maybe an eighth of an inch high. (January 9, 1856)

1 T was often fascinated with word origins but was not always correct in his theories (Gura).

where he was still at work, sporting on this bank, and with excess of energy strewing his fresh designs about. I feel as if I were nearer to the vitals of the globe, for this sandy overflow is something such a foliaceous mass as the vitals of the animal body. You find thus in the very sands an anticipation of the vegetable leaf. No wonder that the earth expresses itself outwardly in leaves, it so labors with the idea inwardly. The atoms have already learned this law, and are pregnant by it. The overhanging leaf sees here its prototype. *Internally*, whether in the globe or animal body, it is a moist thick *lobe*, a word especially

1 applicable to the liver and lungs and the *leaves* of fat (λείβω, *labor, lapsus*, to flow or slip downward, a lapsing; λοβός, globus, lobe, globe; also lap, flap, and many other words); *externally* a dry thin leaf, even as the *f* and *v* are a pressed and dried *b*. The radicals of *lobe* are *lb*, the soft mass of the *b* (single-lobed, or B, double-lobed), with the liquid *l* behind it pressing it forward. In globe, *glb*, the guttural *g* adds to the meaning the capacity of the throat. The feathers and wings of birds are still drier and thinner leaves. Thus, also, you pass from the lumpish grub in the earth to the airy and fluttering butterfly. The very globe continually transcends and translates itself, and becomes winged in its orbit. Even ice begins with delicate crystal leaves, as if it had flowed into moulds which the fronds of water-plants have impressed on the watery mirror. The whole tree itself is but one leaf, and rivers are still vaster leaves whose pulp is intervening earth, and towns and cities are the ova of insects in their axils.

When the sun withdraws the sand ceases to flow, but in the morning the streams will start once more and branch and branch again into a myriad of others. You here see perchance how blood-vessels are formed. If you look closely you observe that first there pushes forward from the thaw-

I see now, in the ruts in sand on hills in the road, those interesting ripples which I only notice to advantage in very shallow running water, a phenomenon almost, as it were, confined to melted snow running in ruts in the road in a thaw, especially in the spring. It is a spring phenomenon. The water, meeting with some slight obstacle, ever and anon appears to shoot across diagonally to the opposite side, while ripples from the opposite side intersect the former, producing countless regular and sparkling diamond-shaped ripples. (February 18, 1860)

ing mass a stream of softened sand with a drop-like point, like the ball of the finger, feeling its way slowly and blindly downward, until at last with more heat and moisture, as the sun gets higher, the most fluid portion, in its effort to obey the law to which the most inert also yields, separates from the latter and forms for itself a meandering channel or artery within that, in which is seen a little silvery stream glancing like lightning from one stage of pulpy leaves or branches to another, and ever and anon swallowed up in the sand. It is wonderful how rapidly yet perfectly the sand organizes itself as it flows, using the best material its mass affords to form the sharp edges of its channel. Such are the sources of rivers. In the silicious matter which the water deposits is perhaps the bony system, and in the still finer soil and organic matter the fleshy fibre or cellular tissue. What is man but a mass of thawing clay? The ball **1** of the human finger is but a drop congealed. The fingers and toes flow to their extent from the thawing mass of the body. Who knows what the human body would expand and flow out to under a more genial heaven? Is not the hand a spreading *palm* leaf with its lobes and veins? The ear may be regarded, fancifully, as a lichen, *Umbilicaria*, on the side of the head, with its lobe or drop. The lip — *labium*, from *labor* (?) — laps or lapses from the sides of the cavernous mouth. The nose is a manifest congealed drop or stalactite. The chin is a still larger drop, the confluent dripping of the face. The cheeks are a slide from the brows into the valley of the face, opposed and diffused by the cheek bones. Each rounded lobe of the vegetable leaf, too, is a thick and now loitering drop, larger or smaller; the lobes are the fingers of the leaf; and as many lobes as it has, in so many directions it tends to flow, and more heat or other genial influences would have caused it to flow yet farther.

1   "And the Lord God formed man of the dust of the ground" (Genesis 2:7).

1   Jean-François Champollion (1790–1832), the French Egyptologist who deciphered the Rosetta stone and launched a widespread interest in the study of hieroglyphics (Irwin).

2   Lights: lungs.

3   The bowels were thought to be the source of compassion and sympathy.

4   "Ye shall find the babe wrapped in swaddling clothes" (Luke 2:12).

5   T once again is reflecting his interest in the archeological discoveries made in the Middle East during his lifetime.

6   As Sattelmeyer (88) points out, T is here giving "a fairly explicit refutation of the contemporary squabbles over the meaning of the geologic record."

7   "As clay is in the potter's hand" (Jeremiah 18:6).

Thus it seemed that this one hillside illustrated the principle of all the operations of Nature. The Maker of this earth but patented a leaf. What Champollion will decipher this hieroglyphic for us, that we may turn over a new leaf at last? This phenomenon is more exhilarating to me than the luxuriance and fertility of vineyards. True, it is somewhat excrementitious in its character, and there is no end to the heaps of liver, lights, and bowels, as if the globe were turned wrong side outward; but this suggests at least that Nature has some bowels, and there again is mother of humanity. This is the frost coming out of the ground; this is Spring. It precedes the green and flowery spring, as mythology precedes regular poetry. I know of nothing more purgative of winter fumes and indigestions. It convinces me that Earth is still in her swaddling-clothes, and stretches forth baby fingers on every side. Fresh curls spring from the baldest brow. There is nothing inorganic. These foliaceous heaps lie along the bank like the slag of a furnace, showing that Nature is 'in full blast' within. The earth is not a mere fragment of dead history, stratum upon stratum like the leaves of a book, to be studied by geologists and antiquaries chiefly, but living poetry like the leaves of a tree, which precede flowers and fruit — not a fossil earth, but a living earth; compared with whose great central life all animal and vegetable life is merely parasitic. Its throes will heave our exuviae from their graves. You may melt your metals and cast them into the most beautiful moulds you can; they will never excite me like the forms which this molten earth flows out into. And not only it, but the institutions upon it are plastic like clay in the hands of the potter.

Ere long, not only on these banks, but on every hill and plain and in every hollow, the frost comes out of the ground like a dormant quadruped from its burrow, and

I see that the sandy soil has been washed far down the hill for its whole length by the recent rains combined with the melting snow, and it forms on the nearly level ground at the base very distinct flat yellow sands, with a convex edge, contrasting with the darker soil there. (March 19, 1859)

seeks the sea with music, or migrates to other climes in clouds. Thaw with his gentle persuasion is more powerful than Thor with his hammer. The one melts, the other but **1** breaks in pieces.

When the ground was partially bare of snow, and a few warm days had dried its surface somewhat, it was pleasant to compare the first tender signs of the infant year just peeping forth with the stately beauty of the withered vegetation which had withstood the winter — life-everlasting, goldenrods, pinweeds, and graceful wild grasses, more obvious and interesting frequently than in summer even, as if their beauty was not ripe till then; even cotton-grass, cat-tails, mulleins, johnswort, hardhack, meadow-sweet, and other strong-stemmed plants, those unexhausted granaries which entertain the earliest birds — decent weeds, **2** at least, which widowed Nature wears. I am particularly attracted by the arching and sheaf-like top of the wool-grass; it brings back the summer to our winter memories, and is among the forms which art loves to copy, and which, in the vegetable kingdom, have the same relation to types already in the mind of man that astronomy has. It is an antique style, older than Greek or Egyptian. Many of the phenomena of Winter are suggestive of an inexpressible tenderness and fragile delicacy. We are accustomed to hear this king described as a rude and boisterous tyrant; but with the gentleness of a lover he adorns the tresses of Summer.

At the approach of spring the red squirrels got under **3** my house, two at a time, directly under my feet as I sat reading or writing, and kept up the queerest chuckling and chirruping and vocal pirouetting and gurgling sounds that ever were heard; and when I stamped they only chirruped the louder, as if past all fear and respect in their mad pranks, defying humanity to stop them. No, you

1 The Norse god of thunder.

2 A widow's mourning costume is known as weeds.

3 Whether T was aware of the fact or not, the squirrels were obviously engaged in a mating ritual.

1 A common name for squirrels, supposedly based on one of their calls.

2 "And the grass which is called forth by the early rains is just growing" (M. Terenti Varronis [Varro], *Rerum Rusticarum* [*On Agriculture*] 2.2.14).

1 don't — chickaree — chickaree. They were wholly deaf to my arguments, or failed to perceive their force, and fell into a strain of invective that was irresistible.

The first sparrow of spring! The year beginning with younger hope than ever! The faint silvery warblings heard over the partially bare and moist fields from the bluebird, the song sparrow, and the red-wing, as if the last flakes of winter tinkled as they fell! What at such a time are histories, chronologies, traditions, and all written revelations? The brooks sing carols and glees to the spring. The marsh hawk, sailing low over the meadow, is already seeking the first slimy life that awakes. The sinking sound of melting snow is heard in all dells, and the ice dissolves apace in the ponds. The grass flames up on the hillsides like a spring fire — 'et primitus oritur herba imbribus primori-

2 bus evocata' — as if the earth sent forth an inward heat to greet the returning sun; not yellow but green is the color of its flame; — the symbol of perpetual youth, the grass-blade, like a long green ribbon, streams from the sod into the summer, checked indeed by the frost, but anon pushing on again, lifting its spear of last year's hay with the fresh life below. It grows as steadily as the rill oozes out of the ground. It is almost identical with that, for in the growing days of June, when the rills are dry, the grass-blades are their channels, and from year to year the herds drink at this perennial green stream, and the mower draws from it betimes their winter supply. So our human life but dies down to its root, and still puts forth its green blade to eternity.

Walden is melting apace. There is a canal two rods wide along the northerly and westerly sides, and wider still at the east end. A great field of ice has cracked off from the main body. I hear a song sparrow singing from the bushes on the shore — *olit, olit, olit* — *chip, chip,*

I see a female marsh hawk sailing and hunting over Potter's Swamp. I not only see the white rump but the very peculiar crescent-shaped curve of its wings. (March 21, 1859)

chip, che char — che wiss, wiss, wiss. He too is helping to crack it. How handsome the great sweeping curves in the edge of the ice, answering somewhat to those of the shore, but more regular! It is unusually hard, owing to the recent severe but transient cold, and all watered or waved like a palace floor. But the wind slides eastward over its opaque surface in vain, till it reaches the living surface beyond. It is glorious to behold this ribbon of water sparkling in the sun, the bare face of the pond full of glee and youth, as if it spoke the joy of the fishes within it, and of the sands on its shore — a silvery sheen as from the scales of a leuciscus, **1** as it were all one active fish. Such is the contrast between winter and spring. Walden was dead and is alive again. **2** But this spring it broke up more steadily, as I have said.

The change from storm and winter to serene and mild weather, from dark and sluggish hours to bright and elastic ones, is a memorable crisis which all things proclaim. It is seemingly instantaneous at last. Suddenly an influx of light filled my house, though the evening was at hand, and the clouds of winter still overhung it, and the eaves were dripping with sleety rain. I looked out the window, and lo! where yesterday was cold gray ice there lay the transparent pond already calm and full of hope as in a summer evening, reflecting a summer evening sky in its bosom, though none was visible overhead, as if it had intelligence with some remote horizon. I heard a robin in the distance, the first I had heard for many a thousand years, methought, whose note I shall not forget for many a thousand more — the same sweet and powerful song as of yore. O the evening robin, at the end of a New England summer day! If I could ever find the twig he sits upon! I mean *he*; I mean *the twig*. This at least is not the *Turdus migratorius*. The pitch pines and shrub **3** oaks about my house, which had so long drooped, sud-

1 A genus of fresh-water fish. In T's time it was considered to include such fish as the dace, roach, minnow, and shiner, but today no fish now included in that genus are known to exist in Massachusetts (Allen, 1910).

2 "For my son was dead, and is alive again" (Luke 15:24).

3 The scientific name for the American robin.

1 Archaic name for a small flock.

denly resumed their several characters, looked brighter, greener, and more erect and alive, as if effectually cleansed and restored by the rain. I knew that it would not rain any more. You may tell by looking at any twig of the forest, ay, at your very wood-pile, whether its winter is past or not. As it grew darker, I was startled by the honking of geese flying low over the woods, like weary travellers getting in late from Southern lakes, and indulging at last in unrestrained complaint and mutual consolation. Standing at my door, I could hear the rush of their wings; when, driving toward my house, they suddenly spied my light, and with hushed clamor wheeled and settled in the pond. So I came in, and shut the door, and passed my first spring night in the woods.

In the morning I watched the geese from the door through the mist, sailing in the middle of the pond, fifty rods off, so large and tumultuous that Walden appeared like an artificial pond for their amusement. But when I stood on the shore they at once rose up with a great flapping of wings at the signal of their commander, and when they had got into rank circled about over my head, twenty-nine of them, and then steered straight to Canada, with a regular *honk* from the leader at intervals, trusting **1** to break their fast in muddier pools. A 'plump' of ducks rose at the same time and took the route to the north in the wake of their noisier cousins.

For a week I heard the circling, groping clangor of some solitary goose in the foggy mornings, seeking its companion, and still peopling the woods with the sound of a larger life than they could sustain. In April the pigeons were seen again flying express in small flocks, and in due time I heard the martins twittering over my clearing, though it had not seemed that the township contained so many that it could afford me any, and I fancied

If you scan the horizon at this season of the year you are very likely to detect a small flock of dark ducks moving with rapid wing athwart the sky, or see the undulating line of migrating geese against the sky. (March 28, 1859)

that they were peculiarly of the ancient race that dwelt in hollow trees ere white men came. In almost all climes the tortoise and the frog are among the precursors and heralds of this season, and birds fly with song and glancing plumage, and plants spring and bloom, and winds blow, to correct this slight oscillation of the poles and preserve the equilibrium of nature.

As every season seems best to us in its turn, so the coming in of spring is like the creation of Cosmos out of **1** Chaos and the realization of the Golden Age.

'Eurus ad Auroram Nabathaeaque regna recessit,
Persidaque, et radiis juga subdita matutinis.'

'The East-Wind withdrew to Aurora and the
        Nabathaean kingdom,   **2**
And the Persian, and the ridges placed under the
        morning rays.
. . . .
Man was born. Whether that Artificer of things,
The origin of a better world, made him from the divine
        seed;
Or the earth, being recent and lately sundered from the
        high
Ether, retained some seeds of cognate heaven.'   **3**

A single gentle rain makes the grass many shades greener. So our prospects brighten on the influx of better thoughts. We should be blessed if we lived in the present always, and took advantage of every accident that befell us, like the grass which confesses the influence of the slightest dew that falls on it; and did not spend our time in atoning for the neglect of past opportunities, which we call doing our duty. We loiter in winter while it is already spring. In a pleasant spring morning all men's sins are forgiven. Such a day is a truce to vice. While such a sun holds out

1   According to Greek mythology, the universe (Cosmos) was created from some unformed original state (Chaos); a Golden Age of innocence, peace, and happiness began soon thereafter (Thomas).

2   An ancient Arab country east of present-day Israel.

3   Ovid, *Metamorphoses* (I, ii, 61–2, 78–81).

In the dry lupine bank pasture, about fifteen rods from the river, apparently travelling up the hill, I see a box tortoise, the first I have found in Concord. . . . The bill is very upright, somewhat like this: A beak like any Caesar's. (May 15, 1856)

1　"And while the lamp holds out to burn / The vilest sinner may return" (Isaac Watts, *Hymns and Spiritual Songs,* I, 88).

2　Once again, the romantic theme of the innocence of childhood.

3　"Enter thou into the joy of thy Lord" (Matthew 25:23).

1 to burn, the vilest sinner may return. Through our own recovered innocence we discern the innocence of our neighbors. You may have known your neighbor yesterday for a thief, a drunkard, or a sensualist, and merely pitied or despised him, and despaired of the world; but the sun shines bright and warm this first spring morning, re-creating the world, and you meet him at some serene work, and see how his exhausted and debauched veins expand with still joy and bless the new day, feel the spring influ-**2** ence with the innocence of infancy, and all his faults are forgotten. There is not only an atmosphere of good will about him, but even a savor of holiness groping for expression, blindly and ineffectually perhaps, like a new-born instinct, and for a short hour the south hillside echoes to no vulgar jest. You see some innocent fair shoots preparing to burst from his gnarled rind and try another year's life, tender and fresh as the youngest plant. Even he **3** has entered into the joy of his Lord. Why the jailer does not leave open his prison doors — why the judge does not dismiss his case — why the preacher does not dismiss his congregation! It is because they do not obey the hint which God gives them, nor accept the pardon which he freely offers to all.

'A return to goodness produced each day in the tranquil and beneficent breath of the morning, causes that in respect to the love of virtue and the hatred of vice, one approaches a little the primitive nature of man, as the sprouts of the forest which has been felled. In like manner the evil which one does in the interval of a day prevents the germs of virtues which began to spring up again from developing themselves and destroys them.

'After the germs of virtue have thus been prevented many times from developing themselves, then the beneficent breath of evening does not suffice to preserve them.

As soon as the breath of evening does not suffice longer to preserve them, then the nature of man does not differ much from that of the brute. Men seeing the nature of this man like that of the brute, think that he has never possessed the innate faculty of reason. Are those the true and natural sentiments of man?' 1

'The Golden Age was first created, which without any
    avenger
Spontaneously without law cherished fidelity and
    rectitude.
Punishment and fear were not; nor were threatening
    words read
On suspended brass; nor did the suppliant crowd fear
The words of their judge; but were safe without an
    avenger.
Not yet the pine felled on its mountains had descended
To the liquid waves that it might see a foreign world,
And mortals knew no shores but their own.
. . . .

There was eternal spring, and placid zephyrs with warm
Blasts soothed the flowers born without seed.' 2

On the 29th of April, as I was fishing from the bank of the river near the Nine-Acre-Corner bridge, standing on 3 the quaking grass and willow roots, where the muskrats lurk, I heard a singular rattling sound, somewhat like that of the sticks which boys play with their fingers, when, 4 looking up, I observed a very slight and graceful hawk, 5 like a nighthawk, alternately soaring like a ripple and tumbling a rod or two over and over, showing the under side of its wings, which gleamed like a satin ribbon in the sun, or like the pearly inside of a shell. This sight reminded me of falconry and what nobleness and poetry are associated with that sport. The merlin it seemed to me 6 it might be called: but I care not for its name. It was the

1 *Works of Mencius,* (book VI, "Kaon Tsze," part 1, chap. VIII, p. 2).

2 Ovid, *Metamorphoses* (I, ii, 89–96, 107–8).

3 In the southwest portion of Concord (Gleason).

4 Bones or clappers that children use as rhythmical instruments.

5 A male marsh hawk.

6 This name is nowadays applied to the falcon.

1 "O death, where is thy sting? O grave, where is thy victory?" (I Corinthians 15:55).

2 Again, T's belief that modern man needs contact with the wild to maintain his sanity and good health.

3 Meadow-hen: T could have been referring to several marsh birds, most probably the coot, but possibly the Virginia rail or the sora rail (Teale, 1946, 262).

most ethereal flight I had ever witnessed. It did not simply flutter like a butterfly, nor soar like the larger hawks, but it sported with proud reliance in the fields of air; mounting again and again with its strange chuckle, it repeated its free and beautiful fall, turning over and over like a kite, and then recovering from its lofty tumbling, as if it had never set its foot on *terra firma*. It appeared to have no companion in the universe — sporting there alone — and to need none but the morning and the ether with which it played. It was not lonely, but made all the earth lonely beneath it. Where was the parent which hatched it, its kindred, and its father in the heavens? The tenant of the air, it seemed related to the earth but by an egg hatched some time in the crevice of a crag; — or was its native nest made in the angle of a cloud, woven of the rainbow's trimmings and the sunset sky, and lined with some soft midsummer haze caught up from earth? Its eyry now some cliffy cloud.

Beside this I got a rare mess of golden and silver and bright cupreous fishes, which looked like a string of jewels. Ah! I have penetrated to those meadows on the morning of many a first spring day, jumping from hummock to hummock, from willow root to willow root, when the wild river valley and the woods were bathed in so pure and bright a light as would have waked the dead, if they had been slumbering in their graves, as some suppose. There needs no stronger proof of immortality. All things must live in such a light. O Death, where was thy sting? O Grave, where was thy victory, then?

Our village life would stagnate if it were not for the unexplored forests and meadows which surround it. We need the tonic of wildness — to wade sometimes in marshes where the bittern and the meadow-hen lurk, and hear the booming of the snipe; to smell the whispering sedge where only some wilder and more solitary fowl builds her nest, and the mink crawls with its belly close to the ground. At the same time that we are earnest to explore and learn all things, we require that all things be mysterious and unexplorable, that land and sea be infinitely wild, unsurveyed and unfathomed by us because unfathomable. We can never have enough of nature. We must be refreshed by the sight of inexhaustible vigor, vast and titanic features, the sea-coast with its wrecks, the wilderness with its living and its decaying trees, the thunder-cloud, and the rain which lasts three weeks and produces freshets. We need to witness our own limits transgressed, and some life pasturing freely where we never wander. We are cheered when we observe the vulture feeding on the carrion which **1** disgusts and disheartens us, and deriving health and strength from the repast. There was a dead horse in the hollow by **2** the path to my house, which compelled me sometimes to go out of my way, especially in the night when the air was heavy, but the assurance it gave me of the strong appetite and inviolable health of Nature was my compensation for this. I love to see that Nature is so rife with life that myriads can be afforded to be sacrificed and suffered to prey on one another; that tender organizations can be so serenely squashed out of existence like pulp — tadpoles which herons gobble up, and tortoises and toads run over in the road; and that sometimes it has rained flesh and **3** blood! With the liability to accident, we must see how little account is to be made of it. The impression made on a wise man is that of universal innocence. Poison is not poisonous after all, nor are any wounds fatal. Compassion is a very untenable ground. It must be expeditious. Its pleadings will not bear to be stereotyped.   **4**

Early in May, the oaks, hickories, maples, and other trees, just putting out amidst the pine woods around the

1 Although fairly common there now, the turkey vulture was not found in Massachusetts in T's day.

2 Richard O'Connor has told me that the dead horse had been thrown in the old cellar hole described in "Former Inhabitants" as "some homestead of the Stratton family," and which is also described in T's *Journal* for January 11, 1857 (IX, 214).

3 "In the consulship of Manius Acilius and Gaius Porcius it rained milk and blood, and . . . frequently on other occasions there it has rained flesh" (Pliny, *Natural History*, II, lvii). There is also a reference in the *Concord Freeman* for March 8, 1844, to a "rain of flesh and blood." (I am indebted to Bradley Dean for these references.)

4 That is, cast into a plate for permanent use.

pond, imparted a brightness like sunshine to the landscape, especially in cloudy days, as if the sun were breaking through mists and shining faintly on the hillsides here and there. On the third or fourth of May I saw a loon in the pond, and during the first week of the month I heard the whip-poor-will, the brown thrasher, the veery, the wood pewee, the chewink, and other birds. I had heard [1] the wood thrush long before. The phoebe had already [2] come once more and looked in at my door and window, to see if my house was cavern-like enough for her, sustaining herself on humming winds with clinched talons, as if she held by the air, while she surveyed the premises. The sulphur-like pollen of the pitch pine soon covered the pond and the stones and rotten wood along the shore, so that you could have collected a barrelful. This is the 'sulphur showers' we hear of. Even in Calidas' drama of [3] Sacontala, we read of 'rills dyed yellow with the golden dust of the lotus.' And so the seasons went rolling on into summer, as one rambles into higher and higher grass.

Thus was my first year's life in the woods completed; [4] and the second year was similar to it. I finally left Walden [5] September 6th, 1847.

---

1 As Allen (1993) has pointed out, T almost invariably confuses the wood thrush and the hermit thrush. And since the wood thrush is a late spring arrival in Massachusetts, it is likely that he is referring to the hermit thrush here.

2 Phoebes often explore barns and sheds, searching for a site to build their nest.

3 Calidas, *Sacontala; or, The Fatal Ring* (translated by Sir William Jones), speech of Dushmanta in act V.

4 T once again reminds us that he has combined the experiences of two years into one for the sake of unity.

5 People often wonder what happened to the cabin after T abandoned it. Zimmer gives a detailed and fascinating later history of both the cabin site and of the cabin itself. The cabin was sold, moved twice, and eventually was incorporated into a barn some miles away, where its particular boards are no longer identifiable. In 1872 a Mrs. Adams from Dubuque, Iowa, on visiting the original site of the cabin, decided it should be marked in some way, and so she gathered up a little cairn of stones. That started a tradition of visitors' adding their own stones to the cairn. Over the years the cairn grew immense, though tourists as often carried away stones, for souvenirs, as added them to the pile. In 1945, in answer to questions raised about the accuracy of the cairn's placement, Roland Robbins (1947) excavated the area and found the foundation of T's cabin only a few feet from the cairn. That site is now marked with granite corner posts and chains. People continue to add to, and subtract from, the cairn. In recent years a new tradition has developed among the children of the area: It is bad luck to pass the cairn without setting a stone on it, even if only a pebble, since all the larger stones in the area have already been placed on the cairn.

CONCLUSION

To the sick the doctors wisely recommend a change of air and scenery. Thank Heaven, here is not all the world. The buckeye does not grow in New England, and the 1 mockingbird is rarely heard here. The wild goose is more 2 of a cosmopolite than we; he breaks his fast in Canada, takes a luncheon in the Ohio, and plumes himself for the night in a southern bayou. Even the bison, to some extent, keeps pace with the seasons, cropping the pastures of the Colorado only till a greener and sweeter grass awaits him by the Yellowstone. Yet we think that if rail fences are pulled down, and stone walls piled up on our farms, bounds are henceforth set to our lives and our fates decided. If you are chosen town clerk, forsooth, you cannot go to Tierra del Fuego this summer: but you may go to 3 the land of infernal fire nevertheless. The universe is wider than our views of it.

Yet we should oftener look over the tafferel of our craft, 4 like curious passengers, and not make the voyage like stupid sailors picking oakum. The other side of the globe 5 is but the home of our correspondent. Our voyaging is only great-circle sailing, and the doctors prescribe for dis- 6 eases of the skin merely. One hastens to southern Africa to chase the giraffe; but surely that is not the game he would be after. How long, pray, would a man hunt giraffes if he could? Snipes and woodcocks also may afford 7 rare sport; but I trust it would be nobler game to shoot one's self

> 'Direct your eye right inward, and you'll find
> A thousand regions in your mind

1   A relative of the horse chestnut. A native of the Midwest, it has become very common since its introduction into New England.

2   Although the mockingbird was indeed rare in New England in T's day, it has in recent years become quite common.

3   A group of islands at the southern tip of South America.

4   Taffrail, the rail around the stern of a ship.

5   On sailing vessels, sailors were often kept busy untwisting old pieces of rope to use in caulking the seams of the ship.

6   The shortest distance between two points on a sphere is the arc of a circular plane passed through the center of the sphere, thus ships (and now airplanes) navigate between any two points on the great circle (Cameron, 1972).

7   Two marsh game birds now no longer legally hunted.

1 William Habington, "To My Honored Friend Sir Ed. P. Knight," which T probably found in Chalmers, *Works of the English Poets* (VI, 468). T has modernized the text and misread "sight" as "right," which Shanley (1971, 402) corrected from the first edition.

2 Hunting for the source of the Nile River was one of the great exploratory challenges of the mid-nineteenth century, as was the search for the Northwest Passage.

3 Sir John Franklin (1786–1847), a British explorer who was lost in the Arctic. Many expeditions were sent out to search for him.

4 Henry Grinnell of New York was the author, advocate, and patron of an American expedition to find Franklin.

5 Mungo Park (1771–1806?) was a Scottish explorer in Africa; Lewis and Clark led an expedition through the Louisiana Purchase to the West Coast; and Sir Martin Frobisher (1535?–1594) was a British navigator and explorer.

6 Elisha Kent Kane, in *The United States Grinnell Expedition in Search of Sir John Franklin* (Philadelphia, 1856, 164), describes the finding of six hundred preserved-meat cans left by Franklin.

7 Doloff finds many parallels between this passage and Byron's *Don Juan* (canto XIV, stanzas 101–2).

8 In T's time the realms of the czar of Russia comprised the largest body of land under one dominion.

9 Charles Wilkes led an expedition to the Antarctic islands of the Pacific from 1839 to 1842.

1 Yet undiscovered. Travel them, and be
Expert in home-cosmography.'

What does Africa — what does the West stand for? Is not our own interior white on the chart? black though it may prove, like the coast, when discovered. Is it the source 2 of the Nile, or the Niger, or the Mississippi, or a Northwest Passage around this continent, that we would find? Are these the problems which most concern mankind? Is 3 Franklin the only man who is lost, that his wife should be 4 so earnest to find him? Does Mr. Grinnell know where he 5 himself is? Be rather the Mungo Park, the Lewis and Clark and Frobisher, of your own streams and oceans; explore your own higher latitudes — with shiploads of preserved meats to support you, if they be necessary; and 6 pile the empty cans sky-high for a sign. Were preserved meats invented to preserve meat merely? Nay, be a Co-7 lumbus to whole new continents and worlds within you, opening new channels, not of trade, but of thought. Every man is the lord of a realm beside which the earthly em-8 pire of the Czar is but a petty state, a hummock left by the ice. Yet some can be patriotic who have no *self*-respect, and sacrifice the greater to the less. They love the soil which makes their graves, but have no sympathy with the spirit which may still animate their clay. Patriotism is a maggot in their heads. What was the meaning of that 9 South-Sea Exploring Expedition, with all its parade and expense, but an indirect recognition of the fact that there are continents and seas in the moral world to which every man is an isthmus or an inlet, yet unexplored by him, but that it is easier to sail many thousand miles through cold and storm and cannibals, in a government ship, with five hundred men and boys to assist one, than it is to explore the private sea, the Atlantic and Pacific Ocean of one's being alone.

> 'Erret, et extremos alter scrutetur Iberos.
> Plus habet hic vitae, plus habet ille viae.'

> Let them wander and scrutinize the outlandish
>   Australians.
> I have more of God, they more of the road.   1

It is not worth the while to go round the world to count the cats in Zanzibar. Yet do this even till you can do 2 better, and you may perhaps find some 'Symmes' Hole' 3 by which to get at the inside at last. England and France, Spain and Portugal, Gold Coast and Slave Coast, all front on this private sea; but no bark from them has ventured out of sight of land, though it is without doubt the direct way to India. If you would learn to speak all tongues and conform to the customs of all nations, if you would travel farther than all travellers, be naturalized in all climes, and cause the Sphinx to dash her head against a stone, even 4, 5 obey the precept of the old philosopher, and Explore 6 thyself. Herein are demanded the eye and the nerve. Only the defeated and deserters go to the wars, cowards that run away and enlist. Start now on that farthest western 7 way, which does not pause at the Mississippi or the Pacific, nor conduct toward a wornout China or Japan, but leads on direct, a tangent to this sphere, summer and winter, day and night, sun down, moon down, and at last earth down too.

It is said that Mirabeau took to highway robbery 'to 8 ascertain what degree of resolution was necessary in order to place one's self in formal opposition to the most sacred laws of society.' He declared that 'a soldier who fights in

1   In his *Journal* for May 10, 1841 (I, 259–60), T tells us that these are the last verses of Claudian's "Old Man of Verona." T has changed Iberos (Spaniards) to Australians to make the reference more appropriate to his time.

2   T was undoubtedly thinking of Charles Pickering, *The Races of Man* (London, 1851), which, according to his *Journal* (V, 392), he read in 1853. Pickering's book, an account of his world tour, amazingly reports (349) on the domestic cats of Zanzibar.

3   Capt. John Cleves Symmes in 1818 proposed that the earth was hollow and open at both poles. A detailed description of his theory can be found in *Blackwood's Magazine* (CCXXVI, 1829, 856–7).

4   A mythical monster of Thebes who killed those unable to solve her riddle. When Oedipus solved it, she dashed her head against a rock, killing herself.

5   "They shall bear thee up in their hands, lest thou dash thy foot against a stone" (Psalms 91:12).

6   The apothegm "Know thyself" has been attributed at various times to nearly all of the great Greek philosophers.

7   T wrote W at the height of the migration to the American West.

8   The Comte de Mirabeau (1749–1791) was a statesman of the French Revolution. In his *Journal* for July 21, 1851 (II, 332–3), T quotes the passage at greater length from *Harper's New Monthly* (I, 648).

1   Robber on foot.

2   The immediate reason for T's leaving Walden was that Emerson planned to go abroad on a lecture tour and wished T to take over the care of his house and family. Later in his *Journal* (III, 214–5) T confessed, "Why I left the woods I do not think I can tell. I have often wished myself back. I do not know any better how I ever came to go there. . . . Perhaps if I lived there much longer, I might live there forever. One would think twice before he accepted heaven on such terms."

3   The path from T's cabin site to the pond is still there, kept open nowadays by visitors who come from all over the world.

4   On sailing vessels, sailors slept before (that is, in front of) the mast. T's Harvard classmate Richard Henry Dana was the author of the celebrated *Two Years Before the Mast*.

5   Channing has said that T refers to a boat trip they took together in 1844 on the Hudson River, when they spent the night in the bow of the ship because there was bright moonlight.

the ranks does not require half so much courage as a **1** foot-pad' — 'that honor and religion have never stood in the way of a well-considered and a firm resolve.' This was manly, as the world goes; and yet it was idle, if not desperate. A saner man would have found himself often enough 'in formal opposition' to what are deemed 'the most sacred laws of society,' through obedience to yet more sacred laws, and so have tested his resolution without going out of his way. It is not for a man to put himself in such an attitude to society, but to maintain himself in whatever attitude he find himself through obedience to the laws of his being, which will never be one of opposition to a just government, if he should chance to meet with such.

2   I left the woods for as good a reason as I went there. Perhaps it seemed to me that I had several more lives to live, and could not spare any more time for that one. It is remarkable how easily and insensibly we fall into a particular route, and make a beaten track for ourselves. I had **3** not lived there a week before my feet wore a path from my door to the pond-side; and though it is five or six years since I trod it, it is still quite distinct. It is true, I fear, that others may have fallen into it, and so helped to keep it open. The surface of the earth is soft and impressible by the feet of men; and so with the paths which the mind travels. How worn and dusty, then, must be the highways of the world, how deep the ruts of tradition and conformity! I did not wish to take a cabin passage, but rather to go **4** before the mast and on the deck of the world, for there I **5** could best see the moonlight amid the mountains. I do not wish to go below now.

I learned this, at least, by my experiment: that if one advances confidently in the direction of his dreams, and endeavors to live the life which he has imagined, he will meet with a success unexpected in common hours. He will put some things behind, will pass an invisible boundary; new, universal, and more liberal laws will begin to establish themselves around and within him; or the old laws be expanded, and interpreted in his favor in a more liberal sense, and he will live with the license of a higher order of beings. In proportion as he simplifies his life, the laws of the universe will appear less complex, and solitude will not be solitude, nor poverty poverty, nor weakness weakness. If you have built castles in the air, your work need not be lost; that is where they should be. Now put the foundations under them.

It is a ridiculous demand which England and America make, that you shall speak so that they can understand you. Neither men nor toadstools grow so. As if that were important, and there were not enough to understand you without them. As if Nature could support but one order of understandings, could not sustain birds as well as quadrupeds, flying as well as creeping things, and *hush* and *whoa*, which Bright can understand, were the best English. As if **1** there were safety in stupidity alone. I fear chiefly lest my expression may not be *extra-vagant* enough, may not wander far enough beyond the narrow limits of my daily experience, so as to be adequate to the truth of which I have been convinced. *Extra vagance!* it depends on how **2** you are yarded. The migrating buffalo, which seeks new pastures in another latitude, is not extravagant like the cow which kicks over the pail, leaps the cowyard fence, and runs after her calf, in milking time. I desire to speak somewhere *without* bounds; like a man in a waking moment, to men in their waking moments; for I am con- **3** vinced that I cannot exaggerate enough even to lay the foundation of a true expression. Who that has heard a strain of music feared then lest he should speak extravagantly any more forever? In view of the future or possible,

1 Then a common farm name for an ox.

2 Neufeldt (1971) discusses T's use of "extravagance" in W. Stern suggests that T splits the word to emphasize its roots — *extra* (outside) and *vagari* (to wander).

3 Berkowitz suggests that T is probably parodying Richard Baxter's *Autobiography* (London, 1696), "as a dying man to dying men."

1 "Insensible perspiration" was coined by the Italian physician Sanctorius (1561–1636) as a synonym for metabolism.

I have never found a satisfactory explanation of this sentence. An early *Journal* version (Princeton edition, I, 429) reads: "In view of the possible and future — we should live quite laxly — and be more straightened behind than before. If there were a true and natural development we should be all defined in front, our outlines dim and shadowy on that side — as the crown of a rising flower shows newly from day to day — and from hour to hour." But that enlightens me, at least, no further.

2 "On prétend que les vers de Kabir ont quatre sens différents: L'illusion (mâyâ), l'esprit (âtmâ), l'intellect (man), et la doctrine exotérique des Védas" (M. Garcin de Tassy, *Histoire de la Littérature Hindout* [Paris, 1839, 279]). The translation is apparently T's.

Kabir (1440–1518) was an Indian mystic and poet.

3 The potato blight, or rot, struck the United States in 1845 and the British Isles in 1846.

we should live quite laxly and undefined in front, our outlines dim and misty on that side; as our shadows reveal **1** an insensible perspiration toward the sun. The volatile truth of our words should continually betray the inadequacy of the residual statement. Their truth is instantly *translated*; its literal monument alone remains. The words which express our faith and piety are not definite; yet they are significant and fragrant like frankincense to superior natures.

Why level downward to our dullest perception always, and praise that as common sense? The commonest sense is the sense of men asleep, which they express by snoring. Sometimes we are inclined to class those who are once-and-a-half-witted with the half-witted, because we appreciate only a third part of their wit. Some would find fault with the morning red, if they ever got up early enough. **2** 'They pretend,' as I hear, 'that the verses of Kabir have four different senses; illusion, spirit, intellect, and the exoteric doctrine of the Vedas;' but in this part of the world it is considered a ground for complaint if a man's writings admit of more than one interpretation. While **3** England endeavors to cure the potato-rot, will not any endeavor to cure the brain-rot, which prevails so much more widely and fatally?

I do not suppose that I have attained to obscurity, but I should be proud if no more fatal fault were found with my pages on this score than was found with the Walden ice. Southern customers objected to its blue color, which is the evidence of its purity, as if it were muddy, and preferred the Cambridge ice, which is white, but tastes of weeds. The purity men love is like the mists which envelop the earth, and not like the azure ether beyond.

Some are dinning in our ears that we Americans, and moderns generally, are intellectual dwarfs compared with the ancients, or even the Elizabethan men. But what is that to the purpose? A living dog is better than a dead lion. **1** Shall a man go and hang himself because he belongs to the race of pygmies, and not be the biggest pygmy that he can? Let every one mind his own business, and endeavor to be what he was made.

Why should we be in such desperate haste to succeed and in such desperate enterprises? If a man does not keep pace with his companions, perhaps it is because he hears a different drummer. Let him step to the music which he **2** hears, however measured or far away. It is not important that he should mature as soon as an apple tree or an oak. Shall he turn his spring into summer? If the condition of things which we were made for is not yet, what were any reality which we can substitute? We will not be shipwrecked on a vain reality. Shall we with pains erect a heaven of blue glass over ourselves, though when it is done we shall be sure to gaze still at the true ethereal heaven far above, as if the former were not?

There was an artist in the city of Kouroo who was **3** disposed to strive after perfection. One day it came into his mind to make a staff. Having considered that in an imperfect work time is an ingredient, but into a perfect work time does not enter, he said to himself, It shall be perfect in all respects, though I should do nothing else in my life. He proceeded instantly to the forest for wood, being resolved that it should not be made of unsuitable material; and as he searched for and rejected stick after stick, his friends gradually deserted him, for they grew old in their works and died, but he grew not older by a moment. His singleness of purpose and resolution, and his elevated piety, endowed him, without his knowledge, with perennial youth. As he made no compromise with Time, Time kept out of his way, and only sighed at a distance

1 "A living dog is better than a dead lion" (Ecclesiastes 9:4).

2 A favorite image of T's, found often in his writings.

3 Many scholars have searched for T's source for this tale. Cameron (1991) has found a possible source in the Indian fable of the Carpenter (or Wood Carver) of the State of Lu, but has been unable to discover where T could have read it. Paul (1958, 353) suggests that "Kouroo was clearly Kuru, Kooroo, or Curu, the nation that fought the Pandoos in the *Mahabharata*, the sacred land that Arjuna was assigned to protect in the *Bhagavad-Gita*. T may have come across it in the *Laws of Menu*, where it is referred to as the country of the Brahmanical sages (see the *Dial*, III [1843], 332). These Brahmins also carried staves."

"I have long thought of it as an allegory of T's own life, of his love for the Beautiful, the True, and the Good, and of his search for Perfection," says Christy (193). "I find in it a veiled suggestion of the reason he went to Walden, of his indifference to criticism and the social standards of his time."

1 Stock: "Stick" seems a more likely reading of this word, though Shanley (1971, 327) accepts the reading of the first edition.

2 In Hindu literature, Kalpa is not a star but a long period of time, cited specifically by some authors as 4,354,560,000 years. The Hindus also knew that over a great period of time the pole star changed. In his *Journal* (Princeton edition, I, 413) T says, "4,320,000,000 years says Murray form 'the grand anomalistic period called a calpa, and fantastically assigned as a day of Brahma.'" Sattelmeyer (242) identifies the source of the internal quotation as Hugh Murray, *Historical and Descriptive Account of British India . . .* (New York, 1832).

3 Woodward points out that a ferule (usually spelled "ferrule") is an iron ring around the end of a staff.

4 A day of Brahma supposedly lasted two billion, one hundred and sixty million years, at the end of which time he slept.

5 In one of the early W manuscripts in the Huntington Library, T adds, "You Boston folks & Roxbury people will want Tom Hyde to mend your kettle," which seems to imply that Hyde was an eastern Massachusetts character either in folklore or fact. Moseley suggests that he might have been derived from Sam Hyde, an early New England trickster. She also points out that his advice to tailors has been attributed to Till Eulenspiegel of German folklore.

because he could not overcome him. Before he had found a stock in all respects suitable the city of Kouroo was a hoary ruin, and he sat on one of its mounds to peel the stick. Before he had given it the proper shape the dynasty of the Candahars was at an end, and with the point of the stick he wrote the name of the last of that race in the sand, and then resumed his work. By the time he had smoothed and polished the staff Kalpa was no longer the pole-star; and ere he had put on the ferule and the head adorned with precious stones, Brahma had awoke and slumbered many times. But why do I stay to mention these things? When the finishing stroke was put to his work, it suddenly expanded before the eyes of the astonished artist into the fairest of all the creations of Brahma. He had made a new system in making a staff, a world with full and fair proportions; in which, though the old cities and dynasties had passed away, fairer and more glorious ones had taken their places. And now he saw by the heap of shavings still fresh at his feet, that, for him and his work, the former lapse of time had been an illusion, and that no more time had elapsed than is required for a single scintillation from the brain of Brahma to fall on and inflame the tinder of a mortal brain. The material was pure, and his art was pure; how could the result be other than wonderful?

No face which we can give to a matter will stead us so well at last as the truth. This alone wears well. For the most part, we are not where we are, but in a false position. Through an infirmity of our natures, we suppose a case, and put ourselves into it, and hence are in two cases at the same time, and it is doubly difficult to get out. In sane moments we regard only the facts, the case that is. Say what you have to say, not what you ought. Any truth is better than make-believe. Tom Hyde, the tinker, standing on the gallows, was asked if he had anything to say. 'Tell the tailors,' said he, 'to remember to make a knot in their thread before they take the first stitch.' His companion's prayer is forgotten.

However mean your life is, meet it and live it; do not shun it and call it hard names. It is not so bad as you are. It looks poorest when you are richest. The faultfinder will find faults even in paradise. Love your life, poor as it is. You may perhaps have some pleasant, thrilling, glorious hours, even in a poor-house. The setting sun is reflected from the windows of the almshouse as brightly as from the rich man's abode; the snow melts before its door as early in the spring. I do not see but a quiet mind may live as contentedly there, and have as cheering thoughts, as in a palace. The town's poor seem to me often to live the most independent lives of any. Maybe they are simply great enough to receive without misgiving. Most think that they are above being supported by the town; but it oftener happens that they are not above supporting themselves by dishonest means, which should be more disreputable. Cultivate poverty like a garden herb, like sage. Do not trouble yourself much to get new things, whether clothes or friends. Turn the old; return to them. Things do not change; we change. Sell your clothes and keep your thoughts. God will see that you do not want society. If I were confined to a corner of a garret all my days, like a spider, the world would be just as large to me while I had my thoughts about me. The philosopher said: 'From an [1] army of three divisions one can take away its general, and put it in disorder; from the man the most abject and vulgar one cannot take away his thought.' Do not seek so anxiously to be developed, to subject yourself to many influences to be played on; it is all dissipation. Humility like darkness reveals the heavenly lights. The shadows of poverty and meanness gather around us, 'and lo! creation

1 *Confucian Analects,* IX, xxv.

1   "And lo! Creation widened in man's view" (Joseph Blanco White, "To Night").

2   A ruler of Lydia in ancient times who was known as the richest of men.

3   "The nearer the bone, the sweeter the flesh" (English proverb).

4   A small tinkling bell.

5   C. B. Cooper (206) suggests that this was probably Senator Robert Toombs, but does not explain why.

6   In 1811, Muhammad Ali Pasha of Egypt ordered the massacre of all the Mamelukes. They were trapped in a citadel, but one escaped by leaping on his horse from the ramparts and fleeing to Syria.

---

1 widens to our view.' We are often reminded that if there

2 were bestowed on us the wealth of Croesus, our aims must still be the same, and our means essentially the same. Moreover, if you are restricted in your range by poverty, if you cannot buy books and newspapers, for instance, you are but confined to the most significant and vital experiences; you are compelled to deal with the material which yields the most sugar and the most starch.

3 It is life near the bone where it is sweetest. You are defended from being a trifler. No man loses ever on a lower level by magnanimity on a higher. Superfluous wealth can buy superfluities only. Money is not required to buy one necessary of the soul.

I live in the angle of a leaden wall, into whose composition was poured a little alloy of bell-metal. Often, in the repose of my mid-day, there reaches my ears a confused

4 *tintinnabulum* from without. It is the noise of my contemporaries. My neighbors tell me of their adventures with famous gentlemen and ladies, what notabilities they met at the dinner-table; but I am no more interested in such things than in the contents of the Daily Times. The interest and the conversation are about costume and manners chiefly; but a goose is a goose still, dress it as you will. They tell me of California and Texas, of England and the

5 Indies, of the Hon. Mr. —— of Georgia or of Massachusetts, all transient and fleeting phenomena, till I am ready

6 to leap from their court-yard like the Mameluke bey. I delight to come to my bearings — not walk in procession with pomp and parade, in a conspicuous place, but to walk even with the Builder of the universe, if I may — not to live in this restless, nervous, bustling, trivial Nineteenth Century, but stand or sit thoughtfully while it goes by. What are men celebrating? They are all on a committee of arrangements, and hourly expect a speech from

somebody. God is only the president of the day, and Web- **1**
ster is his orator. I love to weigh, to settle, to gravitate
toward that which most strongly and rightfully attracts
me; — not hang by the beam of the scale and try to weigh
less — not suppose a case, but take the case that is; to
travel the only path I can, and that on which no power
can resist me. It affords me no satisfaction to commence
to spring an arch before I have got a solid foundation. Let
us not play at kittly-benders. There is a solid bottom eve- **2**
rywhere. We read that the traveller asked the boy if the
swamp before him had a hard bottom. The boy replied **3**
that it had. But presently the traveller's horse sank in up to
the girths, and he observed to the boy, 'I thought you said
that this bog had a hard bottom.' 'So it has,' answered the
latter, 'but you have not got half way to it yet.' So it is with
the bogs and quicksands of society; but he is an old boy
that knows it. Only what is thought, said, or done at a
certain rare coincidence is good. I would not be one of
those who will foolishly drive a nail into mere lath and
plastering; such a deed would keep me awake nights.
Give me a hammer, and let me feel for the furring. Do **4**
not depend on the putty. Drive a nail home and clinch it
so faithfully that you can wake up in the night and think
of your work with satisfaction — a work at which you
would not be ashamed to invoke the Muse. So will help **5**
you God, and so only. Every nail driven should be as
another rivet in the machine of the universe, you carrying
on the work.

Rather than love, than money, than fame, give me
truth. I sat at a table where were rich food and wine in **6**
abundance, and obsequious attendance, but sincerity and
truth were not; and I went away hungry from the inhospi-
table board. The hospitality was as cold as the ices. I
thought that there was no need of ice to freeze them.

1   Daniel Webster (1782–1852), senator from
Massachusetts and the most famous orator of
his day. Gottesman (1737) suggests that T is
playing on the Islamic affirmation "There is no
god but Allah, and Muhammad is his prophet."

2   A children's game of running out onto
thin ice without breaking through.

3   This story was told in the Concord *Yeoman's Gazette* for November 22, 1828, T's most
likely source. Many variations on the tale are
given in Hunt and Maxwell (100–9).

4   The furring are studs to which laths are
nailed. Shanley (1971, 402) has corrected this
from the first edition's "furrowing," although
both spellings are found.

5   It was the custom to invoke the aid of
the Muses whenever one embarked upon a major literary effort.

6   T often complained about the ostentation
of Emerson's dinner table.

1   Emerson, in his journal, as quoted in Edward Emerson (210), also mentions "a divine man dwelt near me in a hollow tree," but I have been unable to trace the allusion further. But see the previous hollow tree allusion, page 223.

2   I have been unable to trace the source of this quotation.

3   A long-lasting itch. Interestingly, the *Dictionary of American English* gives its earliest entry for this term as 1899.

4   When T visited Staten Island in 1843, he was much impressed with the seventeen-year locust (cicada) there, which was not known in Concord.

5   Pellicle: skin.

They talked to me of the age of the wine and the fame of the vintage; but I thought of an older, a newer, and purer wine, of a more glorious vintage, which they had not got, and could not buy. The style, the house and grounds and 'entertainment' pass for nothing with me. I called on the king, but he made me wait in his hall, and conducted like a man incapacitated for hospitality. There was a man in 1 my neighborhood who lived in a hollow tree. His manners were truly regal. I should have done better had I called on him.

How long shall we sit in our porticoes practising idle and musty virtues, which any work would make impertinent? As if one were to begin the day with long-suffering, and hire a man to hoe his potatoes; and in the afternoon go forth to practise Christian meekness and charity with goodness aforethought! Consider the China pride and stagnant self-complacency of mankind. This generation inclines a little to congratulate itself on being the last of an illustrious line; and in Boston and London and Paris and Rome, thinking of its long descent, it speaks of its progress in art and science and literature with satisfaction. There are the Records of the Philosophical Societies, and the public Eulogies of *Great Men!* It is the good Adam contemplating his own virtue. 'Yes, we have done great 2 deeds, and sung divine songs, which shall never die' — that is, as long as *we* can remember them. The learned societies and great men of Assyria — where are they? What youthful philosophers and experimentalists we are! There is not one of my readers who has yet lived a whole human life. These may be but the spring months in the life of the 3 race. If we have had the seven-years' itch, we have not 4 seen the seventeen-year locust yet in Concord. We are 5 acquainted with a mere pellicle of the globe on which we live. Most have not delved six feet beneath the surface, nor leaped as many above it. We know not where we are. Beside, we are sound asleep nearly half our time. Yet we esteem ourselves wise, and have an established order on the surface. Truly, we are deep thinkers, we are ambitious spirits! As I stand over the insect crawling amid the pine needles on the forest floor, and endeavoring to conceal itself from my sight, and ask myself why it will cherish those humble thoughts, and hide its head from me who might, perhaps, be its benefactor, and impart to its race some cheering information, I am reminded of the greater Benefactor and Intelligence that stands over me the human insect.

There is an incessant influx of novelty into the world, and yet we tolerate incredible dulness. I need only suggest what kind of sermons are still listened to in the most enlightened countries. There are such words as joy and sorrow, but they are only the burden of a psalm, sung with a nasal twang, while we believe in the ordinary and mean. We think that we can change our clothes only. It is said that the British Empire is very large and respectable, and that the United States are a first-rate power. We do not believe that a tide rises and falls behind every man which can float the British Empire like a chip, if he should ever harbor it in his mind. Who knows what sort of seventeen-year locust will next come out of the ground? The government of the world I live in was not framed, like that of Britain, in after-dinner conversations over the wine.

The life in us is like the water in the river. It may rise **1** this year higher than man has ever known it, and flood the parched uplands; even this may be the eventful year, which will drown out all our muskrats. It was not always **2** dry land where we dwell. I see far inland the banks which the stream anciently washed, before science began to record its freshets. Every one has heard the story which has **3**

1 D'Avanzo (1981) suggests that this penultimate paragraph of W "summarizes the theme of the entire narrative through symbol and illusion."

2 Muskrats build their houses with the upper chamber above water level and the entrance below. Thus if the water rises high enough, they run the risk of being drowned. T was apparently inspired in this comment by the high waters of 1850 in Concord (*Journal*, II, 18, 33).

3 This story reached print in a number of places (Harding, 1956) in T's day, and he saw it both in Timothy Dwight, *Travels in New England and New York* (New Haven, 1821, II, 398), and in J. W. Barber, *Massachusetts Historical Collections* (Worcester, 1839, 108–9). The story could be true, because long-horned beetles have been known to hatch out from wood after more than fifty years.

1   Saunders points out that this passage echoes that about the maggot in "Economy," but while the earlier passage seems one of cynical disappointment, this is one of affirmation and faith.

2   Names used for a typical British and a typical American citizen, respectively.

3   Jacobs and Jacobs suggest as a source for this, "We have also a more sure word of prophecy; whereunto ye do well that ye take heed, as unto a light that shineth in dark places, until the day dawn, and the day star arise in your hearts" (II Peter 1:19).

4   Friesen suggests many possible sources for this image, among them Emerson, Wordsworth, Tennyson, and the Old and New Testaments.

gone the rounds of New England, of a strong and beautiful bug which came out of the dry leaf of an old table of apple-tree wood, which had stood in a farmer's kitchen for sixty years, first in Connecticut, and afterward in Massachusetts — from an egg deposited in the living tree many years earlier still, as appeared by counting the annual layers beyond it; which was heard gnawing out for several weeks, hatched perchance by the heat of an urn. Who does not feel his faith in a resurrection and immortality strengthened by hearing of this? Who knows what beautiful and winged life, whose egg has been buried for ages under many concentric layers of woodenness in the dead dry life of society, deposited at first in the alburnum of the green and living tree, which has been gradually converted into the semblance of its well-seasoned tomb — heard perchance gnawing out now for years by the astonished family of man, as they sat round the festive board — may unexpectedly come forth from amidst society's most trivial and handselled furniture, to enjoy its perfect summer life at last!

I do not say that John or Jonathan will realize all this; but such is the character of that morrow which mere lapse of time can never make to dawn. The light which puts out our eyes is darkness to us. Only that day dawns to which we are awake. There is more day to dawn. The sun is but a morning star.

APPENDIX
A Hound, a Bay Horse, and a Turtle-Dove

MAP OF WALDEN POND

WORKS CITED

Appendix

A HOUND, A BAY HORSE, AND A TURTLE-DOVE

(page 15) This cryptic passage is one of the most discussed in W. At least three different people attempted to learn T's own interpretation directly from him:

1. When T visited Plymouth, Massachusetts, a year or two after the publication of W, he met there "Uncle Ed" Watson, who asked him what he meant when he said he lost "a hound, a horse, and a dove." T replied, "Well, Sir, I suppose we all have our losses." "That's a pretty way to answer a fellow," replied Uncle Ed.

2. When T's friend B. B. Wiley wrote from Chicago inquiring as to the meaning of the passage, T replied in a letter on April 26, 1857: "How shall we account for our pursuits, if they are original? We get the language with which to describe our various lives out of a common mint. If others have their losses which they are busy repairing, so I have mine, and their hound and horse may *perhaps* be the symbols of some of them. But also I have lost, or am in danger of losing, a far finer and more ethereal treasure which commonly no loss, of which they are conscious, will symbolize. This I answer hastily and with some hesitation, according as I now understand my words."

3. Raysor, speaking of T's love for Ellen Sewall, says, "When Thoreau discovered Miss Ward's knowledge of the affair, he told her that the reference in the first chapter of *Walden* to 'a hound, a bay horse, and a turtle-dove' which he had lost long ago were allusions to the boy Edmund Sewall, to John Thoreau and to Ellen Sewall" (460, which also provides information on T's relationship with the Sewall family). For further details of this interpretation, see Adams (1945). It is only fair to point out, however, that virtually none of the major biographers of T accept this story as fact.

Among the many interpretations offered by various critics are these:

Ralph Waldo Emerson, in his eulogy for T (Centenary Edition, 1918, X, 479), says, "He had many reserves, an unwillingness to exhibit to profane eyes what was still sacred in his own, and knew well how to throw a poetic veil over his experience. All readers of *Walden* will remember his mythical record of his disappointments. . . . His riddles are worth the reading, and I confide that if any time I do not understand the expression, it is yet just. Such was the wealth of his truth that it was not worth his while to use words in vain."

Vivian Hopkins (243n) tells us, "In a late manuscript fragment, Notes on Thoreau, Emerson records Thoreau's own statement from his journal on 'the hound': 'A good book will not be dropped by its author but thrown up. It will be so long a promise that he will not overtake it soon. He will have slipped leash of a fleet hound.' Emerson adds: 'The bay horse might be such command of property as he desired, and the turtle dove might be the wife of his dream.'"

Burroughs (377) says that T states in his *Journal,* "'The ultimate expression or fruit of any created thing is a fine effluence, which only the most ingenuous worshipper perceives at a reverent distance from its surface even.' This 'fine effluence' he was always reaching after, and often grasping or inhaling. This is the mythical hound and horse and turtle-dove which he says in *Walden* he long ago lost, and has been on their trail ever since. He never abandons the search, and in every woodchuck-hole or muskrat den, in retreat of bird, or squirrel, or mouse, or fox that he pries into, in every walk and expedition to the fields or swamps, or to distant woods, in every spring note and call that he listens to patiently, he hopes to get some clew to his lost treasures, to the effluence that so provokingly eludes him."

Samuel Arthur Jones (19–20) says, "To this man Thoreau every created thing was a divine message from its Maker and his. Oh, if he could but catch the meaning of the message or of the messenger. . . . Alas for us all! they had lost them, even as we have: for what is the hound but the divine scent that finds the trail: what the bay horse but sagacity and strength to carry us in pursuit: what the turtle-dove but innocence to secure us the Divine protection? And we have lost them all."

Mark Van Doren (16–7) says, "The parable of the hound, the bay horse, and the turtle-dove is plainly a 'mythical record of disappointments.' . . . It is clear enough that Thoreau's quest was not

for any metaphysical entity, because he wore his metaphysics as comfortably as anyone. It is clear enough that this single disappointment of his life was not an intellectual but an emotional one, and that it arose in the domain of the human relations. His ideal was perfection in human intercourse, and his quest was for an absolutely satisfactory condition of friendship."

Henry Seidel Canby (294) states, "In the symbolic language of the Persian poets which he so often read, he is clearly describing a search for no lost maid or boy, but for that sense of the spiritual reality behind nature, which again and again in his Journal he deplores as something felt in youth, but never quite regained."

Frank Davidson suggests that "The hound, the bay horse, and the turtle-dove seem to be respectively for Thoreau symbols of a wildness that keeps man in touch with nature, intellectual stimulus, and purification of spirit."

Volkman thinks that the three represent Truth, Goodness, and Beauty.

Johnston claims to find T's source for these images in the constellations Canis Major, the greater dog; Pegasus, the flying horse; and Pleiades, the seven doves.

In 1843 T edited passages from the "Chinese Four Books" for the *Dial* (IV, 206), and one passage there resembles his parable remarkably: "If a man lose his fowls or his dogs, he knows how to seek them. There are those who lose their hearts and know not how to seek them. The duty of the student is no other than to seek his lost heart."

Many old ballads, such as "The Twa Corbies," feature a hound, a horse, and a bird, although the bird is usually a falcon rather than a turtledove.

Stein (1959) suggests "The Story of Conn-eda;

or the Golden Apples of Lough Erne," an old Irish folk tale, as a specific source for the images.

Emerson's poem "Forerunners" also hints of the combination of hound, horse, and dove (Centenary Edition, IX, 85–6).

Barbara Johnson (338) suggests that in his choice of symbols T was not thinking of specific losses but rather the sense of loss itself.

John Girdler (110) presents a 118-page analysis of the allusion in his unpublished master's thesis, but much of it is devoted to a refutation of Van Doren's interpretation. In conclusion he states: "Thoreau is an idealist. He is searching for the thing which he thinks will most benefit man, and he is using methods that he believes best suit his genius. Consequently, his fables must, in his own words, be given the 'most generous interpretation.' It is not enough to seek a narrow interpretation of the hound and bay horse allegory for, to quote him again, 'Those thoughts which are "contemporaneous with social and personal connections, though they may be humane and tender, are not the wisest and most universal."'"

Edith Peairs attempts to prove that T's source for these symbols was Voltaire's *Zadig*. I am unconvinced.

By this time it should be obvious that one needs a sense of humor in considering all these critical reactions. Delaney suggests that T was simply telling white lies to give himself an excuse for wandering over other folks' property, and Burr has an amusing spoof of scholarly efforts to solve this puzzle.

In conclusion — and to be serious once again — there is no unanimity on interpretation of these symbols, and each reader is free to interpret them as he wishes.

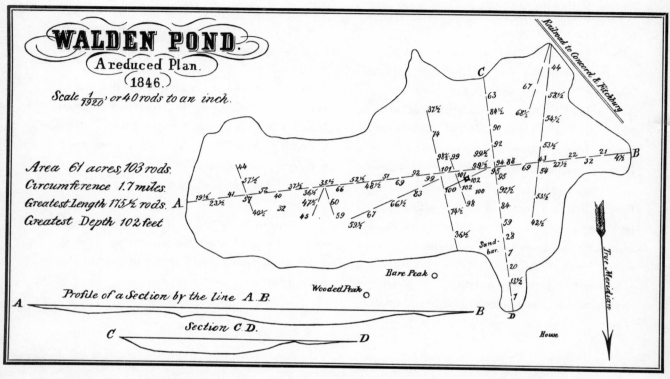

Hovey (104) points out that the lines *AB* and *CD* make a Christian cross and thus reads it as a Christian symbol, but I see it as nothing more than a coincidence. Nowhere else that I know of does T take any interest in the cross as a symbol.

Unfortunately many of the printers over the years have omitted this map. In his *Journal* for January 5, 1855 (VII, 103), T records his astonishment that Emerson's college classmate J. B. Hill of Bangor, Maine, thought the map of Walden was not real but a caricature of coastal survey maps.

Works Cited

Adams, Grace, and Edward Hutter. *The Mad Forties.* New York, 1942.

Adams, Raymond. "Emerson's House at Walden." *Thoreau Society Bulletin* 24 (July 1948), 3–7.

———. "T's Growth at Walden." *Christian Register* 224 (1945), 268–70.

———. "T's Mock-Heroics and the American Natural History Writers." *Studies in Philology* 52 (1955), 86–97.

Adams, Richard P. "Romanticism and the American Renaissance." *American Literature* 18 (1952), 419–32.

Adams, Stephen and Barbara. "T's Diet at Walden." *Studies in the American Renaissance* (1990), 243–60.

Albanese, Catherine. *The Spirituality of the American Transcendentalists.* Macon, 1988.

Alcott, A. Bronson. "Mr. Alcott on T." *Concord Freeman,* Aug. 19, 1880.

Allen, Francis H. "The French Translation of *W.*" *Thoreau Society Bulletin* 38 (1952), 1.

———, ed. T. *T on Birds.* Boston, 1993.

———, ed. T. *W.* Boston, 1910.

Anderson, Charles. *The Magic Circle of W.* New York, 1968.

Anderson, Douglas. "Azads in Concord." In *A House Undivided.* New York, 1990.

Baker, Larry. "'The Ponds' as Linkage." *Thoreau Journal Quarterly* 13 (1981), 21–6.

Balthazor, Ron. "To Play Life." *American Transcendental Quarterly* 7 (1993), 159–70.

Bartlett, John. *Familiar Quotations.* Edited by Emily Morison Beck. Boston, 1980.

Benoit, Raymond. "W as God's Drop." *American Literature* 43 (1971), 122–4.

Berkowitz, Morton. "T and Richard Baxter." *Thoreau Society Bulletin* 131 (1975), 4.

Bickman, Martin. *W: Volatile Truths.* New York, 1992.

Bigelow, Gordon. "T's Melting Sandbank: Birth of a Symbol." *International Journal of Symbology* 2 (1971), 7–13.

Birch, Thomas D., and Fred Metting. "The Economic Design of *W.*" *New England Quarterly* 65 (1992), 587–602.

Blanding, Thomas. "Walton and *W.*" *Thoreau Society Bulletin* 107 (1969), 3.

Blasing, Mutlu. "The Economics of *W.*" *Texas Studies in Literature and Language* 42 (1976), 759–75.

Bode, Carl, ed. T. *Collected Poems.* Baltimore, 1964.

Bonner, Willard. *Harp on the Shore.* Albany, 1985.

———. "T's Other Telegraph Figure." *American Notes and Queries* 7 (1969), 99.

Boone, Joseph Allen. "Delving and Diving for Truth." *ESQ* 27 (1981), 134–46.

Borck, Jim S., and Herbert B. Rothschild, Jr. "Meditative Discoveries in T's 'The Pond in Winter.'"

Texas Studies in Literature and Language 20 (1978), 93–106.

Boudreau, Gordon. "H.D.T., William Gilpin, and the Metaphysical Ground of the Picturesque." *American Literature* 45 (1973), 357–69.

———. "T and Richard C. Trench." *ESQ* 20 (1974), 117–24.

Bradford, Robert W. "T and Therien." *American Literature* 34 (1963), 499–506.

Brenner, Gerry. "T's 'Brute Neighbors.'" *ESQ* 39 (1965), 37–40.

Bridgman, Richard. *Dark T.* Lincoln, 1982.

Broderick, John C. "Imagery in *W.*" *University of Texas Studies in English* 33 (1954), 80–89.

———. "A Lifetime of Waldens." *Thoreau Journal Quarterly* 14 (1982), 10–7.

Brown, Mary Hosmer. *Memories of Concord.* Boston, 1926.

Buckley, Frank. "T and the Irish." *New England Quarterly* 13 (1940), 389–400.

Burr, Michael. "T's Love and Doubt." *American Transcendental Quarterly* 24 (1974), 22–5.

Burroughs, John. "Henry David T." *Century* 2 (1882), 377.

———. "T's Wildness." *Critic* 1 (1881), 74–5.

Bush, Sargent, Jr. "The Ends and Means in *W.*" *ESQ* 31 (1985), 1–10.

Cabot, James Elliot. *A Memoir of Ralph Waldo Emerson.* Boston, 1887.

Cady, Lyman C. "T's Quotations from the Confucian Books in *W.*" *American Literature* 33 (1961), 20–32.

Cameron, Kenneth Walter. "Hawthorne and Concord Legendry." *American Renaissance Literary Report* 5 (1991), 223–6.

———. *The Massachusetts Lyceum during the American Renaissance.* Hartford, 1969.

———. "T and the Folklore of Walden Pond." *ESQ* 3 (1956), 11.

———. "T on the Limitations of Great Circle Sailing." *American Transcendental Quarterly* 14 (1972), 70–1.

Canby, Henry S. *T.* Boston, 1939.

Cavell, Stanley. *The Senses of W.* New York, 1972.

Chase, Harry. "Henry T, Surveyor." *Surveying and Mapping* (1965), 219–22.

Christie, John Aldrich. *T as World Traveler.* New York, 1965.

Christy, Arthur. *The Orient in American Transcendentalism.* New York, 1932.

Clapper, Ronald. "The Development of *W*: A Genetic Text." Ph.D. diss. Los Angeles, 1967.

Commager, Henry Steele. *Theodore Parker.* Boston, 1936.

Conway, Moncure. *Autobiography, Memories and Experiences.* Boston, 1904.

Cook, Reginald L. "Ancient Rites at Walden." *ESQ* 39 (1965), 52–6.

———. "An Encounter with Myth at Walden." *American Transcendental Quarterly* 10 (1971), 41–2.

Cooke, George Willis. *Early Letters of George Wm. Curtis to John S. Dwight.* New York, 1898.

Cooper, C. B., ed. *T. W.* Chicago, 1938.

Cooper, David. "T's *W.*" *Explicator* 51 (1993), 159–62.

Crawford, Bartholow. *Henry David T: Representative Selections.* New York, 1934.

Cronkhite, C. Ferris. "The Transcendental Railroad." *New England Quarterly* 24 (1951), 315–21.

Cummings, Richard O. *The American Ice Harvests.* Berkeley, 1949.

Curtis, George William. "The Editor's Easy Chair." *Harper's Monthly* 49 (1874), 284.

D'Avanzo, Mario. "An Iron Chest in Walden's Depths." *New England Quarterly* 52 (1979), 397–400.

———. "John Field's Well." *Mass. Studies in English* 8 (1982), 4–8.

———. "T's Brick Pillow." *New England Quarterly* 50 (1977), 664–6.

———. "T's Rising River in *W*." *Mark Twain Journal* 20 (1981), 14–5.

———. "T's *W*, Chapter XVI." *Explicator* 29 (1971), 41.

Davidson, Frank. "T's Contribution to Hawthorne's *Mosses*." *New England Quarterly* 20 (1947), 539.

———. "T's Hound, Bay Horse, and Turtle-Dove." *New England Quarterly* 27 (1954), 521–4.

Dean, Debi Kang. "Of Muskrats and Men in *W*." *Concord Saunterer* 18 (1985), 30–5.

Deevey, Edward S. "A Re-examination of T's *W*." *Quarterly Review of Biology* 17 (1942), 1–11.

Delaney, Bill. "Found: One Hound, One Horse, and One Turtle-Dove." *South Dakota Review* (1992), 122–9.

DeMott, Robert. "T and 'Our Cabin.'" *Thoreau Journal Quarterly* 5 (1973), 19–24.

Dhawan, R. K. *Henry D. T: A Study in Indian Influence*. New Delhi, 1985.

Doloff, Steven. "T's Use of Byron in *W*." *Thoreau Society Bulletin* 190 (1990), 2–3.

Domina, Lyle. "'The Beanfield': Microcosm of *W*." *Thoreau Journal Quarterly* 12 (1980), 27–37.

Doudna, Martin. "T and James Freeman Clarke." *Thoreau Society Bulletin* 156 (1981), 1.

———. "T's Stiff Neck." *Concord Saunterer* 15 (1980), 20.

Eddleman, Floyd. "Use of Lemprière's *Classical Dictionary* in *W*." *ESQ* 43 (1968), 62–5.

Eidson, John Olin. *Charles Stearns Wheeler*. Athens, Georgia, 1951.

Emerson, Edward Waldo. *Emerson in Concord*. Boston, 1888.

Emerson, Ralph Waldo. *Journals*. Boston, 1909–14.

———. *The Journals and Miscellaneous Notebooks*. Cambridge, 1960–82.

———. *Writings*. Centenary Edition. Boston, 1903.

Fink, Steven. *Prophet in the Market-Place*. Princeton, 1992.

Friesen, Victor. "T's Morning Star." *Thoreau Society Bulletin* 204 (1993), 1–2.

Girdler, John. "A Study of the Hound, Bay Horse, and Turtle-Dove Allusion in T's *W*." Master's thesis. Los Angeles, 1935.

Gleason, Herbert W. "Map of Concord, Mass., Showing Localities Mentioned by T in his Journals." In *The Writings of Henry David T*. Boston, 1906.

Gottesman, Ronald, et al., eds. *The Norton Anthology of American Literature*. New York, 1979.

Gozzi, Raymond. "An Incoherent Sentence in *W*." *Thoreau Society Bulletin* 95 (1966), 4–5.

———. "The Meaning of the 'Complemental Verses' in *W*." *ESQ* 35 (1964), 79–82.

Griffin, William. "T's Reaction to Horatio Greenough." *New England Quarterly* 30 (1957), 508–12.

Griscom, Ludlow. *Birds of Concord*. Cambridge, 1949.

Gross, Robert. *Books and Libraries in T's Concord*. Worcester, 1988.

———. "The Great Bean Field Hoax." *Virginia Quarterly Review* 61 (1985), 483–96.

Gupta, R. K. "T's Water Privileges in *W*." *Thoreau Journal Quarterly* 8 (1976), 3–16.

Gura, Philip F. *The Wisdom of Words*. Middletown, Connecticut 1981.

Haddin, Theodore. "Fire and Fire Imagery in T's *Journal* and *W*." *South Atlantic Bulletin* 41 (1976), 78–89.

Hahn, Thomas. "T's Myrmidons." *Thoreau Society Bulletin* 147 (1979), 7–8.

Hanley, Wayne. "Geologist Thinks Walden Pond Born Almost as Indians Thought." *Boston Herald*, Jan. 15, 1956.

Harding, Walter. "The Apple-Tree Table Tale." *Boston Public Library Quarterly* 8 (1956), 213–5.

———. "A Check List of T's Lectures." *Bulletin of the New York Public Library* 52 (1948), 78–87.

———. *The Days of Henry T.* Princeton, 1993.

———. "A New Checklist of the Books in Henry David T's Library." *Studies in the American Renaissance* (1983), 151–86.

———. "Parker Pillsbury, the Walden Cabin, and the Underground Railroad." *Thoreau Society Bulletin* 198 (1992), 7–8.

———. "T on the Lecture Platform." *New England Quarterly* 24 (1951), 365–74.

———. "T's Sexuality." *Journal of Homosexuality* 21 (1991), 23–45.

Hawthorne, Nathaniel. *American Notebooks.* Columbus, 1972.

Hayward, Adrian. "The White Pond Tree." *Nature Outlook* 4 (1945), 29–36.

Heinzelman, Kurt. *The Economics of the Imagination.* Amherst, 1980.

Hellenbrand, Harold. "A True Integrity Day by Day." *ESQ* 25 (1979), 71–8.

Hoch, David. "T's Source for the Story of the King's Son." *Thoreau Journal Quarterly* 11 (1970), 10–2.

———. "T's Use of the Hindoos." *Thoreau Society Bulletin* 114 (1971), 1–2.

———. "W: Yoga and Creation." In Robert DeMott and Sanford Marovitz, eds. *Artful Thunder.* Kent, 1975, 85–102.

Hodges, Robert. "The Functional Satire of T's Hermit and Poet." *Satire Newsletter* 8 (1971), 105–8.

Hoeltje, Hubert. "T as Lecturer." *New England Quarterly* 19 (1946), 485–94.

Hopkins, Vivian. *Spires of Form.* Cambridge, 1951.

Hosmer, William. *The Higher Law.* New York, 1852.

Hovey, Allen. *The Hidden T.* Beirut, 1966.

Hudson, Hannah. "Concord Books." *Harper's Monthly* 51 (1875), 29.

Hume, Robert. "February, T, and Spring." *Rendezvous* 2 (1967), 23–6.

Hunt, William, and Allen Maxwell. "The Hat in the Mud Tale." In *The Sunny Slopes of Long Ago.* Dallas, 1966, 100–9.

Hyman, Stanley Edgar. "Henry T in Our Time." *Atlantic Monthly* 178 (1946), 137–46.

Jacobs, Edward C. "Undulations of Walden Pond." *Thoreau Society Bulletin* 173 (1985), 7–8.

Jacobs, Edward and Karen. "W's End and II Peter 1:19." *Thoreau Journal Quarterly* 10 (1978), 30–1.

Irwin, John T. "The Symbol of the Hieroglyphics in the American Renaissance." *American Quarterly* 26 (1974), 103–26.

Johnson, Barbara. *A World of Difference.* Baltimore, 1987.

Johnson, Linck C. "Revolution and Renewal." In Joel Myerson, ed. *Critical Essays on Henry David T's W.* Boston, 1988, 215–35.

Johnston, Kenneth. "T's Star-Spangled Losses." *Thoreau Journal Quarterly* 3 (1971), 10–20.

Jones, Buford. "A Thoreauvian Wordplay and Paradise Lost." *ESQ* 47 (1967), 65–6.

Jones, Joseph. "Transcendental Grocery Bills." *University of Texas Studies in English* 36 (1957), 141–54.

———. "Villages as Universities." *ESQ* 7 (1957), 40–2.

Jones, Samuel Arthur. *T: A Glimpse.* Concord, 1903.

Kappeler, Richard. "The Walden Tool Box of Henry T." *Chronicle of the Early American Industries Association* 41 (1988), 67–9.

Kenner, Hugh. *Bucky.* New York, 1973.

Knott, Robanna Sumrell. "'Reading': W's Third Chapter." *CEA Critic* 55 (1993), 52–60.

Krutch, Joseph W. *Henry David T.* New York, 1948.

Kurtz, Kenneth. "Style in W." *ESQ* 60 (1970), 59–67.

Lambden, William. "Sounds in W." *Colorado Quarterly* 18 (1960), 59–64.

Lane, Lauriat, Jr. "On the Organic Structure of *W*." *College English* 21 (1960), 195–202.

———. "*T*'s *W*: I, Paragraphs 1–3." *Explicator* 29 (1970), 35.

———. "Walden, the Second Year." *Studies in Romanticism* 8 (1969), 183–92.

Langlois, M. A., trans. *Harivansa, ou Histoire de la Famille de Hari*. Paris, 1834.

Leach, Joseph. "*T*'s Borrowing in *W*." *American Notes and Queries* 2 (1943), 171.

Leisy, E. E. "*T*'s Borrowings in *W*." *American Notes and Queries* 2 (1943), 121.

Lincoln Journal. [Renaming of Flint's Pond] March 20, 1986.

Long, Larry. "The Bible and the Composition of *W*." *Studies in the American Renaissance* (1979), 309–53.

Lyon, Melvin E. "Walden Pond as Symbol." *PMLA* 82 (1967), 289–300.

MacDonald, Lawrence. "Henry T — Liberal, Unconventional Nudist." *Sunshine and Health*, 1943.

Madden, Edward. *Civil Disobedience and Moral Law in Nineteenth-Century American Philosophy*. Seattle, 1968.

Masteller, Richard and Jean. "Rural Architecture in Andrew Jackson Downing and Henry David T." *New England Quarterly* 57 (1984), 483–510.

Matson, Peter. *A Place in the Country*. New York, 1977.

Matthews, Kenneth. "Making the Earth Say Beans." *Thoreau Society Bulletin* 143 (1978), 5–6.

Matthiessen, F. O. *American Renaissance*. New York, 1941.

Maxwell, J. C. [Review of *Variorum W*] *Notes and Queries* 210 (1965), 78–9.

McShane, Frank. "*W* and Yoga." *New England Quarterly* 37 (1964), 322–42.

Meigs, Peveril. "The Cove Names of Walden." *Thoreau Society Bulletin* 104 (1968), 5–6.

Meltzer, Milton, and Walter Harding. *A T Profile*. New York, 1962.

Metzger, Charles. *Emerson and Greenough*. Berkeley, 1954.

Michaels, Walter Benn. "Walden's False Bottoms." *Glyph* 1 (1977), 132–49.

Miller, F. DeWolfe. "*T*'s *W*: I, Paragraph 63." *Explicator* 33 (1973), 10.

Minnaert, M. *The Nature of Light and Color in the Open Air*. New York, 1954.

Moldenhauer, Joseph J. "The Extra-vagant Manner." *Graduate Journal* 6 (1964), 132–46.

———. "The Rhetorical Function of Proverbs in *W*." *Journal of American Folklore* 80 (1967), 151–9.

———. "*W* and Wordsworth's Guide to the English Lake District." *Studies in the American Renaissance* (1990), 261–92.

Morison, Samuel E. *The Maritime History of Massachusetts*. Boston, 1921.

Morse, David. *American Romanticism*. New York, 1987.

Moseley, Caroline. "*T*'s Tom Hyde." *Concord Saunterer* 14 (1979), 23–6.

Myers, Douglas. "The Bean-Field and the Method of Nature." *Thoreau Journal Quarterly* 4 (1972), 1–9.

Neufeldt, Leonard. *The Economist: Henry T and Enterprise*. New York, 1989.

———. "Extravagance through Economy." *American Transcendental Quarterly* 11 (1971), 63–9.

———. "The Wild Apple Tree." Ph.D. diss. Urbana, 1966.

Noverr, Douglas. "The Divining of Walden." *Thoreau Journal Quarterly* 4 (1972), 9–14.

O'Connell, Patrick. "The Battle of the Ants." *Thoreau Journal Quarterly* 12 (1980), 12.

O'Connor, Richard. "The Irish Shanties at Walden Pond." *Thoreau Society Bulletin* 182 (1986), 7.

Oelschlaeger, M. Henry. *The Idea of Wilderness*. New Haven, 1991.

Ogden, Marlene, and Clifton Keller. *W: A Concordance*. New York, 1985.

Ohlhoff, Klaus. "A Meaning of the Word 'Walden.'" *Thoreau Society Bulletin* 140 (1977), 4.

Paul, Sherman. *The Shores of America*. Urbana, 1958.

———. "The Wise Silence." *New England Quarterly* 22 (1949), 511–27.

Peairs, Edith. "The Hound, the Bay Horse, and the Turtle-Dove." *PMLA* 51 (1937), 863–9.

Pebworth, Ted-Larry. "Evelyn's Lay Fields, Digby's Spirits, and T's Beans." *Thoreau Society Bulletin* 101 (1967), 6–7.

Pederson, Lee. "T's Rhetoric and Carew's Lines." *Thoreau Society Bulletin* 82 (1963), 1.

Pickard, John B. "The Religion of 'Higher Laws.'" *ESQ* 39 (1965), 68–72.

Poirier, Richard. *A World Elsewhere*. New York, 1966.

Pribeck, Thomas. "A Note on the Winds of Walden." *College English Association Journal* 34 (1991), 354–63.

Pritchard, John Paul. "Cato in Concord." *Classical Weekly* 36 (1942), 3–5.

Proulx, Earl. "Plain Talk." *Yankee* 57 (1993), 18.

Railton, Stephen. *Authorship and Audience*. Princeton, 1991.

Raysor, T. M. "The Love Story of T." *Studies in Philology* 23 (1926), 460.

Rees, Byron, ed. T. *W.* New York, 1910.

Rees, John. "Et in Arcadas T." *ESQ* 23 (1977), 240–3.

Richardson, Robert. *Henry T: A Life of the Mind*. Berkeley, 1986.

Robbins, Roland. *Discovery at Walden*. Stoneham, Mass., 1947.

Robinson, E. Arthur. "T's Buried Short Story." *Studies in Short Fiction* 1 (1963), 16–20.

Rodabaugh, Delmer. "T's Smoke." *Explicator* 17 (1959), 47.

Rohman, David. "An Annotated Edition of Henry David T's *W.*" Ph.D. diss. Syracuse, 1960.

Rose, E. J. "The Wit and the Wisdom of T's 'Higher Laws.'" *Queen's Quarterly* 69 (1963), 555–67.

Ross, Donald, Jr. "Composition as a Stylistic Feature." *Style* 4 (1970), 1–10.

———. "Verbal Wit and *W.*" *American Transcendental Quarterly* 11 (1971), 38–44.

Ross, Francis. "Rhetorical Procedure in T's 'Battle of the Ants.'" *College Composition and Communication* 16 (1965), 14–8.

Rossi, William, ed. T. *W and Resistance to Civil Government*. New York, 1992.

Rusk, Ralph. *Letters of Ralph Waldo Emerson*. New York, 1939.

Ryan, George. "Shanties and Shiftlessness." *Eire* 13 (1978), 54–78.

Salt, Henry S. *Life of Henry David T*. Urbana, 1993.

Sanborn, Franklin Benjamin. *The Life of Henry David T*. Boston, 1917.

———. *Recollections of Seventy Years*. Boston, 1909.

———, ed. T. *W*. Boston, 1909.

Saperstein, Jeffrey. "T's *W.*" *Explicator* 46 (1988), 17–8.

Sattelmeyer, Robert. *T's Reading*. Princeton, 1988.

Saucerman, James. "T's Geologic Sand Image as Symbol." *Northwest Missouri State University Studies* 36 (1976), 3–12.

Saunders, Judith. "Economic Metaphor Redefined." *American Transcendental Quarterly* 36 (1977), 4–7.

———. "T's *W.*" *Explicator* 36 (1978), 4–5.

Sayre, Robert. *T and the American Indians*. Princeton, 1977.

Scanlon, Lawrence. "T's Parable of Baker Farm." *ESQ* 47 (1967), 19–21.

Schultz, Howard. "A Fragment of Jacobean Song in T's *W.*" *Modern Language Notes* 63 (1948), 271–2.